Supplemental Text to accompany

Modern Electronic Communication
by Jeffrey S. Beasley, et al.

Including System Projects

Taken from:

Laboratory Manual with System Project, by Jeffrey S. Beasley and Michael Fairbanks to accompany
Modern Electronic Communication, by Gary M. Miller and Jeffrey S. Beasley, Seventh Edition

Modern Electronic Communication, Eighth Edition
by Jeffrey S. Beasley and Gary M. Miller

Taken from:

Laboratory Manual with System Projects, by Jeffrey S. Beasley and Michael Fairbanks
to accompany *Modern Electronic Communication,* by Gary M. Miller and Jeffrey S. Beasley, Seventh Edition
Copyright © 2002 by Pearson Education, Inc.
Published by Prentice Hall
Upper Saddle River, New Jersey 07458

Modern Electronic Communication, Eighth Edition
by Jeffrey S. Beasley and Gary M. Miller
Copyright © 2005, 2002, 1999, 1996, 1993, 1988, and 1978 by Pearson Education, Inc.
Published by Prentice Hall

This special edition is published in cooperation with Pearson Custom Publishing.

All trademarks, service marks, registered trademarks, and registered service marks are the property of their respective owners and are used herein for identification purposes only.

Printed in the United States of America

10 9 8 7 6 5 4 3 2

ISBN 0-536-21013-6

2006200078

EM/KL

Please visit our web site at *www.pearsoncustom.com*

PEARSON CUSTOM PUBLISHING
75 Arlington Street, Suite 300, Boston, MA 02116
A Pearson Education Company

*Many thanks to Peter Butu of the Chantilly, Virginia campus,
ITT Technical Institute for his editorial review and selection of this textbook.*

PREFACE

This latest edition of the laboratory manual to accompany *Modern Electronic Communication,* seventh edition by Gary Miller and Jeff Beasley introduces the use of Electronics Workbench Multisim into the laboratory experience.

The 22 traditional laboratory experiments provide the student with a working knowledge of the concepts contained in the textbook. They also guide the student through the process of experimenting with communications circuitry. All of the experiments have been performed in a laboratory situation and have been used successfully. Due to the complexity of some of the experiments, you should plan for sufficient time to complete the experiments within your course constraints. Some of the experiments require test equipment that may be limited at your facility. We suggest that you allow your students to work on the Electronics Workbench experiments when the test equipment is not available.

This edition contains eight new experiments developed using Electronics Workbench Multisim. These laboratories have been tested by students and complement the material in the text and the traditional lab experiments. The students will be able to use these experiments to enhance their understanding of various communication system concepts. The CD-ROM packaged with the laboratory manual contains the multisim files for most of the circuits presented in the EWB Multisim labs.

The eight system projects are provided as a tool for the students to show the instructor that they have mastered a communication concept. Individual reports by each student on each system project will indicate the amount of practical knowledge they have gained. However, due to time and course constraints, you may assign each system project to a group of students who will then present the results to the rest of the class. These system projects will also allow your students to experience the pressures of the actual work environment.

PARTS AND EQUIPMENT

Parts Required (quantities greater than one are in parentheses)

Semiconductor Devices:
2N2222 (2), 2N3904 (3), 2N3906, 1N270 (2), 1N4148 (2), ECG222 (2), 1N4001

Integrated Circuits:
LM324 (2), LM339, LM386-3 (2), LM567 (1), LM741 (2), LM5534, 565 (2), 1496 (2), 3028A, 3418 codec (2), 3080E, 7493 (2), 74LS00, 7420 (2), 74LS27, 7474 (2), 7476, 7486, 74121, 74151, 74LS174, 74293 (2), HCT4016, 8038, XR2206, XR2211

Resistors: (1/2 watt except as noted)
4.7*, 10**, 47 (5), 56, 100 (2), 220, 273, 330, 390 (2), 470 (2), 560 (2), 680 (3), 820, 1k (9), 1.2k (2), 1.5k (4), 1.8k, 2.2k (2), 3.3k (5), 3.9k, 4.7k (4), 5.6k, 6.8k (2), 8.2k (2), 9.6k, 10k (13), 12k (2), 15k, 18k, 22k (2), 27k (2), 33k (2), 56k, 68k (5), 100k (3), 120k, 220k, 330k, 390k, 470k (2), 1.5M, 2.2M, 4.7M (2) Potentiometers: 1k, 5k (2), 10k (2), 20k, 50k, 100k

*2 watt
**1 watt

Capacitors: (all values in microfarads, unless noted)
10 µF (1), 4.7 µF (1), 1 µF(1), 33pF, 75pF, 100pF, 220pF, 330pF, 470pF, 500pF, 680pF, 820pF, 0.0068, 0.0047 (3), 0.0033 (2), 0.0022 (2), 0.0015, 0.001 (3), 0.068, 0.047 (4), 0.033, 0.022, 0.015, 0.01 (20), 0.1 (6), 0.22, 0.33, 0.47 (3), 0.68, 1 (2), 2.2, 10 (5), 470 (4), 0.22 µF (1), 0.01 µF (1)

Potentiometers: 25k [10-turn trim] (1)

Inductors: (microhenries unless noted)
1.0, 1.2, 1.5, 1.8, 2.2, 3.3, 4.7, 6.8, 8.2, 10, 12, 15, 18, 22, 27, 33 (2), 47, 68, 82, 100, 150, 220, 330, 470, 1mH (21), 15mH, 27mH, 33mH, 390mH

Miscellaneous Components:
Ceramic filter CFM-455D, 8Ω speaker, toggle switch, toroid core (type T106, mix 2), Magnet wire (4 feet), attenuator pad, fiber optic emitters: MLED-71, MFOE-71, LED HLMP-3200, fiber optic detectors: MRD-721, MFOD-71 (2), fiber optic cable (pcp) three 8 foot lengths of AMP 501232, fiber optic plugs: AMP 228087-1 (3), fiber optic device mounts: AMP 228040-1, AMP 228709-1 (2), microphone P-9930 miniature cartridge, Voltage Regulator 5V, Surface Mount RCA phono jacks (2), Power Jack, Max2606 IC Chip & Proto-Board adapter board, PROTO-Board, Univ PC Board, Stand-offs (4)

Test equipment needed for each experiment (x = required; o = optional)

Experiment / Equipment	1	2	3	4	5	6	7	8	9	10	11	12	13	14	15	16	17	18	19	20	21
Dual Trace Oscilloscope	x	x	x	x	x	x	x	x	x	x	x	x	x	x	x	x	x	x	x	x	x
Dual Voltage Power Supply	x		x		x	x	x	x	x		x	x	x	x		x	x	x	x	x	x
Function Generator	x	x	x	x	x	x	x		2	2	2	2	x	2	x	2	2	x	2	x	2
Volt-ohmmeter (DMM)						x	x	x	x				x			x		x	x	x	
Frequency Counter	x	x	x	x	x	x	x	x	x	x			x		x		x	x		x	
Prototype Board	x	x	x	x	x	x	x	x			x	x	x	x	x		x	x	x	x	x
RF Generator							x						x	x		x					
Pulse Generator																					
Attenuator Pad									x							x					
Spectrum Analyzer		o													o						
Distortion Analyzer						o															
Audio Spectrum Analyzer													o			x					

Acknowledgments

The following companies provided the data sheets used in the Appendix:

Amidon Associates, Inc.
AMP Incorporated
Analog Devices, Inc.
EXAR Corporation
Harris Semiconductor Corporation
Hewlett-Packard Company
Maxim Integrated Products, Inc.
Motorola Semiconductor Products
Murata-Erie North America, Inc.
National Semiconductor Corporation
Raytheon Company
Signetics Corporation

We gratefully acknowledge Mark E. Oliver of Monroe Community College, whose experiments constitute the majority of Part I of this manual.

CONTENTS

Taken from: *Laboratory Manual with System Projects,* by Jeffrey S. Beasley and Michael Fairbanks to accompany *Modern Electronic Communication,* by Gary M. Miller and Jeffrey S. Beasley, Seventh Edition

PART I: LABORATORY EXPERIMENTS

PART II: ELECTRONICS WORKBENCH (EWB) MULTISIM EXPERIMENTS

PART III: SYSTEM PROJECTS

Taken from: *Modern Electronic Communication*, Eighth Edition by Jeffrey S. Beasley and Gary M. Miller

PART IV: TROUBLESHOOTING WITH ELECTRONICS WORKBENCH MULTISIM

PART I

LABORATORY EXPERIMENTS

FREQUENCY SPECTRA OF POPULAR WAVEFORMS

OBJECTIVES:

1. To become acquainted with the Fourier series and its use in representing the frequency spectra of signals commonly used in communication systems.
2. To become familiar with frequency response of ceramic filters.
3. To become familiar with the use of spectrum analyzers.

REFERENCE:

Refer to section 1-6

TEST EQUIPMENT:

Dual-trace oscilloscope
Function generator
Frequency counter
Low-voltage power supply
Spectrum analyzer (if available)

COMPONENTS:

Ceramic filter: Murata-Erie CFM-455D
Signal diode: 1N914/1N4148 or equivalent
Resistors ($\frac{1}{2}$ watt): 1.5 kΩ (2)

THEORY:

The Fourier series is a mathematical tool used to represent any periodic function as an infinite series of sine or cosine functions. In electronics, waveforms of voltage or current are periodic functions which lend themselves to the use of the Fourier series. In the field of electronic communication, the Fourier series is often utilized to explain how signals are filtered and processed within the various blocks and stages that make up a communication system. In its general form,

$$f(t) = A_0 + \sum_{n=1}^{\infty} A_n \cos(n\omega_n t + \phi_n) + \sum_{n=1}^{\infty} B_n \sin(n\omega_n t + \phi_n)$$

Fortunately, most waveforms can be represented in much easier terms. The easiest waveform to represent mathematically is the sine wave itself.

$$e(t) = E_0 + E_{max} \cos(\omega t + \phi)$$

where
E_0 = dc offset
E_{max} = peak value of the sine wave
ω = frequency, radians per second
ϕ = initial phase angle

Other popular waveforms that can be written as a Fourier series are the square wave and triangle wave shown, respectively, in Fig. 2-1(a) and (b).

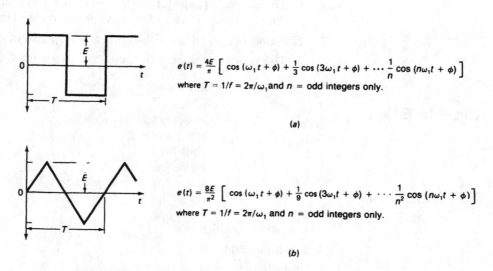

$$e(t) = \frac{4E}{\pi} \left[\cos(\omega_1 t + \phi) + \frac{1}{3}\cos(3\omega_1 t + \phi) + \cdots \frac{1}{n}\cos(n\omega_1 t + \phi) \right]$$
where $T = 1/f = 2\pi/\omega_1$ and n = odd integers only.

(a)

$$e(t) = \frac{8E}{\pi^2} \left[\cos(\omega_1 t + \phi) + \frac{1}{9}\cos(3\omega_1 t + \phi) + \cdots \frac{1}{n^2}\cos(n\omega_1 t + \phi) \right]$$
where $T = 1/f = 2\pi/\omega_1$, and n = odd integers only.

(b)

FIGURE 2-1 Popular waveforms and their Fourier series

If the Fourier series of a waveform is known, its spectral content can be represented on a spectrum diagram. A spectrum diagram is a sketch of voltage (or current) versus frequency in which its individual harmonic amplitudes are plotted as vertical lines (arrows) at each harmonic frequency. For example, for a 60-Hz sawtooth waveform:

$$e(t) = \frac{2E}{\pi} \left[\sin(377t) - \frac{\sin(2 \times 377t)}{2} + \frac{\sin(3 \times 377t)}{3} + \cdots \frac{(-1)^{n+1}\sin(n \times 377t)}{n} \right]$$

Figure 2-2 shows the spectrum of this signal if $E = 10$ V.

Notice that if the peak voltage is negative, it is still displayed as positive, since the negative sign merely denotes a 180° phase shift of that sinusoidal term. A spectrum diagram can be displayed for an unknown signal using a spectrum analyzer. Often, the spectrum analyzer's display is more useful in communication applications than is the more popular oscilloscope display of waveforms.

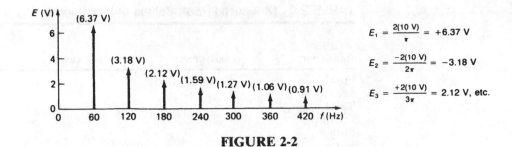

$$E_1 = \frac{2(10 \text{ V})}{\pi} = +6.37 \text{ V}$$

$$E_2 = \frac{-2(10 \text{ V})}{2\pi} = -3.18 \text{ V}$$

$$E_3 = \frac{+2(10 \text{ V})}{3\pi} = 2.12 \text{ V, etc.}$$

FIGURE 2-2

PRELABORATORY:

Determine the theoretical peak values of the first nine harmonics of the two waveforms given in Fig. 2-1, using the given Fourier series and the procedures shown in the theory section. For both of these waveforms, let $E = 5$ V. Compile your data into a table similar to Table 2-1.

PROCEDURE:

1. Build the circuit shown in Fig. 2-3. Connect a function generator to TP_1 and apply a 10-$V_{p\text{-}p}$ 455-kHz sine wave. Connect an oscilloscope at TP_2 and measure V_0. Carefully fine-tune the frequency of the function generator until you produce a maximum output voltage. You should discover five peaks near 455 kHz, but the center peak should be slightly larger than the other two, as sketched in Fig. 2-4. Make sure that you are tuned to the larger center peak frequency. Measure the peak values of V_0 and V_{in} and determine the insertion loss of the filter. You may discover your filter has a gain, rather than a loss due to impedance transformation properties.

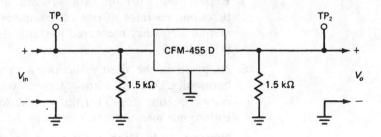

FIGURE 2-3

2. Now set the function generator to produce a ± 5V amplitude 455-kHz square wave such as that shown in Fig. 2.1. Carefully fine-tune the function generator so as to peak the output voltage. Again, you will find five specific frequencies near 455 kHz, where V_o is a maximum. Use the center peak frequency that causes the largest of the five peak voltages to result at TP_2. Measure the largest peak value of V_o at TP_2. Also, measure the frequency of the function generator using a frequency counter. Record these values in Table 2-1.

3. To determine the peak value of the third harmonic, instead of retuning the ceramic filter to resonate at the third harmonic frequency, set the function

TABLE 2-1   Measured Peak Values of Harmonics

HARMONIC	FREQUENCY	SQUARE	OUTPUT VOLTAGE AT TP₂
			TRIANGLE
First			
Second			
Third			
Fourth			
Fifth			
Sixth			
Seventh			
Eighth			
Ninth			

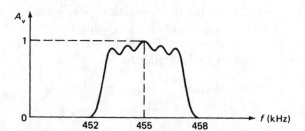

FIGURE 2-4   Typical frequency response of ceramic filter

generator to exactly one-third of the 455-kHz value measured in step 1. Again, you will find five specific frequencies near 455 kHz/3 where V_o is maximum. Again, use the center peak frequency that causes the largest of the five peaks to result in TP₂. Measure V_o at TP₂ and the frequency of the function generator. Record these values in Table 2-1.

4. Repeat step 3 for the fifth, seventh, and ninth harmonics by setting the function generator at one-fifth, one-seventh, and one-ninth of the fundamental frequency measured in step 1. Enter your resulting measurements in Table 2-1.

5. As given in the theory section, a square wave should exhibit no even harmonics. Determine how "perfect" your function generator's square wave is by repeating step 3 for the second, fourth, sixth, and eighth harmonics. Enter your measurements in Table 2-1.

6. Now set the function generator to produce a 10-V$_{p-p}$ triangle wave such as that shown in Fig. 2-1(b). Repeat steps 2–5 to measure the peak amplitudes of the first nine harmonics of the triangle wave. Enter your measurements in Table 2-1.

7. If a spectrum analyzer is available, produce the spectral display of the signal at TP₁ for the square and triangle waveforms. Set the controls so as to clearly display the amplitudes of the first nine harmonics.

REPORT/QUESTIONS:

1. Compare the theoretical values of the prelaboratory section with the measured values obtained in steps 2–6. What factors may have led to discrepancies between theoretical and measured values?

2. Sketch a frequency spectrum diagram for each of the two waveforms shown in Fig. 2-1, using the theoretical values determined in the prelaboratory section.

3. Suppose that the waveform shown in Fig. 2-1(a) is applied to a low-pass filter that exhibits a break frequency of 455 kHz and −20 dB/decade roll-off. Calculate the amplitudes of the first nine harmonics which would be contained in the output signal of the low-pass filter. Sketch the spectrum diagram of the resulting output signal of the filter. Assume that this waveform has a fundamental frequency of 455 kHz and an amplitude, E, of 5 V.

EXPERIMENT 3   NAME _____

TUNED AMPLIFIERS AND FREQUENCY MULTIPLICATION

OBJECTIVES:

1. To investigate the behavior of a negative clamper.
2. To study class C bias and amplification.
3. To understand the theory of frequency multiplication.

REFERENCE:

An application of frequency multiplication can be found in section 5-5 of the text.

TEST EQUIPMENT:

Dual-trace oscilloscope
Sinusoidal function generator
Low-voltage power supply
Prototype board
Frequency counter

COMPONENTS:

Transistor: 2N2222 or equivalent
Signal diode: 1N914/1N4148 or equivalent
Resistors ($\frac{1}{2}$ watt): 1 kΩ, 120 kΩ
Capacitors: 3.3 nF, 1 μF (2)
Inductor: 10 mH

PRELABORATORY:

Determine the resonant frequency of the tank circuit shown in Fig. 3-4 using

$$f_r = \frac{1}{2\pi\sqrt{LC}} \quad f_r = \text{_____}$$

PROCEDURE:

1. Build the circuit of Fig. 3-1. Monitor V_{in} with channel A (1 V/div dc-coupled) of the dual-trace oscilloscope. Monitor V_o with channel B (1 V/div dc-coupled). Apply a 1-V_{p-p} 1-kHz sine-wave signal as V_{in}. You should notice that the waveforms of V_{in} and V_o are identical. Now slowly increase the amplitude of V_{in} and you should notice that V_{in} and V_o are no longer identical with respect to their dc offset. Record V_{in} and V_o waveforms when $V_{in} = 4\ V_{p-p}$.

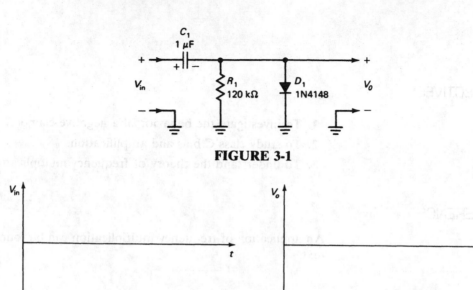

FIGURE 3-1

Also, determine at what critical voltage level of V_{in} the waveforms of V_{in} and V_o no longer possesses the same dc offset. (This level may be a judgment call on your part.) This is the process of negative clamping action. The circuit of Fig. 3-1 can now be disassembled.

Critical level =

2. Negative clamping is often used to bias a transistor for class C amplification. Class C bias puts the Q-point at a point "beyond" cutoff. To create a class C amplifier the diode used in the circuit of Fig. 3-1 is replaced with the base-emitter junction of a transistor. Build the circuit of Fig. 3-2. Monitor V_{in} with channel A (1 V/div dc-coupled) and monitor V_b with channel B (1 V/div dc-coupled). Again, apply a 1-V_{p-p} 1-kHz sine wave as V_{in}. Slowly increase the amplitude of V_{in} and you should notice that V_{in} and V_b behave exactly as V_{in} and V_o did in step 1. Now move channel B (5 V/div dc-coupled) to monitor V_o. Sketch the V_b and V_o waveforms when $V_{in} = 1\ V_{p-p}$. Repeat for V_{in} set at 2 V_{p-p} and 4 V_{p-p}. Measure the pulse-width of the negative pulse in V_o.

From these waveforms notice that it takes a certain initial V_{in} voltage level to force the Q-point to move into the active region from cutoff. This is what is meant by "beyond cutoff" bias in class C amplifiers. The circuit of Fig. 3-2 can now be disassembled.

3. Notice that this amplifier has a voltage gain greater than unity and also has a fairly high efficiency due to the small average collector current level.

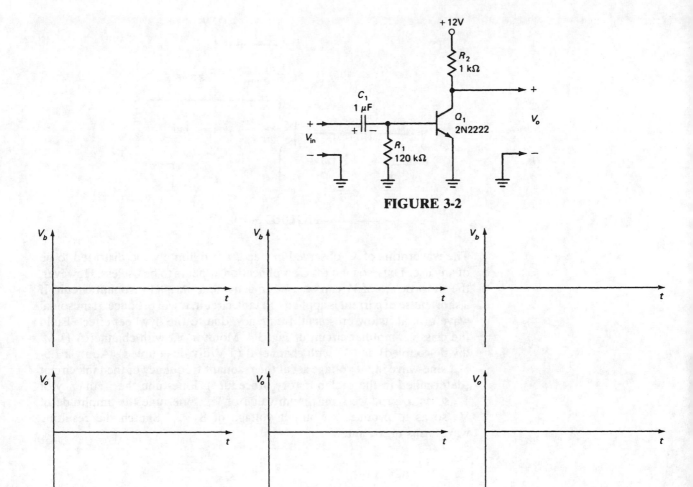

FIGURE 3-2

$V_{in} = 1$ Vp-p

$V_{o(pk)} = $ _____

$V_{in} = 2$ Vp-p

$V_{o(pk)} = $ _____

$V_{in} = 4$ Vp-p

$V_{o(pk)} = $ _____

The small average collector current results from the small duty cycle resulting from negative clamping action as seen in V_o waveforms of step 2. Calculate the duty cycle for each of the waveforms of step 2 using Fig. 3-3 and the equation:

$$\% D = \text{duty cycle} = \frac{\Delta t}{T} \times 100\%$$

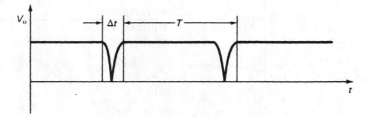

FIGURE 3-3

$V_{in} = 1$ V_{p-p}; $\% D = $ _____

$V_{in} = 2$ V_{p-p}; $\% D = $ _____

$V_{in} = 4$ V_{p-p}; $\% D = $ _____

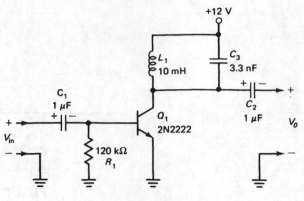

FIGURE 3-4

4. The waveforms of V_o observed in step 2 are definitely too distorted to be of any use. Thus, so far class C amplification appears to be useless. However, the short pulses of V_o can be used to activate a parallel resonant circuit. If a short pulse of current is applied to a tank circuit, it will produce a sinusoidal waveform at its own resonant frequency, due to the flywheel effect. Build the class C amplifier circuit of Fig. 3-4. Monitor V_{in} with channel A (1 V/div dc-coupled) and V_o with channel B (5 V/div dc-coupled). Apply a 1.5-V_{p-p} sine-wave input voltage set at the resonant frequency of the tank circuit (determined in the prelaboratory procedure). Fine-tune the frequency of V_{in} so as to produce a maximum value of V_o. Fine-tune the amplitude of V_{in} so as to produce an output voltage of 8 V_{p-p}. Sketch the resulting waveforms of V_{in} and V_o.

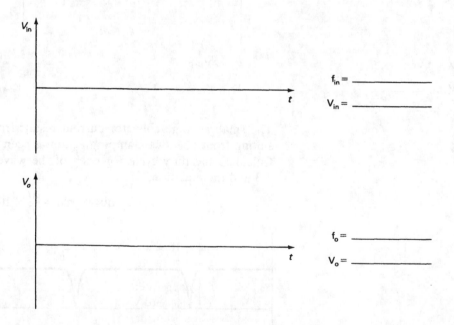

5. The main limitation of a class C amplifier is its narrow bandwidth of frequencies which can be amplified. This is due to the Q of the tank circuit. Fortunately, in most communication applications it is desired for an RF amplifier to have a narrow bandwidth so that it can filter out undesired frequencies. This amplifier is sometimes referred to as a "tuned amplifier" because of this characteristic. Determine the bandwidth of this amplifier by adjusting the frequency of V_{in} above and below the resonant frequency

so as to force V_o to drop 3 dB below its maximum value set in step 4. The bandwidth is simply the difference between the upper and lower 3-dB frequencies. Record these values.

$$f_+ = \text{_____} \qquad f_- = \text{_____} \qquad BW = \text{_____}$$

6. The Q of the tank circuit can be determined using the equation below. Determine this and record your results.

$$Q = \frac{f_r}{BW} \qquad Q = \text{_____}$$

7. Another use of a tuned class C amplifier is in frequency multiplication. In step 4, notice that for each cycle of the sine wave produced in the tank circuit by the flywheel effect, the tank circuit is recharged by another pulse of collector current due to negative clamping action and the fact that the input voltage is exactly matched to the resonant frequency of the tank circuit. However, it is possible to recharge the tank circuit on every other cycle of the sine wave by setting the frequency of V_{in} to exactly one-half of the resonant frequency. Do this with the circuit of Fig. 3-4. Again, fine-tune the frequency of V_{in} so as to produce a maximum value of V_o. Also, adjust the amplitude of V_{in} so as to produce $V_o = 8$ V$_{p-p}$. Record the resulting waveforms of V_{in} and V_o. This is a frequency-doubler circuit.

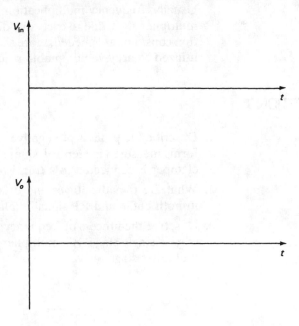

8. Try adjusting the frequency of V_{in} so as to produce ×3, ×4, and ×5 frequency multiplication. Record your resulting input and output voltage amplitudes and frequencies. Measure the input and output frequencies with a counter, if one is available. Also, record your waveform sketches for the ×5 multiplier.

TYPE	V_{in}	f_{in}	V_o	f_o
×3				
×4				
×5				

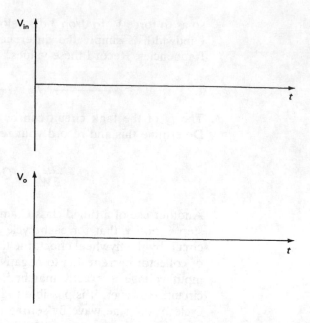

Note that the voltage amplitude decreases over the later cycles of V_o until the next current pulse restores the original amplitude. This distortion can be minimized by the use of higher Q components within the tank circuit. Usually, frequency multiplication greater than 5 is not possible in a single multiplier stage due to excessive distortion of this type. If larger multiplication constants are needed, more than one stage of multiplication is generally utilized to achieve acceptable results.

REPORT/QUESTIONS:

1. Describe the process of negative clamping action as observed in the waveforms measured in step 1. Explain how class C bias results when a negative clamper is connected to a transistor as observed in step 2.

2. What are the advantages and disadvantages of a class C amplifier design in both audio and RF signal applications?

3. Describe the process of frequency tripling in a ×3 multiplier stage. Explain why a single-stage ×7 multiplier stage does not work as well as a ×3 multiplier stage.

LOW-PASS IMPEDANCE TRANSFORMATION NETWORKS

OBJECTIVES:

1. To understand the concept of impedance matching for maximum power transfer.

2. To investigate the use of resonant *LC* networks to produce impedance transformation.

3. To design, build, and test an L-network.

REFERENCES:

Refer to sections 1-7 of the text.

TEST EQUIPMENT:

Dual-trace oscilloscope

Function generator

Frequency counter

Prototype board

COMPONENTS:

Inductors: two selected design values from Table 4-1

Capacitors: two selected design values from Table 4-2

Resistors ($\frac{1}{2}$ watt): 50 Ω, 426 Ω (use 560 Ω in parallel with 1800 Ω), and selected values needed to simulate a specific generator impedance (explained in procedure section)

THEORY:

Most RF circuits are required to deliver power to loads which have impedances quite different than the circuit load value that would optimize circuit output power. For example, a transistor amplifier might require an ac collector load resistance of 3000 Ω to deliver the desired power gain, but the actual load resistance available could well be a 50-Ω antenna. The problem then arises of finding a way to make the

50-Ω load resistance appear as a 3000-Ω load resistance to the transistor. If a resistive matching network is used, the resistors themselves produce a significant power loss in the system. This results even though they are providing the proper match for maximum power transfer. One solution frequently employed is to use a transformer. A second solution that works as long as the frequency of the signal remains relatively constant is to use an *LC* impedance transformation network. Ideal networks, being purely reactive, exhibit zero power loss. Realistic *LC* networks exhibit quite small values of power loss due to the real power dissipated in the pure resistance of the inductor. *LC* networks can be designed for operation at any desired frequency using fairly standard component values. They can be designed to exhibit either low-pass or high-pass filter characteristics. Low-pass filter characteristics are advantageous since they help eliminate unwanted harmonics from the system output.

In this experiment you will design, build, and test the simplest form of these networks, the two-element *LC* network, which is more commonly called the L-network. The name "L" is used because of its resemblance to an upside-down capital "L" when drawn out as a schematic.

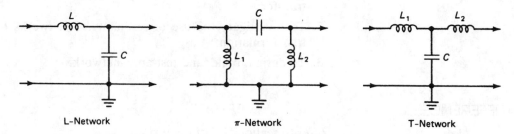

FIGURE 4-1 Typical impedance-matching networks

Other forms of these networks containing three or more elements are quite commonly found in communication systems. These include the T- and II-networks, which also resemble their names, as shown in Fig. 4-1. In summary, these circuits will exhibit the following properties:

1. They will have either low- or high-pass frequency response.
2. They will exhibit close-to-zero power loss.
3. At a desired frequency, their input impedance will be purely resistive and of a predetermined value when loaded with a specified resistive load.

PRELABORATORY:

1. Review electrical circuit theory on series and parallel resonance and read the attached theory material on designing impedance-matching networks with low-pass frequency response characteristics.

2. Calculate the required values of inductance and capacitance in order to build the two specified L-networks in Table 4-2, given the values for Z_{in}, R_L, and f_r. Show all work. Use equations 4-5, 4-8, 4-9, and 4-10 to design your L-networks.

3. Check your L-network designs for accuracy by applying ac circuit theory to your resulting designs. For each of the two circuits designed in step 2, you should show all work as you do the following:

(a) Determine the reactances of each of the L's and C's in your circuit at the given match frequency of 218 kHz.

(b) Combine these reactances with the other resistances (series, parallel, etc.) to determine the input impedance of the circuit at the match frequency of 218 kHz. A few polar-to-rectangular (or vice versa) conversions may be required, so you may need to brush up on your complex-number arithmetic before completing this step.

(c) Your results should be very close to being a purely resistive impedance (small reactive component in rectangular form or a small phase angle in polar form). If this does not happen, you made a mistake in either your original design or your check.

4. The component values available in the laboratory are given in Table 4-1. Select values for L and C which are closest to your calculated values from this table.

PROCEDURE:

1. Show your prepared design and test procedures to the lab instructor for verification that they are accurate and complete. If they are not correct, make corrections and modifications as necessary.

2. Determine the frequency response for both of your L-networks using the function generator to produce the sinusoidal input signal. It is important to simulate the proper internal impedance by adding the proper resistor in series. For example, if your signal generator has an internal impedance of 50 Ω and you want it to act like it has an internal impedance of 426 Ω, place a 376-Ω resistor (470 Ω, in parallel with 1.8 kΩ is close enough) in series with the generator as shown in Fig. 4-2.

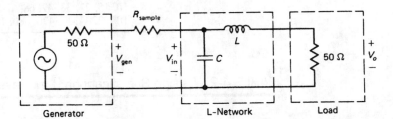

FIGURE 4-2

Consider V_{in} to be on the L-network end of the 376-Ω resistor. Take measurements of V_{in} and V_o at approximately 10 frequencies between 100 kHz and 1.0 MHz. Do not change the amplitude of the generator so as to produce a constant V_{in}, or else you will negate the effect of simulating the proper internal impedance and will not produce the valid frequency response. Calculate the relative decibel output voltage by comparing V_o to its maximum value and convert the ratio to decibels using

$$V_{o(dB)} = 20 \log \left| \frac{V_o}{V_{o_{(max)}}} \right|$$

3. Complete the following test procedures to determine experimentally the frequency at which the input impedance of the L-network is purely resistive. Determine the value of the purely resistive input impedance, R_{in}, at that frequency. Do this for both designs.

(a) At the frequency at which Z_{in} is purely resistive, there cannot be any phase shift between V_{gen} and V_{in} as seen in Fig. 4-2. Thus, experimentally determine the frequency near 218 kHz at which the waveforms of V_{gen} and V_{in} exhibit zero phase difference. Use a frequency counter to measure this frequency and compare to the theoretical value of 218 kHz. For the step-up L-network, use a sample resistor equal to 50 Ω. For the step-down L-network, use a sample resistor equal to 426 Ω (rather than 376 Ω).

(b) At this frequency, if Z_{in} is actually the design value given in Table 4-1, you should find that exactly half of V_{gen} is dropped across the sample resistor. The other half of V_{gen} is dropped across the input of the L-network. Verify that this is true. If you find that this relationship does not hold, measure the amplitudes of V_{gen} and V_{in} and solve for R_{in} using the voltage-divider equation:

$$V_{in} = V_{gen} \frac{R_{in}}{R_{gen} + R_{in}}$$

Compare your results with the theoretical value for R_{in} from Table 4-2.

TABLE 4-1   Standard Design Values

Inductors (μH)	1.0, 1.2, 1.5, 1.8, 2.2, 2.7, 3.3, 4.7, 6.8, 8.2, 10, 12, 15, 18, 22, 27, 33, 47, 68, 82, 100, 150, 220, 330, 470, 1000
Capacitors (nF)	0.1, 0.22, 0.33, 0.47, 0.68, 1.0, 1.5, 2.2, 3.3, 4.7, 6.8, 10, 15, 22, 33, 47, 68, 100, 220, 330, 470, 680, 1000

TABLE 4-2   Design Specifications: Low-Pass L-Section

FIGURE	NETWORK TYPE	Z_{in} (Ω)	R_L (Ω)	OPERATING FREQUENCY (kHz)
4-3	Step-down	426	50	218
4-5	Step-up	50	426	218

REPORT/QUESTIONS:

1. Using the results of step 2 of the test procedure, plot your resulting frequency response curves for both of the designed networks on graph paper by plotting $V_{o(dB)}$ versus frequency. It is not necessary to use semilog graph paper.

2. Write a design report describing what you did and how it worked out. Include all materials from the design procedure and test procedure. If your design procedure had to be modified, be sure to include both the original data and modified data. Explain what was wrong with the original design or procedure.

ADDITIONAL THEORY:

Impedance Transformation Using the L-Section

The L-section shown in Fig. 4-3 is an example of a low-pass tuned circuit, since at high frequencies the capacitor looks like a short and the inductor looks like an open, thus keeping the applied signal from ever reaching the load resistance, R_L.

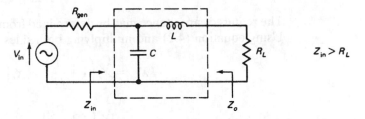

FIGURE 4-3

It is a tuned circuit because there is a particular frequency at which the inductive and capacitive reactances are equal and the circuit resonates, thus producing a maximum signal passed on to the load. If the values of L_p and C (shown in Fig. 4-4) are properly chosen to produce resonance at the frequency of the input signal, the generator will see a parallel resonant circuit in which the load resistance appears to be larger than it really is. Similarly, the load resistance will see a low-pass series resonant circuit made up of L and C. These principles are made obvious by redrawing the circuit of Fig. 4-3 into its parallel equivalent circuit, shown in Fig. 4-4.

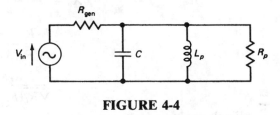

FIGURE 4-4

The series combination of L and R_L can be converted to an equivalent parallel combination by using the following series-parallel conversion equations:

$$R_p = R_L(1 + Q^2) \quad \text{where } Q = \frac{X_L}{R} \tag{4-1}$$

$$L_p = L\left(1 + \frac{1}{Q^2}\right) \tag{4-2}$$

At F_{in}, the frequency of the input signal, we want Z_{in} to be equal to some desired resistance value, R_d. If the values of L and C are chosen properly, X_c and $X_{L,p}$ will cancel at $f = f_{in}$. The impedance of a parallel resonant circuit is very high. Thus at $f = f_{in}$,

$$R_d = Z_{in} = R_p = R_L\left(1 + \frac{X_L^2}{R_L^2}\right) \tag{4-3}$$

$$= \frac{X_L^2 + R_L^2}{R_L}$$

LOW-PASS IMPEDANCE TRANSFORMATION NETWORKS   23

Solving equation (4-3) for X_L, we get

$$X_L^2 = R_L R_d - R_L^2$$

$$X_L = \sqrt{R_L(R_d - R_L)} \tag{4-4}$$

Finally, solving for the required inductance yields

$$L = \frac{\sqrt{R_L(R_d - R_L)}}{2\pi f_{in}} \tag{4-5}$$

The required capacitance may be determined from the fact that $X_c = X_{Lp}$ at resonance. Using equation (4-2) and multiplying both sides by $2\pi f_{in}$, we get

$$X_{Lp} = X_L\left(1 + \frac{1}{Q^2}\right) = X_L\left(1 + \frac{1}{X_L^2/R_L^2}\right)$$

$$= X_L\left(1 + \frac{R_L^2}{R_L^2}\right) = X_L\left(\frac{X_L^2 + R_L^2}{X_L^2}\right)$$

$$= \frac{X_L^2 + R_L^2}{X_L}$$

At $f = f_{in}$,

$$X_c = X_{Lp} = \frac{X_L^2 + R_L^2}{X_L} \tag{4-6}$$

Substituting equation (4-5) into (4-6) yields

$$X_o = \frac{\left[\sqrt{R_L(R_d - R_L)}\right]^2 + R_L^2}{\sqrt{R_L(R_d - R_L)}}$$

$$= \frac{R_L R_d - R_L^2 + R_L^2}{\sqrt{R_L(R_d - R_L)}}$$

$$= \frac{R_L R_d}{\sqrt{R_L(R_d - R_L)}} \tag{4-7}$$

Finally, solving for C gives us

$$C = \frac{1}{2\pi f_{in} X_o}$$

$$= \frac{1}{2\pi f_{in}\left|\dfrac{R_L R_d}{\sqrt{R_L(R_d - R_L)}}\right|}$$

$$= \frac{\sqrt{R_L(R_d - R_L)}}{2\pi f_{in} R_d R_L} \tag{4-8}$$

The L-section shown in Fig. 4-5 is another example of a low-pass tuned circuit for the same reasons as those stated for the circuit in Fig. 4-3. The main difference is that in this circuit if values of L' and C'_s (shown in Fig. 4-6) are properly chosen to produce resonance at the frequency of the input signal, the generator will "see" a series resonant circuit in which the load resistance will appear to be smaller than it is.

Again, a tool that can be used to demonstrate this phenomenon and derive the design equations is the use of series-parallel conversion equations and the series equivalent circuit shown in Fig. 4-6. However, before we get involved in another fairly long derivation as we did with the network of Fig. 4-3, compare the network

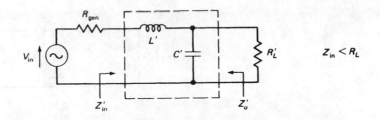

FIGURE 4-5

of Fig. 4-5 with the network of Fig. 4-3. A close inspection reveals that the network of Fig. 4-5 is nothing more than the network of Fig. 4-3 drawn in the reverse direction. Thus, if we think of the load resistance of Fig. 4-3 as the desired input impedance of Fig. 4-5, and if we think of the desired input impedance of Fig. 4-3 as the load resistance of Fig. 4-5, we can immediately devise the design equations. This can be done merely by substituting in the new variable names in for the old variable names in the design equations for Fig. 4-3.

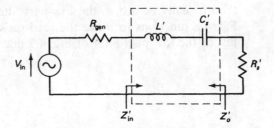

FIGURE 4-6

Since for Fig. 4-3,

$$L = \frac{\sqrt{R_L(R_d - R_L)}}{2\pi f_{in}} \qquad (4\text{-}5)$$

then for Fig. 4-5,

$$L = \frac{\sqrt{R_d'(R_L - R_d')}}{2\pi f_{in}} \qquad (4\text{-}9)$$

Similarly, since for Fig. 4-3,

$$C = \frac{\sqrt{R_L(R_d - R_L)}}{2\pi f_{in}R_d R_L} \qquad (4\text{-}8)$$

then for Fig. 4-5,

$$C = \frac{\sqrt{R_d'(R_L - R_d')}}{2\pi f_{in}R_L' R_d'} \qquad (4\text{-}10)$$

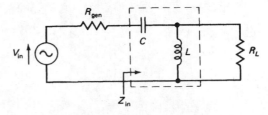

FIGURE 4-7

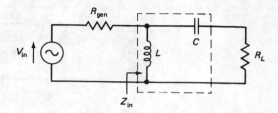

FIGURE 4-8

As stated in the introduction of this experiment, low-pass frequency response characteristics are usually important to eliminate the generation of harmonics from a nonpure sinusoidal input signal. However, this is not to say that high-pass filter L-networks are never found in practice. Examples of a high-pass filter L-network are shown in Figs. 4-7 and 4-8. At low frequencies, the capacitor looks like an open and the inductor looks like a short, thus keeping the input signal from ever reaching the load. The circuit of Fig. 4-7 functions to make the load resistance appear to be smaller than it really is, just as the low-pass filter network of Fig. 4-5 does. The circuit of Fig. 4-8 functions to make the load resistance appear to be larger than it really is, just as the low-pass filter of Fig. 4-3 does.

NAME _____

PHASE-SHIFT OSCILLATOR

OBJECTIVES:

1. To become familiar with the Barkhausen criteria for oscillation.
2. To analyze typical oscillator designs using operational amplifiers.
3. To predict if an amplifier will oscillate by first testing the circuit in the open-loop mode.

REFERENCE:

Refer to section 1-8 of the text.

TEST EQUIPMENT:

Dual-trace oscilloscope
Low-voltage power supply (2)
Function generator
Volt-ohmmeter
Frequency counter
Prototype board

COMPONENTS:

741 Operational amplifier (2)
Resistors ($\frac{1}{2}$ watt): 3.3 kΩ (7), 6.8 kΩ (2)
Capacitors: 0.1 μF (2)

PROCEDURE:

1. Build the circuit of Fig. 5-1. Connect the two power supplies to produce $+V_{cc}$ and $-V_{cc}$, as shown in Fig. 5-2. Also, connect the function generator as V_1.
2. Set the power supplies to produce $+12$ V dc at their output terminals so as to provide ± 12 V dc to the op amp. Connect R_9 to the output of the phase-shift network (C_2 and R_8) by connecting J_2 to TP$_4$. This sets up the

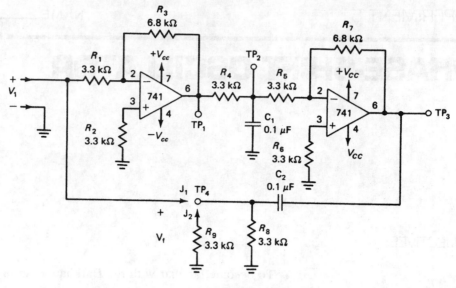

FIGURE 5-1

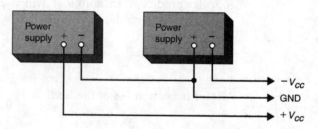

FIGURE 5-2

oscillator for open-loop measurements to be made. R_9 simulates the load that the amplifier would place on the lag network if the oscillator were running closed-loop. It is important that this load be included in the open-loop circuit so that realistic values of A_v and B are obtained.

3. Using the oscilloscope or VOM, perform a dc voltage check at TP_1 and TP_3 to verify that the op amp output voltage levels are at 0 V. If you find +12 V or −12 V at either test point, you probably have a defective op amp, which obviously means that a replacement is necessary.

FREQUENCY (Hz)	V_1 (V)	V_f (V)	ϕ (deg)	LEAD/LAG (+/−)
500				
2000				

STEP 4 DATA

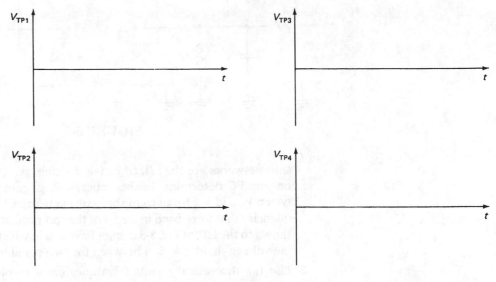

STEP 6 DATA

4. Turn on the function generator and set the generator controls to produce a 100-mV$_{p-p}$ sine wave at a frequency of 1 kHz. Measure V_1 and V_f at approximately 10 equally spaced test frequencies ranging from 500 Hz to 2 kHz. Also determine the phase difference between V_1 and V_f at each of these 10 test frequencies. Do not forget to record whether the phase difference is positive (if V_f leads V_1) or negative (if V_f lags V_1).

5. The oscillator will now be tested for proper closed-loop operation. Disconnect the simulated load resistor, R_9, from TP$_4$. Close the loop by connecting J_1 to TP$_4$. Obviously, there is no longer any need for a generator hookup, so remove it from the circuit. This will remove the generator's internal impedance from acting as a load on the closed-loop system. Measure the frequency of oscillation by connecting the frequency counter at TP$_3$.

6. Sketch the resulting waveforms of the voltages at TP$_1$, TP$_2$, TP$_3$, and TP$_4$. Record with each sketch the voltage amplitude and phase. Let the voltage at TP$_4$ be the phase reference.

7. Turn off both of the power supplies. Check and make sure that all required measurements have been recorded. The circuit can now be disassembled.

REPORT/QUESTIONS:

1. Using the data gathered in step 4, calculate the oscillator's loop gain $(A_v \times B)$ by dividing the open-loop output voltage, V_f, by the applied input voltage, V_1. Do this at each of the 10 test frequencies used in step 4. Record your resulting voltage gain and phase data in tabular form.

2. At what frequencies does the oscillator's measured loop gain exceed unity? At what frequency does the open-loop phase difference between V_f and V_1 equal zero degrees? How do these frequencies compare to the frequency of oscillation measured in step 5?

3. What was the purpose of R_9 in the open-circuit test circuit? Why was 3.3 kΩ chosen as its resistance value?

4. Figure 5-3 shows the two phase-shift networks used in this oscillator design. What kind of filters are they (high-pass or low-pass)? What kind of phase-

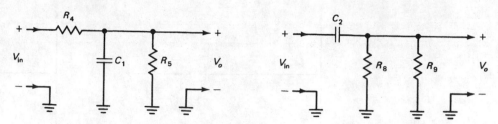

FIGURE 5-3

shift networks are they (lead or lag)? Using circuit theory or using SPICE on your PC, determine the theoretical voltage gain and phase difference between V_0 and V_{in} for each of these two networks. Use the same ten test frequencies that were used in step 4 of the test procedure. Note that the circuit shown to the left of Fig. 5-3 cannot have a gain which exceeds 0.5 due to simple voltage-divider action between the two equal-value resistors.

5. Use the theoretical results from question 4 to plot the voltage gain and phase frequency response curves for each of the two circuits shown in Fig. 5-3. Use two sheets of graph paper, one for the gain plots and one for the phase-angle plots.

6. Find the voltage gain and phase of each of the networks in Fig. 5-3 at the frequency of oscillation measured in step 5 of the test procedure. Do this by simply reading off the values from the graphs generated in question 5.

7. What type of op amp amplifiers (inverting or noninverting) are being used in this oscillator design? Theoretically determine the voltage gain of each of the amplifier stages using the given values for R_1, R_3, R_5, and R_7.

8. Referring to the answers to questions 6 and 7, determine if the oscillator circuit theoretically meets Barkhausen criteria for oscillation at the frequency of oscillation measured in step 5 of the test procedure.

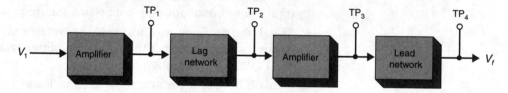

Loop gain $= A_{V1} \times A_{V2} \times A_{V3} \times A_{V4} \geq 1$

Total phase $= \phi_1 + \phi_2 + \phi_3 + \phi_4 = 0$ degrees

LC FEEDBACK OSCILLATOR

OBJECTIVES:

1. To reinforce the concepts of Barkhausen criteria for oscillation.

2. To analyze typical oscillator designs using operational amplifiers.

3. To become familiar with limiting and one application for this process.

REFERENCES:

Refer to section 1-8 of the text.

TEST EQUIPMENT:

Dual-trace oscilloscope
Low-voltage power supply (2)
Function generator
Volt-ohmmeter
Frequency counter
Prototype board
Distortion analyzer (optional)

COMPONENTS:

741 Operational amplifier
Germanium diodes: 1N270, IN34A or equivalent (2)
Inductor: 1 mH
Capacitors: 2.2 nF (2)
Resistors ($\frac{1}{2}$ watt): 330 Ω, 470 Ω, 1 kΩ (2)

PRELABORATORY:

Determine the resonant frequency of the series resonant circuit of Fig. 6-1. Also, determine the theoretical voltage gain of the op amp stage using the given values of R_1 and R_2.

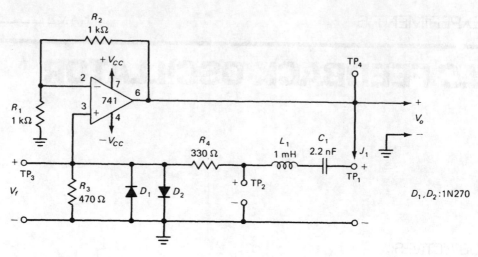

FIGURE 6-1

PROCEDURE:

1. Build the oscillator of Fig. 6-1. Use a pair of needle-nosed pliers to protect the glass body of each germanium diode from being cracked as the leads are bent. Connect the power supplies to the op amp as shown in Fig. 6-1. Adjust each power supply voltage level to 5 V dc to apply ±5 V dc to the op amp.

2. To analyze this oscillator circuit design in the open-loop mode, connect the function generator to TP_1 and make sure that jumper J_1 is not connected to TP_1. Check the dc output voltage of the op amp. If the level is not approximately zero volts, you may have a wiring error or a defective op amp. Repair any faults that are found.

3. Apply a 250-mV$_{p-p}$ sine wave at TP_1 and tune the frequency to approximately the resonant frequency determined in prelab. Monitor V_{TP1} with channel A and monitor V_o with channel B of the oscilloscope. Fine-tune the frequency of the generator so as to produce a maximum signal amplitude at TP_4. Record the generator frequency and the amplitude of V_{TP_1}, V_f, and V_o. Also, record the phase angle of V_f and V_o, letting V_{TP_1} be phase reference.

$$V_{TP_1} = \rule{1.5cm}{0.4pt} \qquad V_f = \rule{1.5cm}{0.4pt} \qquad V_o = \rule{1.5cm}{0.4pt}$$
$$f_{TP_1} = \rule{1.5cm}{0.4pt} \qquad \phi_f = \rule{1.5cm}{0.4pt} \qquad \phi_o = \rule{1.5cm}{0.4pt}$$

4. Reconnect the generator at TP_2 and measure the same amplitudes and phase angles that were measured in step 3. From these measurements, determine the actual voltage gain of the op amp stage. Compare this value to the theoretical value determined in prelab.

$$V_{gen} = \rule{1.5cm}{0.4pt} \qquad V_f = \rule{1.5cm}{0.4pt} \qquad V_o = \rule{1.5cm}{0.4pt}$$
$$A_v = \rule{1.5cm}{0.4pt} \qquad \phi_f = \rule{1.5cm}{0.4pt} \qquad \phi_o = \rule{1.5cm}{0.4pt}$$

5. Now increase the amplitude of the generator voltage until limiting just begins to occur in the waveforms of V_f and V_o. This is the point at which the V_f and V_o waveforms start to look distorted due to the diodes beginning to turn on. Measure the amplitudes and sketch the waveforms of V_{TP_1}, V_f, and V_o at this critical setting.

6. Now the oscillator will be tested for closed-loop operation. Do this by removing the generator connection from TP_1 to avoid loading by the genera-

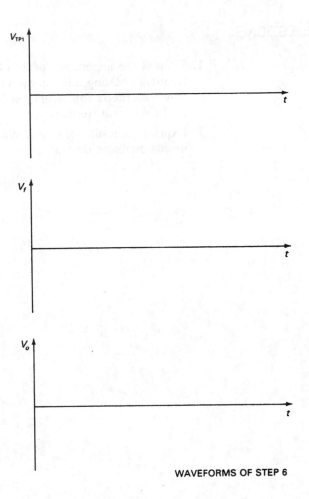

WAVEFORMS OF STEP 6

tor's internal impedance. Also, the jumper J_1 must be connected to TP_1. The circuit should now self-oscillate at the resonant frequency of the series resonant circuit. Measure the amplitude and phase angle of the voltages at TP_2, TP_3, and TP_4. Let the voltage at TP_4 serve as phase reference. Also, measure the frequency of oscillation and note how badly distorted the waveforms appear to be. Note that it may be necessary to use 10:1 probes on the oscilloscope to avoid having the scope's internal impedance from loading down the circuit and possibly keeping it from oscillating.

TP_2: Amplitude = _____   phase = _____

TP_3: Amplitude = _____   phase = _____

TP_4: Amplitude = _____   phase = _____

frequency = _____

disortion comments:

7. Short out the resistor R_4 by connecting a jumper between TP_2 and TP_3. With R_4 out of the circuit, the feedback factor, B, should be much larger.

Again, observe the waveforms at TP_2, TP_3, and TP_4. Note any changes that occur in the waveforms. Remove the R_4 short before proceeding.

8. If a distortion analyzer is available, measure the total harmonic distortion (% THD) of V_o at TP_4.

% THD = _____

REPORT/QUESTIONS:

1. What is the impedance of an ideal series resonant circuit at its resonant frequency? Using this answer and your observations for reference, explain why the criteria for oscillation for the *LC* feedback oscillator is met only at the resonant frequency.

2. Explain the results of step 7. What is the purpose of the germanium diodes in this oscillator design?

NAME _____

COLPITTS RF OSCILLATOR DESIGN

OBJECTIVES:

1. To investigate the theory of operation of a Colpitts oscillator.
2. To follow a "cookbook" design procedure in the fabrication of a working circuit.
3. To reinforce the concepts of Barkhausen criteria for oscillation.

REFERENCE:

Refer to section 1-8 of the text.

TEST EQUIPMENT:

Dual-trace oscilloscope
Low-voltage power supply
Function generator
Volt-ohmmeter
Frequency counter
Prototype board

COMPONENTS:

2N2222 Transistor
Inductors: 8.2 μH, 27 mH
Capacitors: 0.1 μF (3), selected design values for C_1 and C_2 from Table 7-1
Resistors ($\frac{1}{2}$ watt): 680 Ω, selected design values for R_1, R_2, and R_3 from Table 7-1

THEORY:

In this experiment you will design, build, and test a Colpitts oscillator. This oscillator belongs to a class of oscillators called resonant oscillators. This name arises from the fact that they use LC resonant circuits as the frequency determining elements. Again, as in the oscillators of Experiments 5 and 6, Barkhausen criteria must be met for oscillations to occur. Specifically, the product of the loaded voltage gain of the active device's stage and the attenuation of the feedback network must be equal to or slightly larger than unity to sustain oscillations resulting from an undistorted sinusoidal output signal.

$$A_v \times B \geq 1$$

Also, the total phase shift that occurs around the closed loop must be close to 0° to ensure that positive feedback is existing.

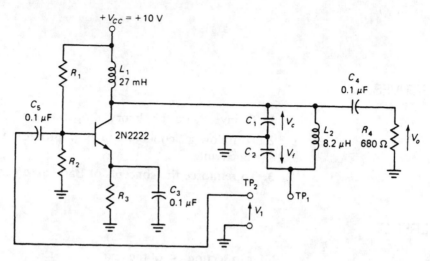

FIGURE 7-1

Figure 7-1 shows the basic Colpitts oscillator layout. It is easily recognized by the capacitor voltage division, which makes up the feedback network. Applying Barkhausen criteria to this circuit, we find

$$\frac{V_c}{B_1} \times \frac{V_f}{V_c} \geq 1$$

where

$$A_v = \frac{V_c}{B_1} \quad \text{and} \quad B = \frac{V_f}{V_c} = \frac{C_1}{C_2}$$

In other words, when the circuit is in the open-loop configuration, V_f must be equal to or slightly greater in amplitude to V_1. Also, V_f must be in phase with V_1. If these two conditions are met, then when the loop is closed, the circuit will oscillate. The amplitude criteria are fairly easily met. The voltage-divider action of C_1 and C_2 must yield an attenuation, B, that is the reciprocal of the voltage gain of the transistor amplifier stage, A_v.

$$A_v \geq \frac{1}{B}$$

Meeting the phase criteria is more difficult. The collector-to-emitter voltage of a common-emitter amplifier is 180° out of phase with the base-to-emitter voltage if the collector load is a pure resistance. The feedback scheme of obtaining V_c and V_f in opposite directions with respect to ground causes the additional 180° phase shift required to bring V_f to the desired 0° phase relationship. The load on the transistor's collector looks purely resistive when the circuit is resonant. Thus there is no additional phase shift created within the closed-loop system. At resonance, the tank circuit ideally looks like an infinitely large resistance in parallel with R_4. In practice, the equivalent parallel resistance is small enough to decrease the load slightly below 680 Ω, due to the Q of the inductor in the tank circuit, so circuit response may be slightly altered from what is ideally expected.

PRELABORATORY DESIGN:

Design the Colpitts oscillator circuit of Fig. 7-1 using the following design procedures. Draw a schematic of the final design in your lab report along with each of your design calculations.

1. *General design rules*: For the final design, use only a single component in each component location. Pick the value of the component from the list of standard value components available in the lab given in Table 7-1. Do this by selecting the standard value that comes closest to each of your design values.

TABLE 7-1 Standard Values of Resistors and Capacitors Available for Use as Design Values

Resistors (Ω):	10, 15, 22, 27, 33, 47, 68, 82,
	100, 150, 220, 270, 330, 470, 680, 820
	1 k, 1.5 k, 2.2 k, 2.7 k, 3.3 k, 4.7 k, 6.8 k, 8.2 k
	10 k, 15 k, 22 k, 27 k, 33 k, 47 k, 68 k, 82 k,
	100 k, 150 k, 220 k, 270 k, 330 k, 470 k, 680 k, 820 k
Capacitors (nF):	0.1, 0.22, 0.47, 1.0, 2.2, 4.7, 10, 22, 47, 100, 220, 470

2. *Dc design*: Determine the values of R_1, R_2, and R_3 to meet the following conditions. Assume that $V_{BE} = 0.5$ V.
   (a) The emitter current, I_E, is approximately 3.75 mA.
   (b) The current through the voltage-divider resistors, R_1 and R_2, is approximately one-tenth the value of I_E.
   (c) $V_{CE} = 5.5$ V. Assume that the 27-mH inductor is ideal (negligible winding resistance).

3. *Ac design:* Assume that the collector load is just R_c. Assume that the tank circuit impedance is too large to produce any noticeable loading on the amplifier stage. Also, assume that the amplifier's input impedance, reflected back through the tank circuit, does not produce any appreciable loading on the output of the amplifier stage.
   (a) Determine A_v of the amplifier stage using the values of R_1, R_2, and R_3 determined in the dc design. Use the equations given below to approximate the transistor's base-emitter ac resistance and the voltage gain of the amplifier stage:

$$A_v = -\frac{r_c}{r_e'} = -\frac{R_4}{r_e'} \quad \text{where } r_e' \cong \frac{0.025}{I_E}$$

   (b) Select single standard values of C_1 and C_2 to achieve a value of B such that $A_v \times B = 10$, and to cause the frequency of oscillation to be 1.8 MHz ± 200 kHz.

PROCEDURE:

1. Show the completed design and drawing to the lab instructor for verification that it is complete and accurate. The design and drawing should be completed before coming to the lab and is due for inspection at the beginning of the laboratory session.

2. Assemble the circuit on the prototype board. Leave the circuit in the open-loop configuration by leaving the jumper between TP_1 and TP_2 disconnected. Connect the power supply, generator, and oscilloscope to the circuit to make open-circuit measurements.

3. Using the volt-ohmmeter, measure V_{BE}, V_{CE}, and V_E. Determine if the transistor is biased close to the theoretical values used in the design procedures. Document the original data, changes to the circuit design, and final test data.

4. The generator should initially be tuned close to the theoretical resonant frequency of 1.8 MHz. Apply a 20 mV_{p-p} signal at TP_2 and determine the frequency that causes V_c to be of maximum amplitude. Record this frequency. You should use 10:1 probes on the scope to avoid having the scope load down the circuit.

5. At this test frequency, measure the voltage amplitude and frequency of the voltages V_1, V_c, and V_f. Also, record the phase angles of these voltages with respect to V_1.

VOLTAGE	AMPLITUDE	FREQUENCY	PHASE
V_1			
V_c			
V_f			

6. Using the data gathered in step 5, determine if $A_v \times B$ exceeds unity. Show your calculations.

7. If $A_v \times B$ is less than 1, make necessary changes to the circuit in order to cause the product to exceed unity. If the product does exceed unity, close the loop by disconnecting the generator and hooking up a jumper between TP_1 and TP_2. Measure the amplitude, frequency, and phase of the three voltages V_1, V_c, and V_f. Again, make sure that these waveforms are being measured with 10:1 scope probes.

8. Carefully measure and record the waveshape of the oscillator's output voltage. Does it look at all distorted? If it does, consult the troubleshooting chart in Fig. 7-2 and make changes to A_v and B to produce the most undistorted output voltage waveform. An easy way to decrease A_v without changing the bias conditions is to place an unbypassed emitter resistance between the emitter resistor and transistor's emitter. Try values between 10 and 100 Ω.

   (a) If this resistor is too large, the oscillator will not oscillate.
   (b) If this resistor is too small, the output voltage waveform will remain distorted.

9. Determine a final set of component values that will yield an apparently undistorted sinusoidal signal of desired frequency and record the final schematic in your report.

Symptom #1:   With loop closed, the oscilloscope shows no output signal.

Possible causes:

  (a) No d.c. power supplied.
  (b) 1:1 scope probe loading down the circuit.
  (c) Insufficient voltage gain in amplifier stage.
  (d) Feedback voltage division too small.

Symptom #2:   With loop closed, the oscilloscope display as shown below:

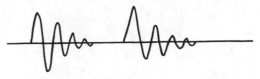

Possible causes:
  (a) Way too much voltage gain.
  (b) Feedback voltage division way too large.

Symptom #3:   With loop closed, the oscilloscope display as shown below:

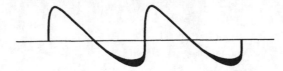

Possible causes:
  (a) Slightly too much voltage gain.
  (b) Feedback voltage division slightly too large.

If the output signal of the oscillator is an undistorted sinewave, then $A_r \times B$ is probably somewhere between 1.0 and 2.0.

FIGURE 7-2 Troubleshooting chart

10. Demonstrate to the lab instructor that your Colpitts oscillator is working properly in producing an undistorted output waveform in the closed-loop configuration.

REPORT/QUESTIONS:

1. Draw the ac and dc equivalent circuits for your final working Colpitts oscillator.

2. Explain how your Colpitts design operates, using the results of your measurements and conclusions that you have devised based on positive-feedback concepts and Barkhausen criteria.

HARTLEY RF OSCILLATOR DESIGN

OBJECTIVES:

> 1. To investigate the theory of operation of a Hartley oscillator.
> 2. To follow a "cookbook" design procedure in the fabrication of a working circuit.
> 3. To become familiar with the characteristics of toroid coils and the procedures associated with hand-winding coils.
> 4. To reinforce the concepts of Barkhausen criteria for oscillation.

REFERENCE:

> Refer to section 1-8 of the text.

TEST EQUIPMENT:

> Dual-trace oscilloscope
> Low-voltage power supply
> Function generator
> Volt-ohmmeter
> Frequency counter
> Prototype board

COMPONENTS:

> 2N2222 Transistor
> Capacitors: 0.001 μF, 0.1 μF (3)
> Resistors ($\frac{1}{2}$ watt): selected design values for R_1-R_5 from Table 7-1
> Toroid core: iron powder type T-106, mix 2 (Polamar or Amidon)
> Magnet wire: AWG No. 20 varnish-coated, 4-ft length

THEORY:

> The Hartley oscillator design, shown in Fig. 8-1, operates in the same manner as the Colpitts, except that the voltage division is accomplished at the inductive half of the

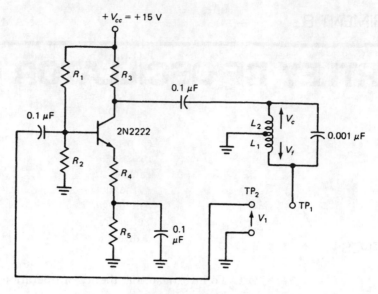

FIGURE 8-1

tank circuit instead of at the capacitive half. To make the results agree more closely with theory, the RF choke has been replaced with a fixed collector resistor, R_3. The tank circuit inductance, shown in Fig. 8-1 as L_1 and L_2, is fabricated by winding the apropriate number of turns on an iron-powder toroid core. The voltage division is accomplished by connecting a tap at the correct location between the ends of the coil. Iron-powder toroids are circular, doughnut-shaped devices fabricated by bonding very fine iron particles together. They make it possible to build a certain value inductor with fewer turns than would be required without an iron core. They also produce very predictable values of resulting inductance. The toroid shape confines the magnetic field within its circular border and therefore reduces the magnetic coupling from accidentally resulting between coils in neighboring circuits. Winding a single coil on one core simplifies construction and makes the desired voltage division in the feedback network much easier to produce. To find the number of turns needed for type T-106 mix 2 cores, the following relation holds:

$$N = 100 \sqrt{\frac{L \times 10^6}{135}}$$

where L is the design value of total inductance in henrys.

The location of the tap can be obtained by applying transformer principles. Since the upper and lower parts of the coil are wound on the same core, the flux cutting each turn is the same. Therefore, the voltage per turn is constant, allowing the following relationship to hold for the feedback attenuation factor:

$$B = \frac{V_f}{V_c} = \frac{N_1}{N_2}$$

where

N_1 = number of windings for L_1

N_2 = number of windings for L_2

$N = (N_1 + N_2)$ = total number of windings in the toroid coil

The major drawback to toroids is that the powdered iron exhibits loss, which appears as a resistor in parallel with the tuned tank circuit. For the T-106 mix 2 variety, the equivalent parallel resistance, R_P, is given by

$$R_P = \frac{K}{N^2}$$

where $K = 619.2 \times 10^3 \ \Omega\text{-turns}^2$

N = total number of turns

This resistance, R_P, is in parallel with R_c in the ac equivalent circuit. The required tap location can be calculated once the voltage-divider ratio, B, is determined. Three turns is about the smallest practical number for obtaining predictable voltage division. When designing the transistor amplifier portion of the oscillator, the best results are usually achieved with gains in the range 5 to 20. Low values of voltage gain create a problem of obtaining the desired voltage division, B, which is very difficult to adjust. High values of voltage gain are hard to obtain repeatedly or predictably from the transistor at high frequencies. They also require the voltage division, B, to be unreasonably small and difficult to achieve.

PRELABORATORY DESIGN:

Design the Hartley oscillator circuit of Fig. 8-1 using the following design procedures. Draw a schematic of your final design in your lab report along with each of your design calculations.

1. *General design rules:* For the final design, use only a single component in each component location. Pick the value of the component from the list of standard value components available in the lab given in Table 7-1 of the Colpitts oscillator experiment. Do this by selecting the standard value that comes closest to each of your design values.

2. *Ac design:*
   (a) Determine the value of inductance, L, required to obtain oscillation at 1.8 MHz $\pm$ 200 kHz.
   (b) Determine the total number of turns required to achieve this total inductance.
   (c) Select a tap location that will yield a value of B somewhere in the range 0.18 to 0.25.
   (d) Calculate the equivalent parallel resistance, R_P, of the coil at resonance.
   (e) Calculate the value of voltage gain, A_v, of the amplifier to create $A_v \times B$ to be between 1.0 and 1.1.
   (f) Select a trail value of R_4 so that R_4 is approximately 15 times greater than the transistor's base-emitter dynamic resistance, r_e'. Use a dc emitter current value of 3.75 mA. Approximate r_e' using

$$r_e' \cong \frac{.025}{I_E}$$

   (g) Calculate the value of ac collector resistance, r_c, required to yield the desired A_v, using

$$A_v = \frac{r_c}{r_e' + r_e} = \frac{R_P \| R_3}{r_e' + R_4}$$

   (h) Using the r_c found in step (g) and the equivalent parallel resistance, R_P, found in step (d), calculate a trial value of R_3.

$$r_c = \frac{R_3 R_P}{R_3 + R_P}$$

3. *Dc design:*
   (a) Select values of R_1, R_2, and R_5, which when used with R_3 and R_4 from the ac design yields the following dc conditions. Assume that $V_{BE} = 0.5$ V.
      (1) Dc emitter current: $I_E = 3.75$ mA.
      (2) $V_{CE} = 6.0$ V.
      (3) The current through the voltage-divider resistors, R_1 and R_2, is approximately one-tenth the value of I_E.
   (b) Make sure that R_5 is set at least 10 times as large as R_4.

PROCEDURE:

1. Show the completed design and drawing to the lab instructor for verification that they are complete and acceptable.

2. Assemble the oscillator circuit using the prototype board. Set up the circuit in the open-loop configuration by leaving TP_1 and TP_2 disconnected.

3. Using the volt-ohmmeter, measure V_{BE}, V_{CE}, and V_E to determine if the transistor is biased properly for amplification to occur. Document the original data, any changes made to the circuit design, and final dc data.

4. The generator should be initially tuned close to the theoretical resonant frequency of 1.8 MHz. Apply a 200-mV$_{\text{p-p}}$ signal at TP_2 and determine the frequency at which V_c is of maximum amplitude. Use 10:1 scope probes to make sure that the scope's internal impedance does not alter the waveforms being observed due to loading.

5. At this frequency, measure the voltage amplitude, frequency, and phase of V_c, V_f, and V_1, using V_1 as phase reference.

6. Using the data gathered in step 5, decide if $A_v \times B$ is greater than unity.

7. If $A_v \times B$ is less than 1, make necessary changes to the circuit design to cause the product to exceed unity and repeat steps 2–6. If $A_v \times B$ is greater than 1, close the loop by connecting a jumper between TP_1 and TP_2 and disconnect the generator from the circuit. Measure the amplitude, frequency, and phase angle of the three voltages as was done in step 5. Again, use 10:1 scope probes.

8. Carefully measure and record the waveshape of the oscillator's output voltage. If the output waveform is not a clean sine wave, but shows distortion, or if there is no output waveform present, consult the troubleshooting chart in Fig. 7-2. Make appropriate modifications. Record all changes made to your design. An easy way to change the voltage gain of the amplifier stage without changing the bias conditions or the resonant frequency is to alter the value of R_4.

9. Determine a final set of values for the circuit that will yield an apparently undistorted sinusoidal signal of the desired frequency.

10. Demonstrate to the lab instructor that your Hartley oscillator is working properly in producing an undistorted output waveform in the closed-loop configuration.

REPORT/QUESTIONS:

1. Draw the ac and dc equivalent circuits for the oscillator stage.

2. Explain how your circuit operates, using the results of your measurements and conclusions you have devised based on positive-feedback concepts and Barkhausen criteria.

SWEPT-FREQUENCY MEASUREMENTS

OBJECTIVES:

1. To use the VCG swept-frequency capability of a signal generator to obtain the frequency response of a circuit.
2. To use a detector in a swept-frequency measurement setup.
3. To use a swept-frequency measurement procedure to obtain the insertion loss of a ceramic filter in decibels.

REFERENCE:

Ceramic filters are discussed in section 4-3 of the text.

TEST EQUIPMENT:

Dual-trace oscilloscope: must be able to produce a Y versus X display with variable sensitivity on both axes

Function generators (2); one must have a VCG input jack

50-Ω Selectable attenuator pad; refer to Fig. 9-7

Low-voltage power supply

Frequency counter

COMPONENTS:

Ceramic filter: Murata-Erie Type CFM-455D

Resistors ($\frac{1}{2}$ watt): 50 Ω, 100 Ω, 1.5 kΩ (2), 10 kΩ (3)

Capacitor: 0.1 μF

Germanium diode: 1N270, 1N34A, or equivalent

THEORY:

Swept-frequency measurement techniques are used extensively in the design and testing of RF and microwave components. This technique allows the technician to observe the entire frequency response of a circuit in real time on oscilloscopes.

A swept-frequency measurement setup can be thought of as one where constant amplitude signals of different test frequencies are applied to a test circuit in successive time intervals. The results of each of these successive measurements are then observed on an oscilloscope.

Implicit in this technique is the assumption that the rate at which the test frequency is changed can be ignored. This criterion can be met in almost all cases where the sweep frequency is no greater than one-hundredth of the lowest test frequency. In some noncritical applications, the sweep frequency can be as high as one-tenth the lowest test frequency.

The simplest form of a swept-frequency setup is shown in Fig. 9-2. This form of measurement displays the complete test sine wave and achieves a waveform such as the bandpass filter in the left column of Fig. 9-4. The peak values of the sine waves form the frequency response curve with respect to the zero volt axis for the filter under test. The portion of the display below the zero volt line is simply the mirror image of the top-half.

The major drawback to this display method is that the display instrument used for the resulting display must have a frequency response significantly greater than that of the highest frequency to be displayed. This method is obviously useless with an X-Y recorder at RF frequencies; however, it may prove useful for a high-quality oscilloscope at low RF frequencies.

A less ambiguous display and one that is compatible with low-frequency oscilloscopes and X-Y recorders is shown in the right column of Fig. 9-4. This display is obtained by inserting a diode peak detector at the output of the circuit under test. This peak detector generates a voltage amplitude that is proportional to the peaks of the RF sine waves passed by the test circuit and creates the desired bandpass filter response display. In this case the oscilloscope used does not have to display the RF frequencies, only the low-frequency sweep signal.

Within the procedure of this experiment, you will use both methods to display the bandpass characteristics of a ceramic RF filter. Limitations and calibration of the display will be illustrated. The ceramic bandpass filter used as a sample test device in this experiment is designed for use in a standard AM broadcast band receiver's intermediate-frequency circuits. The device has a specified center frequency of 455 kHz and a total-5-dB bandwidth of 30 kHz. It exhibits a typical 2-dB ripple and 2-dB insertion loss in the bandpass region and a very large (greater than 50 dB) attenuation cutoff in the stop band. These filters are fairly expensive and fragile, so handle them with care. These filter characteristics are specified between a 1.5-kΩ source and a 1.5kΩ load, so make sure that the circuit given in Fig. 9-2 is used for testing this device.

PROCEDURE:

1. Build the test circuit shown in Fig. 9-1. Most function generators that are designed for sweeping capability will provide the user with an input jack. The name of the jack varies with the manufacturer of the generator. Some of the more popular names used are VCG (voltage-controlled generator) input, VC input, or FM (frequency-modulated) input. As the names imply, the instantaneous voltage level that is applied to this input jack will determine a certain amount of deviation in the output frequency of the generator. The exact amount of frequency change that occurs will also vary from one generator to another.

2. Adjust the RF generator to produce a 400-mV$_{p-p}$ sine wave at a test frequency of 450 kHz. Now apply a series of eight different positive dc voltage

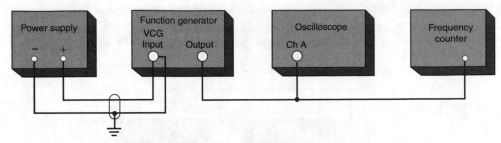

FIGURE 9-1 Determination of the deviation rate

levels to the VCG input jack and note the resulting output frequency of the RF generator. Consult the manual of the generator to make sure that you do not exceed the maximum allowable VCG input voltage before nonlinearity or damage results in the RF generator.

VCG INPUT VOLTAGE (V)	OUTPUT FREQUENCY (kHz)

3. Repeat step 2 using a negative dc voltage applied to the VCG input jack. Simply reverse the leads of the power supply to create a negative voltage at the VCG input jack of the generator.

VCG INPUT VOLTAGE (V)	OUTPUT FREQUENCY (kHz)

4. Plot the graph of the output frequency versus VCG input voltage for your generator. It should be a near-linear function. From your graph, determine your generator's resulting deviation rate, K_f, by reading off the slope of the straight line or using the following equation:

$$K_f = \frac{\Delta f}{\Delta V_{VCG}} = \frac{f_{max} - f_{min}}{V_{max} - V_{min}}$$

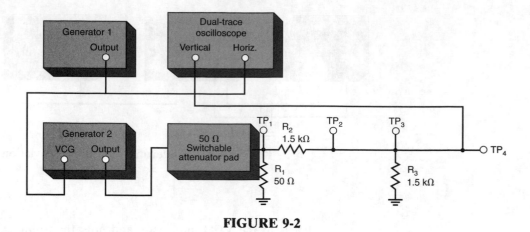

FIGURE 9-2

5. From the graph or the equation of step 4, determine the minimum and maximum dc voltages at the VCG input jack that would cause the output frequency to be 400 kHz and 500 kHz, respectively, assuming that the generator's frequency dial remains set at 450 kHz.

6. Calculate the peak-to-peak voltage swing necessary to sweep the output frequency of the generator between 400 and 500 kHz. Do this simply by finding the difference between the maximum and minimum VCG voltages in step 5.

7. Construct the test circuit of Fig. 9-2. In Fig. 9-2, we shall refer to generator 1 as the sweep generator since it controls the rate and amount of frequency deviation that occurs. We shall refer to generator 2 as the RF generator since its output frequency range must be kept significantly higher than that of the sweep generator.

   Adjust the 50-Ω attenuator pad switches so that no attenuation (0 dB) exists within the pad. Apply a 1-V_{p-p}, 450-kHz sine wave from the RF generator to the vertical input of the oscilloscope. Put the oscilloscope into its Y versus X mode of operation (time-base disabled). Make sure that the vertical and horizontal inputs are dc coupled. In this mode the scope is displaying the vertical input signal versus the horizontal input signal. Since the sweep generator of Fig. 9-2 is turned off, there should be no horizontal sweep, making the display a vertical line. Horizontally position the line in the middle of the screen. Also, adjust the vertical sensitivity so that vertical line fills up most of the screen, but remains calibrated.

8. Turn on the sweep generator and adjust so as to produce a 5-Hz triangle output waveform. This should form a horizontally shifting vertical line display on your scope. If your sweep generator has a dc offset control, make sure that it is either turned off or set to exactly zero volt offset. Now adjust the amplitude of the sweep generator to the p-p value determined in step 5. Since this linearly changing triangle waveform is being applied to the VCG input of the RF generator, it must be allowing the output frequency of the RF generator to deviate in a linear fashion, from a minimum of 400 kHz to a maximum of 500 kHz. Since this triangle voltage is also being applied to the horizontal input of the oscilloscope, the horizontal axis must represent the frequency output signal of the RF generator. Thus the horizontal scale of the scope display can now be calibrated in terms of frequency. Increase the sweep frequency from 5 Hz to a value that causes the display to appear as a solid rectangle. Adjust the horizontal scale factor of your scope so that

the width of the resulting rectangular display just fills up the screen. You may need to uncalibrate the horizontal sensitivity control to do this.

9. Now insert the ceramic filter between TP₂ and TP₃ by removing the jumper and connecting the input of the filter to TP₂ and the output of the filter at TP₃. Now you should see a display similar to that given in Fig. 9-4 (a). Sketch this display. Label the vertical axis with the appropriate voltage scale and the horizontal axis with the appropriate frequency scale.

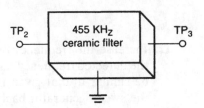

FIGURE 9-3

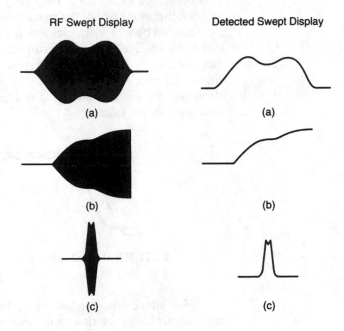

RF Swept Display   Detected Swept Display

(a)   (a)

(b)   (b)

(c)   (c)

FIGURE 9-4

10. Repeat step 9 with the filter connected using each of the following ranges of frequencies to be swept. The full width of the horizontal scale should represent each of the following frequency ranges:
    (a) 430 kHz to 470 kHz
    (b) 200 kHz to 700 kHz

    You should produce displays similar to those given in the left column of Fig. 9-4(b) and (c). Before proceeding to step 11, restore the original display obtained in step 9.

11. Now remove the jumper between TP₃ and TP₄. Replace the jumper with the diode peak detector shown in Fig. 9-5. Make sure that the vertical input of the oscilloscope is dc coupled. You should now see a display similar to the right-hand column of Fig. 9-4(a). Sketch this display. Again, label the vertical axis with the appropriate voltage scale and the horizontal axis with the appropriate frequency scale.

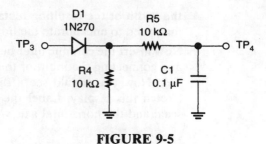

FIGURE 9-5

12. Increase the frequency of the sweep generator until the double image of the detected frequency response just becomes apparent. This display should be similar to that given in Fig. 9-6. Record this sweep frequency. Return the sweep generator back to 5 Hz before proceeding.

13. Frequency response curves are usually presented as graphs of gain in decibels versus the logarithm of frequency (Bode magnitude plots). In the ideal system, the amplitude of the signal coming out of the filter under test would be detected by a logarithmic detector and the resulting amplitude read off directly in decibels. Such detectors do exist and are referred to as square-law detectors. The test setup that we are using in this experiment uses a linear detector that yields a display in voltage amplitude rather than in decibels. We are also sweeping frequency in a linear fashion rather than in a logarithmic fashion.

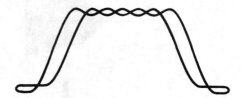

FIGURE 9-6 Double-image detected display

An alternative method of vertical calibration for both linear and logarithmic displays that does make use of decibels uses the in-line switchable attenuator, shown in Fig. 9-7. In this method the switchable attenuator is placed in the signal path between the generator and the circuit under test. The circuit under test is then temporarily removed and replaced by a short circuit between TP_2 and TP_3. With the attenuator first set at no attenuation (0 dB), the detected display is set for a straight horizontal line corresponding to 0 dB at the top of the display of the scope. Also, the vertical deflection controls are adjusted so that total attenuation is then displayed as a horizontal line at the bottom of the scope display. Then successive steps of attenuation are switched in and the corresponding shift downward of the horizontal line on the scope display is then noted by showing a series of horizontal lines at each downward position as shown in Fig. 9-8. In this way the vertical display is then calibrated directly in decibels.

The temporary short between the input and output of the circuit under test represents a 0-dB loss filter. After resetting the attenuator to 0-dB attenuation, the filter to be tested is then placed back into the test circuit between TP_2 and TP_3 instead of the short and its vertical response

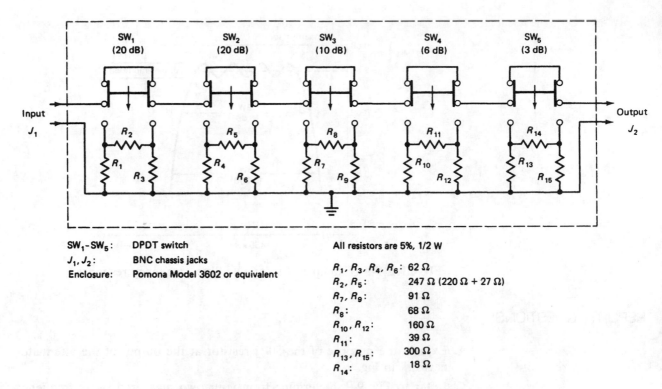

SW₁–SW₅: DPDT switch
J₁, J₂: BNC chassis jacks
Enclosure: Pomona Model 3602 or equivalent

All resistors are 5%, 1/2 W

R_1, R_3, R_4, R_6: 62 Ω
R_2, R_5: 247 Ω (220 Ω + 27 Ω)
R_7, R_9: 91 Ω
R_8: 68 Ω
R_{10}, R_{12}: 160 Ω
R_{11}: 39 Ω
R_{13}, R_{15}: 300 Ω
R_{14}: 18 Ω

FIGURE 9-7 Schematic of a 50-Ω selectable attenuator pad

read out directly in decibels. This is done by superimposing the successive decibel horizontal lines on the detected filter response. Refer to Fig. 9-8. Not only is the response of the filter displayed, but also its insertion loss and other important characteristics.

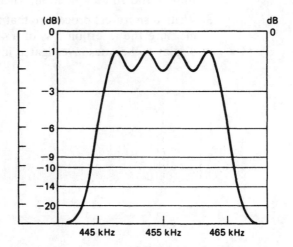

FIGURE 9-8 Sample detected frequency response

Complete the test procedure above for the 455-kHz ceramic filter. Calibrate the vertical axis in decibels, ranging from 0-dB maximum to a minimum of −20 dB of gain. Note that the decibel scale will not be linear but will resemble that shown in Fig. 9-8.

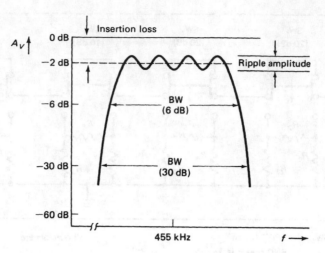

FIGURE 9-9 Example of a ceramic filter frequency response

REPORT/QUESTIONS:

1. Explain the purpose of the 50-Ω resistor at the output of the attenuator network in Fig. 9-2.

2. Refer to Fig. 9-9. Determine from your own measured swept-frequency display the following specifications for your 455-kHz ceramic filter.
   (a) Insertion loss in decibels
   (b) 6-dB bandwidth
   (c) Ripple amplitude

3. What is the hazard of using a swept-frequency display such as the one investigated in this experiment with respect to the validity of data?

4. Describe how the peak detector circuit operates. Why do the displays in steps 9 and 10 look filled in, whereas the one in Step 11 does not?

5. Write a short test procedure that a test technician could follow in order to measure the insertion loss of a 455-kHz filter using the swept-frequency display techniques investigated in this experiment.

NONLINEAR MIXING PRINCIPLES

OBJECTIVE:

To become acquainted with the process of creating new frequencies by mixing two signals of different frequencies together in a nonlinear device.

REFERENCE:

Refer to section 2-2 of the text.

TEST EQUIPMENT:

Dual-trace oscilloscope
Function generator (2)
Frequency counter

COMPONENTS:

Resistors ($\frac{1}{2}$ watt): 1 kΩ, 1.5 kΩ (4)
Germanium diode: 1N270, 1N34A, or equivalent
Ceramic filter: CFM-455D or equivalent

THEORY:

When two sinusoidal signals of different frequencies, f_1 and f_2, are applied simultaneously to a nonlinear amplifier, a nonlinear mixing action occurs, resulting in the creation of several output frequencies which include:

1. The first and second harmonics of the original frequencies: $f_1, f_2, 2f_1$, and $2f_2$.
2. The sum and difference frequencies: $(f_1 + f_2)$ and either $(f_1 - f_2)$ or $(f_2 - f_1)$, whichever produces a positive result.
3. 0 Hz (dc offset).

One method of proving this principle is to feed the complex output signal of the mixer through a sharp bandpass filter tuned to each of the expected output frequencies, and then check for the presence of a sinusoidal signal of that particular frequency at the output of the bandpass filter. However, sharp filters, such as ceramic or crystal filters, are not available for all bandpass frequencies. Manufacturers of these devices have ample supplies available only for standard bandpass frequencies that are used in radio designs such as 455 kHz or 10.7 MHz. Thus, an alternate method that will be used in this experiment is to carefully select the two frequencies, f_1 and f_2, so that only one of the predicted output frequencies of nonlinear mixing ends up being near the standard bandpass frequency of 455 kHz. We shall use a 455 kHz ceramic filter to isolate this frequency from all the other frequencies produced by nonlinear mixing.

PRELABORATORY:

Using the theory of nonlinear mixing, list each of the frequencies contained in the output of a nonlinear amplifier, if the input signal frequencies being mixed together are set at each of the values listed in steps 2 and 3 of the test procedure for this experiment. For each output, circle the output frequency component that falls within the bandpass of the ceramic filter. Also, for each case, sketch a spectrum diagram showing what a spectrum analyzer would display as the output signal spectrum of the nonlinear mixer.

PROCEDURE:

1. Build the mixer stage shown in Fig. 10-1. The nonlinear I-V characteristics of the germanium diode make it function as a nonlinear mixer.

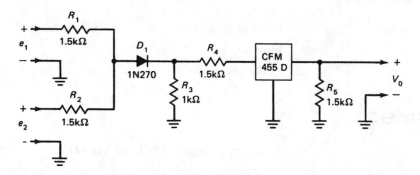

FIGURE 10-1

2. Set the amplitudes of e_1 and e_2 at 10 V_{p-p}. Set the frequency of e_1 to 455 kHz and the frequency of e_2 to 200 kHz. Monitor the output voltage using the oscilloscope. Carefully fine-tune the frequency of one of the two input generators so that the output voltage reaches a maximum amplitude. Once the amplitude is peaked, measure the output voltage amplitude and frequency.

3. Repeat step 2 using each of the following input frequencies:
   a. f_1 = 200 kHz and f_2 = 455 kHz
   b. f_1 = 227.5 kHz and f_2 = 300 kHz
   c. f_1 = 300 kHz and f_2 = 227.5 kHz
   d. f_1 = 355 kHz and f_2 = 100 kHz
   e. f_1 = 755 kHz and f_2 = 300 kHz
   f. f_1 = 295 kHz and f_2 = 80 kHz

REPORT/QUESTIONS:

1. Which outputs—$f_1, f_2, 2f_1, 2f_2, (f_1 + f_2)$, or $(f_1 - f_2)$—were of the largest amplitude?

2. If step 2 was completed using $f_1 = 682.5$ kHz and $f_2 = 227.5$ kHz, what problem would occur in looking for the output difference frequency component of $(f_1 - f_2) = 455$ kHz?

3. In step 3 (f), the only output frequency that would be within the bandpass of the ceramic filter would be $(f_1 + 2f_2)$, which is one of the smaller, usually ignored, output frequencies. How many decibels down is this output frequency compared to the simple sum and difference frequency outputs that are produced by nonlinear mixing action? How can these "extra" nonlinear modulation products be kept to a minimum amplitude level?

4. The frequency component referred to in question 3 is named a "third-order" frequency component since the sum of the two harmonics, $1f_1$ and $2f_2$, is 3. What three other third-order components could result from nonlinear mixing?

5. Research: What is meant by the third-order intercept spec of a nonlinear mixer?

NAME _____

RF MIXERS AND SUPERHETERODYNE RECEIVERS

OBJECTIVES:

   1. To analyze an RF mixer/IF amplifier system.

   2. To determine experimentally the transconductance of a field-effect transistor using gathered frequency response data as reference.

   3. To become familiar with the principles of operation of the superheterodyne receiver design.

REFERENCE:

   Refer to sections 3-5, 3-6, and 3-7 of the text.

TEST EQUIPMENT:

   Dual-trace oscilloscope

   Low-voltage power supply (2)

   Function generators (3); one must be able to be amplitude modulated

   Frequency counter

COMPONENTS:

   Dual-gate FET: Type ECG222, 3N204, or equivalent

   Germanium diode: 1N270, 1N34A, or equivalent

   Integrated circuit: LM386-3

   Inductors: 33 μH (2)

   Capacitors: Ceramic disk: 0.001 μF, .05 μF (2), 0.1 μF (3)
   silver mica: 0.0033 μF (2)
   electrolytic: 10 μF (3), 470 μF

   Resistors: 4.7 Ω (2 watt), 10 Ω (1 watt), 22 kΩ (3), 100 kΩ ($\frac{1}{2}$ watt)

   Potentiometer: (10-turn trim) 5 kΩ

   Speaker: 8 Ω

THEORY:

This two-stage circuit is a typical RF mixer and first IF (intermediate-frequency) amplifier stage used in superheterodyne receiver designs. This circuit uses ECG222 dual-gate, N-channel field-effect transistors as the active elements. Q_1 serves as the mixer and Q_2 serves as a fairly selective amplifier.

PRELABORATORY:

Calculate the theoretical resonant frequencies for both tank circuits (the RF amplifier circuit and the IF amplifier circuit) in Fig. 12-1 using the given values of L and C. Also predict the frequency of V_{TP_5} if V_{LO} is at 1.7 MHz and V_{RF} is at 1.2 MHz.

PROCEDURE:

1. Build the circuit given in Fig. 12-1. Turn on the power supply and adjust for 3 V dc. Connect a function generator to TP_1. Apply a 50-mV$_{p\text{-}p}$ sine wave at TP_1. Use a test frequency that is approximately equal to the resonant frequency calculated in the prelab exercise. Temporarily short TP_2 to ground.

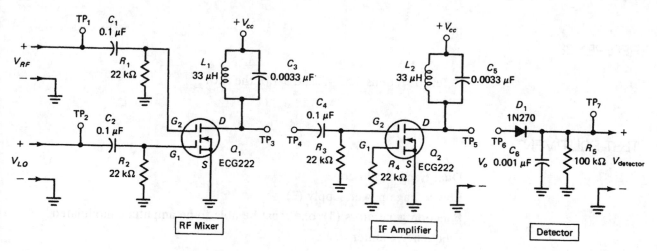

FIGURE 12-1 RF mixer-IF amplifier with detector

2. Test the RF mixer stage as an amplifier by measuring V_{RF} and V_0 at TP_1 and TP_3, respectively. Take a series of measurements at different frequencies to determine the frequency response of the mixer stage near the resonant frequency. Include enough measurements to be able to determine at what two frequencies the gain drops down 10 dB from its maximum value at the resonant frequency. Use approximately ten data points in addition to measuring the resonant frequency. Use a frequency counter to read each test frequency accurately. The output waveform at low frequencies may be distorted due to the mixer trying to resonate at harmonics of the input frequency. This effect is greatly magnified if the RF amplifier is overdriven.

3. Connect the function generator to TP_4. Now test the IF amplifier stage as amplifier by measuring V_{in} and V_o at TP_4 and TP_5, respectively. Again, take a series of measurements at different test frequencies to determine the

frequency response of the IF amplifier stage near the resonant frequency. Again, include enough measurements to be able to determine at what two frequencies the gain drops down 10 dB from its maximum value at the resonant frequency. Determine the resonant frequency of the IF amplifier stage. If the resonant frequency is more than 10 kHz away from the resonant frequency of the RF mixer stage, fine-tune either tank circuit so as to produce exactly the same resonant frequency in both stages. Do this by adding a small parallel capacitance across the tank circuit in the amplifier that has the larger resonant frequency. Record the value of the added capacitance necessary to produce equal values of resonant frequency and which stage was modified.

4. Connect the generator back to TP_1 and connect a jumper between TP_3 and TP_4. Now test the RF-IF amplifier system as a cascaded amplifier by measuring V_{in} and V_o at TP_1 and TP_5, respectively. Use the same test procedure used in steps 2 and 3 when testing the stages individually. Also record the resonant frequency of the cascaded system. You should find that the cascaded amplifier offers a larger voltage gain at the resonant frequency and a smaller bandwidth.

5. Connect a second function generator to TP_2. Set V_{RF} (at TP_1) to an amplitude of 200 mV$_{p-p}$ at a frequency of 1.2 MHz. Set V_{LO} (at TP_2) to an amplitude of 2 V$_{p-p}$ at a frequency of 1.7 MHz. Monitor the output voltage at TP_5. Fine-tune the frequency of V_{LO} while keeping the frequency of V_{RF} constant, to produce a maximum output voltage at TP_5. Using the frequency counter, measure the frequencies of V_{RF}, V_{LO}, and the voltage at TP_5. Record these frequencies.

6. Increase and decrease the amplitude of V_{LO} to determine the value of V_{LO} that yields a saturated value of V_o. This means that further increases in V_{LO} do not significantly increase the amplitude of V_o. Do not, however, allow the amplitude of V_{LO} to exceed 10 V$_{p-p}$. Record this critical value of V_{LO}. Now, with V_{LO} set at this critical value, vary V_{RF} from 0 V to 200 mV$_{p-p}$ in 40-mV steps and record V_o at each setting. Record your measurements in tabular form.

7. Return V_{RF} back to 200 mV$_{p-p}$. Now vary V_{LO} from 0 V to the critical value measured in step 6, using approximately five increments. Record V_o at each setting.

8. In the next step we shall simulate the reception of an AM broadcast station by an AM receiver using the superheterodyne design. Hook up the test configuration as shown in Fig. 12-2. A jumper should be connected between TP_5 and TP_6. Make sure that the scope is set up to trigger on the intelligence signal (function generator 3). Also, make sure that the function generator that can be amplitude modulated is connected up as the RF generator at TP_1.

9. Again, set V_{RF} to 200 mV$_{p-p}$ at a frequency of 1.2 MHz and V_{LO} at 2 V$_{p-p}$ at a frequency of 1.7 MHz. Monitor the voltage at TP_5 and fine-tune the frequency of V_{LO} until the output amplitude is at a maximum. Now switch the RF generator over to the AM mode. Apply a 1-kHz sinusoidal intelligence signal to the AM input jack of the RF generator. Carefully increase the amplitude of the intelligence signal until the waveform of the RF generator output shows approximately 100% modulation. (The positive and negative envelopes should just barely touch.) You should see that the output of the IF amplifier at TP_5 is another AM waveform that has a carrier frequency of 500 kHz rather than the original 1.2 MHz. You should also see that the output of the diode detector is the original 1-kHz intelligence

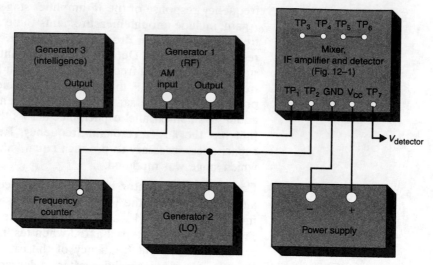

FIGURE 12-2 Superheterodyne receiver setup

signal mixed in with some noise. Sketch the waveforms observed at TP_5 and TP_7.

10. Build the audio amplifier in Fig. 12-3. Connect the input of the audio amplifier stage to TP_7. Connect the audio output to the speaker. Apply +12 V dc to this circuit using a second power supply. Adjust the volume control potentiometer to a comfortable listening level. You should be able to hear the original 1-kHz intelligence signal as the detected signal produced by the diode detector. Prove this by varying the frequency of the audio oscillator and note the shift in the frequency of the detected signal TP_7 and the audible output of the speaker.

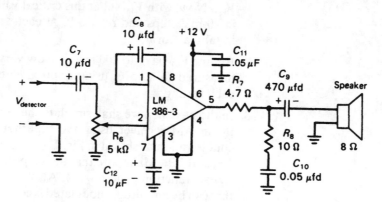

FIGURE 12-3 Audio amplifier stage

11. If you are close to a local AM broadcast transmitter, you may be able to receive the AM signal with this superheterodyne receiver system. Disconnect the AM signal generator from TP_1. In its place, connect an antenna. If there is no outside antenna connection available in your laboratory, try a 6- to 10-ft piece of unshielded wire instead. Carefully tune the frequency of the V_{LO} generator between 950 and 2150 kHz while observing the signal at TP_7. Try to peak the amplitude of the detected signal at TP_7 by fine-tuning the frequency of the V_{LO} generator. If a signal can be observed on

the scope display, you should be able to hear the audio signal with the speaker if the volume is increased high enough. Record the final frequency of V_{LO}. Using mixing principles, determine the carrier frequency of the received AM broadcast station.

12. Try to receive the same AM broadcast station received in step 11 by setting the local oscillator less than the RF carrier frequency by approximately 500 kHz.

REPORT/QUESTIONS:

1. The conversion gain of the mixer stage is defined as the output voltage in decibels (with respect to its input RF voltage level) with the local oscillator voltage held constant at some given value. Calculate the conversion gain using each of the values of V_o measured in step 6. Tabulate the results of step 6, including conversion gain in the tabulation.

2. Calculate the decibel voltage gain for each of the measured voltages in steps 2, 3, and 4. Tabulate your results.

3. Using a single sheet of linear graph paper, draw an overlay of each of the following plots. Calibrate the vertical axis in decibels.
   (a) The mixer-stage decibel voltage gain (down 10 dB on each side of the resonant frequency) vs. frequency.
   (b) The IF amplifier stage decibel voltage gain (down 10 dB on each side of the resonant frequency) vs. frequency.
   (c) The system decibel voltage gain vs. frequency. [Use the same frequency range as in parts (a) and (b).]

4. Using three sheets of linear graph paper, graph each of the following:
   (a) V_o versus V_{RF}, with V_{LO} held constant at its critical value. (step 6)
   (b) V_o versus V_{LO}, with V_{RF} held constant at 200 mV$_{p-p}$. (step 7)
   (c) Conversion gain in decibels versus V_{RF}, with V_{LO} held constant at its critical value.

5. Determine the transconductance, g_m, of the RF mixer FET using the frequency response data and the following procedure:
   (a) Using the frequency response data and assuming that the capacitor values are accurate, calculate the equivalent parallel inductance of the inductor.

$$f_r = \frac{1}{2\pi\sqrt{LC}}$$

   (b) Using the 3-dB bandwidth of the frequency response curve, calculate the Q of the tank circuit in the mixer stage.

$$f_r = BW \times Q$$

   (c) Using the results of step (b) and tank circuit theory, find the parallel resistance of the tank circuit in the mixer stage.

$$R_p = QX_L.$$

   (d) Using the mixer stage's voltage gain at the resonant frequency and the results of step (c), find the transconductance of the FET.

$$A_v = g_m R_p$$

6. Summarize the principles of operation of the superheterodyne receiver investigated in steps 9–12.

7. Explain why it was possible to pick up the same radio station in steps 11 and 12 with two different local oscillator frequency settings. (Use example numbers to describe the mixing action that occurs in each of the two cases.)

CASCODE AMPLIFIERS

OBJECTIVES:

1. To build and test an RF cascode amplifier with simulated AGC (automatic gain control).
2. To obtain an understanding of cascode amplifier operation.
3. To compare and evaluate data of discrete and integrated circuit configurations which perform the same function.

REFERENCE:

An IF amplifier stage using the 3028 can be found in section 3-5 of the text.

TEST EQUIPMENT:

Dual-trace oscilloscope
Low-voltage power supplies (2)
Function generator
Volt-ohmmeter
Prototype board

COMPONENTS:

Ceramic filter: CFM-455D or equivalent
3028A Cascode amplifier integrated circuit
Transistors: 2N2222 (3)
Diode: 1N4001 (2)
Capacitors: 0.1 μF (10)
Resistors ($\frac{1}{2}$ watt): 470 Ω (2), 680 Ω (2), 1 kΩ (5), 1.5 kΩ (5), 2.2 kΩ (3), 3.3 kΩ, 7.5 kΩ (4), 12 kΩ (4)

Potentiometer: 10 kΩ (10-turn trim)

PRELABORATORY:

Using your textbook and other technical references, explain what the difference is between a cascaded amplifier configuration and a cascode amplifier. Explain what causes a cascode amplifier to offer a high input impedance and low input capacitance at high frequencies.

PROCEDURE:

1. Build the discrete amplifier configuration shown in Fig. 13-1. Turn on the dc supply and adjust V_{cc} for exactly +10 V dc. Take dc bias voltage measurements at each of the test points given. Record each of your measurements.

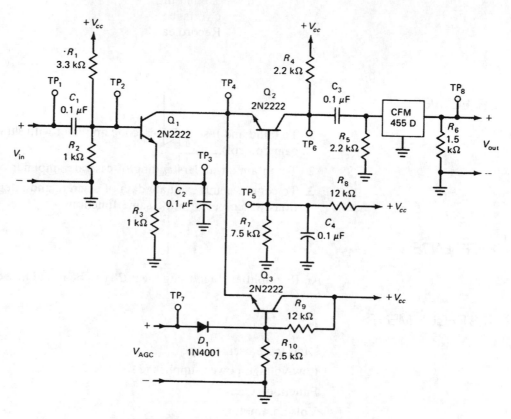

FIGURE 13-1 Discrete cascode amplifier

2. Apply a 455-kHz, 40-mV$_{p-p}$ sine wave at the RF input of the amplifier. Monitor the output voltage of the ceramic filter at TP$_8$. Fine-tune the generator so as to maximize the output voltage at TP$_8$. Sketch the waveforms observed at TP$_1$, TP$_6$, and TP$_8$.

3. Using approximately eight equal increments, increase V_{in} from 40 mV$_{p-p}$ to the value where any additional increase does not result in any appreciable increase in the filter's output voltage. For each increase, measure the amplitude of the voltages at TP$_1$, TP$_6$, and TP$_8$. Record your data in tabular form. Also, determine what level of V_{in} causes the voltage at TP$_6$ to become distorted due to clipping.

4. Repeat step 3, except this time decrease V_{in} from 40 mV$_{p-p}$ down to zero in four equal decrements. The voltage at TP$_6$ should remain unclipped at these settings.

5. Set V_{in} back to 40 mV$_{p-p}$. Turn on the AGC supply. Set the AGC voltage to approximately 4 V dc. Increase this voltage in 100-mV steps until you reduce the voltage gain of the stage to zero. At each new setting, measure

the voltage at TP_1, TP_6, and TP_8. You should end up with approximately five sets of data. If not, return the AGC voltage back to 4 V dc and take smaller increments until you end up with at least five AGC voltage settings before reducing the gain to zero. Note any AGC voltage settings that cause distortion or oscillations to occur in the voltage waveform at TP_6.

6. Build the amplifier configuration given in Fig. 13-2 or Fig. 13-3 depending if you have the 3028 (Fig 13-2) or CA3086 (Fig. 13-3) integrated circuit. Turn on the two power supplies and adjust them for ±5 V dc. Adjust the 10-kΩ potentiometer so that the AGC voltage at pin 1 (3028), pin 2 (3086) is close to zero. Take dc voltage readings at each of the eight pins of the 3028A integrated circuit. Record each of your measurements.

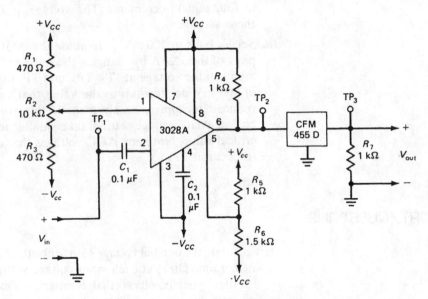

FIGURE 13-2 Integrated-circuit cascode amplifier

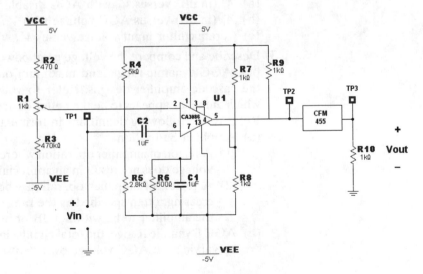

FIGURE 13-3

7. Apply a 455-kHz, 100-mV$_{p-p}$ sine wave at the RF input of this amplifier. Monitor the output voltage of the ceramic filter at TP$_3$. Fine-tune the generator to maximize V_o at TP$_3$. Sketch the waveforms observed at TP$_1$, TP$_2$, and TP$_3$.

8. Using approximately eight equal increments, increase V_{in} from 100 mV$_{p-p}$ to the value where any additional increase does not result in any appreciable increase in filter output voltage. For each increase, measure the amplitude of the voltage at TP$_1$, TP$_2$, and TP$_3$. Record your data in tabular form. Also, note what input voltage level causes the waveform at TP$_2$ to become distorted due to clipping.

9. Repeat step 8, except this time decrease V_{in} from 100 mV$_{p-p}$ down to zero in four equal decrements. The voltage at TP$_2$ should not be distorted at these settings.

10. Set V_{in} back to 100 mV$_{p-p}$. Increase the AGC voltage (positive polarity) at pin 1 of the 3028A by changing the setting of the 10 kΩ pot. Take measurements of the voltage at TP$_1$, TP$_2$, and TP$_3$ with the AGC voltage increasing in 200 mV dc steps up to the value that causes the voltage at TP$_3$ to be reduced to approximately zero. If this voltage drops drastically at one critical AGC voltage setting, take smaller increments of V_{AGC} around this critical value. Note any AGC voltages that cause distortion or oscillations to occur at TP$_3$.

REPORT/QUESTIONS:

1. Calculate the decibel voltage gain for both of the cascode amplifiers (including ceramic filter) at each input voltage setting used in steps 3, 4, 8, and 9. Tabulate your results so that comparisons can easily be made.

2. On three sheets of graph paper, plot each of the following for both of your amplifiers. Put both amplifier curves on the same graph:
   (a) A_v (in dB) versus V_{in} with AGC disabled
   (b) A_v (in dB) versus AGC voltage with V_{in} at initial setting
   (c) Ceramic filter input voltage versus V_{in} with AGC disabled

3. Describe and compare the voltage gain, power gain, saturation characteristics, AGC dynamic range, and maximum output power level for both of the cascode amplifier designs. Refer to your data and graphs. Conclude which amplifier appears to be the better design and defend your conclusion. Refer to the following definitions in formulating your evaluation.
   (a) Amplifier Saturation
      (1) A region of amplifier operation where an increase in the input signal voltage does not result in an appreciable increase in output voltage.
      (2) A region of amplifier operation where the amplifier's gain is decreasing; often specified as the range of V_{in} that causes the gain of the amplifier to be within 3 dB of its maximum value.
   (b) AGC Dynamic Range: the total change in amplifier decibel gain caused by varying the AGC voltage over its useful range.

SIDEBAND MODULATION AND DETECTION

OBJECTIVES:

1. To become familiar with the 1496 balanced mixer.

2. To build and evaluate a balanced modulator that produces double-sideband suppressed carrier.

3. To build and evaluate a product detector that extracts the intelligence from a single-sideband suppressed carrier signal.

REFERENCE:

Refer to Chapter 4 of the text.

TEST EQUIPMENT:

Dual-trace oscilloscope: must have a Y vs X display capability

Function generator (2)

Low-voltage power supply (2)

Frequency counter

Spectrum analyzer (if available)

COMPONENTS:

1496P integrated circuit (2)

CFM-455D ceramic filter

Capacitors: 0.005 μF (3), 0.1 μF (4), 1.0 μF (2)

Resistors ($\frac{1}{2}$ watt): 47 Ω (5), 100 Ω (2), 1 kΩ (8), 3.3 kΩ (4), 6.8 kΩ (2), 10 kΩ (2)

Potentiometer: 10 kΩ (10-turn trim)

THEORY:

A balanced modulator (Fig. 14-1) is typically used to generate a double-sideband suppressed carrier signal in an SSB transmitter that uses the filter method of design. Nonlinear amplification causes the creation of first and second harmonics of the

f_c (carrier) $\longrightarrow$ $\bigotimes$ $\longrightarrow$ (DSB-SC) $\begin{cases} f_i, 2f_i \\ (f_c + f_i) \\ (f_c - f_i) \end{cases}$

f_i (intelligence)

FIGURE 14-1 Balanced modulator function

intelligence input signal, the simple sum and difference frequency components, and a dc component. The first and second harmonics of the carrier input signal, which are normally produced in mixing action are suppressed in a balanced modulator. In the 1496, this is done by signal cancellation due to the symmetrical arrangement of the differential amplifier stage as shown in Fig. 14-2. A spectrum diagram of the output signal reveals the presence of the lower and upper sidebands but no RF carrier frequency component (Fig. 14-3).

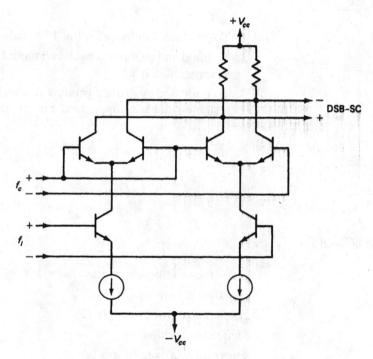

FIGURE 14-2 1496 balanced modulator circuitry

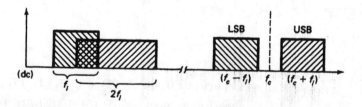

FIGURE 14-3 Balanced modulator typical output spectrum

To produce single sideband, a sharp filter that exhibits a fairly constant passband response and steep roll-off skirts is needed to attenuate all frequencies produced by a balanced modulator except for the desired sideband. A ceramic filter such as the one used in Experiments 2 and 9 may fit these design requirements.

A balanced modulator followed by a low-pass filter is typically used to recreate the original intelligence signal in an SSB receiver. Again, the balanced mixer's nonlinear amplification causes the creation of the first and second harmonics of the input SSB signal, the simple sum and difference frequencies of the two input signals, and a dc signal. Again, the first and second harmonics of the input carrier signal are suppressed by the balanced modulator. This time, however, since the frequencies of the SSB input and carrier input signals are fairly close to each other, the difference frequency components end up being much smaller than any of the other frequencies produced by mixing action. These difference frequencies are exactly equal to the original intelligence frequencies. For example, if upper sideband is being supplied to the SSB input of the balanced modulator, the frequency spectra shown in Fig. 14-4 will result in the output signal.

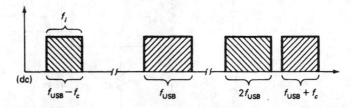

FIGURE 14-4 SSB detector output spectra before filtering

It is very easy to filter out the original intelligence from this complex signal because of the large frequency difference between the difference frequencies and all other output frequency components produced by mixing action. A similar result occurs if lower sideband is being supplied to the balanced modulator. All that is necessary is a simple RC low-pass filter that has a sufficiently large time constant at all RF frequencies. The balanced modulator, low-pass filter, and RF carrier oscillator make up what is known as a product detector in an SSB receiver.

PRELABORATORY:

Using the theory described above and in your text, draw the spectrum diagrams of the output signals that would result in each of the following designs.

1. The output double-sideband suppressed carrier signal if a 475-kHz sinusoidal RF carrier is mixed with a 20-kHz audio sine-wave signal in a balanced modulator.

2. The output double-sideband suppressed carrier signal if a 435-kHz sinusoidal RF carrier is mixed with a 20-kHz audio sine-wave signal in a balanced modulator.

3. The output signal if a USB signal having a frequency range of 455 kHz–460 kHz is mixed with a 460-kHz sinusoidal RF carrier in a balanced modulator.

4. The output signal if an LSB signal having a frequency range of 450 kHz–455 kHz is mixed with a 450 kHz sinusoidal RF carrier in a balanced modulator.

5. If the output signal of either design 3 or 4 above is passed through a low-pass filter that totally attenuates all signals above 100 kHz but passes all frequencies below 50 kHz, sketch the resulting output spectra of the low-pass filter.

PROCEDURE:

1. Build the balanced modulator circuit shown in Fig. 14-5. Apply ± 10 V dc to the circuit. Apply a 2 V_{p-p}, 400-kHz sine wave at TP_1. This signal represents the input RF carrier. Monitor V_o at TP_3 with the oscilloscope. Adjust the carrier null potentiometer, R_2, for a minimum-amplitude 400-kHz sine wave. At the optimum precise setting it should null the carrier to zero amplitude and increase the carrier on either side of the null setting.

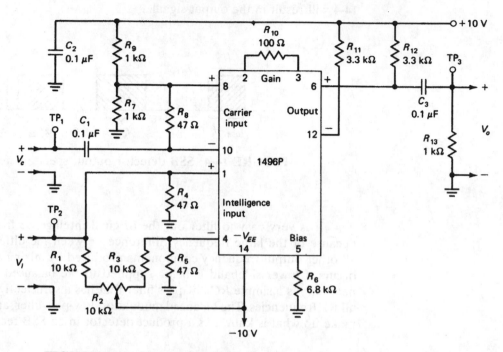

FIGURE 14-5 DSB-SC generator using a 1496P balanced modulator

2. Apply a 150-mV_{p-p} 200-Hz sine wave at TP_2. This signal represents the input audio intelligence signal. Again, monitor TP_3 with the oscilloscope. Use 10:1 probes to avoid loading. The output signal at TP_3 should look like a "fuzzy" 400-kHz sine wave if the signal is being viewed with a small horizontal time scale, such as 0.5 μs/div, and is being triggered by the RF carrier signal. Sketch the observed signal at TP_3.

3. A better, more informative waveform can be displayed by placing the horizontal time scale at a much larger setting, such as 0.5 ms/div and by externally triggering the scope with the audio intelligence signal. Do this by observing the signal at TP_3 with channel A and the signal at TP_2 with channel B. The observed DSB-SC signal will probably be slightly distorted. Make small adjustments to the carrier null potentiometer, R_2, and to the intelligence and carrier amplitudes in order to produce a clean waveform such as that shown in Fig. 14-6. The two interwoven envelopes should be near-perfect sine waves that have a frequency of 200 Hz. The peak envelope voltages should all be equal to one another. Sketch the resulting waveform.

4. Determine the effect on the resulting DSB-SC waveform if changes are made in the frequencies of the carrier signal or the intelligence signal. Also, determine the effect of changing the gain resistance, R_{10}, to 47 Ω and to 1 kΩ. Return the display back to its original form as in step 3 before proceeding.

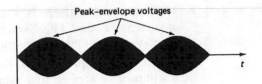

Peak–envelope voltages

FIGURE 14-6 DSB-SC waveform showing no distortion

5. Observe and sketch the resulting swept-frequency display of the DSB-SC signal by applying the DSB-SC signal to the vertical input of the scope and applying the intelligence signal to the horizontal input of the scope. Place the scope in A versus B mode. Set the vertical and horizontal sensitivities to fill the screen with the display. You should note a double triangle or "bow-tie" shaped swept display. Notice the effect on the screen of changing the amplitude of the carrier and intelligence signals. Notice that when distortion occurs, the two triangles will no longer have straight sides. Try adjusting the value of the carrier null potentiometer. You should notice that the two triangles are symmetrical when the carrier has been nulled. Again, return the display to its original form as in step 3 before proceeding.

6. The double-sideband suppressed carrier signal will now be applied to a ceramic filter to produce true SSB. Recall from Experiment 9 that the CFM-455D has a 3-dB bandwidth of approximately 20 kHz and a center frequency of 455 kHz. Adjust the intelligence signal frequency to exactly 20 kHz and the RF carrier frequency to exactly 435 kHz. The DSB-SC signal should now have an upper sideband frequency of 455 kHz and a lower sideband frequency of 415 kHz. Build the circuit in Fig. 14-7 and connect it to the output of the balanced modulator circuit by connecting TP_3 and TP_4 together. Monitor the output voltage at TP_5. It should be a clean sine wave, since only the upper sideband frequency component makes it through the filter. Adjust the carrier frequency so that the voltage at TP_5 is at maximum amplitude. Measure its frequency with a counter.

$$f_{USB} = \text{\underline{\hspace{2cm}}} \qquad f_{carrier} = \text{\underline{\hspace{2cm}}}$$

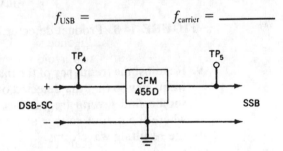

FIGURE 14-7 Ceramic filter to create SSB from DSB-SC

If a spectrum analyzer is available, observe the spectral content of the signals at TP_3 and TP_5. Sketch the spectral displays.

7. Repeat step 6, but this time allow only the lower sideband frequency component of the DSB-SC signal to make it through the ceramic filter. Since you cannot change the bandpass frequency range of the ceramic filter, you must change the frequency of the RF carrier signal entering the balanced modulator to align the lower sideband frequency with the bandpass.

$$f_{LSB} = \text{\underline{\hspace{2cm}}} \qquad f_{carrier} = \text{\underline{\hspace{2cm}}}$$

If a spectrum analyzer is available, observe the spectral content of the signals at TP$_3$ and TP$_5$. Sketch the spectral displays. Return to the scope display of step 6 before continuing.

8. The SSB signal produced at the output of the ceramic filter in steps 6 and 7 will now be applied to a balanced modulator. Build the circuit shown in Fig. 14-8. Connect the output of the ceramic filter to the detector's input by connecting TP$_5$ and TP$_6$ together with a jumper. The RF carrier driving the balanced modulator at TP$_1$ should also be connected to the RF carrier input of the detector at Tp$_7$. Adjust the amplitude of V_c to approximately 3.5 V$_{\text{p-p}}$. Observe the output waveform of the product detector at TP$_8$ with channel A of the oscilloscope. Monitor the original intelligence signal with channel B of the oscilloscope. Use 10:1 probes.

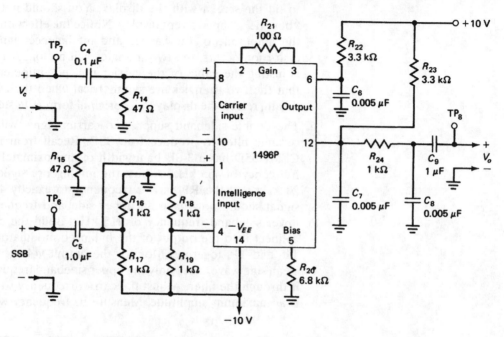

FIGURE 14-8 Product detector using a 1496P balanced modulator

9. Readjust the frequency of the intelligence for 200 Hz. Adjust the RF carrier frequency so that the detected output frequency signal is a maximum. You should find several frequencies within the bandpass of the ceramic filter where the output voltage at TP$_8$ peaks, but select the largest peak. Sketch the resulting waveforms.

10. Readjust the frequencies of the intelligence for 20 kHz. Again, adjust the RF carrier frequency so that the detected output signal is a maximum. You should find only two distinct frequencies within the bandpass of the filter where the output voltage at TP$_8$ is at a maximum. These frequencies are those that cause just the upper sideband or just the lower sideband to fall within the bandpass of the filter.

11. Adjust the audio function generator to produce a 20-kHz triangle wave instead of a sine wave. You should find that the output voltage at TP$_8$ remains as a sine wave. Also, you should find that the output voltage of the detector at TP$_8$ will peak at several settings of the RF carrier. This is because only part of the upper sideband or lower sideband frequencies produced at the balanced modulator output are being passed by the

20-kHz-bandwidth ceramic filter. This should also happen if a square-wave intelligence signal is being used.

12. Now adjust the intelligence signal to produce a 200-Hz triangle wave. Now the first 100 harmonics of the triangle wave's fundamental frequency can be within the 20-kHz bandwidth of either the upper sideband or lower sideband at the output of the balanced modulator. Thus, if we tune the RF carrier so that just the upper sideband or lower sideband frequency component is passed by the ceramic filter, the product detector should recreate the original triangle wave with minimal distortion. Tune the carrier to produce an output signal at TP_8 that is least distorted. Sketch the original and recreated intelligence signals.

13. Repeat step 11 using a square-wave intelligence signal.

14. Repeat step 12 using a square-wave intelligence signal.

REPORT/QUESTIONS:

1. Draw a sketch of the frequency spectra of the DSB-SC signals produced in steps 6 and 7. Label all important frequencies on the horizontal axis. Explain why a sine wave at 455 kHz was observed at the output of the ceramic filter in each case.

2. Draw a sketch of the frequency spectra of the DSB-SC signals produced in step 11 when a 20-kHz triangle wave or a 20-kHz square wave was used as the intelligence signal. Draw a sketch of the frequency spectra of the output signal of the product detector. Explain why the output signal of the product detector was not a close replica of the input triangle or square-wave intelligence signal in steps 11 and 13.

3. Draw a sketch of the frequency spectra of the DSB-SC signals produced in steps 12 and 14 when a 200-Hz triangle or square wave was used as the intelligence signal. Draw a sketch of the frequency spectra of the output signal of the product detector. Explain why the output signals of the product detector in steps 12 and 14 were close replicas of the input triangle or square-wave intelligence signals.

FREQUENCY MODULATION: SPECTRAL ANALYSIS

OBJECTIVES:

1. To become familiar with spectral displays of frequency modulated carriers at different values of modulation index.

2. To calculate the frequency deviation of an FM waveform by viewing its waveshape on an oscilloscope.

3. To determine the bandwidth of an FM signal using a spectrum analyzer and using Carson's rule.

REFERENCE:

Refer to section 5-3 of the text.

TEST EQUIPMENT:

Dual-trace oscilloscope

Function generator (2); one must have a VCG input to produce FM.

Audio Spectrum Analyzer (HP3580A or equivalent)

50 ohm Attenuator Pad (such as given in Figure 9-7)

THEORY:

Frequency modulation is defined as a type of angle modulation in which the instaneous frequency of a carrier is caused to vary by an amount proportional to the modulating signal amplitude. The spectral display of an FM signal is much more complicated than that of an AM or SSB signal. This is because each modulating frequency creates an infinite number of side-frequency components on either side of the carrier frequency component. Fortunately, inspection of the infinite series reveals that the higher-ordered side-frequency components have very small, negligible amplitudes. This effect can be shown by use of a mathematical tool known as the Bessel function, which is given in tabular form in Table 15-1. This table also allows us to predict the effective bandwidth of the FM signal. Carson's rule also can be used to predict the effective bandwidth of the FM signal. Carson's rule states that:

$$BW = 2 (\delta + f_i) \qquad (15\text{-}1)$$

TABLE 15-1 FM Side Frequencies from Bessel Functions

x (m_f)	J_0 (CARRIER)	J_1	J_2	J_3	J_4	J_5	J_6	J_7	J_8	J_9	J_{10}	J_{11}	J_{12}	J_{13}	J_{14}	J_{15}	J_{16}
0.00	1.00	—	—	—	—	—	—	—	—	—	—	—	—	—	—	—	—
0.25	0.98	0.12	—	—	—	—	—	—	—	—	—	—	—	—	—	—	—
0.5	0.94	0.24	0.03	—	—	—	—	—	—	—	—	—	—	—	—	—	—
1.0	0.77	0.44	0.11	0.02	—	—	—	—	—	—	—	—	—	—	—	—	—
1.5	0.51	0.56	0.23	0.06	0.01	—	—	—	—	—	—	—	—	—	—	—	—
2.0	0.22	0.58	0.35	0.13	0.03	—	—	—	—	—	—	—	—	—	—	—	—
2.5	-0.05	0.50	0.45	0.22	0.07	0.02	—	—	—	—	—	—	—	—	—	—	—
3.0	-0.26	0.34	0.49	0.31	0.13	0.04	0.01	—	—	—	—	—	—	—	—	—	—
4.0	-0.40	-0.07	0.36	0.43	0.28	0.13	0.05	0.02	—	—	—	—	—	—	—	—	—
5.0	-0.18	-0.33	0.05	0.36	0.39	0.26	0.13	0.05	0.02	—	—	—	—	—	—	—	—
6.0	0.15	-0.28	-0.24	0.11	0.36	0.36	0.25	0.13	0.06	0.02	—	—	—	—	—	—	—
7.0	0.30	0.00	-0.30	-0.17	0.16	0.35	0.34	0.23	0.13	0.06	0.02	—	—	—	—	—	—
8.0	0.17	0.23	-0.11	-0.29	-0.10	0.19	0.34	0.32	0.22	0.13	0.06	0.03	—	—	—	—	—
9.0	-0.09	0.24	0.14	-0.18	-0.27	-0.06	0.20	0.33	0.30	0.21	0.12	0.06	0.03	—	—	—	—
10.0	-0.25	0.04	0.25	0.06	-0.22	-0.23	-0.01	0.22	0.31	0.29	0.20	0.12	0.06	0.03	0.01	—	—
12.0	0.05	-0.22	-0.08	0.20	0.18	-0.07	-0.24	-0.17	0.05	0.23	0.30	0.27	0.20	0.12	0.07	0.03	0.01
15.0	-0.01	0.21	0.04	-0.19	-0.12	0.13	0.21	0.03	-0.17	-0.22	-0.09	0.10	0.24	0.28	0.25	0.18	0.12

n OR ORDER

Source: E. Cambi, *Bessel Functions*, Dover Publications, Inc., New York, 1948. Courtesy of the publisher.

where δ represents the deviation in carrier frequency.

The index of FM modulation, m_f, determines how many non-negligible side frequency components appear in the FM signal spectra. It can be determined by:

$$m_f = \frac{\delta}{f_i} \tag{15-2}$$

In this experiment, you will be measuring the waveform and spectral display of an FM signal when the modulation index is set at various levels.

PROCEDURE:

1. Adjust the RF generator to produce a 20 kHz, sinewave with an amplitude of 3Vp-p. Adjust the audio generator to produce a 500 Hz sinewave. Then reduce its amplitude down to zero.

2. Connect the audio generator up to the FM input jack (VCG) of the rf generator as shown in Figure 15-1. Also connect the output of the rf generator to the oscilloscope and spectrum analyzer as shown. Let the scope trigger on the carrier signal. Increase the amplitude of the intelligence signal at TP1 while watching the RF carrier at TP3 begin to blur due to FM action taking place. You may need to place 20 to 30 dB of attenuation between TP2 and TP3 to keep the modulation index down to the low levels as requested in the following steps.

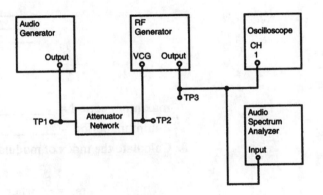

FIGURE 15-1

3. Tune in the RF carrier signal on the oscilloscope with the vertical sensitivity set at 0.5V per division and the horizontal sensitivity set at 10 microseconds per division. This should allow you to see approximately two periods of the rf carrier waveform.

4. Carefully tune in the RF generator output signal with the spectrum analyzer so that you can see the carrier frequency component and the first six or seven side frequency components on each side of the carrier. If you are using an HP-3580A spectrum analyzer, the following settings should suffice.

Center Frequency: 20.000 kHz.   **Frequency Span/Div.:** 1 kHz./div.
Resolution BW: 100 Hz.   **Sweep Mode:** repetitive
Display Smoothing: medium setting   **Amplitude Mode:** linear
Sweep Time/Div.: 2 sec./div.   **Amplitude Ref Level:** 0 dB
    Input Sensitivity: +10 dB

5. Fine tune the spectral display so that the carrier frequency component is in the center of the display. Now disconnect the modulating signal from the VCG input of the rf generator. Measure the amplitude of the carrier frequency component in terms of vertical divisions. Sketch the resulting displays of your spectrum analyzer and oscilloscope. Make sure that you measure the period of the sinewave on the scope display.

6. Now reconnect the intelligence signal to the VCG input jack of the rf generator and slowly increase the amplitude from zero. You should see the amplitude of the carrier frequency component begin to diminish, while the first and second order side frequency components begin to grow in amplitude. Continue to slowly increase the amplitude of the intelligence signal until the carrier frequency component reduces down to exactly zero amplitude while the side frequency components continue to grow. You should now be able to see five upper and five lower side frequency components on your spectral display. Sketch your resulting spectral and waveform displays. Carefully measure the amplitudes of each of the visible frequency components on your spectral display.

7. Measure the minimum and maximum periods of the blurry sinewave displayed on your oscilloscope, as shown in Figure 15-2. Invert these values to get the maximum and minimum values of carrier frequency.

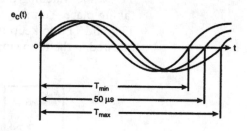

FIGURE 15-2

maximum period = _____   minimum frequency = _____

minimum period = _____   maximum frequency = _____

8. Calculate the index of modulation of this FM signal using:

$$m_f = \frac{\delta}{f_i}, \text{ where } \delta = \frac{f_{max} - f_{min}}{2}$$

9. Based upon the results of steps 7 and 8, determine what the maximum and minimum periods need to be in order to produce a modulation index of exactly 1.5.

minimum frequency = _____   maximum period = _____

maximum frequency = _____   minimum period = _____

10. Carefully adjust the amplitude of the signal at TP2 in order to produce these corresponding values of minimum and maximum periods. Sketch the resulting spectral and waveform displays. Accurately measure the amplitude and frequency of each frequency component in the spectral display.

11. This time, determine what the maximum and minimum periods need to be in order to produce a modulation index of exactly 5.0.

minimum frequency = _____   maximum period = _____

maximum frequency = _____   minimum period = _____

12. Carefully adjust the amplitude of the signal at TP2 in order to produce these corresponding values of minimum and maximum periods. Sketch the resulting spectral and waveform displays. Accurately measure the amplitude and frequency of each frequency component in the spectral display.

13. One more time, determine what the maximum and minimum periods need to be in order to produce a modulation index of exactly 8.0.

    minimum frequency = _____   maximum period = _____

    maximum frequency = _____   minimum period = _____

14. Carefully adjust the amplitude of the signal at TP2 in order to produce these corresponding values of minimum and maximum periods. Sketch the resulting spectral and waveform displays. Accurately measure the amplitude and frequency of each frequency component in the spectral display.

REPORT/QUESTIONS:

1. Make a table like that shown in Table 15-2. To enter each theoretical value, simply copy the value of J from the Bessel table given in Table 15-1. To calculate each value for J from your measured data, simply divide each spectral component's amplitude from steps 10, 12, and 14 by the unmodulated carrier's amplitude, which was measured in step 5. Enter each calculated result in your table.

TABLE 15-2

FREQUENCY COMPONENT	J-TERM	$m_f = 1.5$		$m_f = 5.0$		$m_f = 8.0$	
		THEORETICAL	CALCULATED	THEORETICAL	CALCULATED	THEORETICAL	CALCULATED
Carrier	J0						
First-Order	J1						
Second-Order	J2						
Third-Order	J3						
Fourth-Order	J4						
Fifth-Order	J5						
Sixth-Order	J6						
Seventh-Order	J7						
Eighth-Order	J8						
Ninth-Order	J9						
Tenth-Order	J10						
Eleventh-Order	J11						
Twelfth-Order	J12						

2. How close are your theoretical and measured values in question 1? Comment on any causes for discrepancies.

3. What are the theoretical values of m_f which cause the carrier amplitude to diminish to zero amplitude? In step 8, the smallest of these critical values of m_f should have been calculated. How close was it? What might have caused any discrepancies?

4. Consider the spectral display of step 12 to be the actual display of an FM radio station under test, where each vertical division represents 100Vrms. What would be the resulting output power if this signal was measured across a 50 ohm load?

5. Repeat question 4 for the spectral display of step 5. The power level should be the same regardless of what m_f is set at. How close are they?

6. Calculate the resulting bandwidths for each of the spectral displays of steps 6, 10, 12, and 14 by use of Carson's rule. Compare your results to those revealed by spectral displays. Record your results in tabular form such as shown in Table 15-3.

TABLE 15-3

STEP	MODULATION INDEX	BANDWIDTH (SPECTRAL INSPECTION)	BANDWIDTH (CARSON'S RULE)
6	2.4		
10	1.5		
12	5.0		
14	8.0		

PHASE-LOCKED LOOPS: STATIC AND DYNAMIC BEHAVIOR

OBJECTIVES:

1. To become familiar with the phase-locked loop (PLL) and its major subsystem building blocks.
2. To study the static and dynamic behavior of the phase-locked loop.

REFERENCE:

Refer to section 6-5 of the text.

TEST EQUIPMENT:

Dual-trace oscilloscope: must have a Y vs X display capability

Low-voltage power supply (2)

Function generator (2); one must have a VCG input for swept-frequency operation

Volt-ohmmeter

Frequency counter

Prototype board

COMPONENTS:

Integrated circuit: 565 phase-locked loop (2)

Capacitors: 0.001 μF (5), 2.2 nF, 0.1 μF, 10 μF

Resistors ($\frac{1}{2}$ watt): 680 Ω (5), 820 Ω, 2.2 kΩ, 3.3 kΩ (1), 4.7 kΩ (2), 10 kΩ, 33 kΩ (2)

PRELABORATORY:

Calculate the free-running frequency of the PLL's voltage-controlled oscillator using the timing resistor and timing capacitor values given in Figs. 16-1 and 16-2. Use the equation given in the data sheet for the 565 PLL included in the Appendix.

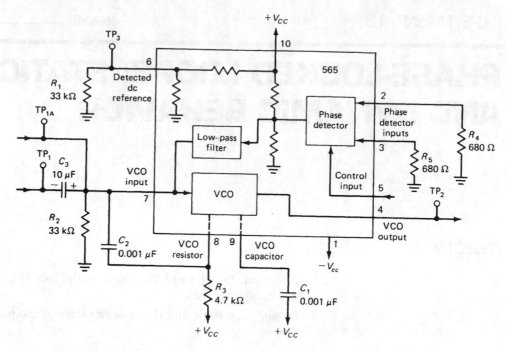

FIGURE 16-1 VCO static and dynamic test circuit

PROCEDURE:

VCO Static Tests

1. Build the circuit given in Fig. 16-1. Apply the power supply voltages and adjust for ±7 V dc. Monitor the VCO output voltage at TP_2 using the oscilloscope. Measure and record the waveform of the VCO output signal, noting the amplitude and frequency.

2. Note the effect on the free-running VCO output waveform by introducing each of the following changes, one at a time. Use a frequency counter to measure the frequency at TP_2 and observe the signal with an oscilloscope. Make sure that each alteration is restored back to its original form before proceeding to the next step.
   (a) Decrease the timing resistor, R_3, to 2.2 kΩ.
   (b) Increase the timing capacitor, C_1, to 2.2 nF.
   (c) Load the VCO output with a capacitative load by placing a series RC load between TP_2 and ground. Let $R = 680$ Ω and $C = 0.001$ μF.
   (d) Increase each of the phase detector input resistors, R_4 and R_5, one at a time, to 3.3 kΩ.
   (e) Decrease the load resistance at the detected dc reference output (TP_3) to 820 Ω.
   (f) Reduce each of the supply voltages by 2 V, one at a time.

3. Measure the reference dc voltage level at the phase detector output by connecting the scope through a 10:1 probe to TP_3. Apply a dc voltage level equal to the reference to TP_{1A} (no coupling capacitor). If a third low-voltage power supply is not available to do this, simply feed the V_{cc} power supply voltage through a 10-kΩ potentiometer acting as a voltage divider. Increase and decrease the applied voltage above and below the reference voltage level in 0.5-V steps. At each setting, measure the resulting VCO output frequency. Disconnect the dc voltage before proceeding.

VCO Dynamic Tests

4. Connect a function generator at TP_1. Apply a 2-Hz, 4-V_{p-p} sine wave as the VCO input voltage at TP_1. Sketch the resulting VCO output waveform displayed at TP_2. You will need to use your imagination in showing the motion of the resulting display. You are observing an FM waveform.

   (a) Carefully increase and decrease the amplitude of the function generator and note the effect upon the FM output signal at TP_2. Return back to 4 V_{p-p} before proceeding.

   (b) Carefully increase and decrease the frequency of the function generator and note the effect on the FM output signal at TP_2. Return to 2 Hz before proceeding.

Phase-Detector Static Tests

5. Build the phase detector circuit shown in Fig. 16-2. Connect the test equipment to the phase detector test circuit as shown in Fig. 16-3. Use the scope to monitor the input voltage at TP_1 on channel A and to monitor the VCO output voltage at TP_4 on channel B. Use a VOM to monitor the difference voltage between TP_2 and TP_3 of the phase detector. Again, use power supply voltages of ± 7 V dc.

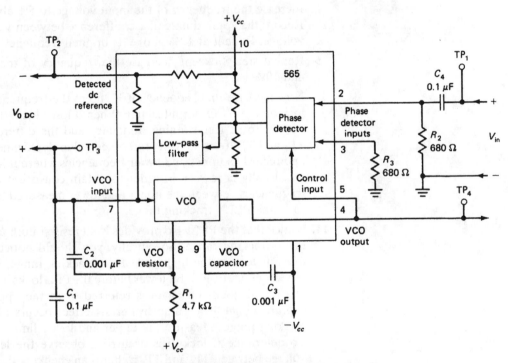

FIGURE 16-2 Phase-detector test circuit

6. With no voltage applied at TP_1, measure the difference voltage between TP_2 and TP_3 with the VOM. This value is the reference level of the phase detector output. Also, measure the free-running frequency of the VCO by measuring the frequency of the VCO output signal at TP_4 using the oscilloscope.

7. Apply a 0.5-V_{p-p} square wave at a frequency approximately equal to that of the VCO output at TP_4. Vary the frequency of this input signal and you

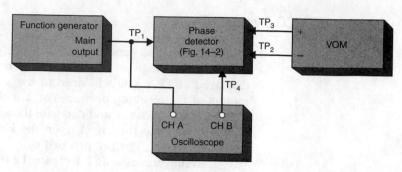

FIGURE 16-3 Phase-detector static test circuit configuration

should see that the VCO output signal will "track" the frequency of the input signal as long as it is fairly close to the free-running frequency. Also, the difference voltage measured with the VOM should vary as long as tracking is taking place. Adjust the frequency of the input voltage so that the difference voltage equals the reference voltage value measured in step 6. Record the waveforms of the input voltage and the VCO output signal under these conditions. Note the amplitudes, frequencies, and approximate phase difference between the two waveforms.

8. Increase the frequency of the input voltage to 5% above its original value. Record the approximate phase difference between V_{in} and the VCO output voltage. Repeat at 10% above its original frequency.

9. Repeat step 8 except decrease the frequency of the input voltage by 5% and 10%.

10. Now increase the frequency of V_{in} up to the frequency at which it loses its lock on the VCO output signal. When it loses lock, the VCO output signal returns to its free-running frequency and the difference voltage between TP_2 and TP_3 returns to its reference value determined in step 6. Measure and record its upper and lower frequencies where it loses lock. A few trials are usually necessary in order to obtain consistent results. This range of frequencies between the upper and lower measured frequencies is referred to as the PLL's tracking range.

11. Notice that the PLL also provides hysteresis at both upper and lower limits of its tracking range. Specifically, you should notice that when the PLL loses its lock at the high end of the tracking range, you need to decrease the frequency of V_{in} a bit lower before the PLL locks back up. The frequency at which it locks up again is referred to as the upper end of the PLL's capture range. The same hysteresis effect occurs at the low end of the tracking range. Measure the upper and lower limits of the capture range. To determine if lockup is occurring, observe the level of the difference voltage between TP_2 and TP_3 rather than checking the stability of the VCO output signal. Note that when measuring the low end of the capture range, there may be a few false triggers before true capture actually occurs. Again, several attempts will be necessary to yield consistent results. Record your results.

Phase Detector Dynamic Tests

12. A swept-frequency display can be used to measure simultaneously the capture and tracking frequency ranges of a PLL. To do this, the frequency of V_{in} is slowly swept linearly above and below the complete tracking range.

The PLL responds by repeatedly locking up and losing lock as the applied frequency of V_{in} is swept. Refer to the test configuration of Fig. 16-4. The vertical deflection of the display represents the value of the detected dc voltage from the phase detector, which should vary linearly about its reference value. The sweep signal, being triangular instead of ramp, permits us to see hysteresis at both ends of the tracking range. This permits us to measure the capture and tracking ranges. Refer to Experiment 9 for procedures for frequency calibration of the horizontal axis when producing a swept-frequency display using a generator that provides a VCG input jack. Set up the test configuration of Fig. 16-4 and measure the tracking and capture ranges of the PLL. Adjust the sweep generator for a 2.5-V_{p-p} triangle wave at a frequency of 20 Hz. Set the RF generator for a 500-mV_{p-p} sine wave at the VCO's free-running frequency. Make sure that the scope inputs are dc coupled to avoid distorting the display. Your resulting display should look similar to the one shown in Fig. 16-5. Make slight alterations to the amplitude and frequency settings to produce optimum results. Sketch your resulting display.

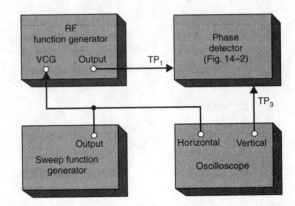

FIGURE 16-4 Phase-detector dynamic test configuration

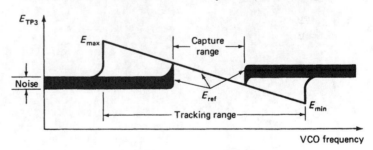

FIGURE 16-5 Typical swept-frequency display of phase detector

REPORT/QUESTIONS

1. Based on the results of each of the changes made in step 2, comment on the stability of a PLL's VCO when it is in the free-running state.

2. Plot the VCO output frequency versus dc input voltage for the measurements made in step 3. From your graph determine the VCO's deviation constant by determining the slope of the resulting linear graph.

$$K_f = \frac{\Delta f_{VCO}}{\Delta V_{TPIA}} = \frac{f_{max} - f_{min}}{V_{max} - V_{min}}$$

3. Explain the difference between the two frequency-modulated waveforms observed in step 4. What characteristic of the observed FM waveform was changing in each case? Refer to pages 187–188 of your text to help answer this question.

4. Plot the relative phase difference between V_{in} and the VCO output voltage versus frequency using the results of steps 8 and 9 of the phase detector static tests. From your graph determine the phase detector's deviation constant by determining the slope of the resulting linear graph.

$$K_\phi = \frac{\Delta_\phi}{\Delta f_{VCO}} = \frac{\phi_{max} - \phi_{min}}{f_{max} - f_{min}}$$

5. Explain what is meant by each of the following specifications of a PLL:
   (a) Free-running frequency
   (b) Tracking range
   (c) Capture range

FM DETECTION AND FREQUENCY SYNTHESIS USING PLLs

OBJECTIVES:

1. Further familiarization with phase-locked-loop operation.

2. To be acquainted with two popular applications of phase-locked loops: FM detection and frequency synthesis.

REFERENCE:

Refer to sections 6-5 and 7-5 of the text.

TEST EQUIPMENT:

Dual-trace oscilloscope
Low-voltage power supply (2)
Function generators (2); one must have a VCG input to produce FM
Frequency counter

COMPONENTS:

Integrated circuits: 565 (2), 7493 (2), 7420
Transistor: 2N2222
Capacitors: 0.001 μF (4), 0.1 μF (3), 10 μF
Resistors ($\frac{1}{2}$ watt): 680 Ω (4), 4.7 kΩ (2), 10 kΩ, 33 kΩ (2)

PROCEDURE:

1. Build the FM detector circuit shown in Fig. 17-1. Apply ± 10 V dc to this circuit and measure the free-running frequency of the VCO part of the 565 PLL by measuring the frequency of the VCO output waveform at TP$_4$ with a frequency counter.

free-running frequency = _____

2. Connect a function generator that has VCG capability to the phase detector input at TP$_1$. This generator will serve as the FM signal generator. Connect

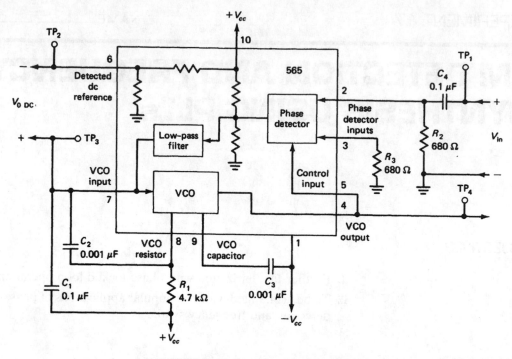

FIGURE 17-1 FM detector using a 565 PLL

channel A of the dual-trace oscilloscope to monitor the output of the FM generator. Connect channel B of the oscilloscope to monitor the VCO output signal at TP_4. Set the FM generator to produce a 500-mV$_{p-p}$ sine wave at the same frequency as the free-running frequency of the VCO part of the PLL. You should see the PLL lock up to the FM generator's frequency by observing both waveforms of the oscilloscope lock up at the same frequency.

3. Connect a second function generator as an intelligence signal by connecting it to the VCG input jack of the RF generator. Set the intelligence signal generator to produce a 100-mV$_{p-p}$ sine wave at a frequency of 20 Hz. You should see both waveforms on the oscilloscope frequency modulate. As long as the deviation of the FM signal does not cause the VCO output of the PLL to exceed its tracking range, the waveforms should remain frequency locked together.

4. Now connect channel A of the scope to monitor the original intelligence signal at the VCG jack of the RF generator. Connect channel B of the oscilloscope to monitor the detected dc reference signal at TP_3. Sketch the waveforms observed on the oscilloscope.

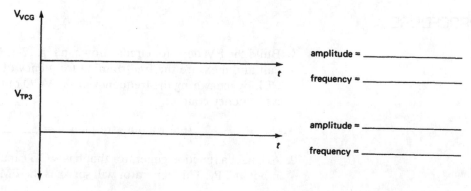

amplitude = _____

frequency = _____

amplitude = _____

frequency = _____

5. Increase and decrease the amplitude of the intelligence signal. Note the effect the amplitude changes have on the signals observed at TP_4 and TP_3. Return to the original amplitude setting before proceeding.

6. Increase and decrease the amplitude of the FM signal. Again, note the effect the amplitude changes have on the signals observed at TP_4 and TP_3. Return to the original amplitude setting before proceeding.

7. Increase the intelligence signal frequency and watch the waveform at TP_3. You will discover a critical frequency where the phase-locked loop can no longer follow the variations in frequency of the RF generator. Record this frequency and return the intelligence generator back to 20 Hz.

8. Set the intelligence generator to produce a 50-mV_{p-p} 20 Hz square wave. Sketch the resulting detected signal at TP_3. It should exhibit overshoot and ringing. Measure the ringing frequency. It should be fairly close to the same frequency as the critical frequency measured in step 7.

9. Build the frequency synthesizer circuit shown in Fig. 17-2. Leave jumpers J_1, J_2, J_3, and J_4 disconnected from any test points. Apply ±5 V dc to this circuit. Again, check the VCO output at TP_9 and measure the free-running frequency.

free-running frequency = _____

10. Connect a function generator to act as a master oscillator at TP_{10}. Connect channel A of the dual-trace oscilloscope at TP_{10} and channel B at TP_9. Connect jumper J_1 to ground. This causes the binary counter to be engaged to count up to its maximum value as a MOD-256 counter. This particular divide-by ratio, N, which is 256 in this case, determines the multiple that the output frequency is with respect to the input frequency. Even though the digital divider is dividing by 256, the value of $N = 256$ causes the input frequency to be multiplied by 256 to create the output frequency. Thus, by providing a constant input frequency through the design of a single, stable oscillator, we can produce a stable but variable output frequency simply by changing the value of N in the digital divider network. This can be done easily through the use of proper digital logic gates and appropriate switches which would be set properly either manually or perhaps by a microcontroller computer. This offers an alternative to the expensive use of multiple-crystal oscillators to create stable but multiple operating frequencies in receiver and transmitter designs.

Apply a 0.5-V_{p-p} sinusoidal signal to the synthesizer circuit at TP_{10}. Use an input frequency fairly close to the free-running frequency divided by 256. Observe the waveforms of V_{in} and V_o at TP_{10} and TP_9, respectively. Verify that f_o/f_{in} is equal to 256, using a frequency counter to measure f_o and f_{in}. You should notice that the loop locks up for output frequencies within a certain range about the free-running frequency. This range is again referred to as the tracking range. Measure the tracking and capture ranges of the closed-loop system, using the same techniques that were used in steps 10 and 11 of Experiment 16. The tracking and capture ranges should be measured with respect for f_o, not f_{in}. Also, measure the duty cycle of the output signal of the digital divider at TP_{11}.

duty cycle = _____

11. Connect jumpers J_1 to TP_1, J_2 to TP_2, J_3 to TP_7, and J_4 to TP_8. This makes the counter into a MOD-195 counter. If you are unfamiliar with MOD

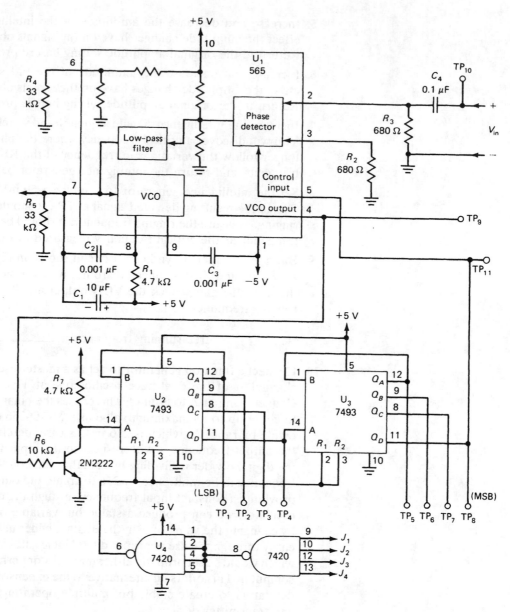

FIGURE 17-2 Frequency synthesizer using a 565 PLL

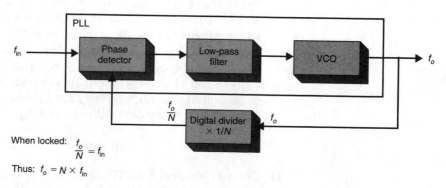

When locked: $\dfrac{f_o}{N} = f_{in}$

Thus: $f_o = N \times f_{in}$

FIGURE 17-3 Frequency synthesizer block diagram

counters and digital dividers, refer to a digital electronics text to review how the divide-by-195 function occurs with the 7420 NAND gate controlling the reset inputs of the dividers. Verify that $f_o = 195 \times f_{in}$ by measuring the frequencies, f_{in} and f_o, with a frequency counter when f_{in} is set at approximately 1/195th of the free-running frequency. Again, measure the tracking range of the loop and the duty cycle of the output signal of the digital counter at TP_{11}. Note that it may be possible for the PLL to lock up at input frequency ranges other than $1/195$ of f_o. These "false" tracking ranges are usually quite small and unstable in nature.

12. Connect J_1 to TP_1, J_2 to TP_2, J_3 to TP_6, and J_4 to TP_8. Vary the frequency of V_{in} until the phase-locked loop locks up. Again, measure f_o and f_n with the counter and experimentally determine what the value of N now is for the digital divider. Determine theoretically what N is by following one of the procedures described below.

(a) Review what signals cause the NAND gate to reset the counter, express this as a digital count in binary notation, and convert to decimal notation.

(b) If you are patient and determined, you may be able to carefully count how many pulses of the input signal to the digital counter it takes to produce one complete pulse at the output. If your oscilloscope has delayed sweep capability, it should be helpful to you in your counting process!

Again, measure the duty cycle of the output signal of the digital divider and the tracking range of the synthesizer. Be prepared to demonstrate to the lab instructor that you understand how the frequency synthesizer operates.

13. Try a small-value duty-cycle case. Connect the jumpers properly for a divide-by-139 counter. Calculate the free-running frequency divided by 139 and set f_{in} at this frequency value. Slowly vary the frequency, f_{in}, until you notice that the loop is back in lock. Again, measure f_o and f_{in} to verify that $N = 139$. Measure and record the duty cycle and tracking range as done in previous steps. You should find that at low duty cycles, the tracking range is very narrow, making the system more unstable.

REPORT/QUESTIONS:

1. Describe how the phase-locked loop can be used successfully to detect an FM signal. Explain how it works.

2. Explain why in step 6 there was very little if any effect of changing the amplitude of the FM signal on the amplitude of the detected output signal.

3. Describe how the phase-locked loop can be used successfully to synthesize a range of output frequencies by using a single stable oscillator and digital counter. Explain how the circuit works. Also, state its advantage over the use of multiple-crystal oscillators in a "channelized" radio.

4. Research: A limitation of this synthesizer design is its noncontinuous frequency ranges that can actually be synthesized. How can this limitation be removed through the addition of mixers? (Refer to Chapter 8 in your text.)

NAME _____

PULSE-AMPLITUDE MODULATION AND TIME-DIVISION MULTIPLEXING

OBJECTIVES:

1. To investigate pulse-amplitude modulation techniques.
2. To investigate time-division multiplexing.

REFERENCE:

Refer to sections 9-5 and 9-6 of the text.

TEST EQUIPMENT:

Dual-trace oscilloscope
Power source for +5 V dc and + 12 V dc
Audio frequency function generator
TTL-compatible signal source

COMPONENTS:

Integrated circuits: 74LS27, 74LS174, HCT4016
Capacitors: 0.033 μF, 0.68 μF
Resistors ($\frac{1}{2}$ watt): 1 kΩ (3), 2.2 kΩ (3), 8.2 kΩ

PROCEDURE:

1. Examine the pulse-amplitude modulator circuit shown in Fig. 18-1. The HCT4016 is a bilateral switch used to sample each of three voice channels and a dc voltage used for synchronizing the receiver. By using a ring counter to select channels of the HCT4016, time-division multiplexing of a pulse-amplitude modulated signal is achieved. Three voice channels will be simulated using dc voltages or the function generator with a voltage divider. Point D is connected to a dc voltage for synchronization.

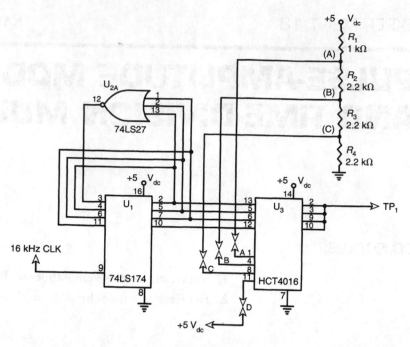

FIGURE 18-1

2. Construct the pulse-amplitude modulator. The dc voltage divider is simulating input signals. Apply power and a 16-kHz TTL-compatible clock signal. Examine the signal at TP_1. Trigger on pin 13 of U_3. The dc levels from the voltage divider should appear one after the other in a repeating sequence. Draw the signal at TP_1 below.

3. Disconnect the dc power supply from the voltage divider, and connect the function generator at points A, B, and C as shown in Figure 18-2. Set the generator frequency to 200 Hz with the amplitude at 5 V_{p-p}. Notice that R_5, R_6, and C_1 provide the signal with a dc offset. Measure the ac and dc voltages at points A, B, and C.

$V_A =$ _____ V_{p-p} $V_A =$ _____ V_{dc}

$V_B =$ _____ V_{p-p} $V_B =$ _____ V_{dc}

$V_C =$ _____ V_{p-p} $V_C =$ _____ V_{dc}

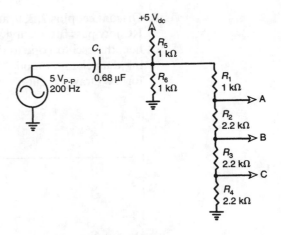

FIGURE 18-2

4. Using the function generator, apply a TTL-compatible clock signal to the 74174 ring counter. Set the clock frequency to approximately 2 Hz. Examine the signal at TP_1 with the oscilloscope. Trigger the oscilloscope with the signal at point A. The display should change at half-second intervals. Describe the signal observed at TP_1.

_____

_____

_____

5. At this point, we should have proper time-division multiplexing, but the PAM is not acceptable because the sample frequency is much too low. Determine the minimum sample rate to meet the Nyquist rate criterion for the modulating signal frequency.

Minimum sample rate = _____

6. We will be using a sample rate of 4 kHz on each channel. Since there are four channels, the ring counter will be clocked at a rate of 16 kHz. Connect a TTL-compatible 16-kHz clock signal to the counter.

7. Connect one channel of the oscilloscope to point A and the other channel to TP_1. Trigger on point A. Overlap the two waveforms and observe how the modulating signal is being sampled. Also observe how time-division multiplexing is achieved by interleaving the four channels in time. Draw the waveforms in the space below. Compare the signal at TP_1 to those at points B and C in the same manner.

8. Disconnect pins 2, 3, 9, and 10 of U_4 from each other. Connect pin 2 to an RC low-pass filter using a 0.033-μF capacitor and an 8.2-kΩ resistor. Connect the oscilloscope to the output of the low-pass filter and to point A using dual-channel mode. Trigger on point A and compare the two waveforms. Draw the filter output in the space below.

9. Reduce the clock frequency to 250 Hz and again observe the filtered pin 2 waveform. Use point A to trigger the oscilloscope. Draw the waveform in the space below.

10. Reconnect pins 2, 3, 9, and 10 of the 4016, and leave the circuit built for use in the next experiment.

SUMMARY:

Pulse-amplitude modulation (PAM) is a simple analog form of pulse modulation. It is commonly used as a first step in pulse-code modulated systems. By sampling several channels in a regular sequence, the channel samples can be carried on a single line and further processed in a time-sharing arrangement. This is time-division multiplexing, a commonly used means of transmitting digital signals in multichannel systems. Sampling rates must be selected to satisfy the Nyquist criterion for acceptable reproduction. A low-pass filter removes the sample frequency and harmonics which result from the sampling process.

QUESTIONS:

1. What is the minimum sample rate for a signal frequency of 4 kHz?
   (a) 2 kHz
   (b) 4 kHz
   (c) 6 kHz
   (d) 8 kHz

2. What is the function of the voltage applied to point D?
   (a) It is the clock input to the 4016.
   (b) It will synchronize the receiver.
   (c) It provides the ramp voltage to the comparator.
   (d) It resets the ring counter.

3. What is the function of the NOR gate?

   (a) It loads the ring counter for proper operation after a few clock counts.
   (b) It truncates the counter.
   (c) It gives the counter a mod 4 count.
   (d) It provides receiver synchronization.

4. What would the clock speed for U_1 need to be if the number of voice channels were increased from three to seven?

   (a) 8 kHz
   (b) 16 kHz
   (c) 32 kHz
   (d) 64 kHz

5. What would be seen at TP_1 if the jumper connecting U_1 pin 7 to U_{2A} pin 1 opened near U_{2A}? Assume that the ring counter has been operating properly.

   (a) TP_1 will show a signal that is the sum of all four inputs.
   (b) TP_1 will show a signal that is the difference between the inputs.
   (c) TP_1 will show no signal at all.
   (d) There will be no change in the signal at TP_1.

6. What is the purpose of the network made up of C_1, R_5, and R_6?

   (a) They are a voltage divider for the ac voltage.
   (b) They give the ac signal a dc offset.
   (c) They act as a delay line to synchronize the clock.
   (d) They integrate the incoming waveform.

7. In step 9, was the filtered pin 2 waveform an acceptable reconstruction of the original intelligence signal from point A?

   (a) Yes
   (b) No
   (c) They cannot be compared because they are not related to each other.

NAME _____

PULSE-WIDTH MODULATION AND DETECTION

OBJECTIVES:

1. To observe two types of pulse-time modulation waveforms.
2. To test and evaluate a pulse-width modulator.
3. To test and evaluate a pulse-width demodulator.

REFERENCE:

Refer to section 9-6 of the text.

TEST EQUIPMENT:

Dual-trace oscilloscope
Low-voltage power supply (2)
Function generator (2)
Volt-ohmmeter
Frequency counter

COMPONENTS:

Integrated circuits: 565, 1496P, 7486
Transistor: 2N2222
Capacitors: 4.7 nF (2), 0.01 μF (2), 0.1 μF (6), 0.47 μF (2), 10 μF, 470 μF
Resistors ($\frac{1}{2}$ watt): 47 Ω, 100 Ω, 390 Ω (2), 680 Ω, 1 kΩ (5), 3.3 kΩ, 4.7 kΩ (2), 5.6 kΩ, 10 kΩ (4), 33 kΩ
Potentiometers: (10-turn trim) 5 kΩ (2)

THEORY:

A type of modulation often used when transmitting low-frequency signals over a long distance via telephone lines or fiber optic scale is pulse-time modulation. In PTM, the amplitude of the intelligence signal is converted to variations in pulse length or variations in pulse position of the carrier signal. These two types of PTM are referred to as pulse-width modulation and pulse-position modulation, respectively. The wave shapes of PWM and PPM are given in Fig.19-1.

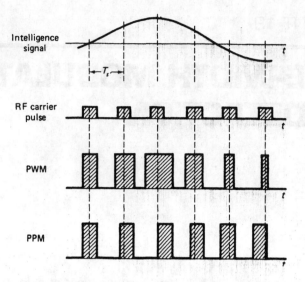

FIGURE 19-1 PWM and PPM waveforms

The amplitude of the carrier pulses remains constant in either PWM or PPM. Thus pulse-time-modulated signals exhibit the same advantages that are exhibited by frequency-modulated signals: noise immunity and low distortion. In addition, pulse signals are easily reproduced if they do get noisy and distorted. This is not possible if analog signals are used.

One possible method of generating PWM and PPM uses the phase-locked loop and digital Exclusive-Or gate as given in Fig. 19-2. The PLL is designed to lock up

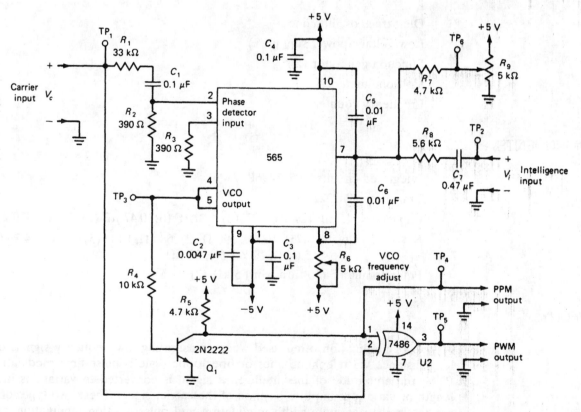

FIGURE 19-2 PWM modulator stage

near the frequency of the carrier. The carrier frequency is applied to the phase detector input, thus causing it to lock up at the carrier frequency. The intelligence signal is applied to the reference input of the VCO and causes the VCO's output signal to shift its phase with respect to the reference phase by an amount proportional to the amplitude of the intelligence signal. This fits the definition of pulse-position modulation. If the VCO output signal is fed into a switching transistor, the output of the switching transistor can be described as being a TTL-compatible PPM signal. To create PWM, the original RF carrier pulse and the PPM signal are fed into the two inputs of an Exclusive-Or gate. Its output will be "high" only during the time when the RF carrier pulse and PPM signals are at different logic states. Since the two signals are synchronized by the PLL, the Exclusive-Or output signal will be "high" only during the time of phase difference between the RF carrier pulse and the PPM pulse. This creates PWM. Refer to Fig. 19-1 to verify this.

A method that successfully demodulates the PWM signal uses a 1496 balanced modulator as given in Fig. 19-3. If the 1496 product detector that was investigated in Experiment 14 is slightly altered so that the differential amplifier transistors act as switching transistors, the pulse signal produced at its output will exhibit a dc offset that will vary as a function of the phase difference between its two inputs. Thus if the two input signals are the PWM signal and the original RF carrier pulse, the output voltage of the product detector will resemble the original intelligence signal. Fortunately, all of the other frequency components produced by the mixing action of the switching transistors in the 1496 are much higher frequencies than the original intelligence signal. Therefore, if the complex output signal of the 1496 is passed through a simple low-pass filter, the original intelligence signal will be recreated.

PRELABORATORY:

Calculate the free-running frequency of the PLL found in the PWM modulator of Fig. 19-2 if R_6 is adjusted to 3 kΩ using the information given in the Appendix for the 565 integrated circuit.

PROCEDURE:

1. Build the circuit given in Fig. 19-2. Apply ±5 V dc and measure the VCO output frequency at TP$_3$. Adjust R_9 so as to produce approximately 3.5 V dc at TP$_6$. Adjust R_6 to produce exactly 15 kHz at TP$_3$.

2. Apply a 3 V, 15 kHz positive square wave at TP$_1$. This will function as the RF carrier pulse that is to be modulated by this circuit. Observe the waveform at TP$_3$. Use 10:1 scope probes to avoid loading of the signal by the scope. You should be able to see the PLL lock up as the RF carrier frequency is adjusted near 15 kHz. Measure the PLL's tracking and capture ranges as in steps 10 and 11 of Experiment 16.

	minimum	maximum
capture range:	_____	_____
tracking range:	_____	_____

3. Set the RF carrier back at 15 kHz. This should be approximately in the middle of the tracking range. If not, readjust R_6 and repeat step 2 to make

it so. Now apply a 2-V_{p-p}, 2-kHz sine wave at TP$_2$. This will function as the intelligence signal. Observe the signal at TP$_3$. Notice that as the intelligence signal amplitude is varied, the display will blur. This is due to the intelligence signal introducing phase shift into the PLL's VCO's output signal. This is pulse-position modulation.

4. Observe the waveform at TP$_4$ with channel A of the oscilloscope. This is a TTL-compatible PPM waveform. Now observe the intelligence signal at TP$_2$ with channel A and observe the PPM signal at TP$_4$ with channel B. Trigger the oscilloscope with the intelligence signal. Increase the amplitude of the intelligence signal to approximately 5 V_{p-p}. Carefully adjust the trigger level of the oscilloscope and the frequency of the intelligence signal in order to produce a stable display. Sketch the resulting display. It should look similar to the sketch given in Fig. 19-1.

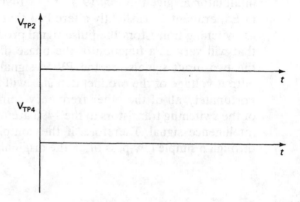

5. Temporarily disconnect the intelligence signal from TP$_2$. Observe the output of the Exclusive-Or gate at TP$_5$ with channel B and observe the original RF carrier pulse at TP$_1$ with channel A. Let the RF carrier pulse serve as the trigger signal for the scope. The waveform at TP$_5$ should be a square wave at exactly twice the frequency of the RF carrier pulse. Fine-tune the frequency of the RF carrier pulse. It should vary the duty cycle of the output waveform at TP$_5$. Adjust the frequency such that a duty cycle of approximately 50% is produced. Measure the frequency of the RF carrier pulse. It should be approximately in the center of the PLL's tracking range.

6. Reconnect the intelligence signal at TP$_2$. Adjust the amplitude between zero and 5 V_{p-p}. You should notice that the intelligence signal causes the pulse duration of the output signal of the Exclusive-Or gate to vary. This is seen as a blurring effect on the waveform at TP$_5$. This is pulse-width modulation.

7. Move the channel A probe to TP$_2$. Observe the waveform at TP$_5$ with channel B with the intelligence signal serving as the trigger signal for the oscilloscope. Adjust the amplitude of the intelligence signal to approximately 2 V_{p-p}. As in step 4, carefully adjust the trigger level of the scope and the frequency of the intelligence signal in order to produce a stable display. Sketch the resulting PWM display. It should look similar to the sketch given in Fig. 19-1. Do not disassemble this circuit before proceeding to step 8.

8. Build the PWM demodulator circuit given in Fig. 19-3. Connect the output signal of the PWM modulator to the input of the PWM demodulator by connecting a jumper between TP$_5$ and TP$_8$. Also, provide the balanced

modulator with the RF carrier pulse input by connecting a jumper between TP_1 and TP_7. Apply $\pm5V$ dc to both circuits. The RF carrier should still be set at 3-V amplitude at a frequency near 15 kHz that causes approximately 50% duty cycle to exist at the modulator output at TP_5. The balanced modulator may capacitively load the RF carrier pulse, so do not expect the waveform at TP_1 to remain as a clean square wave as was observed in preceding steps.

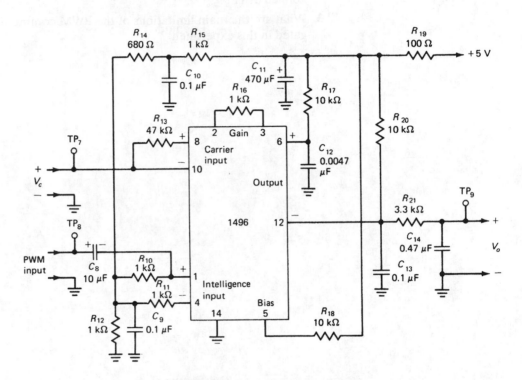

FIGURE 19-3 PWM demodulator

9. Adjust the amplitude of the intelligence signal to 1 V_{p-p} at a frequency of 30 Hz. Observe the waveform at TP_9. It should be a clean replica of the original intelligence signal. Fine-tune the amplitude and frequency of the carrier signal to produce optimum results. Verify that the system is working properly by temporarily disconnecting each of the two jumpers connected in step 8, one at a time. The output waveform of the demodulator at TP_9 should disappear if either of the two jumpers is disconnected. With the jumpers reconnected, adjust the frequency of the RF carrier pulse above and below the PLL's tracking range as was measured in step 2. You should see that when the PLL goes out of lock, the output signal of the demodulator at TP_9 disappears again. Readjust the frequency of the RF carrier pulse such as to produce 50% duty cycle at TP_5 before proceeding.

10. Determine the range of the intelligence frequencies that can be reproduced successfully by the PWM demodulator without any resulting distortion. Take data so as to be able to sketch the frequency response of the PWM digital communication system, i.e. V_{TP_x} vs. frequency.

11. Determine the maximum and minimum amplitudes of both the intelligence signal and the RF carrier pulse that allow the output signal at TP_9 to remain undistorted.

REPORT/QUESTIONS:

1. Provide a brief explanation of how the intelligence signal applied at TP_2 of Fig. 19-2 is encoded as variations in pulse width in the output waveform at TP_5.

2. How does the 1496 balanced modulator stage shown in Fig. 19-3 function to detect the original information signal from the encoded PWM signal applied at TP_8?

3. What are the main limitations of the PWM communication system investigated in this experiment?

NAME _____

PULSE-CODE MODULATION AND TIME-DIVISION MULTIPLEXING

OBJECTIVES:

    1. To investigate pulse-code modulation techniques.

    2. To investigate analog-to-digital conversion techniques.

    3. To investigate time-division multiplexing.

REFERENCE:

    Refer to section 8-3 of the text.

TEST EQUIPMENT:

    Dual-trace oscilloscope

    Power source for +5 V dc and + 12 V dc

    Audio frequency function generator

    TTL-compatible signal source

COMPONENTS:

    Integrated circuits: 74LS00, 7474 (2), 7476, 74121, 74151, 74293 (2), LM339

    Transistors: 2N3904, 2N3906

    Capacitors: 270 pF, 680 pF, 0.003 μF, 0.0068 μF

    Resistors ($\frac{1}{2}$ watt): 1 kΩ (2), 2.2 kΩ (2), 4.7 kΩ, 6.8 kΩ, 10 kΩ,

                    1 kΩ potentiometer

PROCEDURE:

    1. Pulse-code modulation (PCM) is the process of encoding information into a binary code for processing or transmission. Its major advantage over analog modulation techniques is its superior noise immunity. The most common implementation of PCM converts pulse-amplitude modulated (PAM) signals to digital code. The PAM samples are usually time-division multiplexed, and the analog-to-digital conversion is referred to as quantizing.

2. Examine the ramp generator of Figure 20-1. Q_1 charges capacitor C_4 with constant current to produce a linear ramp. The one-shot resets the ramp generator by turning on Q_2 with a very short duration positive pulse applied to the base of Q_2. This discharges C_4, making C_4 ready for the next cycle. Resistor R_8 and capacitor C_2 differentiate the pulse to the base of Q_2. This allows an extremely short discharge time for C_4 by putting Q_2 quickly into saturation.

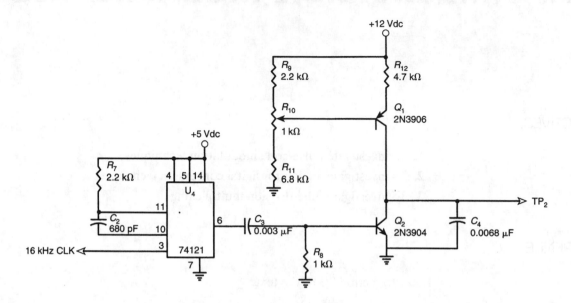

FIGURE 20-1

3. Construct the circuit of Figure 20-1, apply a TTL-compatible 16-kHz clock signal to the one-shot, and observe the waveform at TP_2. Adjust R_{10} so that the voltage ramps from near ground to +5 V. This ramp will provide the quantizing level voltages for the pulse-code modulator. Draw the signal in the space below.

4. Examine the pulse-code modulator of Fig. 20-2. U_{12} is a divide-by-16 counter used to provide the system with the three clock rates required. U_5 makes a comparator. One input is from the PAM circuit from Experiment 18, and the other is from the ramp generator. The output will be high as long as the sample voltage is larger than the ramp voltage. U_7 is a mod 16 counter clocked at a rate 16 times greater than the sample clock. The sample voltage will be represented by one of the 16 binary codes from the counter. The counter is clocked through a NAND gate which is enabled as long as the comparator output is high. When the ramp voltage exceeds the sample voltage, the comparator output goes low, inhibiting the clock to the counter. U_8 and U_9 are used as parallel registers to temporarily hold the code from the counter. U_{10} converts the parallel output of the counter to serial for transmission to the receiving circuit.

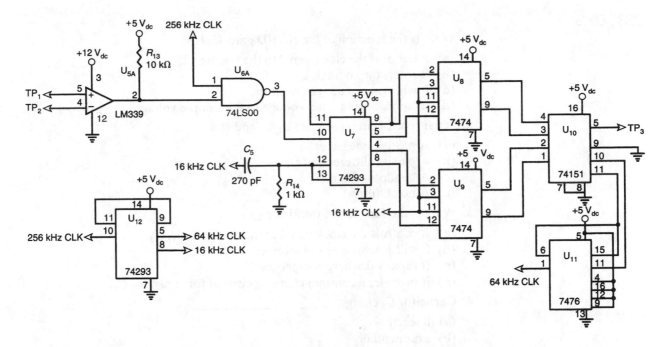

FIGURE 20-2

5. Construct the pulse-code modulator, and connect to TP$_1$ (from Experiment 18) and TP$_2$. Temporarily disconnect the function generator from points A, B, and C. Apply the dc voltage divider to these points as in Figure 18-1. Make sure the clock signals are connected, as indicated, at every point needing clock. Apply power and observe the signal at TP$_3$. Use the signal at pin 10 of the U$_1$ ring counter to trigger the oscilloscope. You should see a digital pulse train representing the voltages from the voltage divider in sequence. Draw the pulse pattern in the space below.

6. Remove the clock signal and power from the circuit. Remove the dc voltage divider and replace it with the function generator as in Fig. 20-2. Observe the signal at TP$_3$. You should again see a digital pulse train, but there should be no consistent pattern. It is not possible to observe this signal clearly because it is no longer periodic.

SUMMARY:

Pulse-code modulation (PCM) is the method most used in the telephone industry for transmitting signals from one place to another. The digital form is preferred due to its superior immunity to noise. In this experiment you have investigated one method of converting pulse-amplitude modulated signals to PCM. Notice that by using time-division multiplexing, a single analog-to-digital converter can process multiple channels, and that signals can be transmitted over a single pair of wires. The digital signals can also be easily used to modulate an LED or laser for fiber optic transmission. Using modern digital electronics, thousands of voice circuits can be carried on a single optical fiber.

QUESTIONS:

1. What is the function of the NAND gate, U_6?

   (a) It controls the clock signal to the counter, U_7.
   (b) It resets the counter, U_7.
   (c) It will synchronize the receiver.
   (d) It compares the ramp voltage to the sample voltage.

2. What type of circuit is made by C_3 and R_8?

   (a) A passive integrator
   (b) A passive differentiator
   (c) A bandpass filter
   (d) A notch filter

3. What is the function of transistor Q_1?

   (a) It controls the clock signal to the comparator, U_5.
   (b) It will synchronize the receiver.
   (c) It rapidly discharges capacitor C_4.
   (d) It provides a constant charging current for capacitor C_4.

4. Capacitor C_4 charges _____.

   (a) linearly
   (b) exponentially
   (c) when transistor Q_2 turns on
   (d) when the one-shot output is high

5. What would the clock rate for U_{11} be if seven voice channels were encoded instead of three?

   (a) 32 kHz
   (b) 64 kHz
   (c) 128 kHz
   (d) 256 kHz

6. Under what condition will the counter U_7 stop counting?

   (a) The synchronizing signal arrives at the comparator, U_5.
   (b) Transistor Q_1 stops conducting.
   (c) The ramp voltage exceeds the sample voltage at comparator U_5.
   (d) The output of NOR gate U_2 goes low.

7. What would be one method of reducing quantizing error in this system?

   (a) Increase the clock rate to the counter, U_7.
   (b) Increase the ramp voltage from C_4 to $+8$ V.
   (c) Reduce the value of capacitor C_5.
   (d) Increase the amplitude of the audio signals from Experiment 18.

DIGITAL COMMUNICATION LINK USING DELTA MODULATION CODECS

OBJECTIVES:

1. To become familiar with the process of delta modulation encoding and decoding in a data communication link.

2. To become familiar with the operating principles of the 3418 Continuously Variable Slope Delta Modulator integrated circuit.

REFERENCE:

Refer to section 9-6 of the text.

TEST EQUIPMENT:

Dual-trace oscilloscope

Function generator

Square-wave generator

Low-voltage power supply

COMPONENTS:

3418 codec integrated circuit (2)

324 op amp integrated circuit

Toggle switch

Resistors ($\frac{1}{2}$ watt): 560 Ω (3), 1 kΩ (4), 1.5 kΩ, 3.3 kΩ (9), 10 kΩ (5), 18 kΩ, 22 kΩ (4), 27 kΩ, 68 kΩ (5), 100 kΩ (4), 120 kΩ, 390 kΩ, 1.5 MΩ, 2.2 MΩ, 4.7 MΩ (4)

Capacitors: 33 pF., 75 pF., 220 pF., 470 pF. (2), 820 pF. (2), 1000 pF., .047 μF. (8), 0.1 μF. (4), 0.33 μF., 10 μF. (3)

THEORY:

The 3418 is a popular codec integrated circuit that uses delta modulation, sometimes referred to as slope modulation, to encode an analog signal into a digital format. It does this by transforming each sampled segment of the analog signal into a digital instruction that states whether the analog signal's amplitude is increasing or decreasing. Then when the 3418 is set up as a decoder, it simply reconstructs the analog signal by following the given instructions of increment or decrement. The rough edges of the reconstructed analog output signal are smoothed out by a low-pass filter. Obviously, the higher the sampling rate (clock) is, the easier it is for the low pass filter to recreate a near-perfect replica of the original analog signal.

In this experiment, the 3418 is first set up as an encoder. In this mode the continuously variable slope delta (CVSD) encoding scheme is observed. With CVSD, the step size is increased during periods of maximum slope and reduced during periods of minimum slope. Next, a complete process of encoding digital data and subsequent decoding of this data back into its original analog form is observed. Two 3418 codecs are necessary to perform this task. Finally, a telephone voice data link is built and analyzed.

PROCEDURE:

1. Build the circuit given in Fig. 21-1. Connect a 5 V, 16 kHz positive square wave to the clock input at TP2. Close switch S1 to apply a +5 V dc level at the EN/DE control input at TP3. This sets up the codec as an encoder. In other words, it will encode the analog signal applied at TP1 into a digital format, as described in the theory section of this experiment.

2. Observe the digital output signal at TP5. Sketch the square waveform, making note of its amplitude and frequency.

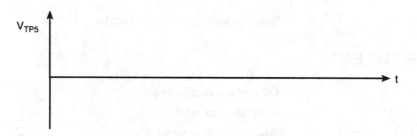

3. Now apply an analog signal at TP1. Connect the function generator at TP1. Connect channel 1 of your scope to TP1 and channel 2 to TP5. Set the function generator frequency to produce a 50 Hz sinewave. Trigger on channel 1. Also invert channel 2 of your scope. Slowly increase the amplitude of the sinewave from zero to approximately 6 Vp-p. Notice that as the amplitude increases, the square wave at TP5 begins to change into a varying duty cycle pulse. You may need to slightly alter the frequency of the sinewave in order to create a stable display of the waveform of TP5 on your scope. Carefully sketch both waveforms, making note of exactly where the duty cycle of the pulse is a maximum, a minimum, and 50%.

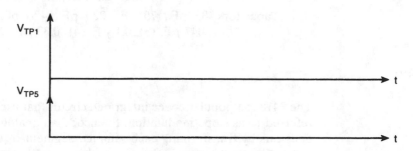

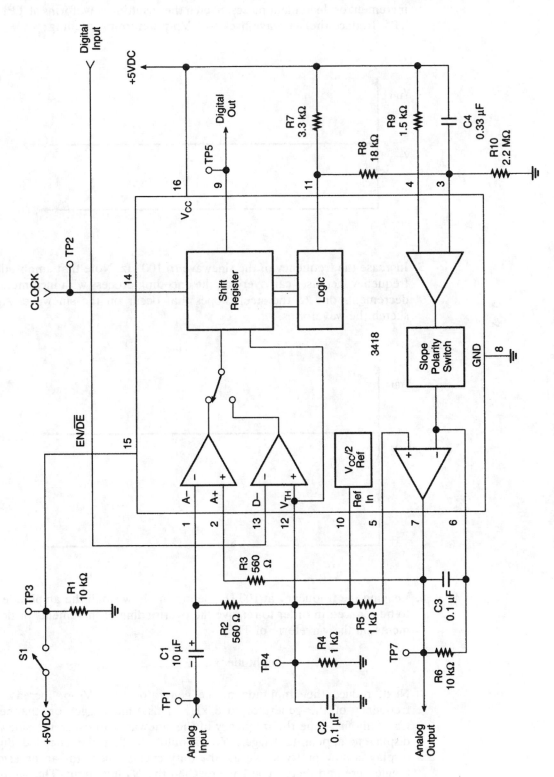

FIGURE 21-1 Encoding configuration of the 3418 codec

4. Now increase the sinewave to 7 Vp-p. Notice that the steeper slopes of the sinewave forces the encoded digital waveform to become overloaded with increment or decrement pulses. Sketch the resulting waveforms at TP1 and TP5. Reduce the sinewave back to 6 Vp-p before proceeding.

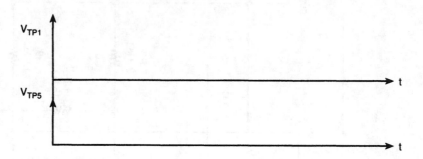

5. Increase the frequency of the sinewave to 100 Hz. Note that amplitude or frequency increases can overload the encoding process with increments or decrements due to the steep slopes that occur on the sinewave. Again sketch the waveforms.

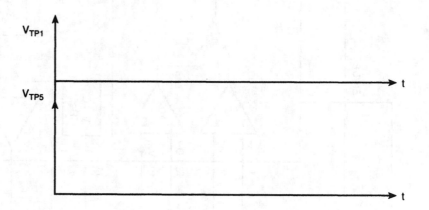

6. Leaving the frequency at 100 Hz, determine how small the amplitude has to be reduced in order to remove the overloading of increments or decrements on the waveform of TP5.

amplitude = _____

7. Next, reduce the amplitude of the generator to 3 Vp-p. Increase the frequency of the generator to 8 kHz. This time trigger on channel 2. Carefully fine-tune the frequency of the sinewaves to cause the sinewave display to appear to trigger. You should see that the encoded digital display is now pretty stable at 50% duty cycle, except for an occasional toggle here and there. You have reached the Nyquist limit. The sampling of the analog input only happens once for every half-cycle of the sinewave. Thus, the encoded digital signal is no longer an accurate representation of the analog information.

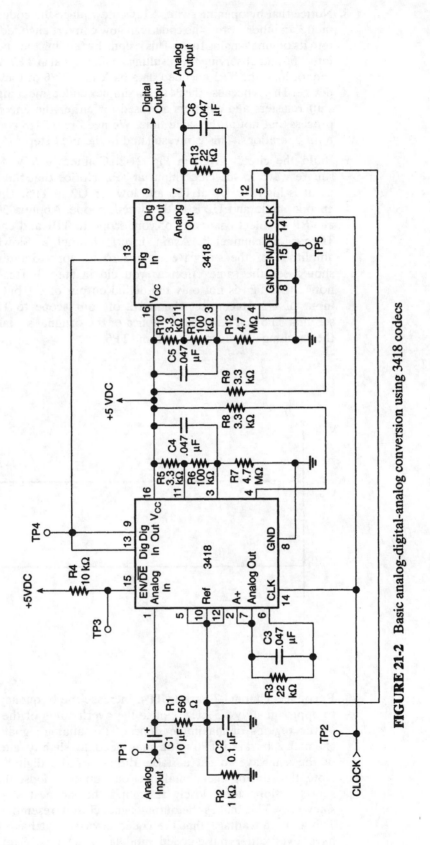

FIGURE 21-2 Basic analog-digital-analog conversion using 3418 codecs

8. Notice that by opening switch S1, we now place the codec into the decode mode. In other words, the codec can now convert encoded digital data back into its original analog form. This is done by feeding the encoded digital data into TP6 and observing the resulting analog signal at TP7. Unfortunately we cannot loop the TP5 encoded data back into TP6 of the same 3418 codec device. This is because the 3418 is a simplex codec, meaning that the internal shift registers and counters are used for either the encoding or decoding process, but not at the same time. We need two 3418 codec devices to do both operations. This is investigated in the next step.

9. Build the circuit given in Fig. 21-2. Connect a 5 V, 50 kHz positive square wave to the clock input at TP2. Notice that the EN/DE control input is high for U1 at TP3 and low for U2 at TP5. Thus, U1 is in the encode mode and U2 is in the decode mode. Apply a 500 Hz sinewave at TP1. Connect channel 1 of your scope to TP1 and channel 2 to TP4. Trigger on channel 1. Again, invert channel 2. Slowly increase the amplitude of the sinewave from zero to approximately 3 Vp-p. You should see the same effect as you did in step 3. This time, however, notice that TP4 is not only the digital output of U1 but also the digital input of U2. Reconnect channel 2 of your scope to TP6. You should see that TP6 is a fairly close replica of the original signal at TP1. Sketch the resulting waveforms at TP1 and TP6.

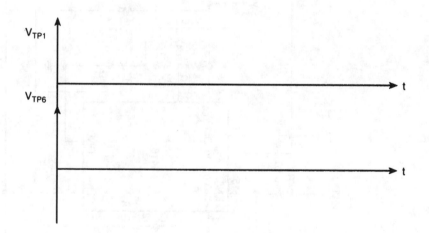

10. Reconnect channel 2 back to TP4. Increase the frequency of the sinewave to approximately 1.5 kHz. Notice the overloading of the digital encoding at the regions of maximum slope of the analog signal. Now reconnect channel 2 back to TP6. You may need to slightly alter the frequency of the sinewave to get a stable display of the digital "noise" at TP6. Note that during the digital overload time periods, the analog output shows a slope that closely resembles the steepest slopes of the input sinewaves. This makes the output signal closely resemble the input signal. This is an advantage that the codec devices that have CVSD encoding have over other pulse-coded modulated devices. Sketch the resulting waveforms at TP1 and TP6.

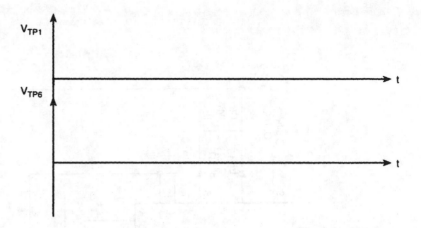

11. Sketch the resulting waveforms at TP1 and TP6 if the analog input is a 3 Vp-p, 1.5 kHz triangle wave.

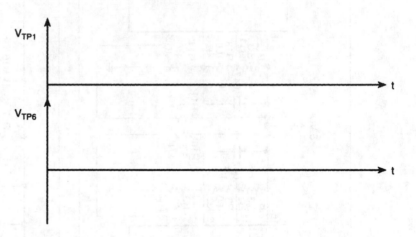

12. Repeat step 11 for a 3 Vp-p, 1.5 kHz square wave. Note that square wave slopes are very hard to reproduce.

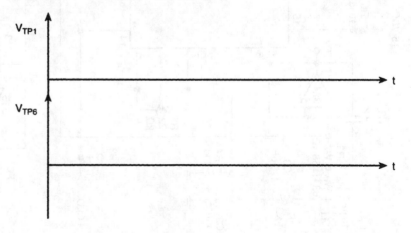

13. To make this digital communication link useful for voice communication, two improvements need to be made. First, the digital noise in the output waveform must be removed without affecting the basic waveshape of the desired signal. This can be done by the addition of an active low-pass filter in the output. Secondly, any high-frequency information in the input voice signal must not cause the encoding codec to be pushed past its Nyquist

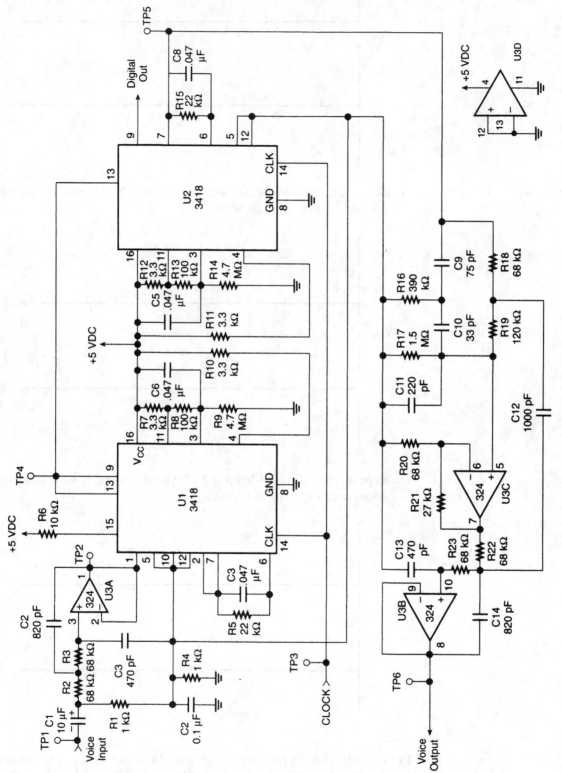

FIGURE 21-3 Telephone voice communication link using 3418 codecs

limit (half the clock rate). This is done by the addition of another active low-pass filter at the input. These two improvements are designed into the circuit of Fig. 21-3.

14. Build the test circuit of Fig. 21-3. Connect a 5 V, 50 kHz, positive square wave to the clock input at TP3. Again, U1 is set up as the encoder and U2 as the decoder. Apply a 2 Vp-p, 200 Hz sinewave at TP1. Connect channel 1 of your scope to TP1 and channel 2 to TP6. You should now see that most all of the digital "noise" has been removed by the filter. Sketch the resulting waveforms at TP1 and TP6.

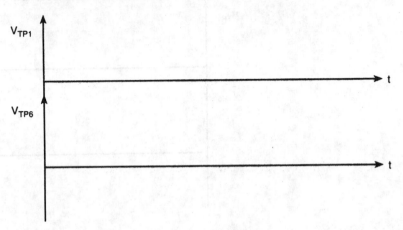

15. Repeat step 14 for a 2 Vp-p triangle wave at TP1.

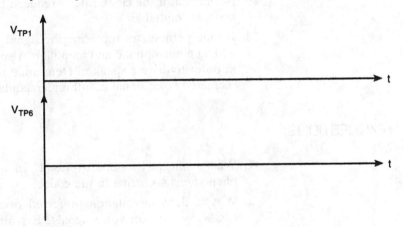

16. Repeat step 14 for a 2 Vp-p square wave at TP1.

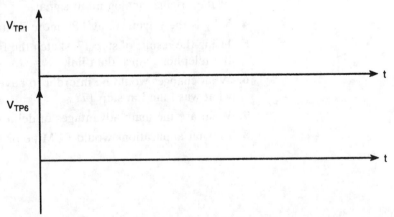

17. Reset the signal generator at TP1 as a 2 Vp-p sinewave. Determine the frequency response of this digital communication link by taking the output voltage readings at frequencies ranging from 10 Hz to 5 kHz. Calculate the output voltage in dB at each frequency, referenced to its maximum value.

18. Reset the signal generator at TP1 as a 2 Vp-p sinewave. Reduce the clock rate to 10 kHz. Notice the effect on the output waveform at TP6. Sketch the resulting waveforms.

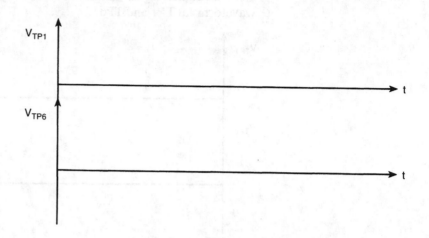

19. Notice that if the clock rate is reduced any further, the output waveform becomes unusable.

20. If time permits, try replacing the signal generator with a voice signal, by adding a microphone and amplifier. Also, amplify the output signal at TP$_6$ in order to drive a speaker. Determine the lowest clock rate at which the recreated voice signal is still understandable.

REPORT/QUESTIONS:

1. What is meant by slope overioad? In which steps did you discover this phenomena occurring in the codec?

2. Why is delta modulation preferred over basic pulse coded modulation (PCM) systems for voice signals? Explain.

3. State why in steps 12–16 the reconstructed square wave is not a close replica of the original analog input signal.

4. Why is the waveform at TP6 more distorted in step 18 than in step 14?

5. Using the results of step 17, sketch the frequency response curve in dB for the telephone voice data link.

6. What changes would be in order to have a wider frequency response than what was found in step 17?

7. What are the main advantages of delta modulation over PCM systems?

8. In what applications would PCM be preferred over delta modulation?

EWB MULTISIM—dB MEASUREMENTS IN COMMUNICATIONS

OBJECTIVES:

1. To become acquainted with the use of Electronics Workbench Multisim in simulating dB measurements in communications circuits.
2. To understand dB measurement using the EWB multimeter set to the dB mode.
3. To explore the characteristics of a T-type passive attenuator circuit.
4. To explore the procedure for setting the dB levels in a system.

VIRTUAL TEST EQUIPMENT:

AC voltage source

Multimeter

Virtual resistors, capacitors

INTRODUCTION:

This exercise introduces the reader to the techniques for making audio signal level measurements using Electronics Workbench Multisim simulations. Obtaining signal level measurements and measuring signal path performance are common maintenance, installation, and troubleshooting practices in all areas of communications. Communication networks require that proper signal levels are maintained to ensure minimum line distortion and cross-talk. This section examines the techniques for making dB (decibel) measurements on various passive circuits and setting the levels for a system.

PRELABORATORY:

1. Review Section 1-2, the dB in Communications in your text.
2. Review the Chapter 11 Troubleshooting with Electronics Workbench Multisim in your lab manual—Audio Signal Level and Distortion Measurements.

PROCEDURE:

You will be required to make dB level measurements on passive attenuator circuits and perform a system-wide calibration of the levels.

Part I: Measuring the Insertion Loss Provided by Passive Resistive Attenuators Circuits

1. The EWB Multisim implementation of a test circuit for making dB measurements is provided in Fig. 22-1. This circuit contains an AC signal source, a 600 load, and two multimeters. The top multimeter (XMM1) is measuring the dB level and the bottom multimeter (XMM2) is being used to measure the voltage across the load. Construct the circuit and set the AC voltage source to 2.188 V at 1kHz. Measure the voltage and dB levels across $R2$. Record your value. Note: Make sure you set your multimeter to measure AC.

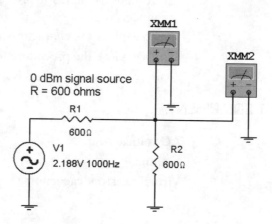

FIGURE 22-1

2. Explain how the voltage measured across $R2$ equates to 0 dBm (*Hint:* Refer to Audio Signal Level Measurements in your lab manual.)

3. Construct the circuit shown in Fig. 22-2. This circuit includes a 600 Ω, 0-dBm voltage source and a 600-Ω T-type attenuator that has been inserted into the path between the signal source and the 600-Ω load resistance. Measure the amount of insertion loss provided by the T-type attenuator. This requires that you measure the dB levels at both the input and output of the attenuator. The insertion loss will be the difference in the two measurements.

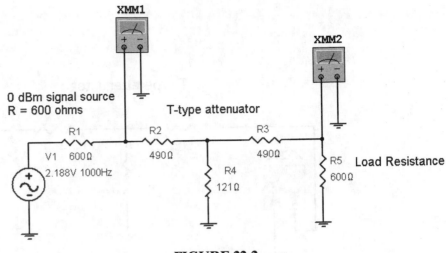

FIGURE 22-2

dB level measured at the attenuator input   _____

dB level measured at the attenuator output   _____

insertion loss (input–output)   _____

4. Repeat step 3 for the resistor values provided for the T-type attenuator in Table 22-1.

TABLE 22-1

R2	*R3*	*R4*	INPUT LEVEL (dB)	OUTPUT LEVEL (dB)	INSERTION LOSS (dB)
230	230	685			
69*	69	258			
588	588	12			
312	312	422			
563	563	38			

*Why does the input level for this attenuator not equal 0 dBm?

5. Verify that the measured resistance for the T-type attenuator values listed in Table 22-1 equal 600Ω. Connect the test circuit as shown in Fig. 22-3.

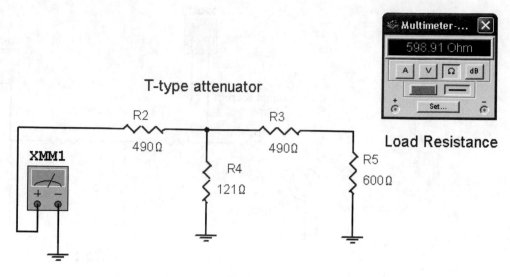

FIGURE 22-3

Repeat step 5 for the resistor values provided in Table 22-2. Make sure that the T-type attenuator is terminated with a 600-Ω resistor. The resistor R5 is the termination resistor in Fig. 22-3.

TABLE 22-2

R2	R3	R4	INPUT RESISTANCE (Ω)
230	230	685	
69	69	258	
588	588	12	
312	312	422	
563	563	38	

Part II: Setting System Wide dB Levels

This exercise demonstrates the procedure for setting dB levels in a communications system. This example is for a broadcast facility where the audio levels are being set to a predefined level throughout the system. The system is shown in Fig. 22-4. The audio outputs for a tone generator, production audio, VCR1, and a satellite feed are shown. These devices are inputted into a passive rotary switch. The output of the switch feeds the station studio transmitter link (STL). The levels' input to the rotary switch (TP1) must be set to 0 dBm. The level to the STL (TP2) must be set to +8 dBm. A 1-kHz tone is used to calibrate the system. Level adjustment is provided by the virtual potentiometer connected in the feedback paths for the operational amplifiers.

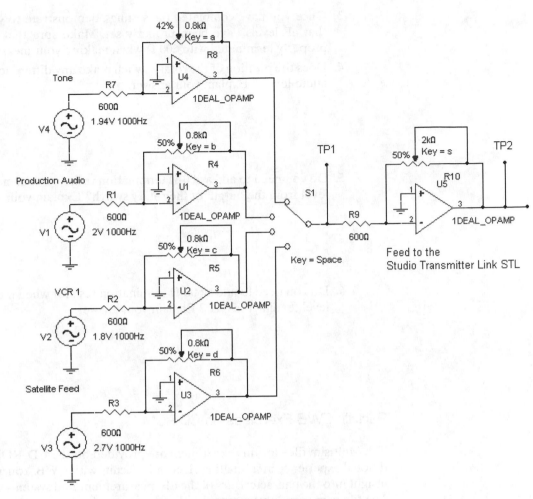

FIGURE 22-4

1. Open the file **Lab22-Part2** found on your EWB CD-ROM. This file contains the circuit shown in Fig. 22-4.
2. Set the levels according to Table 22-3.

TABLE 22-3

DEVICE	OUTPUT LEVEL	LEVEL CONTROL KEY
Tone	0 dBm	**A** increase, **a** decrease
Production Audio	0 dBm	**B** increase, **b** decrease
VCR1	0 dBm	**C** increase, **c** decrease
Satellite Feed	0 dBm	**D** increase, **d** decrease
Rotary Switch	0 dBm	None
STL	+ 8 dBm	**S** increase, **s** decrease

3. Once you have completed the settings, demonstrate to your lab instructor that all levels have been properly set. Make sure that the multimeter is properly terminated with 600 Ω when making your measurements.

4. Does the position of the rotary switch make any difference when setting the audio levels? Explain your answer.

5. Do you need to add a 600-Ω termination resistor when measuring the audio level from the output of the rotary switch? Explain your answer.

6. Do you need to add a 600-Ω termination resistor when measuring the audio level feeding the STL? Explain your answer.

Part III: EWB Exercises on CD-ROM

The Multisim files for this experiment are provided on the CD-ROM to give you additional experience in simulating electronic circuits with EWB. You will also gain more insight into the characteristics of the dB measurement and system-wide level settings. The file names and their corresponding figure number are listed.

FILE NAME
Lab22-Fig22-1
Lab22-Fig22-2
Lab22-Fig22-3
Lab22-Part2

SMITH CHART MEASUREMENTS USING THE EWB MULTISIM NETWORK ANALYZER

OBJECTIVES

1. To become acquainted with the use of the Electronics Workbench Network Analyzer
2. To understand impedance measurements.
3. To explore the impedance characteristics of transmission lines and impedance matching for antennas.

VIRTUAL TEST EQUIPMENT:

AC voltage source

Multimeter

Virtual resistors, capacitors, inductors

Virtual network analyzer

INTRODUCTION:

The concept of using a Smith chart has been introduced in Chapter 12 of the your text. This important impedance calculating tool is now reintroduced using Electronics Workbench Multisim simulations. Multisim provides a network analyzer instrument that contains the Smith chart analysis as one of its many features. A network analyzer is used to measure the parameters commonly used to characterize circuits or elements that operate at high frequencies. This exercise will focus on the Smith chart and the z-parameter calculations. Z-parameters are the impedance values of a network expressed in its real and imaginary components. Refer back to Section 12-8 of your text for additional Smith chart examples and a more detailed examination of its function.

PRELABORATORY:

1. Review Section 12-8, the Smith Chart in your text.
2. Review the lab manual section—Troubleshooting with Electronics Workbench Multisim, Ch.12-Network Analyzer and Ch. 15-Testing Lossy and Low-Loss Waveguide.

PROCEDURE:

You will be required to make impedance measurements on various resistive, RC, and RL circuits and transmission lines using the EWB network analyzer.

Part I: Using the Network Analyzer

1. Begin the exercise by constructing the circuit shown in Fig. 23-1. This circuit contains a 50-Ω resistor connected to port 1 (*P1*) of the network analyzer; port 2 (*P2*) is terminated with a 50-Ω resistor. The first circuit being examined by the network analyzer is a simple resistive circuit. This example provides a good starting point for understanding the setup for the network analyzer and how to read the simulation results.

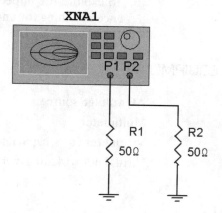

FIGURE 23-1

2. Start the simulation. The impedance calculations performed by the network analyzer are very quick and the start simulation button will quickly reset. Before you look at the test results, predict what you will to see. Based on the information you learned in Section 12-8, and the fact that you are testing a resistor, you would expect to see a purely resistive result. Double-click on the network analyzer to open the instrument. You should see a Smith chart similar to the result shown in Fig. 23-2.

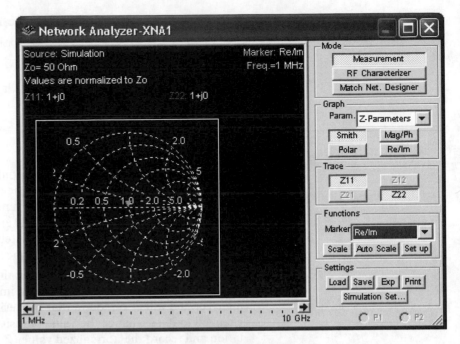

FIGURE 23-2

The Smith chart indicates the following:

$Z_o = 50\ \Omega$

Values are normalized to Z_o

$Z_{11} = 1 + j0$

The $Z_{11} = 1 + j0$ value indicates that the input impedance for the network being analyzed is purely resistive and its normalized value is 1, which translates to 50 Ω. Recall that the values on a Smith chart are divided by the normalized resistance. Notice the marker on the Smith chart is located at 1.0 on the real axis. The 1.0 translates to 50 Ω, and this value is obtained by multiplying the Smith chart measured resistance of 1 Ω by the characteristic impedance of 50 Ω to obtain the actual resistance measured. In this case the computed resistance is 50 Ω.

The frequency at which this calculation was made is shown in the upper-right corner of the Smith chart screen. In this case a frequency of 1.0 Mhz was used. The frequency range for the simulation is shown at the bottom of Figure 23-2 and is adjusted by clicking on the left and right arrows. You can adjust the frequency to see how the impedance values change through the frequency range. Of course an ideal resistor will not be frequency-dependent. The frequency range, used in the network analysis, is set by clicking on the Simulaton Set button at the bottom of the network analyzer screen. You will notice the following:

Start Frequency	1 MHz
Stop Frequency	10 GHz
Sweep Type	Decade
Number of points per decade	25
Characteristic impedance Z_o	50 Ω

The start and stop frequency provides control of the frequency range when testing a network. The sweep type can be specified to be plotted in either a decade or linear form, but most of the time use the decade form. The number of points per decade enables the user to control the resolution of the plotted trace displayed, and the characteristic impedance Z_o provides for user control of the normalizing impedance.

3. Change the characteristic impedance of the network analyzer to 75 Ω. This will require changing the characteristic impedance setting for the network analyzer and will also require that the resistor connected to port 2 (P2) be changed to 75 Ω. Change the value of resistor R1 to 75 Ω. Restart the simulation and record the normalized value (Z_{11}); convert the normalized value to actual resistance. Repeat this for the resistor R1 values provided in Table 23-1. Record the measured normalized network impedance and calculate the actual resistance.

TABLE 23-1

$R1$ (Ω)	NETWORK IMPEDANCE Z_{11}	RESISTANCE
75		
50		
100		
600		
300		

Part II: Measuring Complex Impedances With the Network Analyzer

The next two Multisim exercises provide examples of using the Multisim network analyzer to compute the impedances of RC and RL networks. These exercises will help you better understand the Smith chart results when analyzing complex impedances.

1. Construct the circuit shown in Fig. 23-3. This is a simple RC network of R = 25 Ω and C = 6.4 nF. The network analyzer is set to analyze the frequencies from 1 MHz to 100 MHz. The results of the simulation are shown in Fig. 23-4. At 1 MHz, the normalized input impedance to the RC network shows that Z_{11} = .5 − j.497. Multiplying these values by the normalized impedance of 50 Ω yields approximately a Z of 25 − j25, which is the expected value for this RC network at 1 MHz. Verify this by calculating the capacitive reactance (X_c) of the 6.4 nF capacitor at 1 MHz. Record your result.

X_c = _____

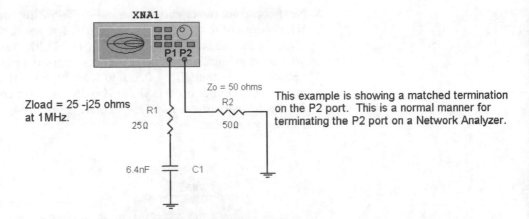

FIGURE 23-3

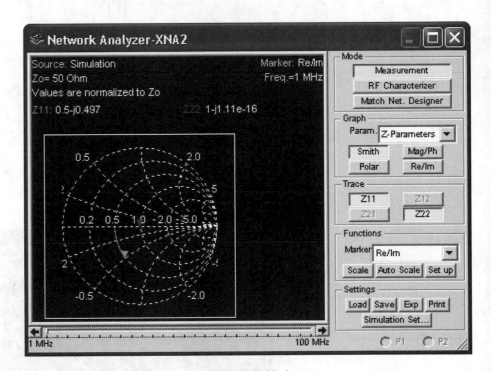

FIGURE 23-4

2. Repeat step 1 to measure the impedance of the RC networks specified in Table 23-2 for the frequencies listed.

TABLE 23-2

R_1 (Ω)	C_1	**FREQUENCY**	**NETWORK IMPEDANCE, Z_{11}**
25	6.4 nF	100 kHz	
25	6.4 nF	100 MHz	
10	10 pF	1 MHz	
10	10 pF	100 MHz	
50	50 nF	100 kHz	

3. Next construct the circuit shown in Fig. 23-5. This circuit contains a simple RL network of $R = 25\ \Omega$ and $L = 4.0\ \mu\text{H}$. The network analyzer is set to analyze the frequencies from 1 MHz to 10 GHz. The results of the simulation are shown in Fig. 23-6. At 1 MHz, the normalized input impedance to the RL network shows that $Z_{11} = 0.5 + \text{j}0.5$. Multiplying these values by the normalized impedance of 50 Ω yields $Z = 25 - \text{j}25$, which is the expected value for this RL network at 1 MHz. Calculate X_L of the 4-μH inductor at 1 MHz. Record your value.

$$X_L = \underline{\hspace{2cm}}$$

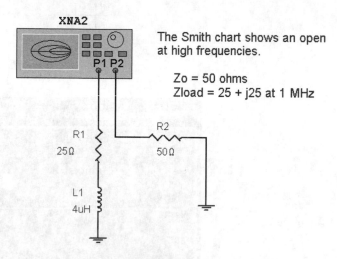

FIGURE 23-5

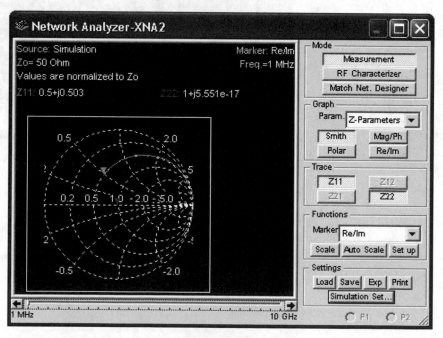

FIGURE 23-6

4. Measure the impedance of the RL networks specified in Table 23-3 for the frequencies listed.

TABLE 23-3

R_1 (Ω)	L_1	FREQUENCY	NETWORK IMPEDANCE, Z_{11}
25	4 μH	10 kHz	
25	4 μH	100 kHz	
25	4 μH	10 MHz	
25	4 μH	100 MHz	
25	4 μH	1 GHz	

5. What observation can you make about the RL network of step 4 at low and high frequencies? (*Hint:* Express your observation in terms of the changes in the inductance value).

low frequencies:

high frequencies:

Part III: Transmission and Waveguide Impedance Measurements

1. Part III provides the student with the opportunity to explore the properties of a low-loss waveguide. Begin by opening the **Lab23-Fig 23-7** file on your CD-ROM. This circuit contains a sample waveguide attached to the network analyzer. The circuit is shown in Fig. 23-7. Both ends of the waveguide are connected to the ports of the network analyzer.

L-band 1 - 2G
56 ohms

The Z parameters
are along the unit circle
which indicates R = 0
or nearly zero in this case.

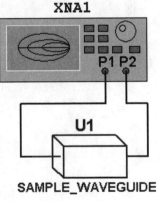

FIGURE 23-7

Before starting the simulation change, click on the network analyzer. Set the characteristic impedance of the network analyzer to 50 Ω and change the number of points per decade to 200, the start frequency to 1 GHz, and the stop frequency to 2 GHz. This change provides a smoother plot of the simulation results and a realistic frequency range for the waveguide. Start the simulation and view the results on the network analyzer. You should see a result similar to the one shown in Fig. 23-8.

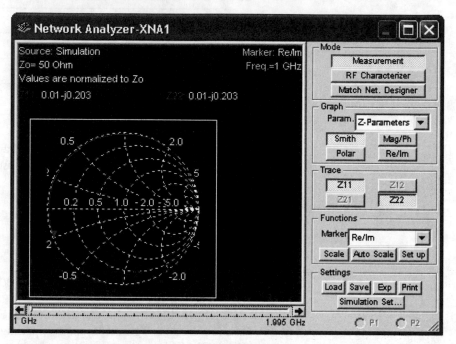

FIGURE 23-8

The plot of the data is along the outside perimeter of the Smith chart. This indicates that the line is low loss. Move the frequency marker on the network analyzer to 1 GHz. The input impedance of the waveguide at 1 GHz is $Z_{11} = 0.01 - j0.203$ or very little resistive loss.

2. Begin step 2 by opening the **Lab23-Part3_6** file on your CD-ROM. This circuit contains several waveguides and a network analyzer. Connect each waveguide to the network analyzer and record the normalized resistance of the waveguide. This is the point where the resistance and reactance terms for Z_{11} are minimum. Also record the frequency at which the measurement was made. For example, the minimum resistance and reactance, Z_{11}, for waveguide A is $0.01 - j0.008$ at 1.122 GHz. Complete this information for the

waveguides listed in Table 23-3 and provided in the file **Lab23-Part3_6.** Limit the frequency sweep of the waveguide to 500 MHz to 2 GHz.

WAVEGUIDE SECTION	NETWORK IMPEDANCE, Z_{11}	FREQUENCY
A		
B		
C		
E		
F		
G		

3. Based on the measurements made in step 2, which waveguide has the greatest loss? Record your answer.

   _____

4. Based on your measurements made in step 2, what frequency are the waveguide sections A-E designed to carry? Record your answer.

   _____

5. Based on your measurements, what frequency is waveguide G designed to carry? Record your answer. (*Hint:* This is the frequency of the waveguide when the resistance and reactance are at a minimum.)

   _____

6. Connect the network analyzer to waveguide H and sweep it from 1 GHz to 2 GHz. Explain what the Smith Chart is showing when the frequency is set to 1.12 GHz.

Part IV: EWB Exercises on CD-ROM

The Multisim files for this experiment are provided on your EWB CD-ROM so you can gain additional experience simulating electronic circuits with EWB and gain more insight into the characteristics of impedance measurements using the network analyzer.

FILE NAME
Lab23-Fig23-1
Lab23-Fig23-3
Lab23-Fig23-5
Lab23-Fig23-7
Lab23-Part1_Step3_75_ohms
Lab23-Part3_6

TONE DECODER

OBJECTIVES:

1. To investigate frequency sensing and detection.
2. To investigate the bandwidth and sensitivity of a tone decoder.
3. To build and test a tone decoder circuit.

REFERENCE:

An application of tone sensing can be found in section 11-2 of the text.

TEST EQUIPMENT:

Dual-trace oscilloscope

Sinusoidal function generator

Low-voltage power supply

Prototype board

COMPONENTS:

Integrated circuit: 567

Capacitors: 10 μF, 4.7 μF, 1 μF, 0.22 μF, 0.01 μF

Resistors: 1 kΩ

Potentiometers: (10-turn trim) 25 kΩ

PRELABORATORY:

Calculate the f_o, and bandwidth for the circuit shown in Fig. 24-1. Use the equations shown in the data sheet for the LM567 Tone Decoder included in the Appendix (assume the potentiometer is 10 kΩ).

$f_o =$ _____

BW = _____

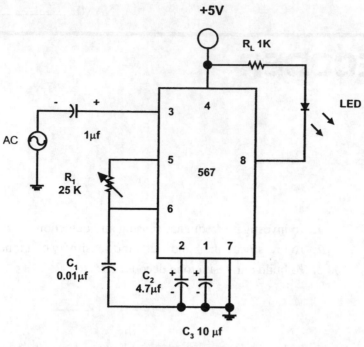

FIGURE 24-1

PROCEDURE:

1. Build the tone decoder circuit shown in Fig. 24-1.

2. Apply the DC power to the circuit, but do not apply a signal from the function generator yet.

3. Connect channel 1 of your oscilloscope to pin 5 of the LM567 and adjust R_1 until the free-running frequency of the decoder is the same as your calculated f_o.

4. Set the function generator frequency to equal the calculated f_o and set the output voltage level to 1.0-V rms. Connect the function generator to the input of the circuit.

5. Reduce the function generator voltage level to the minimum voltage that will still have the LED lit.

6. Slowly increase the frequency of the generator until the LED turns off. This is the upper-lock frequency.

   Record the frequency: _____

7. Slowly decrease the frequency of the generator until the LED turns back on. Continue to decrease the frequency until the LED turns off. This is the lower-lock frequency.

   Record the frequency: _____

8. Subtract the lower-lock frequency from the upper-lock frequency to get the bandwidth, and divide the bandwidth by f_o to get the Bandwidth %.

$$Bandwith \ \% \ = \ \frac{bandwith}{f_0} * 100$$

Bandwidth % = _____

9. Increase the voltage level of the function generator, and repeat steps 6 through 8.

Bandwidth % = _____

10. Demonstrate to your instructor that the tone decoder will detect the presence of a signal by lighting an LED when the function generator frequency is adjusted to within the bandwidth of the tone detector and there is sufficient voltage level.

REPORT/QUESTIONS:

1. What is the Bandwidth % of the tone decoder at the minimum input voltage level?
2. What happened to the bandwidth when the input voltage was increased?

PART II

ELECTRONICS WORKBENCH (EWB) MULTISIM EXPERIMENTS

SIMULATION OF ACTIVE FILTER NETWORKS

OBJECTIVES:

1. To become acquainted with the use of Electronics Workbench Multisim for simulating Active Filter Networks.
2. To understand frequency response measurements using the EWB Bode plotter.
3. To measure the frequency response and phase of an active filter and compare the simulation results with the experimental results.

VIRTUAL TEST EQUIPMENT:

Dual-trace oscilloscope
AC voltage source
Bode plotter
Power supplies
Virtual resistors, capacitors
Simulation model of the 741 operational amplifier

THEORY:

The computer simulation of electronics circuits provides a way to verify the functionality and performance characteristics of your circuit prior to its fabrication and assembly. Many simulation models of both active (e.g., op-amps and transistors) and passive (resistors, capacitors, and inductors) devices are available and provide accurate simulation results. For example, in this experiment the 741 operational amplifier is specified for the operational amplifier. EWB Multisim includes a model of the 741 available for use in the simulation. Using this model, instead of an ideal operational amplifier, enables you to obtain computer simulation results that more closely resemble your experimental results.

PRELABORATORY:

1. Review your experimental results from Experiment 1–Active Filter Networks.

PROCEDURE:

In this exercise you will be required to build an active filter circuit using Electronics Workbench Multisim. You will be asked to make both frequency and phase measurements on the circuit, and to compare your simulation results with those obtained in the experimental portion of Experiment 1.

Note: Do not forget to apply basic troubleshooting techniques when performing a computer simulation. Visual checks and power supply voltage verification are still a must.

Part I: Plotting the Output Magnitude for the Butterworth Second Order Low-Pass Active Filter

1. The EWB Multisim implementation of a Butterworth Second Order Low-Pass Filter is provided in Fig. E1-1. Your first step is to construct this filter in EWB Multisim. After completing your design, start the simulation and use the oscilloscope to verify that the circuit is functioning properly. To do this, connect the oscilloscope to both the input and output of the filter and verify that the output sine wave is 180° out of phase with respect to the input sine wave. The output signal will also be attenuated with respect to the input (gain less than 1). The connections you need to make to the oscilloscope are shown in Fig. E1-1.

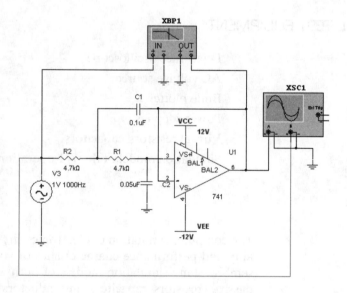

FIGURE E1-1

2. EWB Multisim provides a Bode plotter for making frequency and phase response measurements. A Bode plot graphs the output magnitude and phase as a function of the input signal frequency. Connect the Bode plotter as shown in Fig. E1-1. To use the Bode plotter, double-click on it and set the sweep frequency to an initial value (**I**) of 500 mHz and a final value (**F**) of 20 kHz. Both the Vertical and Horizontal settings should be set to Log. Adjust the initial and final level settings for the vertical axis as needed to display the data results. For this exercise click on the Magnitude button. The settings for the Bode plotter and the expected simulation results are shown in Fig. E1-2.

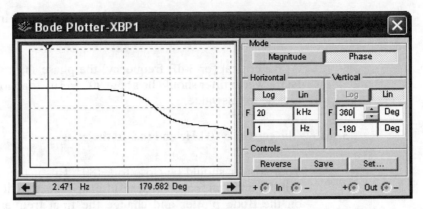

FIGURE E1-2

3. Use the slider on the Bode plotter to measure the critical frequency. This will be the point where the plot drops from 0 dB to −3 dB. Record the value.

4. Move the slider to 1 kHz and record the dB level.

5. Move the cursor to 10 kHz and record the dB level.

6. Calculate and record the dB level difference for 1 kHz and 10 kHz.

This is the amount in dB that the magnitude of the output voltage is being attenuated. Is this value correct? For assistance, refer back to Part I of Experiment 1 (the experimental lab) for a discussion on the Butterworth Second Order Filter.

Part II: Plotting the Output Phase for the Butterworth Second Order Low-Pass Active Filter

1. In this exercise you will make phase measurements on the Butterworth Second Order Low-Pass Filter provided in Fig. E1-1 using the EWB Bode plotter. Your first step is to double-click on the Bode plotter and select on the phase mode by clicking on the Phase button. Change the initial (**I**) phase setting to −180° and final (**F**) phase setting to 360°. The settings for the Bode plotter and the expected simulation results are shown in Fig. E1-3. You may need to rerun the simulation after making the changes.

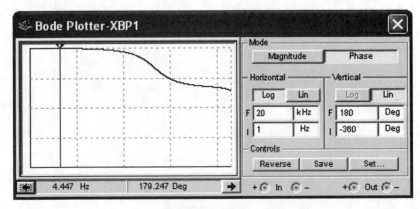

FIGURE E1-3

2. Move the slider to the critical frequency you measured in step 3 of Part I. Record the amount of phase shift, in degrees. _____

> At the critical (or 3-dB frequency) the phase shift of a second order Butterworth filter should be about 90°. Verify that your measurement is close to this value.

3. Move the cursor to 10 kHz and record the phase. _____

> Your answer should be close to −180°. This is the amount of phase shift for an ideal second order Butterworth active filter. Double-click on the Bode plotter and change the final frequency to 500 kHz. Restart the simulation and you will see that the phase shift actually exceeds 180°. This is due to the additional contributions in phase shift provided from the LM741. The simulation for the LM741 models its behavior on real operating characteristics including the non-ideal characteristics such as the increased phase shift.

Part III: Additional EWB Exercise on CD-ROM

The active filter networks for EWB Experiment 1 are provided on the CD-ROM so that you can gain additional experience simulating electronic circuits with EWB and gain more insight into the characteristics of active filter networks. The file names and their corresponding figure numbers are listed.

FILE NAME
Lab1-low_pass_filter
Lab1-high_pass_filter
Lab1-bandpass_filter
Lab1-notch_filter

USING THE SPECTRUM ANALYZER IN THE SIMULATION AND ANALYSIS OF COMPLEX WAVEFORMS

OBJECTIVES:

1. To become acquainted with the use of Electronics Workbench Multisim in analyzing complex waveforms.
2. To understand the operation of the EWB spectrum analyzer.
3. To measure and analyze the spectral content of a sinusoid, a triangle wave, and a square wave.

VIRTUAL TEST EQUIPMENT:

Dual-trace oscilloscope
Function generator
Spectrum analyzer
Virtual resistor

THEORY:

The method of analyzing complex repetitive waveforms is known as Fourier analysis. It permits any complex wave to be represented by a series of sine or cosine waves. The application of Fourier analysis, when using digital sampling oscilloscopes and spectrum analyzers, is provided through the use of the fast Fourier transform (FFT). Examples of using the FFT are presented through the use of the EWB Multisim virtual spectrum analyzer. Refer back to the theory section in Experiment 2, which mathematically defines the relationships for the sine wave, the square wave, and the triangle wave.

PRELABORATORY:

1. Review Section 1-6, Information and Bandwidth in your text.
2. Review your experimental procedures and results from Experiment 2– Frequency Spectra of Popular Waveforms.

PROCEDURE:

You will be asked to use the EWB Multisim virtual spectrum analyzer to examine simple and complex waveforms. You will gain a better understanding of the use of the spectrum analyzer, including the setup and configuration of the instrument.

Note: Make sure you have Section 1-6 from your text available for reference when working on this laboratory.

Part I: Using the EWB Spectrum Analyzer and the Spectral Analysis of a Sine Wave

1. The first step is to assemble the test setup shown in Fig. E2-1. The setup includes an oscilloscope and a spectrum analyzer, each connected to the output of a function generator. The function generator will be used to generate the waveforms being analyzed.

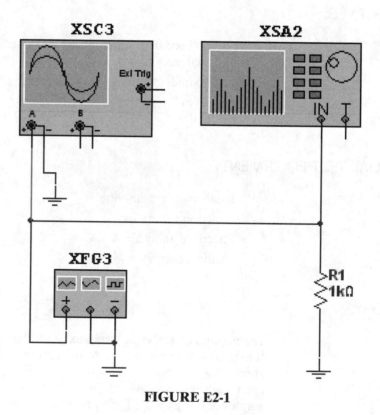

FIGURE E2-1

2. Double-click on the function generator. You should see the panel display of the function generator as shown in Fig. E2-2.

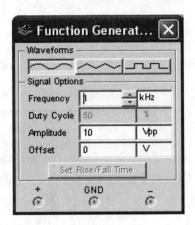

FIGURE E2-2

3. Notice that you have the choice of outputting either a sine wave, a triangle wave, or a square wave. Click on the sine wave. Set the amplitude to 10 Vpp and the offset to 0 V and set the frequency to 1 kHz.

4. Start the simulation. Double-click on the oscilloscope and verify that you are outputting a 1-kHz sine wave. Next, double-click on the spectrum analyzer. You should see a display similar to the one shown in Fig. E2-3. Change the settings to match those shown in the figure using the guidelines outlined in the following steps.

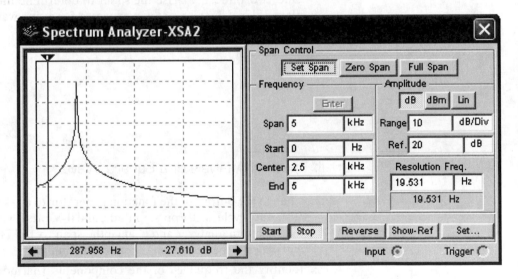

FIGURE E2-3

5. Click on the Set Span button. This provides the user with the ability to set the Span and Frequency controls. Set the Span to 5 kHz, the Start frequency to 0 kHz, the End to 5 kHz, then click on Enter. The center frequency is automatically calculated. The span setting controls the frequency range displayed by the spectrum analyzer.

6. Set the amplitude to dB and the range to 10 dB/Div.

7. Set the Resolution Frequency to 19.531 Hz. This setting defines how many data points are to be used by the spectrum analyzer to display the frequency spectra. The smaller the resolution frequency, the better and more accurate the display. The smallest resolution frequency for the EWB spectrum analyzer is determined by the equation $f\_end/1024$ ($2^{10} = 1024$) where f_end is the end frequency of the span. In this example, the end frequency equals 5 kHz, therefore the minimum frequency resolution is 4.8828 Hz. (*Important:* The resolution frequency specified must be a multiple of the minimum resolution frequency such as two times, four times, six times, etc. The 19.531-Hz resolution frequency specified is four times 4.8828 Hz.)

8. Calculate the minimum resolution frequency for the following, given an end frequency of:

END FREQUENCY	MINIMUM RESOLUTION FREQUENCY
100 kHz	
455 kHz	
108 MHz	
433 MHz	

9. How many frequency components are displayed by the spectrum analyzer? One, two, three, . . . ? Use the slider to determine the frequency of the displayed signal. Is this what you expected for a sine wave? Record and justify your answer.

_____

Part II: Spectral Analysis of a Square Wave

1. Change the output of the function generator to a 1-kHz square wave with a 50% duty cycle, a 10Vpp amplitude, and 0-V offset voltage. Double-click on the spectrum analyzer and change the span to 15 kHz. Start the simulation and observe the results on the spectrum analyzer.

2. Identify the frequency of the components (harmonics) being displayed, their dB levels, and harmonic number. Do this by placing the slider directly over each harmonic. You should be seeing the 1st through 13th harmonics. The 1st harmonic is 1 kHz, the 3rd harmonic is 3 kHz, and so on.

frequency   ____ ____ ____ ____ ____ ____ ____

harmonic   ____ ____ ____ ____ ____ ____ ____

dB value   ____ ____ ____ ____ ____ ____ ____

3. Which harmonic frequency has the greatest amplitude (dB value)?

                                                 _____

4. How many dB down is the 7th harmonic relative to the 1st harmonic?

                                                 _____

5. How many dB down is the 3rd harmonic relative to the 1st harmonic?

                                                 _____

Part III: Spectral Analysis of a Triangle Wave

1. Change the output of the function generator to a 1-kHz triangle wave with a 50% duty cycle, a 10-V amplitude, and 0-V offset voltage. Double-click on the spectrum analyzer and change the span to 15 kHz. Start the simulation and observe the results on the spectrum analyzer.

2. Identify the frequency of the components (harmonics) being displayed, their dB levels, and harmonic number. Do this by placing the slider directly over each harmonic. You should be seeing the 1st through 13th harmonics. The 1st harmonic is 1 kHz, the 3rd harmonic is 3 kHz, and so on.

frequency	____	____	____	____	____	____	____
harmonic	____	____	____	____	____	____	____
dB value	____	____	____	____	____	____	____

3. Which harmonic frequency has the greatest amplitude (dB value)?

                                                 _____

4. How many dB down is the 11th harmonic relative to the 1st harmonic?

                                                 _____

5. How many dB down is the 5th harmonic relative to the 1st harmonic?

                                                 _____

Part IV: Additional EWB Exercise on CD-ROM

This EWB laboratory has demonstrated that complex waveforms, such as a square wave or a triangle wave, generate multifrequency components called harmonics. It demonstrated how the spectrum analyzer can be used to observe and analyze the spectral content of a square wave. The simulation files for this exercise are provided on the CD-ROM.

FILE NAME
Lab2-sine_wave
Lab2-square_wave
Lab2-triangle_wave

SIMULATION OF CLASS C AMPLIFIERS AND FREQUENCY MULTIPLIERS

OBJECTIVES:

1. To become acquainted with the use of Electronics Workbench Multisim in simulating class C amplifiers and frequency multiplier circuits.

2. To understand resonant circuits.

3. To analyze the class C amplifier and the frequency multiplier circuit.

VIRTUAL TEST EQUIPMENT:

Dual-trace oscilloscope   AC voltage source

Bode plotter   Virtual 2N2222A transistor

Virtual resistor   Virtual capacitor

Virtual inductor

PRELABORATORY:

1. Review Section 1-6, Information and Bandwidth in your text.

PROCEDURE:

You will simulate a class C amplifier using EWB Multisim. You will use the EWB instruments to measure the operating characteristics of the amplifier.

1. Construct the class C amplifier provided in Fig. E3-1. This is the same circuit provided in Experiment 3, Fig. 3-4. Connect the EWB instruments to the amplifier as shown in Fig. E3-1.

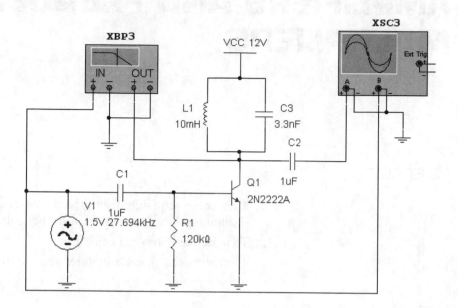

FIGURE E3-1

2. Calculate the resonant frequency of the tank circuit made up of $L1$ and $C3$. Use the equation $f_r = \dfrac{1}{2\pi\sqrt{LC}}$. Record your answer.

_____

3. Use the cursor on the Bode plotter to determine the resonant frequency of the class C amplifier. The resonant frequency, f_r, is the point on the plot where the amplitude is maximum. Record your answer and compare the test results obtained with the Bode plotter to the answer calculated in question 2. Your Bode plot should be similar to Fig. E3-2.

_____

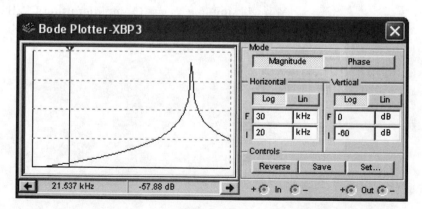

FIGURE E3-2

4. Use the Bode plotter to determine the bandwidth of the tank circuit. To determine the bandwidth, move the cursor so that it is sitting directly over the peak magnitude. Record the resonant frequency and amplitude value in dB in the table provided. Next, move the marker to the left of the peak until the magnitude drops 3 dB of the peak value. Record the −3-dB frequency which will be indicated as $f(-)$. Repeat this procedure to determine the −3-dB frequency to the right of the peak magnitude and record your measurement. This point will be indicated as $f(+)$. Use the −3-dB measured frequencies to determine the bandwidth BW using the equation, $BW = f(+) - f(-)$.

f_r	$f(+)$	$f(-)$	BW

5. Use the measured values obtained from the Bode plotter to determine the Q of the amplifier. Record your answer.

$$Q = f_r/BW$$ _____

Part II: Frequency Multiplication

You will experiment with the use of the tank circuit to provide frequency multiplication. The tank circuit, or parallel resonant LC circuit, can be pulsed by a fast switch such as a transistor to turn the tank on and off.

1. Construct the circuit shown in Fig. E3-3. Double-click on the square-wave generator and change the frequency to 503.5 Hz. Set the duty cycle to 5 and the voltage to 5 V as shown in Fig. E3-4.

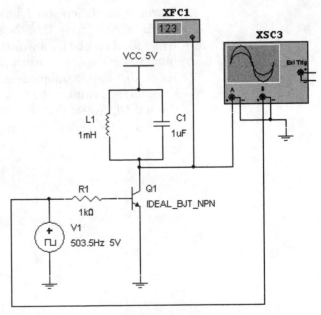

FIGURE E3-3

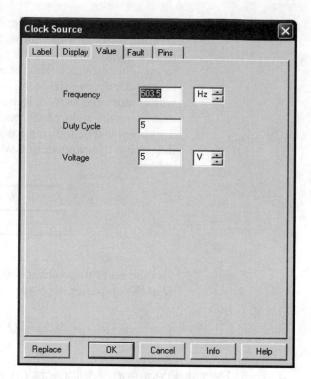

FIGURE E3-4

2. The inductor $L1$ and the capacitor $C1$ used in the tank circuit have ideal characteristics. The use of these components will not provide an accurate simulation of a tank circuit in a real environment. Therefore, to provide a more accurate model, double-click on $L1$, click on the **Fault** tab, select **Leakage,** click on **1 2,** and set the leakage resistance to 500 Ω. Next, double-click on $C1$, click on the **Fault** tab, select **Leakage,** click on **1 2,** and set the leakage resistance to 750 kΩ.

3. Start the simulation and double-click on the oscilloscope. You should see a display similar to Fig. E3-5. Notice that the tank circuit pulsing is controlled by an ideal npn BJT transistor, which has been configured as a switch. The input to the transistor switch is a short duration pulse. This causes the transistor to saturate, momentarily connecting the collector to the emitter (ground) and causing the tank circuit to oscillate at a frequency defined by $L1$ and $C1$. Notice that the oscillation decays over time. This is due to the leakage of the inductor and capacitor.

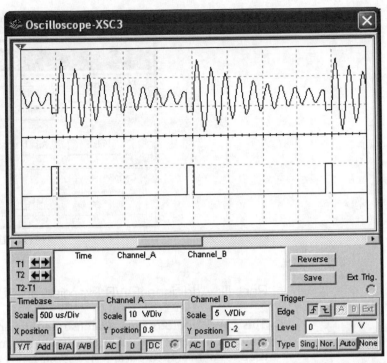

FIGURE E3-5

4. Use the values of $L1$ and $C1$ to calculate the resonant frequency of the tank.

$$f_r = \frac{1}{2\pi 1 \overline{LC}}$$

_____

5. Use the cursors on the oscilloscope to measure the frequency of oscillation. This can be done by setting one cursor at the beginning of the cycle for a sine wave and setting the other cursor at the end of the cycle. The difference, in time (T), is displayed as $T2 - T1$ on the oscilloscope. Use the equation $f = \frac{1}{T}$ to calculate the frequency. Record your answer and compare the measured frequency to the calculated frequency. They should be close in value.

_____

6. Change the frequency of the square-wave pulse to 2.516 kHz, which is one-half the resonant frequency of the tank circuit. Set the duty cycle to 25 and the voltage to 3.0 V. You should observe that the output frequency is twice the input frequency. The tank circuit is being used to double the frequency.

_____

7. Set the frequency of the square-wave to 2.516 kHz. Attach a frequency counter to the output of the frequency multiplier. Double click on the frequency counter icon and change the sensitivity to 1V, the trigger level to 1V. Select "Freq" and AC coupling as shown in Fig. E3-6. Compare your measured value to the calculated value obtained in Step 4. Use the frequency counter to determine the period of the output signal.

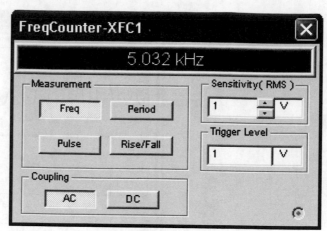

FIGURE E3-6

Part III: Additional EWB Exercise on CD-ROM

This EWB laboratory has demonstrated the analysis and simulation of a class C amplifier and the development of a frequency multiplier. The EWB instruments were used to confirm theoretical results. Your EWB CD-ROM contains the simulation files for this exercise and the full implementation of the frequency doubler.

FILE NAME
Lab3-classC_amplifier
Lab3-tank_circuit
Lab3-frequency_doubler

SIMULATION OF A PHASE-SHIFT OSCILLATOR

OBJECTIVES:

1. To become acquainted with the use of Electronics Workbench Multisim in simulating and analyzing oscillator circuits.

2. To understand the phase-shift oscillator circuit.

3. To analyze the phase-shift oscillator and to better understand the feedback signal path in an oscillator circuit.

VIRTUAL TEST EQUIPMENT:

Dual-trace oscilloscope   AC voltage source

Virtual 741 op-amp   Virtual resistor

Virtual capacitor   DC voltage source

PRELABORATORY:

1. Review Section 1-8, Oscillator Circuits in your text.

PROCEDURE:

You will construct and simulate a phase-shift oscillator circuit using EWB Multisim. To gain a better understanding of the operation of the circuit, you will use the EWB instruments to verify the operation and make measurements.

Part I: Analyzing and Testing the Components of the Phase-Shift Oscillator

Construct the phase-shift oscillator circuit provided in Fig. E5-1. This is the same circuit provided in Experiment 5, Fig. 5-1. Connect the EWB instruments to the amplifier as shown in Fig. E5-1. Notice that the circuit contains a virtual switch so that the feedback path can be opened. You can flip or rotate the components by selecting **Edit** from the Multisim menu and clicking on the desired change. Notice that the 741 op amps have been vertically shifted from their default orientation.

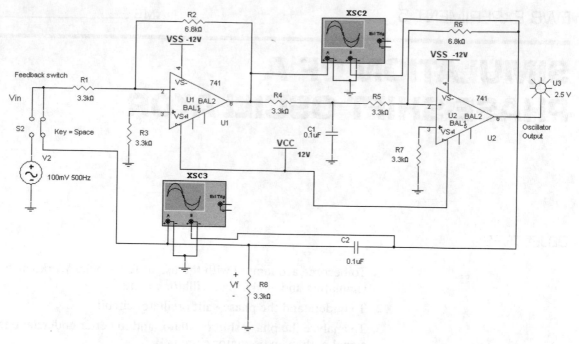

FIGURE E5-1

1. Use the EWB Multisim virtual multimeter to verify that the voltages to the operational amplifiers are set to ±12 V dc. Double-click on the AC voltage source and set the voltage amplitude to 100 mV at a frequency of 500 Hz.

2. Set the double-pole single-throw (DPST) feedback switch so the feedback path from the oscillator is opened and the 500 Hz AC voltage source is connected to the input of operational amplifier $U1$ through resistor $R1$. The position of the virtual switch can be toggled by pressing the space bar on your keyboard. The circuit window in Multisim must be the active window for the space bar to change the switch. The two switch positions provide a way to test the operational amplifiers in an open-loop configuration. The switch can then be repositioned to close the feedback loop so that the oscillator can be tested.

3. Start the simulation and verify that $U1$ and $U2$ are working properly. Use the oscilloscope to measure and record the peak-to-peak voltage level of the signals at the output of $U1$ pin 6 ($U1$-6) and $U2$ pin 6 ($U2$-6).

$U1$-6 _____ $U2$-6 _____

4. Next, use the oscilloscope to measure the phase difference of the input voltage V_{in} to the feedback voltage V_f. Refer back to Fig. E5-1 for the location of V_{in} and V_f in the circuit. Connect V_{in} to channel A and V_f to channel B on the oscilloscope. Set the feedback switch so that the feedback loop is open and the AC voltage source is connected to the circuit. You will need to connect a 3.3-kΩ resistor ($R9$) in parallel with $R8$. The resistor $R9$ is being used to simulate the resistive load that the input operational amplifier places on the network if the oscillator is operating in the closed-loop mode.

Use the cursors on the oscilloscope to measure the time difference from the peak of the V_{in} input signal to the peak of the V_f feedback signal at each frequency. Use cursor $T1$ for V_{in} and cursor $T2$ for V_f. An example of the cursor placement for this measurement is provided in Fig. E5-2.

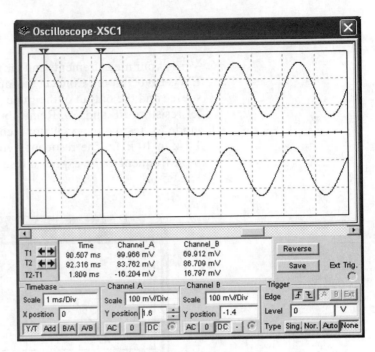

FIGURE E5-2

Use the following equation to calculate the amount of phase shift. Record the time and phase difference for V_{in} to V_f for the input frequencies of 500 Hz, 1000 Hz, 1500 Hz, and 2000 Hz in Table E5-1.

$$Phase\ shift = [(T2 - T1)\ /\ period] \times 360°$$

A difference of 1.8 ms is shown in Fig. E5-2, which equates to a phase shift of

$$[1.8\ ms\ /\ 2\ ms] \times 360° = 324°$$

TABLE E5-1   Test Results on the Phase Shift Circuit

FREQUENCY (Hz)	$T1(V_{in})$	$T2(V_f)$	$T2 - T1$	PHASE SHIFT
500				
1000				
1500				
2000				

5. Review the phase shift test results in Table E5-1 and explain what happens to the phase shift at 500, 1000, 1500, and 2000 Hz. At what frequency is the Barkhausen criteria for oscillation met in regards to the phase shift.

6. Verify your measurements and the results obtained in steps 4 and 5 with the EWB Bode plotter. Connect the input of the Bode plotter to the AC voltage source and the output of the Bode plotter to the node connecting the parallel resistors $R8$ and $R9$. Remember, $R9$ must be added in the open loop mode for testing the oscillator feedback. Sweep the open loop circuit from 1 Hz to 10 kHz. The resonant frequency of the circuit is indicated by the peak frequency. The expected result from the bode plot test is provided in Fig. E5-3.

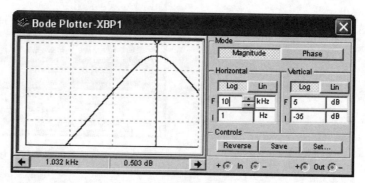

FIGURE E5-3

Record the frequency of the peak value in step 6.   _____

Record the phase of the peak frequency.   _____

Is the phase result consistent with the Barkhausen criteria? Why?

Part II: EWB Simulation of the Phase-Shift Oscillator

1. Change the feedback switch so that the loop for the oscillator is closed. $R8$ should now connect to the 3.3-kΩ resistor on the input of $U1$. This closes the feedback loop. Restart the simulation and observe the output of the oscillator. It may take up to .04 s of simulation time for the oscillation to start. Determine the oscillating frequency. Is this the frequency you expected; why?

2. Connect a 3.3-kΩ resistor in parallel with $R8$. The addition of this resistor alters the feedback signal, which in turn prevents the circuit from maintaining oscillation. Double-click on the oscilloscope and restart the simulation. Press the space bar twice to toggle the feedback switch. This will momentarily start the oscillator. View the output of the oscillator to see the effect changing the feedback path has on the circuit. You should be seeing a damped sine wave similar to Fig. E5-4. Why does the circuit no longer maintain oscillation?

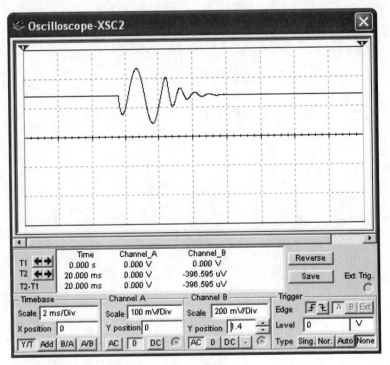

FIGURE E5-4

Part III: EWB Exercises on CD-ROM

This EWB laboratory has demonstrated the operation of the phase shift oscillator. The EWB CD-ROM contains the simulation files for this exercise.

FILE NAME
Lab5-phase_shift_oscillator
Lab5-phase_shift_test
Lab5-damped_osc
Lab5-phase_shift_Bode

NAME _____

SIMULATION OF AN *LC* FEEDBACK OSCILLATOR

OBJECTIVES:

1. To become acquainted with the use of Electronics Workbench Multisim in simulating and analyzing oscillator circuits.

2. To understand the LC feedback oscillator circuit.

3. To analyze the LC feedback oscillator and develop a better understanding of the requirements for testing the feedback signal path in an oscillator circuit.

VIRTUAL TEST EQUIPMENT:

Dual-trace oscilloscope   AC voltage source

Virtual 741 op-amp   Virtual resistor

Virtual capacitor   DC voltage source

Virtual inductor   Bode plotter

Virtual switch

PRELABORATORY:

1. Review Section 1-8, Oscillator Circuits in your text.

PROCEDURE:

You will construct and simulate an LC oscillator circuit using EWB Multisim. You will use the EWB instruments to verify the operation of the oscillator, and you will conduct tests and make measurements to gain a better understanding of the operation of the circuit.

Part I: Analyzing and Testing the Components of the LC Oscillator

Construct the LC oscillator circuit provided in Fig. E6-1. This circuit is similar to the circuit provided in Experiment 6, Fig. 6-1. Connect the EWB instruments to the amplifier as shown in Fig. E6-1. The instruments include the Bode plotter and the oscilloscope. The circuit contains a virtual switch so that the feedback path can be opened and closed as needed for testing.

Note: In some circumstances you may need to change the orientation of a component. You can flip or rotate the components by selecting the component and then select Edit orientation from the Multisim menu and clicking on the desired change. Notice that the 741 op amps have been vertically flipped from their default orientation.

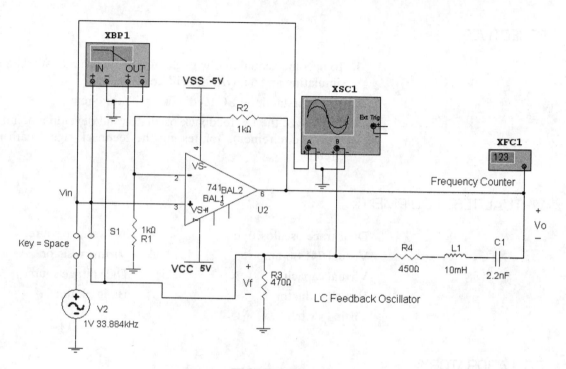

FIGURE E6-1

1. Construct the LC oscillator circuit shown in Fig. E6-1 in EWB Multisim. Connect the switch and the instruments to the circuit as shown.

2. Calculate the resonant frequency of the LC oscillator circuit shown in Fig. E6-1 using the equation below and record the value.

$$f = \frac{1}{2\pi\sqrt{L_1 C_1}}$$ _____

3. Use the EWB Multisim virtual multimeter to verify that the voltages to the operational amplifiers are set to ±5-V dc. Double-click on the AC voltage source and set the voltage amplitude to 1.0 V at the frequency calculated in step 1. You will need to start the simulation to make the voltage measurements.

4. Verify your resonant frequency calculation from step 2 with the EWB Bode plotter. Connect the input of the Bode plotter to the AC voltage source and the output to the oscillator output, V_f. Make sure to conduct the test with the feedback switch set to the AC voltage source (feedback open). Sweep the open loop circuit from 10 kHz to 100 kHz. The resonant frequency of the circuit is indicated by the peak frequency on the Bode plot. The expected result from the bode plot test is provided in Fig. E6-2.

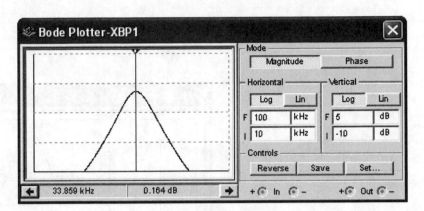

FIGURE E6-2

Record the peak frequency value measured with the Bode plotter and compare your result with the frequency calculated in step 2.

5. Next, use the oscilloscope to measure the phase difference of the input voltage to the op amp V_{in} to the feedback voltage V_f. Refer back to Fig. E6-1 for the location of V_{in} and V_f in the circuit. Connect the input voltage to channel A and V_f to channel B on the oscilloscope. Set the feedback switch so that the feedback loop is open and the AC voltage source is connected to the circuit.

Use the cursors on the oscilloscope to measure the time difference from the peak of the V_{in} input signal to the peak of the V_f feedback signal. Use cursor $T1$ for V_{in} and cursor $T2$ for V_f. An example of the cursor placement for this measurement is provided in Fig. E6-3.

Use the following equation to calculate the amount of phase shift. Record the time and phase difference for V_{in} to V_f for the input frequencies of 10 kHz, 25 kHz, 33.9 kHz, 65 kHz, and 100 kHz in Table E6-1.

$$Phase\ shift = [(T2 - T1)\ /\ period] \times 360°$$

where the period of a 10 kHz sine wave is 1/10 kHz = 100 μs.

A difference of 77.8 μS is shown in Fig. E6-3, which equates to a phase shift of

$$[77.8\ μS\ /\ 100\ μs] \times 360° = 280°$$

TABLE E6-1 Test Results on the Phase Shift Circuit

FREQUENCY (kHz)	$T1(V_{in})$	$T2(V_f)$	$T2 - T1$	PHASE SHIFT
10				
25				
33.9				
65				
100				

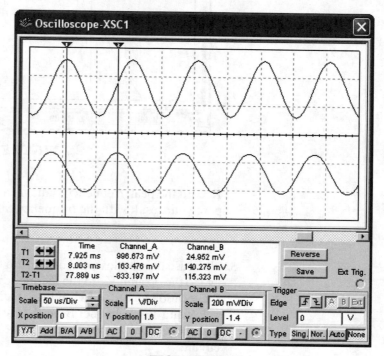

FIGURE E6-3

Part II: EWB Simulation of the LC Oscillator

1. Change the feedback switch so that the loop for the oscillator is closed. Restart the simulation and observe the output of the oscillator. It may take up to .02 s of simulation time for the oscillation to start. Determine the oscillating frequency. Is this the frequency you expected; why?

2. Change $R3$ to 300 Ω and restart the simulation. What change do you observe with the oscillator? Why do you think this happened? Note: You will need to help start the oscillation by momenarily switching the input which opens and closes the feedback path.

3. Change $R3$ to 470 Ω and restart the simulation. You will need to help start the oscillator by momentarily switching the input which opens and closes the feedback path. Change the time base on the oscilloscope to 200 μs/div to better see the output signal as shown in Figure E6-4. What change do you observe with the oscillator? Why do you think this happened?

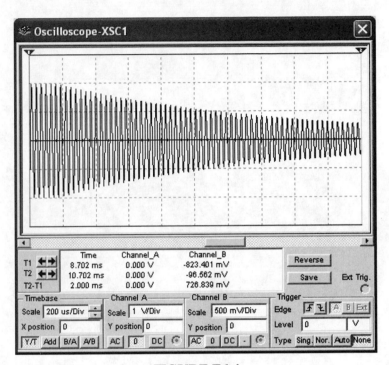

FIGURE E6-4

Part III: EWB Exercises on CD-ROM

This EWB laboratory has demonstrated the operation of the LC oscillator. The EWB CD-ROM contains the simulation files for this exercise.

FILE NAME
Lab6-LC_oscillator
Lab6-LC_R3_300
Lab6-LC_R4_480

PERCENTAGE OF MODULATION MEASUREMENT OF AN AMPLITUDE MODULATED WAVEFORM

OBJECTIVES:

1. To become acquainted with the use of Electronics Workbench Multisim in simulating and measuring amplitude modulated waveforms.
2. To understand the EWB oscilloscope.

VIRTUAL TEST EQUIPMENT:

Dual-trace oscilloscope   AC voltage source
Virtual resistor   AM source

PRELABORATORY:

1. Review the amplitude modulation material in Chapters 2 and 3 of your text.
2. Review Experiment 11.

PROCEDURE:

You will use EWB Multisim to conduct tests on the simulation of an AM signal. You will use the EWB instruments to measure modulation level and frequency.

Part I: Trapezoidal Measurements of the AM Waveform

Construct the test circuit provided in Fig. E11-1. This circuit consists of an AM source, an AC voltage source, a resistive load, and an oscilloscope. The modulation (intelligence) frequencies for the AM source and the AC voltage must be equal. The wattmeter will be used in part 4 to measure the transmit power, P_t.

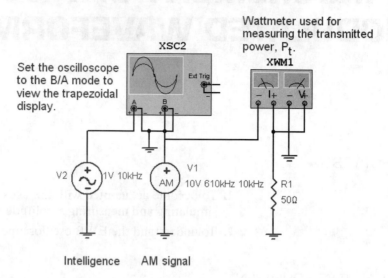

FIGURE E11-1

1. Double click on the AM source and set the carrier frequency to 610 kHz, the modulation frequency (intelligence) to 10 kHz, the modulation index to 0.5, and the carrier amplitude to 1 V. The settings are shown in Fig. E11-2. Set the modulation frequency (intelligence) of the AC voltage source to 10 kHz and the amplitude to 1 V.

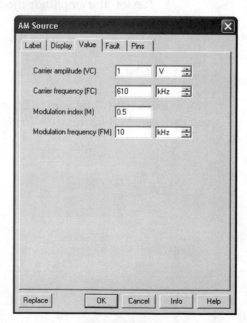

FIGURE E11-2

2. Double-click on the oscilloscope and set the display mode to B/A. This setting can be found in the lower left corner of the oscilloscope front panel. Set the scale for both channels A and B to 1 V/div. Start the simulation and observe the display on the oscilloscope. You should see a trapezoidal display similar to the one shown in Fig. E11-3. The A and B text will not be displayed on the oscilloscope.

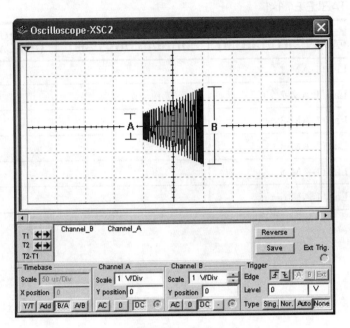

FIGURE E11-3

3. Use the techniques presented in the text to measure the percentage of modulation of the AM waveform. The maximum and minimum levels for the AM waveform are indicated as B and A in Fig. E11-3. These two values can be used to calculate the percentage of modulation (m) for the AM waveform. The equation for calculating the percentage of modulation is

$$\%m = \frac{B - A}{B + A} \times 100\%$$

For this example, $B = 3.0$V and $A = 1.0$V. Using these values to calculate the percentage of modulation gives

$$\%m = \frac{3 - 1}{3 + 1} \times 100\% = 50\%$$

4. In this step, you will open a Multisim file on your EWB CD-ROM. You are to measure the percentage of modulation of the AM source for each simulation. Record your measurements in Table E11-1. You are also to calculate and measure the output power for each multisim file. Refer back to Section 2-4 of the text for help with calculation Pt.

TABLE E11-1

FILE NAME (FROM EWB LAB CD-ROM)	PERCENTAGE OF MODULATION (%*m*)	OUTPUT POWR (PT) CALCULATED	OUTPUT POWER (PT) MEASURED
Lab11-AM-1			
Lab11-AM-2			
Lab11-AM-3			
Lab11-AM-4			
Lab11-AM-5			
Lab11-AM-6			

PART III

SYSTEM PROJECTS

DIGITAL COMMUNICATION USING FREQUENCY-SHIFT KEYING

OBJECTIVES:

1. To become familiar with modems.

2. To analyze the XR2206 function generator and observe how it can be used to encode digital information into an FSK signal.

3. To analyze the XR2211 FSK decoder and observe how it can be used to convert an FSK signal back into digital data.

REFERENCE:

Refer to section 10-2 of the text.

TEST EQUIPMENT:

Dual-trace oscilloscope

Function generator

Frequency counter

Low-voltage power supply (2)

COMPONENTS:

Integrated circuits: XR2206, XR2211

Capacitors: 0.0047 μF, 0.022 μF, 0.033 μF, 0.1 μF (5), 1 μF (2), 10 μF

Resistors: 220 Ω, 3.9 Ω, 4.7 kΩ (4), 10 kΩ (2), 18 kΩ, 100 kΩ, 220 kΩ, 470 kΩ (2)

Potentiometers: (10-turn trim) 1 kΩ (2), 10 kΩ, 50 kΩ

THEORY:

One form of modulation of digital signals onto an RF carrier uses a technique called "frequency-shift keying" (FSK). Early forms of radio-teletype used such a form of modulation. Today, this digital modulation technique is quite obsolete in its basic form although the general principles of FSK are used in more advanced data encoding techniques.

In FSK, the two digital logic states, "1" and "0," are converted to a constant-amplitude sine wave that is shifted between two possible frequencies. These two frequencies are referred to as the "mark" and "space" frequencies. These frequencies are usually in the audio-frequency spectrum. Popular mark/space frequency pairs are 1070/1270 Hz, 2025/2225 Hz, and 2125/2290 Hz. For example, the mark frequency of 2025 Hz might represent the binary "1" and the space frequency of 2225 Hz might represent the binary "0." In a radio transmitter, if an FSK signal is fed into the microphone input and single-sideband modulation is used, the RF carrier at the output of the transmitter will then be shifted between the corresponding RF mark and space frequencies. Refer to Fig. SP1-1.

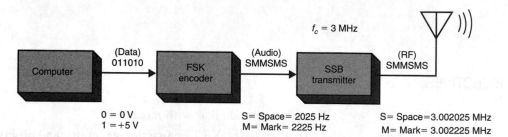

FIGURE SP1-1   FSK encoder and transmitter

Note that the resulting SSB output signal ends up being an elementary form of FM, since only a single sine wave actually modulates the RF carrier at a time. Being FM makes it quite immune to noise interference. This is the main advantage of using FSK in a digital communications system. As seen in Fig. SP1-2, the SSB receiver would detect the original audio frequencies and the FSK decoder would then convert them back to the original digital format.

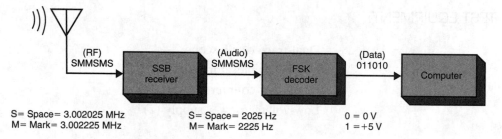

FIGURE SP1-2   Digital communication receiver and decoder

In some digital communications systems, regardless if radio or telephone wires are being used to send the FSK signals, there is a need for two-way communications to occur simultaneously. Thus the FSK encoding and decoding are needed at both ends of the communications link. If this is being done, "modems" are used (Fig. SP1-3). "Modem" is an acronym for a device that contains an FSK encoder or modulator and an FSK decoder or demodulator. In this laboratory exercise, the XR-2206 FSK modulator and the XR-2211 FSK demodulator are investigated.

PRELABORATORY:

1. Using the data sheets for the XR2206 and the given mark and space frequencies of 2025 and 2225 Hz, respectively, determine the theoretical values for R_1 and R_2 in the FSK encoder of Fig. SP1-4.

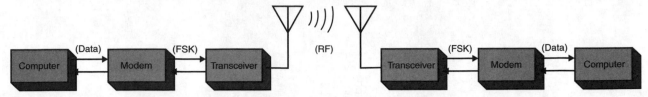

FIGURE SP1-3 Digital communications link using modems

2. Using the design notes for the XR2211 found in the Appendix and the given mark and space frequencies used above, determine the required values for R_9, C_{11}, R_8, C_9, and C_8 for the FSK decoder of Fig. SP1-5. These are listed as R_o, C_o, R_1, C_1, and C_f, respectively, on the XR2211 data sheets.

PROCEDURE:

1. Build the circuit given in Fig. SP1-4. Apply 10 V dc to the circuit. Place a jumper between TP_1 and ground. Monitor the output voltage at TP_3 with an oscilloscope. Adjust R_4 for a 1 $V_{p\text{-}p}$ amplitude.

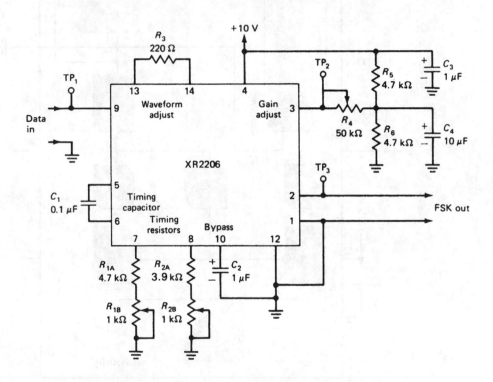

FIGURE SP1-4 XR2206 FSK modulator stage

2. Measure the frequency of the signal at TP_3 with a frequency counter. Adjust R_{2B} for a frequency of exactly 2225 Hz.
3. Open the jumper between TP_1 and ground. Adjust R_{1B} for a frequency of exactly 2025 Hz at TP_3.
4. Apply a 2-V dc voltage at TP_1. Decrease the voltage at TP_1 until you notice the frequency of V_o at TP_3 changing to the alternate value. Determine the critical voltage at TP_1 where the frequency switching occurs.

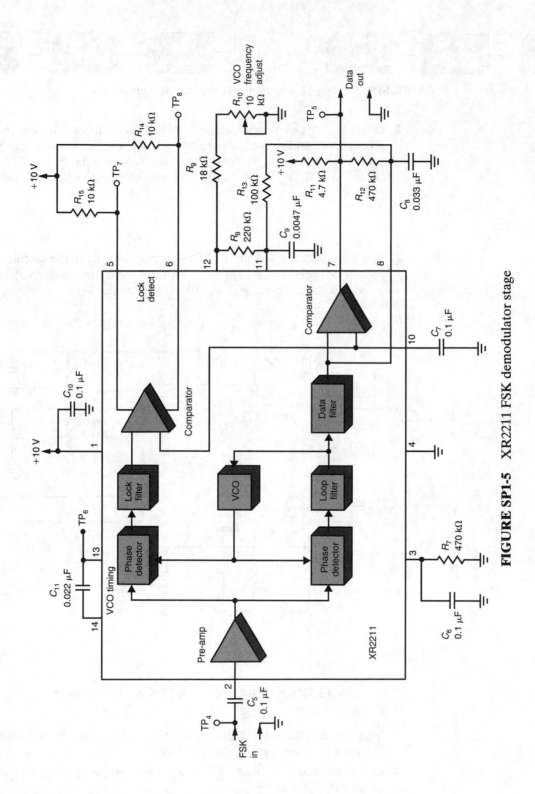

FIGURE SP1-5 XR2211 FSK demodulator stage

5. Apply a 3 V positive square-wave at TP_1. Adjust the frequency for approximately 2 Hz. Notice the output waveform switching between the mark and space frequencies at TP_3. The square-wave generator is simulating a computer sending digital data. The voltage at TP_3 is the encoded FSK signal. Do not disassemble this circuit before proceeding.

6. Build the circuit given in Fig. SP1-5. Notice that the XR2211 is actually a phase-locked-loop similar to the 565 used in Experiments 16 and 17, except that it is specifically designed for use in decoding FSK signals. This is seen in the fact that the VCO output signal is fed back through two separate loops. The standard loop that is used in all PLLs is the phase detector followed by a loop low-pass filter. In addition to this, the XR2211 has a separate phase detector that drives a lock filter. Both loop and lock filters drive separate comparators that cause output signals at pins 5, 6, and 7 to be binary in nature. The data output at pin 7 is the result of converting the FSK mark and space frequencies back into digital form. The lock-detect outputs switch into their active states each time the XR2211 senses mark and space frequencies at its input.

7. Apply 10 V dc to the circuit. Apply a 100-mV$_{p-p}$ sine wave at a frequency of 2125 Hz at TP_4. Observe the waveform at TP_6 with channel A of the oscilloscope. Observe the dc voltage at TP_7 with channel B. You should notice that when the XR2211 locks up, the waveform at TP_6 should stabilize and the dc voltage at TP_7, jumps to a digital "low state." Then when the sine wave is removed at TP_4, the waveform at TP_6 should free-run and the voltage at TP_7 should jump up to 10 V. TP_8 is just the complement logic state of TP_7.

8. Now observe the waveform at TP_5 with channel B. Note what happens when the frequency of the generator is slowly increased and decreased between 2.0 and 2.3 kHz. Measure the critical frequency at which the voltage at TP_5 changes states. It should be approximately 2.125 kHz. If not, adjust R_{10} to make it 2.125 kHz. You will find that there is a small amount of hysteresis at TP_5. In other words, the frequency at which a low to high transition occurs is different from that at which a high to low transition occurs. Adjust R_{10} so that 2.125 kHz is the average of these two critical frequencies.

9. Decrease the amplitude of the function generator. Determine the sensitivity of the FSK decoder. In other words, determine the minimum amplitude at TP_4 which guarantees that successful decoding takes place. Remove the generator from TP_4 before proceeding.

10. Now connect a jumper from TP_3 of Fig.SP1-4 to TP_4 of Fig. SP1-5. The output FSK signal from the FSK encoder is now being applied to the FSK decoder. Apply a 20-Hz, 3-V positive square wave at TP_1. Observe the FSK output at TP_3. It should slowly switch back and forth between the mark and space frequencies. If it doesn't switch states, you may need to fine-tune R_{10} to make it happen.

11. Observe the original digital data (square wave) at TP_1 with channel A and the recreated digital data at TP_5 with channel B. Sketch the resulting waveforms.

12. Increase the baud rate of the digital data by increasing the frequency of the function generator. Determine the highest square-wave frequency that can be sent through this simple digital communications link. Again, fine-tuning R_{10} may make this upper frequency limit a bit larger.

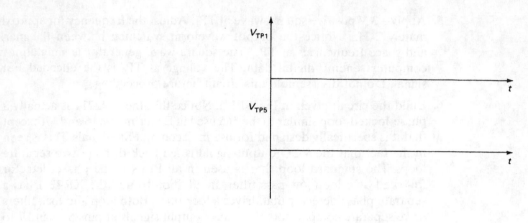

REPORT/QUESTIONS:

1. Calculate the maximum baud rate that the digital communications link could handle without any errors resulting.

2. In your own words, write a brief theory of operation section for the digital communications link analyzed in this experiment. Assume that this system is being sold as a product to the technical public and that this theory section is to be incorporated as part of a manual for the product.

3. For the manual described in question 2, write a technical test procedure for calibration of the FSK encoder for generation of 2025/2225 Hz FSK. Also, write a test procedure for calibration of the FSK detector for successful detection of 2025/2225 Hz FSK. Assume that this procedure is to be read and followed by a bench technician who has a function generator, oscilloscope, and power supply at the test bench.

NAME _____

FIBER OPTICS COMMUNICATION LINK

OBJECTIVES:

1. To become familiar with fiber optic cable, splicing, and connecting procedures.
2. To build and test a fiber optic link.
3. To examine performances for speed and attenuation.

REFERENCE:

Refer to Chapter 17 of the text.

TEST EQUIPMENT:

Dual-trace oscilloscope
Function generator
Low-voltage power supply (2)

COMPONENTS:

Refer to documentation for RSR Electronics Projects #08SPK1 and #OK-120.

PRELABORATORY:

Splice four 6-inch-long fiber cables using different techniques. Refer to RSR Electronics Project #08SPK1.

PROCEDURE/REPORT:

Conduct various experiments detailed in RSR Electronics manual #OK-120.

SYSTEM PROJECT 3 NAME _____

FIBER OPTICAL SYSTEM

OBJECTIVES:

1. To learn to deal with a complete operating device as opposed to sections of the device as performed in normal experiments.
2. To display critical thinking skills in performing analysis of the project's operating parameters.
3. To display ability to select the appropriate method and points to verify circuit and system operation.
4. To gain valuable troubleshooting techniques through construction and testing of each project.

REFERENCE:

Refer to Chapter 17 of the text.

COMPONENTS:

Refer to documentation for RSR Electronics Project #OK-726.

TEST EQUIPMENT:

Dual-trace oscilloscope
Dual-voltage power supply
Volt-ohmmeter
Function generator
RF generator
Frequency counter

PROCEDURE:

When directed by your instructor perform the following steps and prepare a report covering your findings for each of the systems detailed herein.

1. Construct the receiver and transmitter of a fiber optic voice system following directions in the documentation for RSR Electronics Project #OK-726.

2. Verify the operation of the system by transmitting and receiving a 1-kHz test tone.

3. Submit for approval by your instructor your plan for testing the system limitations. Include a block diagram and predicted results for each circuit you will evaluate.

4. Analyze the system by finding its limitations.
   (a) The maximum audio input without distortion.
   (b) The largest signal level without distortion.
   (c) The power requirement for normal operation.

5. Write a complete report which provides an overview of the major parts of the system (block diagram), details of the procedures used to measure the performance of the system, and the methods used to overcome difficulties in operating the devices. The report should include your projected values for stage gain as well as your actual values. Any deviation of more than 10% within a circuit requires further testing and evaluation.

AM COMMUNICATION SYSTEM

OBJECTIVES:

1. To learn to deal with a complete operating device as opposed to sections of the device as performed in normal experiments.
2. To display critical thinking skills in performing analysis of the project's operating parameters.
3. To display ability to select the appropriate method and points to verify circuit and system operation.
4. To gain valuable troubleshooting techniques through construction and testing of each project.

REFERENCES:

Refer to Chapters 2 and 3 of the text.

TEST EQUIPMENT:

Dual-trace oscilloscope

Dual-voltage power supply

Volt-ohmmeter

Function generator

RF generator

Frequency counter

PROCEDURE:

When directed by your instructor perform the following steps and prepare a report covering your findings for each of the systems detailed herein.

1. Submit schematic diagrams for an AM TX and RX to your instructor for approval. Extra components such as trimmer capacitors or variable inductors need the approval of your instructor.
2. Construct the AM receiver with previously provided components.
3. Construct the AM transmitter with an output power of less than 10 mW from previously provided components.
4. Tune your transmitter to 1 MHz.
5. Modulate the carrier with 1 kHz.

6. Using your receiver tune in the transmitted signal.

7. Submit for approval by your instructor a detailed list of the functional tests you plan to perform to verify the operating parameters of the system. This list will include a block diagram and projected values for each circuit you plan to test.

8. Perform a system analysis of your equipment to include the items listed below if applicable to your circuit.

   (a) The dc power requirements of each circuit.
   (b) Ac minimum and maximum signal levels (voltage, frequency) as appropriate for the circuit.
   (c) The transmission range based on your calculations for the TX output power and the RX MDS.
   (d) The deviation between transmitted and received frequency.
   (e) Receiver audio stage gain and bandwidth.
   (f) Receiver RF stage gain and bandwidth.
   (g) Local oscillator bandwidth, frequency deviation, and Q.
   (h) Modulator signal levels for 0 and 100% modulation.

9. Write a complete report which provides an overview of the major parts of the system (block diagram), details of the procedures used to measure the performance of the system, and the methods used to overcome difficulties in operating the devices. The report should include your projected values for stage gain as well as your actual values. Any deviation of more than 10% within a circuit requires further testing and evaluation.

NAME _____

FM COMMUNICATION SYSTEM

OBJECTIVES:

1. To learn how to deal with a complete operating device as opposed to sections of the device as performed in normal experiments.
2. To display critical thinking skills in performing analysis of the project's operating parameters.
3. To display ability to select the appropriate method and points to verify circuit and system operation.
4. To gain valuable troubleshooting techniques through construction and testing of each project.

REFERENCES:

Refer to Chapters 5 and 6 of the text.

TEST EQUIPMENT:

Dual-trace oscilloscope
Dual-voltage power supply
Volt-ohmmeter
Function generator
RF generator
Frequency counter

PROCEDURE:

When directed by your instructor perform the steps and prepare a report covering your findings for each of the systems detailed herein.

1. Submit schematic diagrams for an FM TX and RX to your instructor for approval. Extra components such as variable capacitors and inductors need the approval of your instructor.
2. Construct the FM receiver with previously provided components.
3. Construct the FM transmitter with an output power of less than 10 mW from previously provided components.
4. Tune your transmitter to 10 MHz.
5. Modulate the carrier with 1 kHz.

6. Using your receiver tune in the transmitted signal.

7. Submit for approval by your instructor a detailed list of the functional tests you plan to perform to verify the operating parameters of the system. This list will include a block diagram and projected values for each circuit you plan to test.

8. Perform a system analysis of your equipment.

   (a) The dc power requirements of each circuit.
   (b) Ac minimum and maximum signal levels (voltage, frequency) as appropriate for the circuit.
   (c) The transmission range based on your calculations for the TX output power and the RX MDS.
   (d) The deviation between transmitted and received frequency.
   (e) Receiver audio stage gain and bandwidth.
   (f) Receiver RF stage gain and bandwidth.
   (g) Local oscillator bandwidth, frequency deviation, and Q.
   (h) Modulator signal frequency for 0 and 100% modulation.

9. Write a complete report which provides an overview of the major parts of the system (block diagram), details of the procedures used to measure the performance of the system, and the methods used to overcome difficulties in operating the devices. The report should include your projected values for stage gain as well as your actual values. Any deviation of more than 10% within a circuit requires further testing and evaluation.

EWB MULTISIM—BPSK DIGITAL COMMUNICATION SYSTEM

OBJECTIVES:

1. To become acquainted with the use of Electronics Workbench Multisim for simulating and measuring of a BPSK digital communications link.
2. To understand digital communications.
3. To gain valuable troubleshooting techniques by developing a simulation of a digital communications link.
4. To gain valuable insight into the block diagram of a digital communication system.

REFERENCES:

Refer to Chapter 10, section 10-2 of the text, and the Chapter 10 Troubleshooting with Electronics Workbench Multisim section in the lab manual.

VIRTUAL TEST EQUIPMENT:

AC voltage source
Dual-trace oscilloscope
Clock source

PROCEDURE:

When directed by your instructor, perform the following steps covering the findings for each system detailed herein.

1. Develop a block diagram of a BPSK (binary phase shift keying) transmit receive circuit. Submit the block diagram to your instructor for approval. Verify that the blocks you are proposing to use are available in Electronics Workbench Multisim.
2. Use Electronics Workbench Multisim to develop the simulation of the BPSK transmit receive circuit developed in step 1.
3. Use basic troubleshooting techniques to verify that each block is performing the function specified by the block. Use the oscilloscope to obtain traces of the signal path in both the transmit and receive circuits.

4. Write a technical description for each of the stages used in your design. Include pictures of the traces obtained in step 3 to show that each block is performing the task expected. Include a description of the technical requirements for each stage. For example, specify the required gain of the receiver RF input stage.

5. Write a troubleshooting procedure for the BPSK transmit receive block diagram. Explain how a fault in one stage can affect other stages and how the fault can be isolated and detected. Include a flow chart that describes the symptom(s) and suggested blocks to check. You only need to identify eight symptoms, checks, and possible failures.

SYMPTOM	CHECKS	POSSIBLE FAILURE

NAME _____

DUAL-TONE MULTIPLE-FREQUENCY KEYBOARD DECODER

OBJECTIVES:

1. To learn how to deal with a complete operating system rather than dealing with discrete parts of a system.
2. To display critical thinking skills in performing analysis of the project's operating parameters.
3. To display the ability to select an appropriate method for verifying circuit and system operation.
4. To gain valuable troubleshooting experience through construction and testing of each project.

REFERENCES:

An application of tone sensing can be found on p. 469 of the text.

The appendix of the lab book has the data sheet for an LM567 Tone Decoder.

Experiment 24: Tone Decoder lab.

TEST EQUIPMENT:

Dual-trace oscilloscope

Low-voltage power supply

Prototype board

PRELABORATORY:

1. Design a system that will decode and identify which one of four keys has been depressed. Use a dual-tone multiple-frequency format such that selecting any of the four keys will deliver two different frequencies to a tone decoder network. Refer to the data sheet (in the appendix) under typical applications "tone decoder" to get an idea how to detect and decode the dual frequency signal. Decide how to display which key is being decoded. (For instance, use 4 LEDs to indicate which key has been pressed.)

2. Design a system that will deliver four different two-frequency combinations to the Tone Decoder system.

Hint: Use 555 Timers. If you are really creative you can use more than one frequency determining capacitor for each 555. Two different capacitors can be connected in parallel through two single-pole single-throw switches. Selecting one key switch connects one of the capacitors from ground to the frequency generator circuit, and selecting a different key switch will connect a different capacitor from ground to the frequency generator circuit. A complete dual-tone generation system can be designed with two 555 timers, four different frequency determining capacitors, and four single-pole single-throw switches.

3. Show your design to your instructor for approval.

PROCEDURE:

1. Build the two circuits that you have designed. Connect the output of the dual-tone generator circuit through a single channel medium to the input of the dual-tone decoder circuit. Make sure that the input voltage level to the dual-tone decoder circuit is low so that the Bandwidth % is sufficiently narrow. Demonstrate to your instructor that it works to the design specifications.

2. Write a complete report that provides an overview of the major parts of the system. Include a block diagram and details of the operating parameters including a table of the frequency combinations chosen. Also include a discussion on difficulties encountered and how they were overcome. The report should also compare measured center frequencies and bandwidths to calculated values.

SINGLE-CHIP FM TRANSMITTER

OBJECTIVES:

1. To objective of this project is for the student to experiment with the construction of a single-chip FM transmitter system using the MAXIM 2606 integrated circuit.
2. To gain experience working with surface mount device (MAX 2606)
3. To gain experience assembling components on a project board.

REFERENCES:

Modern Electronic Communication, 8th edition by Miller and Beasley, chapter 5, section 5-7.

TEST EQUIPMENT:

Dual-trace Oscilloscope   DC Voltage Source
Function Generator   FM Receiver

COMPONENTS:

Capacitors: 10uF, 0.47UF, 2200pF, 1000pF, 0.01uF, 1uF, 0.33uf, 0.1uF
Resistors: 22K_ (2), 1K_ (2), 270 _, 4.7 K_,
100K_ square potentiometer, 10K_ square potentiometer
Inductor 390nH
Voltage Regulator 5V
Surface Mount RCA phono jacks (2), Power Jack
Max2606 IC Chip & Proto-Board adapter board.
PROTO-Board, Univ PC Board
Stand-off's (4)

PROCEDURE:

Assemble an FM transmitter using the MAX2606 and required parts following the schematic provided in Fig. SP8-1. This is a low-power FM transmitter operating in the FM band (88-108 MHz). A schematic is provided in Figure SP8-1 that shows all the components required for assembling the project. The circuit runs off a single power supply (3-5 V). The left and right audio channels from your audio player (e.g. CD, MP3, IPOD etc.) connect via the RCA phono jacks to resistors R3 and R4. Resistors R3 and R4 are used to combine the left and right audio channels before inputting the signal input the MAX 2606. Potentiometer R2 is used for the volume control. The MAX 2606 is a voltage-controlled oscillator with an integrated varactor. The nominal frequency of oscillation is set by L1 (390 nH). This inductor value places the center frequency of the transmitter at 100 MHz. A 350 nH inductor can be used in place of the 390 nH inductor with minimal shifting of the transmit center frequency. Potentiometer R1 is used for tuning the transmitter to the desired channel. Potentiometer R1 connects to Tune input (pin 3) of the MAX 2606 IC. The tune input drives a voltage controlled oscillator with an integrated varactor. An FM antenna connects to pin 6 through a 1000 pF capacitor.

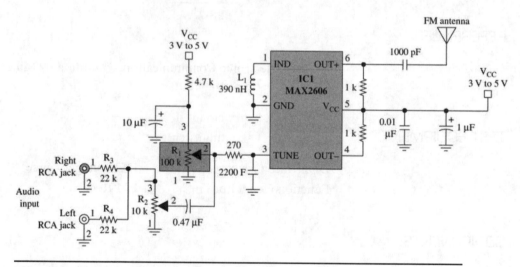

FIGURE SP8-1 The MAX 2606 single-chip FM transmitter.

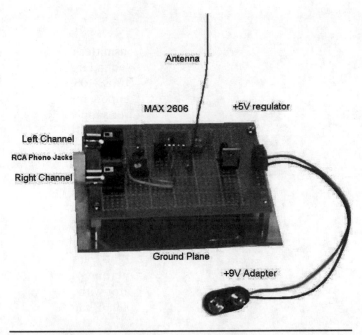

FIGURE SP8-2 An example of an assembled FM transmitter. Note: The antenna is about 4" in length.

Circuit Construction, Operation, and Troubleshooting

1. Assemble the circuit similar to the example provided in Figure SP8-2.

2. Perform a continuity check of your assemble board prior to applying power.

3. Verify that power is being properly provided to the circuit. The example provided in Figure SP8-2 uses a 9V battery with a +5V regulator on board to provide power to the circuit.

4. Tune your FM radio to a frequency that does not have a signal. Turn on the transmitter and tune the FM transmitter (using R1) until the FM receiver goes quiet. FM receivers will go quiet in the presence of an FM carrier.

5. Apply a signal to the audio inputs and experiment with the transmitter.

PART IV

TROUBLESHOOTING WITH ELECTRONICS WORKBENCH MULTISIM

This text presents computer simulation examples of troubleshooting and analyzing electronic communications circuits and concepts using Electronics Workbench Multisim. Examples are presented for each chapter on an important topic covered in that chapter. Electronics Workbench provides a unique opportunity for you to examine electronic circuits and concepts in a way that reflects techniques used for analyzing and troubleshooting circuits and systems in practice. The use of Electronics Workbench provides you with additional hands-on insight into many of the fundamental communication circuits, concepts, and test equipment while improving your ability to perform logical thinking when troubleshooting circuits and systems. The test equipment tools available in Electronics Workbench reflect the type of tools that are commonly available on well-equipped test benches.

1

TROUBLESHOOTING WITH ELECTRONICS WORKBENCH™ MULTISIM— UNDERSTANDING THE FREQUENCY SPECTRA

An introduction to many fundamental concepts in communications was presented in Chapter 1 of the text. The topics included the dB, noise, oscillators, *LC* circuits, and frequency spectra. The first Electronics Workbench example in this text reinforces the concepts presented in the section on understanding the frequency spectra. This particular example demonstrates that a complex waveform such as a square wave generates multifrequency components called harmonics. A spectrum analyzer is used in Electronics Workbench to observe and analyze the spectral content of a square wave.

To begin this exercise, start Electronics Workbench Multisim and open the file called **Fig. T1-1** that is found on the Electronics Workbench (EWB) Multisim CD-ROM packaged with the lab manual. It is a simple circuit containing a 1 kHz square-wave generator connected to a 1 kΩ resistive load. The circuit is shown in Fig. T1-1.

Begin the simulation by clicking on the **start simulation** button. Verify that the function generator is outputting a 5-V square wave at 1 kHz by viewing the trace with the oscilloscope. The oscilloscope display can be opened by double-clicking on the oscilloscope icon. The oscilloscope display is shown in Fig. T1-2. Measurement features for the oscilloscope are introduced in the next section of the lab manual, Troubleshooting with Electronics Workbench Multisim-AM Measurements.

Next, double-click on the spectrum analyzer. In a few seconds, the spectrum analyzer will sample and build the image shown in Fig. T1-3. Each spike in the waveform shows a frequency component or harmonic of the square wave. The concept of a square wave containing multiple frequency components was presented in the text in Section 1-6. An oscilloscope image of a 1-kHz square wave and its corresponding FFT spectrum were presented in the text.

The spectrum analyzer provides a cursor that can be positioned to measure the frequency of each component. In this case, the cursor has been positioned next to the 3-kHz spike, which is the third harmonic of a 1-kHz square wave. The spectrum analyzer provides settings for the frequency span, start, center, and end frequencies. These adjustments provide the user with the capability of selecting the frequency range for conducting a measurement. Additional experiments are presented in the text that demonstrate additional features of the Electronics Workbench tools. Three exercises requiring the use of Electronics Workbench™ Multisim are provided below.

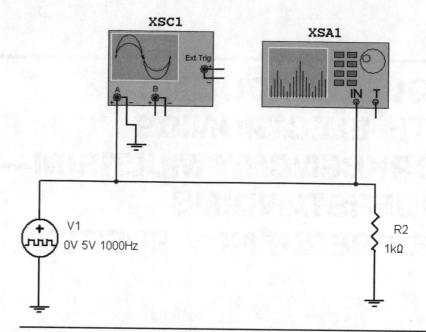

FIGURE T1-1 The Multisim component view of the test circuit used to demonstrate the frequency spectra for a square wave.

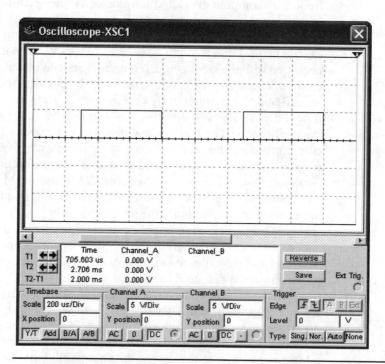

FIGURE T1-2 The Multisim oscilloscope image of the square wave from the function generator.

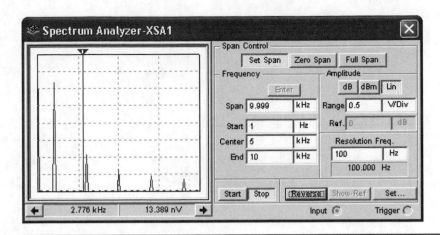

FIGURE T1-3 The Multisim spectrum analyzer view of a 1-kHz square wave.

ELECTRONICS WORKBENCH™ EXERCISES

1. Use the cursor on the spectrum analyzer to identify the seventh and ninth harmonics for the circuit provided in **Fig T1-1.**

2. The circuit provided in **T1-4** on your CD can be used to demonstrate the effect a bandlimited channel has on the spectral content of a square wave. Discuss the observed changes in the circuit as compared to the circuit provided in **Fig T1-1.**

3. The circuit provided in **T1-5** on your CD contains a 100-kHz square wave. Change the settings on the spectrum analyzer so that the first, third, fifth, seventh, and ninth harmonics are displayed on the screen. The solution is provided on your EWB **multisim file T1-5-solution.**

2

TROUBLESHOOTING WITH ELECTRONICS WORKBENCH™ MULTISIM— AM MEASUREMENTS

Chapter 2 presented the modulation processes for producing an AM signal. Electronics Workbench™ Multisim can be used to simulate, make measurements, and troubleshoot AM modulator circuits, such as the simple transistor modulator shown in Fig. 2-10. To begin this exercise, open **Fig T2-1** found in your EWB Multisim CD. You should have a circuit that looks like the one shown in Figure T2-1.

Begin the simulation by clicking on the start simulation switch. View the simulation results by double-clicking on the oscilloscope. You will obtain an image similar to the one shown in Figure T2-2. Is this an example of amplitude modulation? You can freeze the display by turning the simulation off or pressing pause. A record of the im-

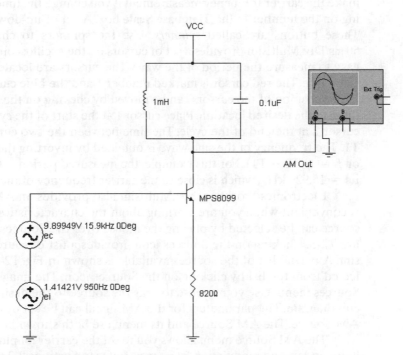

FIGURE T2-1 The Multisim component view for the simple transistor amplitude modulator circuit.

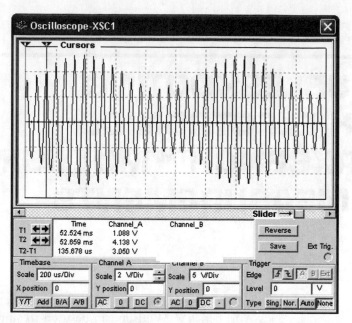

FIGURE T2-2 The Multisim oscilloscope control panel.

age is continually being saved. You can horizontally shift the displayed screen by adjusting the **Slider,** as shown in Figure T2-2. Use Eq. 2-5 from the textbook to determine the modulation index for this simulation. You should obtain a percentage modulation of about 33 percent.

Can you measure the frequency of the carrier from the display? It is easier to make the carrier frequency measurement if you change the timebase settings by clicking on the number in the **Timebase Scale** box. A set of up-down buttons will appear. These buttons are called *spinners*. Use the spinners to change the timebase to 50 ms/Div. Multisim provides a set of cursors on the oscilloscope display that makes it easy to measure the period of the wave. The cursors are located at the top of the oscilloscope. The red cursor is marked number 1 and the blue cursor is marked number 2. The position of the cursors can be moved by clicking on the triangles and dragging them to the desired location. Place cursor 1 at the start of the cycle for a sine wave and cursor 2 at the end of the cycle. The time between the two cursors is shown as **T2 − T1.** The frequency of the sine wave is obtained by inverting the value of the T2 − T1, or $f = 1/(T2 - T1)$. For this example, the measured period is 62.8 μs and $f = 1/62.8$ μs = 15.924 kHz, which is close to the carrier frequency of the generator (15.9 kHz).

Electronics Workbench™ Multisim also provides an AM source. This feature is convenient when you are learning about the characteristics of an AM signal. The source can be selected by placing the mouse over the Sources icon, as shown in Figure T2-3. Clicking on the Sources icon provides a list of sources available in Multisim. A partial list of the sources available is shown in Fig. T2-4. A source can be selected from the list by clicking on the Sources icon. The image will open behind the Sources menu. Use your mouse to drag the source to the desired location on the circuit diagram. The parameters for the AM signal can be set by double-clicking on the AM Source. The AM Source and its menu are both shown in Fig. T2-5.

The AM Source menu allows you to set the carrier amplitude, frequency, modulation index, and modulation frequency. Refer to Sections 2-2 through 2-4 in the textbook for a review of amplitude modulation fundamentals. In this case, the carrier am-

FIGURE T2-3   The Sources icon in Electronics Workbench™ Multisim.

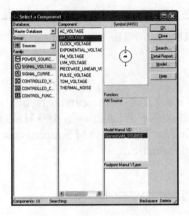

FIGURE T2-4   A partial list of the sources provided by Multisim and the location of the AM Sources icon.

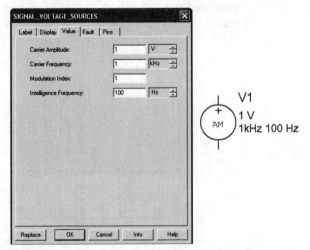

FIGURE T2-5   The AM Source and the menu for setting its parameters.

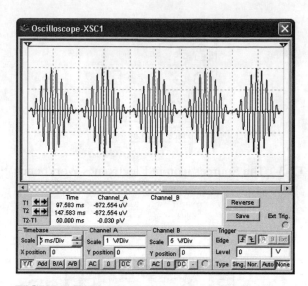

FIGURE T2-6 The output of the AM Source.

plitude is set to 1 V, the carrier frequency is 1000 Hz, the modulation index is 1, and the modulation frequency is 100 Hz. The AM waveform produced by the source is shown in Fig. T2-6. The AM Source is used in the Electronics Workbench exercises that follow this section.

ELECTRONICS WORKBENCH™ EXERCISES

1. Open **T2-7** on your EWB CD. Determine the modulation index.
2. Open **T2-8** on your EWB CD. Use the cursors on the oscilloscope to verify that the carrier frequency is 15 kHz.
3. Open **T2-9** on your EWB CD. Add the display of the input signals of the modulating circuit to the channel B input of your oscilloscope so that both the AM signal and the intelligence signal are displayed. Use the scale controls and the Y position so that both traces are easily viewed. Print out the traces displayed on the oscilloscope.

3

TROUBLESHOOTING WITH ELECTRONICS WORKBENCH™ MULTISIM—AM DEMODULATION

This chapter explored the circuits used for receiving and detecting an AM signal. The diode detector shown in Figure T3-1 is an example of a circuit that can be used to recover the intelligence contained in an AM carrier. **Fig T3-1** found on the EWB Multisim CD is provided to help you investigate further the operation of a diode detector.

Open **Fig T3-1** on your EWB CD. This circuit contains an AM source with a carrier frequency of 100 kHz being modulated by a 1-kHz sinusoid. The modulation index is 50 percent. Open the AM source by double-clicking on the **AM** icon. Click on the **value** tab. It should show that the carrier amplitude is 3 V, the carrier frequency is 100 kHz, the modulation index is 0.5 (50 percent), and the modulating frequency is 1 kHz. These values can be changed by the user to meet the needs of a particular simulation. Click the **start simulation** button and observe the traces on the oscilloscope.

The AM source is connected to the channel A input and the output of the detector is connected to the channel B input. The oscilloscope traces from the diode detector are shown in Figure T3-2. There appears to be a little carrier noise on the

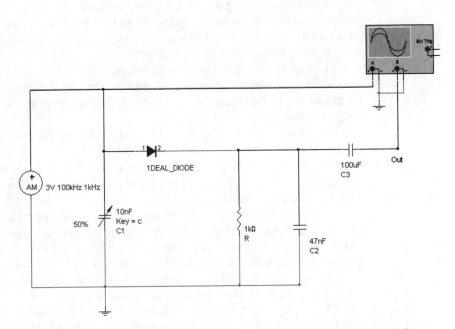

FIGURE T3-1   An AM diode detector circuit as implemented with Electronics Workbench Multisim.

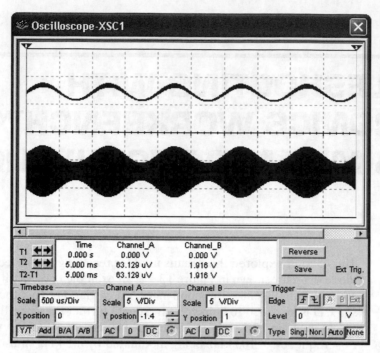

FIGURE T3-2 Oscilloscope output traces from the diode detector.

recovered 1-kHz sinusoid. How can this noise be removed? (This question is addressed in Exercise 3.) Was a 1-kHz sinusoid recovered? Use the cursors to verify that a 1-kHz signal was recovered. Measure the modulation index of the AM source as shown in Figure T3-2. Compare your measurement to the expected 50 percent value set in the AM source.

Capacitor 1 in Figure T3-1 is called a *virtual capacitor*. Double-click on **C1** and select the **value** tab. The information about the virtual capacitor shows that this is a 10-nF capacitor; pressing **c** on the keyboard increases the capacitance value by 5 percent, and pressing **C** decreases the value by 5 percent. Experiment with this adjustment and see if changing the capacitance value affects the recovered signal. Make sure that you click on the schematic window to enable control of the virtual components. Adjustments to the virtual capacitor are not active if another window, such as the oscilloscope window, is currently selected.

Next, open **T3-3.** This circuit looks the same as **Fig T3-1** except that this circuit contains a fault. Use the oscilloscope to view the traces in the circuit. Good troubleshooting practice says: *Always perform a visual check of the circuit and check the vital signs. Checking vital signs implies that you must check power-supply voltages and also examine the input signals.*

Start the simulation of the circuit and view the output and input traces. Notice that the input AM envelope looks the same, whereas the output is significantly different. This circuit does not show a power supply, but just in case, visually check that the ground connections are in place. The input signal (the AM envelope) and the ground connections are good, so the problem rests with a component. Verify that the output coupling capacitor is allowing the signal to pass properly from the detector to the output. Do this by connecting the oscilloscope A and B channels to each side of C3. You will notice that the signal is the same on both sides, which indicates that C3 is good. Electronics Workbench Multisim provides a feature that allows for the addition of a component fault in a circuit. Double-click on each of the components and check the setting under the **Fault** tab. You will discover that R1 is shorted. Change the fault setting back to **none,** which means no fault, and simulate the circuit again. The circuit should now be operational.

Additional insight into troubleshooting with Electronics Workbench " Multisim is provided in the EWB exercises below.

ELECTRONICS WORKBENCH™ EXERCISES

1. Open **T3-4** found on your EWB CD. Determine if this circuit is working properly. If it is not, find the fault. Describe why this fault would have caused the output waveform you observed.

2. Open **T3-5** found on your EWB CD. Determine if this circuit is working properly. If it is not, find the fault. Describe why this fault would have caused the output waveform you observed.

3. Open **T3-6** found on your EWB CD. Adjust the virtual capacitors C1 and C3 to provide an output waveform that contains minimal RF noise. This process requires that you adjust C1 and then C3 and keep repeating this sequence until an optimized output is obtained.

4

TROUBLESHOOTING WITH ELECTRONICS WORKBENCH™ MULTISIM—SINGLE SIDEBAND GENERATION

This section extends understanding of single-sideband systems as implemented in Electronics Workbench™ Multisim. Open **Fig T4-1** on your EWB Multisim CD. This circuit contains two sine-wave generators that are input into a multiplier module. A multiplier circuit produces the sum and difference of the input frequencies on its output. For this example, the sum is 3 MHz + 1 MHz = 4 MHz, and the difference is 3 MHz − 1 MHz = 2 MHz. Start the simulation and observe the inputs to the multiplier and the complex output waveform using the oscilloscope. The circuit is shown in Figure T4-1.

Next, open the spectrum analyzer, which is connected to the output of the multiplier. The spectrum analyzer shows that frequencies of 2 MHz and 4 MHz are produced. This is shown in Figure T4-2. This is called a double-sideband spectrum. Use the cursor to determine the frequencies of each spectral component.

It is necessary to remove one of the sidebands in an SSB (single-sideband) system. This can be accomplished by passing the output of the multiplier through a filter.

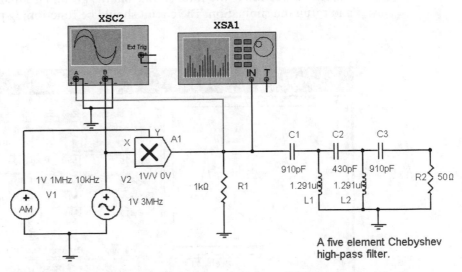

A five element Chebyshev high-pass filter.

FIGURE T4-1 A multiplier plus SSB filter as implemented with Electronics Workbench™ Multisim.

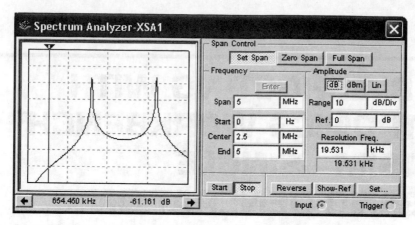

FIGURE T4-2 The double-sideband output spectrum for the multiplier circuit.

In this example, a five-element Chebyshev high-pass filter has been provided to remove the lower-sideband component. This filter has a 20-dB upper cutoff frequency of about 2.6 MHz. Therefore, frequencies below 2.6 MHz should be significantly attenuated. Connect the spectrum analyzer to the output of the filter and restart the simulation. Verify that the output contains only the upper-sideband component. The sideband at 2 MHz has been significantly reduced, but the upper sideband is still present. The result is shown in Figure T4-3.

The next part of this exercise provides you with the opportunity to troubleshoot a filter circuit. Open **T4-4** on your EWB CD. Start the simulation and use the spectrum analyzer to observe the output spectrum. Note that the spectrum analyzer is connected to the output of the filter. Is the circuit working as expected? If not, use the spectrum analyzer and the oscilloscope to check the waveform. Don't forget to perform a visual check of the circuit for potential problems. You will discover that both the upper and lower sidebands are present on the output. What circuit removes the lower sideband? Shouldn't the filter remove the lower sideband? Careful inspection of the filter shows that the ground is missing. Replace the ground and rerun the simulation. The circuit should be functioning properly.

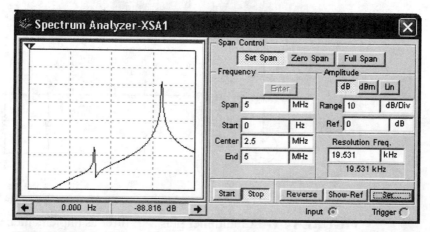

FIGURE T4-3 The multiplier circuit with the lower sideband removed.

ELECTRONICS WORKBENCH™ EXERCISES

1. Open **T4-5** in your EWB CD. This circuit contains a tunable high-pass filter. Use the **(a/A)** and **(b/B) keys** to adjust the inductance values to optimize the performance of the filter. Record your settings and comment on the effect that changing the inductance values has on the output. ($L_1 = 35\%$, $L_2 = 55\%$)

2. Open **T4-6** in your EWB CD. This circuit contains a fault. In this exercise, assume that you have been told that the circuit does not appear to be working properly. You may need to refer back to the waveforms in the multisim file **Fig T4-1** for a properly functioning circuit to help guide you with your troubleshooting. Confirm that the circuit is not working properly and find the cause of the problem. Once you find the problem, record the fault and the circuit behavior generated by the fault. Correct the fault and rerun the simulation to verify that the problem has been corrected.

3. Open **T4-7** in your EWB CD. This circuit contains a fault. Use your troubleshooting techniques to find the problem. Once you find the problem, record the fault and the circuit behavior observed. Correct the fault and re-run the simulation to verify that the problem has been corrected.

5

TROUBLESHOOTING WITH ELECTRONICS WORKBENCH™ MULTISIM—GENERATING AND ANALYZING THE FM SIGNAL

The concept of generating a frequency-modulated signal was introduced in this chapter. This exercise has been developed to help you better understand the concept of generating and analyzing a frequency modulated signal. To begin this exercise, open **Fig. T5-1,** which can be found on your EWB Multisim CD. This circuit, shown in Figure T5-1, contains a voltage-controlled oscillator (VCO) that is being driven by a 1-V, 10-kHz triangle wave. The triangle wave is being generated by the function generator. Double-click on the function generator to see the settings. The function generator can produce a sinusoid, triangle, or square wave. The frequency, duty cycle, and offset voltage are adjustable.

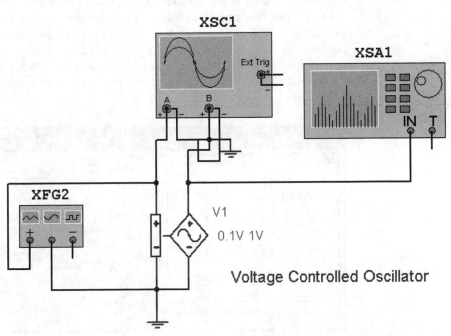

FIGURE T5-1 A frequency-modulation circuit using a voltage-controlled oscillator, as implemented in an Electronics Workbench™ Multisim circuit.

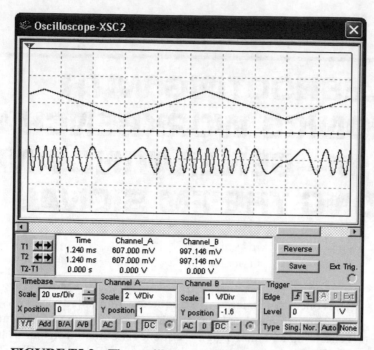

FIGURE T5-2 The oscilloscope display of the 10-kHz triangle wave and the output of the VCO.

Double-click on the VCO to check its settings. The control and frequency arrays are used to specify the ranges for the VCO. In this example, an input voltage of 0 V produces a 100-kHz sinusoid, whereas a 1-V input produces a 200-kHz sinusoid.

The output of the VCO, as viewed with an oscilloscope, is provided in Figure T5-2. Channel A (top) is the 10-kHz triangle waveform and channel B (bottom) is the VCO output. Notice that as the voltage increases, the VCO frequency increases. Experiment with the circuit and see how the VCO output is affected by inputting a square wave. A square-wave input produces a frequency shift keying (FSK) output.

Close **Fig T5-1** and open the **T5-3** file on your EWB CD. The VCO has been replaced with an FM source. Double-click on the FM source to see the settings. The car-

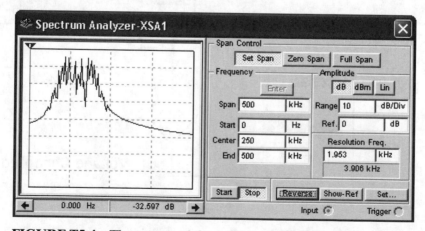

FIGURE T5-4 The output of the voltage-controlled oscillator as viewed with a spectrum analyzer.

rier frequency is 150 kHz, the modulation index is 5, and the signal frequency is 10 kHz. Start the simulation and observe the display on the spectrum analyzer. You should see a picture similar to Figure T5-4. Notice the spectral width of the signal. Recall from Sec. 5-3 in the text that the bandwidth of an FM signal can be estimated by Carson's rule.

For this example, the input frequency is 10 kHz and the modulation index is 5. The estimated BW is 2(50 kHz + 10 kHz) = 120 kHz. This is a noisy signal, but a quick estimate shows that the 3-dB bandwidth is approximately 120 kHz, which agrees with the estimate using Carson's rule.

ELECTRONICS WORKBENCH™ EXERCISES

1. Open the file **T5-5** on your EWB CD. Use Carson's rule to estimate the bandwidth of the FM signal and then compare your result with the measurement obtained with the spectrum analyzer. You will need to double-click on the FM source to view the settings. (~120 kHz)

2. Open the file **T5-6** on your EWB CD. Use Carson's rule to estimate the bandwidth of the FM signal and then compare your result with the measurement obtained with the spectrum analyzer. You will need to double-click on the FM source to view the settings. (~53.4 kHz)

6

TROUBLESHOOTING WITH ELECTRONICS WORKBENCH™ MULTISIM—FM RECEIVER FUNCTIONAL BLOCKS

This section gives you a more thorough understanding of the functional blocks within an FM receiver and additional experience troubleshooting electronic communications circuits. Open the file **Fig T6-1** on your EWB Multisim CD. This is an implementation of an FM receiver using Multisim. Each of the building blocks for the FM receiver is identifed. A picture of the Multisim circuit is provided in Figure T6-1.

A 100-kHz FM signal is being generated by the FM source. The FM carrier is being modulated by a 1-kHz signal and the modulation index is 5. The voltage level has been set to 5 μV to simulate the RF input level that might be received.

The second stage is the RF amplifier, which has a gain of 20,000 V/V. The huge gain is required to provide enough signal voltage for the next stage. The mixer stage follows the RF amplifier and is used to down-convert the 100-kHz frequency to 10 kHz, which is the IF frequency for this circuit. The local oscillator frequency has been set to 110 kHz. The outputs of the mixer are 10 kHz and 210 kHz, which are the difference and sum of the input and local oscillator frequencies. The next stage is the IF amplifier, which includes a bandpass filter that passes the 10-kHz difference and rejects the 210-kHz sum. C_1 and L_1 are used to create the bandpass filter. You can view the Bode plot of the bandpass filter by opening the file **T6-2** on your EWB CD. Start the simulation and open the Bode plotter. You should see a plot similar to the file shown in Figure T6-3.

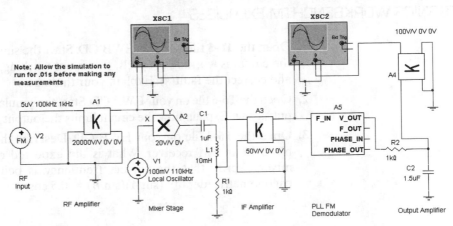

FIGURE T6-1   An implementation of an FM receiver using Multisim.

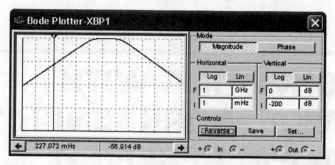

FIGURE T6-3 The frequency plot of the bandpass filter.

This filter provides a 3-dB bandpass of 140 Hz to 22 kHz. The 210-kHz signal is approximately 80 dB down. You can verify this by sliding the cursor along the frequency plot response of the bandpass filter. The frequency and corresponding dB value is shown at the bottom of the Bode plotter window. Close the Bode plot file and reopen the **Fig T6-1** file.

The output of the bandpass filter is next amplified within the IF amplifier with a gain of 24 V/V. The output of the IF amplifier connects to the PLL FM demodulator. The PLL has been set up to lock to the 10-kHz frequency-modulated signal. The output of the PLL FM demodulator circuit is taken from LPF$_{out}$, which is the filtered error voltage output for the PLL. This output is amplified by the output amplifier stage, which has a gain of 200 V/V.

Start the simulation and observe the output. You will notice that a 1-kHz sinusoid is produced, which is the original modulating signal. This simulation may be a little slow and you must let the simulation run for about 2 ms of simulation time for the circuit to stabilize. Become familiar with this circuit; you will next be asked to troubleshoot a faulty version of it.

Open the file **T6-4** on your EWB CD. Start the simulation and observe the output on the oscilloscope. Use your oscilloscope to follow the signal through the circuit. You will find that resistor R2, which connects the output of the PLL to the output amplifier, is open. Double-click on the resistor, R2, and correct the fault by clicking on the **fault** tab and resetting the fault to none. Rerun the simulation to verify that the problem has been corrected.

ELECTRONICS WORKBENCHTM EXERCISES

1. Open the **T6-5** file on your EWB CD. Start the simulation and determine if the circuit is working properly. If it is not working, troubleshoot the circuit and correct the fault(s). Explain your findings.

2. Open the **T6-6** file on your EWB CD. Start the simulation and observe the output signals. Explain how the circuit limits the output level to ±5 V.

3. Open the **T6-7** file on your EWB CD. Describe the purpose of this circuit block in an FM receiver. What is the expected output frequency of the mixer? Verify that the correct frequency is being output by using the trigonometric identity $(\sin A)(\sin B) = 0.5 \cos(A - B) - 0.5 \cos(A + B)$.

TROUBLESHOOTING WITH ELECTRONICS WORKBENCH™ MULTISIM—MIXER AND SQUELCH CIRCUITS

In this section, we first review the concept of a multiplier circuit or, as it is sometimes called, a mixer. Open **Fig T7-1** in your EWB Multisim CD. In this circuit, 20- and 21-MHz sine waves are being input into a mixer stage. The circuit is shown in Figure T7-1. Recall that when two frequencies are mixed together, we should see the sum and differences of the A and B frequencies at the output of the mixer stage.

$$\sin A \times \sin B = 0.5 \cos (A - B) - 0.5 \cos (A + B)$$

Start the simulation and examine the output of the mixer with the oscilloscope. You should see a complex signal containing the product of the A and B frequencies. The oscilloscope trace of the complex signal is shown in Figure T7-2. The figure shows a high-frequency sine wave riding on top of a lower-frequency sine wave. Use the os-

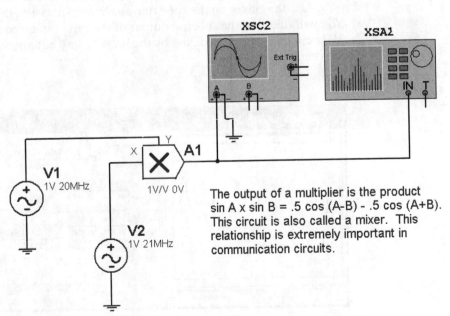

The output of a multiplier is the product sin A x sin B = .5 cos (A-B) - .5 cos (A+B). This circuit is also called a mixer. This relationship is extremely important in communication circuits.

FIGURE T7-1   The mixer circuit as implemented with Multisim.

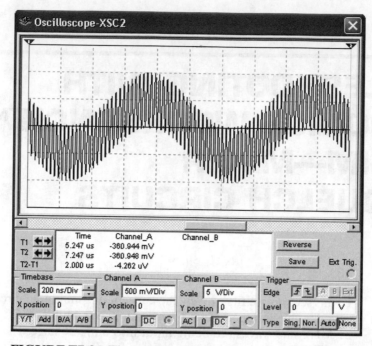

FIGURE T7-2   The output of the mixer as viewed with an oscilloscope. The input frequencies to the mixer are 20 and 21 MHz.

cilloscope to measure the period and determine the frequency of each sine-wave component. You should find that this complex signal contains a 1-MHz and a 41-MHz component.

You can use the spectrum analyzer to verify the frequency components at the output of the mixer. Start the simulation and double-click on the spectrum analyzer module. You should see a spectral display similar to that shown in Figure T7-3.

Use the cursor on the spectrum analyzer to measure the frequency components. You will find that the spectral output of the mixer stage contains a 1-MHz and a 41-MHz component, as predicted by the $\sin A \times \sin B$ equations and by the analysis with the oscilloscope.

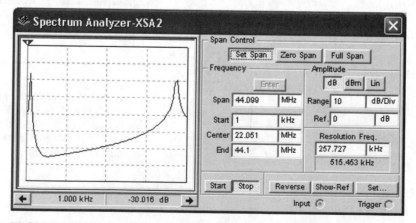

FIGURE T7-3   The output of the mixer as viewed by a spectrum analyzer.

Change the input frequencies so that both inputs are 20 MHz and the amplitudes of each sine wave are equal. What trace do you expect to see on the oscilloscope and on the spectrum analyzer? Start the simulation and see if you are correct. You should find that the oscilloscope shows a 40-MHz sine wave and the spectrum analyzer shows a 40-MHz frequency component. We are seeing the $A + B$ frequency term, whereas the $A - B$ frequency term is zero.

The next exercise provides an opportunity to experiment with a squelch circuit, as implemented with Multisim. Squelch circuits are commonly used in communication receivers to turn off (squelch) the output signal when the signal strength of the received signal is low and noisy or not present. This minimizes annoying noise problems when listening to radio transmissions as they are keyed on and off. Open **Fig T7-4** in your EWB CD to experiment with the squelch circuit.

The input audio signal for the squelch circuit, shown in Figure T7-4, is provided by a 2-kHz sine-wave generator. This signal feeds an amplifier stage and an automatic gain control (AGC) circuit. The AGC circuit uses a simple half-wave rectifier and an RC filter to provide the AGC voltage. The AGC voltage is fed to a 1-kΩ potentiometer that provides squelch adjustment. The signal from the potentiometer feeds two inverters whose outputs are connected to an analog switch, which connects the audio signal to the output amplifier. If sufficient AGC voltage is present (indicating a strong signal), the analog switch will be turned on and the 2-kHz audio signal is passed through to the output amplifier. If the AGC voltage is low or not present (indicating a poor-quality signal or no carrier), the analog switch is turned off. This disconnects the 2-kHz audio signal from the output amplifier.

Start the simulation and double-click on the oscilloscope (XSC1) to view the amplifier output. You should see a sine wave on both the input (Ch. B) and output (Ch. A) of the amplifier stage. A virtual potentiometer has been provided for squelch-level adjustment. It should be set to 40 percent. You can squelch the 100-mV sine wave by ad-

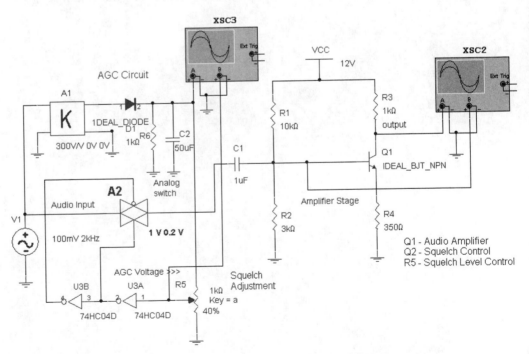

FIGURE T7-4 An example of a squelch circuit as implemented with Multisim.

justing the squelch control to 0 percent. To adjust the squelch level, press *a* to decrease and *A* to increase the resistance of the potentiometer.

Return the squelch setting to 40 percent, stop the simulation and change the sine-wave input level from 100 mV to 10 mV. This change simulates a weak receive signal. A squelch control setting of 40 percent will reject weak signals. Verify this by starting the simulation and viewing the signals on the oscilloscope. The oscilloscope will show a flat line or no signal with the control set to 40 percent. Change the squelch control to 50 percent, and the signals should return. Returning the squelch control to 40 percent will reject the signal. In other words, you now have adjustable squelch control.

Experiment with this circuit. Use the multimeter to examine voltage levels throughout the circuit. View the output of the AGC circuit with the oscilloscope. View both the AC and DC components to understand the AGC signal better.

ELECTRONICS WORKBENCH™ EXERCISES

1. Open the file **T7-5** in your EWB CD. You have discovered that this squelch circuit is not working. Troubleshoot the squelch circuit to determine the cause of the failure. Correct the fault and rerun the simulation. Report on your findings.

2. Open the file **T7-6** in your EWB CD. You have been told that this squelch circuit is working but does not have the range of control that it previously had. Troubleshoot the squelch circuit to determine the cause of the failure. Correct the fault and rerun the simulation. Report on your findings.

3. Open the file **T7-7** in your EWB CD. You discovered that the squelch circuit is not working. You suspect that an employee at the facility dropped a screwdriver into the receiver cabinet while power was on. Troubleshoot the squelch circuit to determine the cause of the failure. Correct the fault(s) and rerun the simulation. Report on your findings.

8

TROUBLESHOOTING WITH ELECTRONICS WORKBENCH™ MULTISIM—SAMPLING THE AUDIO SIGNAL

Proper sampling of the input signal is an extremely important process when converting an analog signal to a digital format. This Electronics Workbench™ Multisim exercise has been developed to advance your understanding of the sampling process and to reinforce the importance of properly selecting the sample frequency. Examples are provided to demonstrate the properly sampled signal and the components generated by aliasing when the sample frequency is inadequate.

Start this exercise by opening the file **Fig T8-1** found on your EWB Multisim CD. This circuit contains a function generator that supplies the sample frequency ($f_s = 5$ kHz) and a sine-wave generator that provides the analog signal ($f_i = 1$ kHz) being sampled. The Multisim circuit is shown in Figure T8-1.

Start the simulation and observe the traces on the oscilloscope. Trace A is the input sine wave and trace B is the sampled signal (also called a pulse-amplitude-modulated [PAM] signal). The oscilloscope traces are shown in Figure T8-2.

Experiment with the sample frequency. Double-click on the function generator and set the sample frequency to 12 kHz. Restart the simulation and notice the improvement in the sampled signal due to the significant increase in the sample frequency. The Nyquist sampling theorem states that the sample frequency (f_s) must be at least twice the highest input frequency. What happens if the sample frequency does not satisfy the Nyquist criteria? Open the file **T8-3** on your EWB CD. Notice that a spectrum analyzer has been connected to the output. The sample frequency (f_s) has been set to 6 kHz and the input frequency (f_i) is 4 kHz. Start the simulation and observe the display of frequencies on the spectrum analyzer. The signal you should see on the spectrum analyzer is shown in Figure T8-4.

Use the cursor to determine the frequencies displayed. You will see the following: 2 kHz, 4 kHz, 6 kHz, 8 kHz, and 10 kHz. Where did these frequencies come from? The sample frequency is 6 kHz. The input frequency is 4 kHz. Therefore, you have the following.

Frequency	Origination
$(6 - 4)$ kHz = 2 kHz	$f_s - f_i$
4 kHz	Input signal
$(6 + 2)$ kHz = 8 kHz	Sum of the sample frequency (f_s) and the 2-kHz ($f_s - f_i$) frequency
$(6 + 4)$ kHz = 10 kHz	Sum of the sample frequency (f_s) and the input frequency (f_i)

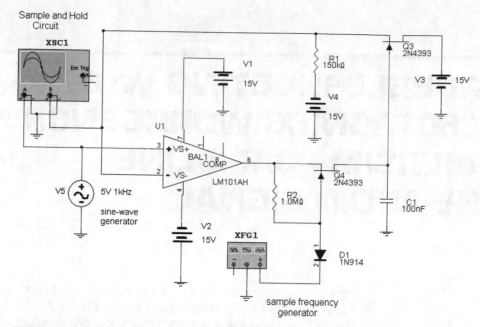

Sample and Hold
Circuit

FIGURE T8-1 A sample-and-hold circuit as implemented in Electronics
Workbench™ Multisim.

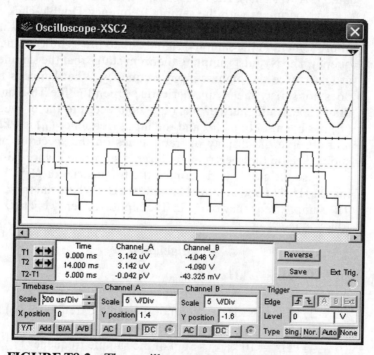

FIGURE T8-2 The oscilloscope traces for the sample-and-hold circuit.

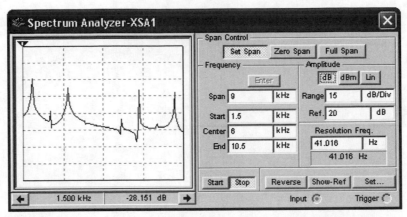

FIGURE T8-4 The spectrum of a signal that contains aliased frequencies due to improper selection of the sampling frequency.

This example demonstrates the importance of properly selecting the sample frequency. The input signals in communications systems are typically more complex than a simple sine wave and contain many harmonic frequencies. This example underscores the importance of incorporating antialiasing filters in sampling circuits to ensure that the maximum input frequency never exceeds $f_s/2$. If the Nyquist criteria is not met, aliasing frequencies will be generated, leading to a decrease in system performance.

One of the Electronics Workbench™ exercises that follows further investigates the sample-and-hold circuit and provides you with the opportunity to examine the spectral content of a signal generated by a sample-and-hold circuit. Additionally, two of the exercises have faults incorporated in the circuit and provide you with the opportunity to troubleshoot the circuit.

ELECTRONICS WORKBENCH™ EXERCISES

1. Open the file **T8-5** on your EWB CD. Use the spectrum analyzer to determine the frequencies generated in the sampled signal. The input frequency is 5 kHz. Where did the 3-kHz signal come from?

2. Open the file **T8-6** on your EWB CD. This circuit contains a fault. Start the simulation and use the oscilloscope to isolate the fault. When you discover the fault, double-click on the component, click on the **fault** tab, and set the faults to none. Restart the simulation and see if you have repaired the circuit. Specifiy what component(s) you repaired.

3. Open the file **T8-7** on your EWB CD. This circuit contains a fault. Start the simulation and use the oscilloscope to isolate the fault. When you discover the fault, double-click on the component, click on the **fault** tab, and set the faults to none. Restart the simulation and see if you have repaired the circuit. Specifiy what component(s) you repaired.

9

TROUBLESHOOTING WITH ELECTRONICS WORKBENCH™ MULTISIM—SEQUENCE DETECTOR

In this section, we examine a circuit used to detect a unique binary data sequence. This circuit is called a sequence detector. Once the unique binary sequence is detected, an output signal is triggered. Circuits such as this one are often used in communications to detect the beginning of a serial data stream. These type of circuits are frequently discussed in digital design textbooks, and you are encouraged to refer to these texts for the steps to implement sequence detectors.

This section examines the method for testing the sample sequence generator shown in Fig T9-1. This circuit has been designed to detect a sequence of three consecutive 1s (1 1 1). The objective of this section is to demonstrate how to test the sequence detector circuit using the Multisim Word Generator and Logic Analyzer.

To begin, open the Multisim file **Fig T9-1** using Electronics Workbench™ Multisim. The circuit should look similar to Figure T9-1 except the word generator is labeled XWG1 and the logic analyzer is labeled XLA1. Double-click on the word generator to open its control panel. An example of the window displayed is provided in Figure T9-2. The Multisim word generator provides for 32-bit words to be programmed into the generator. Over 16,000 32-bit numbers can be entered. In this case we will be using only the first data bit (D0) for the simulation of a serial data stream so the en-

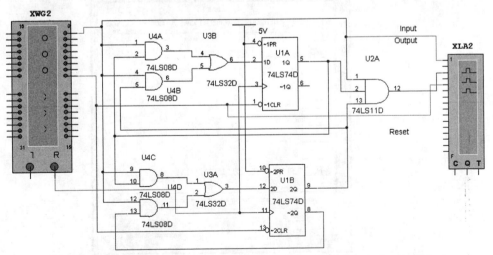

FIGURE T9-1 A "1 1 1" sequence detector circuit as implemented in Electronics Workbench™ Multisim.

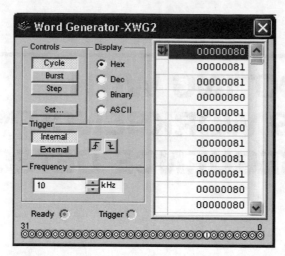

FIGURE T9-2 The control panel for the Multisim word generator.

tries shown will have data values only in the D0 position. The data values displayed are in hexadecimal. The 80_H translates to 1000000 in binary. The 81_H translates to 10000001.

There are several options for running the simulation. The option selected in Figure T9-2 is the cycle. This mode will run the simulation through the entire set of more than 16,000 data values. Another useful option is the step. In this mode, the simulation will proceed one clock cycle at a time. In this mode, clicking on the Multisim pause button will let the simulation proceed for one more clock cycle.

Double-click on the logic analyzer icon to display the selected traces from the sequence detector. Start the simulation and let the simulation fill the logic analyzer's screen. You should see an image similar to that shown in Figure T9-3. You should also see the input data, the output, the reset pulse, and the internal clock (clock). The traces have been relabeled in Figure T9-3.

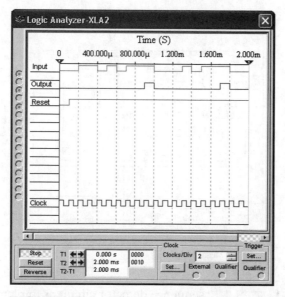

FIGURE T9-3 The simulation results as displayed by the Multisim logic analyzer.

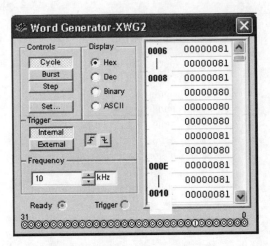

FIGURE T9-4 The two sets of three consecutive 1s in the Multisim simulation.

Notice that the sequence detector has detected the presence of two occurrences of three consecutive 1s. Careful examination of the word generator file shows that three consecutive 1s appear beginning at 0006–0008 and again at 000E–0010. This is shown in Figure T9-4.

This exercise has demonstrated how to use the Multisim word generator and the logic analyzer for examining the traces from a sequence detector circuit. The following Electronic Workbench™ Multisim exercises will also investigate your understanding of the material presented in this section.

ELECTRONIC WORKBENCH™ EXERCISES

1. Open the Multisim file **Fig T9-1** and determine if another sequence of three consecutive 1s appears in the simulation. (data sequence 0025–0027)

2. Open the Multisim file **T9-5** and determine if the circuit is working properly. If it is not, determine which circuit has a fault. Correct the fault and verify that the circuit is working properly.

3. Open the Multisim file **T9-6** and determine if the circuit is working properly. If it is not, find and correct the fault.

10

TROUBLESHOOTING WITH ELECTRONICS WORKBENCH™ MULTISIM—BPSK TRANSMIT-RECEIVE CIRCUIT

This chapter presented techniques for encoding digital data for transmission. In this exercise, you will have the opportunity to use Electronics Workbench™ Multisim to gain a better understanding of several important communication building blocks, including generation of a BPSK signal, a coherent carrier recovery circuit, a mixer, and recovering a BPSK encoded signal. The circuit used in this example is shown in Figure T10-1.

To begin this exercise, open the file **Fig T10-1** on your EWB Multisim CD. This circuit contains a BPSK generating circuit and a receiver based on the block diagrams provided in Figs. 10-5 and 10-6.

A 1-kHz sine wave is used to simulate the carrier frequency. The 1-kHz sine wave is fed to an inverting operational amplifier with a gain of −1. The op amp provides a 180° phase shift of the sine wave. This result is shown in Figure T10-2.

Both phases of the sine-wave signal are fed into a 1-of-2 selector constructed with two analog switches. The control of the analog switches is provided by a 500-Hz square wave, which is used to represent the digital data. In this case, the digital data is an alternating 1 0 pattern. The square wave is inverted by the 74HC04 inverter, and the inverted and noninverted signals are used to select which phase is being output. Start the simulation and view the output of the BPSK generating circuit with oscilloscope XCS1. Notice that the phase is alternating, based on which analog switch is selected.

The BPSK generated signal is next input into a BPSK receiver that consists of a coherent carrier recovery circuit, a mixer or multiplier stage, and a low-pass filter. This circuit is discussed in Sec. 10-2 in the text. The BPSK received signal is connected to both inputs of a multiplier stage. The purpose of this circuit is to square the input signal so that only a $+\sin 2\nu t$ term is created. The $+\sin 2\nu t$ term indicates that the new signal, which is twice the original frequency, has been created and the new signal does not alternate-phase. Connect the oscilloscope to the output of the multiplier and you will observe that a 2-kHz signal has been generated. Why was a 2-kHz signal created? Recall that $(\sin A) \times (\sin B) = 0.5 \cos(A - B) - 0.5 \cos(A + B)$. For this example, the $A - B$ term (1 kHz − 1 kHz) will go to zero, whereas the $A + B$ term will equal 2 kHz.

The output of the multiplier is fed to a voltage-controlled oscillator, which has been set to output a 1-kHz signal. This circuit is being used to simulate a phase-locked-loop circuit, where the internal VCO on the PLL phase-locks to the 2-kHz signal and the output is preset to generate a 1-kHz sine wave.

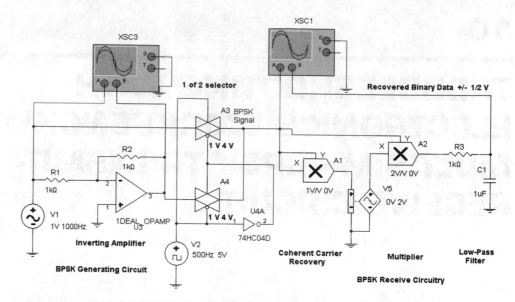

FIGURE T10-1 A BPSK transmit-receive circuit as implemented in Electronics WorkbenchTM Multisim.

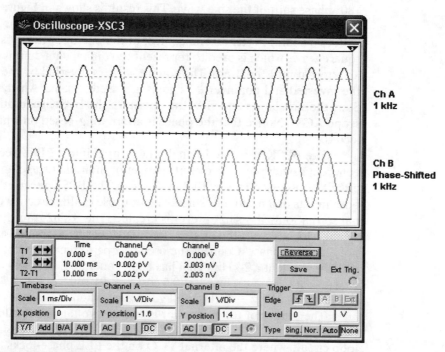

FIGURE T10-2 The phase relationship for the input and output of an inverting amplifier.

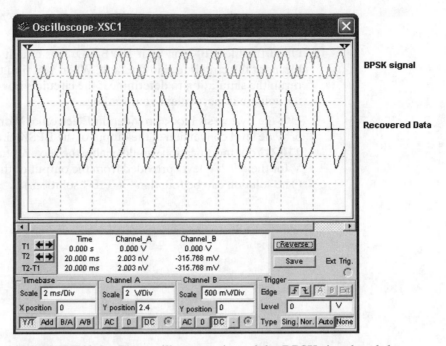

FIGURE T10-3 The oscilloscope view of the BPSK signal and the recovered data.

The recovered carrier and the BPSK signal are both input into a multiplier. Once again, this is a (sin A) $\times$ (sin B) circuit. As mentioned in Sec. 10-2, the output of this circuit will be either

$$\sin A \times \sin A = 0.5 - 0.5\cos(2A)$$

or

$$\sin A \times -\sin A = -0.5 + 0.5\cos(2A)$$

The low-pass filter consisting of R_3 and C_1 (Figure T10-1) removes the high-frequency term, leaving only the ± 0.5-V term. This result can be viewed by connecting the oscilloscope (XSC1) to the output of the recovery circuit. Notice in Figure T10-3 that the oscilloscope is showing a ± 0.5-V output, which is exactly what was predicted. The output is changing with the change in phase of the BPSK signal.

This exercise has demonstrated how a BPSK digital communications block can be constructed and analyzed using Electronics Workbench™ Multisim. Be sure to use the oscilloscope to verify that you have gained a complete understanding of the signal path for both the generating and receiver sides of a BPSK digital communications system. You will need a thorough understanding of this circuit to complete the Electronics Workbench™ Multisim exercises in this chapter.

ELECTRONICS WORKBENCH™ EXERCISES

1. Open the file **T10-4** on your EWB CD. This circuit contains a fault. Troubleshoot the circuit to find the fault. When you find the fault, correct it and rerun the simulation to determine if the circuit is now working properly. If

it is not, then continue troubleshooting the circuit. After you are done, explain your findings.

2. Open the file **T10-5** on your EWB CD. This circuit contains a fault. Troubleshoot the circuit to find the fault. When you find the fault, correct it and rerun the simulation to determine if the circuit is now working properly. After you are done, explain your findings.

3. Use the hysteresis block provided in Electronics Workbench™ Multisim to provide level conversion of the output of the BPSK circuit provided in the file **T10-1.** Your modification should enable the receiver to output $+5.0$ V and 0.0 V for the ± 0.2-V level provided from the output of the RC (R_3 and C_1) filter. (The solution can be found in Fig T10-1 solution.)

11

TROUBLESHOOTING WITH ELECTRONICS WORKBENCH™ MULTISIM—AUDIO SIGNAL MEASUREMENTS

This exercise introduces the techniques for making audio-signal-level and distortion measurements using Electronics Workbench™ Multisim simulations. Obtaining signal-level measurements and measuring signal-path performance are common maintenance, installation, and troubleshooting practices in all areas of network communications. Communication networks require that proper signal levels are maintained to ensure minimum line distortion and crosstalk. This section examines the techniques for making dB (decibel) and THD (total harmonic distortion) measurements.

To begin the execise, open the file **Fig T11-1** on your Electronics Workbench™ Multisim CD. The circuit is shown in Figure T11-1. This circuit contains an ac signal source, a 600-Ω load, and two multimeters. Start the simulation and double-click on both multimeters. The bottom multimeter is measuring the dB level, and the top multimeter is used to measure the voltage across the load. Recall from Sec. 1-2 that 0.774 V across a 600-Ω load represents 0 dBm. The example provided in Fig. T11-1 shows a 0-dBm measurement. Note the voltage value specified on the ac voltage source. If we are measuring 0 dBm, then why isn't the value 0.774 V? Why is the level from the 0-dBm signal source set to 2.188 V? Careful examination of the circuit shows that the output impedance of the signal generator is 600 Ω. The load resistance is also 600Ω, and the combination of the two resistors forms a voltage divider of two equal-value resistors; therefore, only half of the original signal generator voltage (≈ 1.094 V) appears across the load. This still is not the expected value of 0.774 V. Why the difference? Recall that power measurements, including dB measurements, require that the ac signal be expressed in terms of its rms value. If you multiply 1.084 V by 0.707, then you will obtain the expected 0.774 V measured across the 600-Ω load, and this explains how the -0.011-(~0) dB value is obtained.

Total harmonic distortion (THD) measurements provide a measure of distortion that takes all significant harmonics into account. Electronics Workbench™ Multisim provides an instrument that measures THD. Open the file **T11-2** on your EWB CD. Double-click on the distortion analyzer. You will see an image similar to the one shown in Figure T11-3.

The distortion analyzer provides modes for measuring THD and SINAD (see Sec. 1.4 for a discussion on SINAD). This exercise focuses on the THD measurement. Notice that the control panel allows the user to specify the fundamental frequency of the signal being measured. For example, if you are measuring the THD of a 1-kHz signal, then you would set the fundamental frequency to 1 kHz. The instrument also pro-

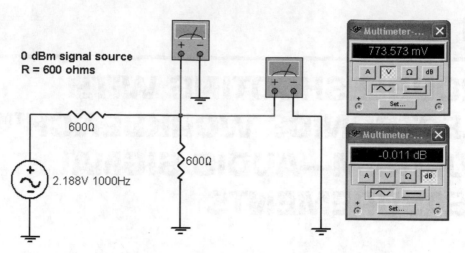

FIGURE T11-1 The Multisim circuit used to demonstrate the dB measurements.

vides for the number of harmonics being measured. Click on the set button. For this example, the number of harmonics being measured is 10.

Double-click on the waveform generator and verify that the frequency is 1 kHz and a sinusoid has been selected. Start the simulation and observe the value of the THD. You should see 0.000 percent. This is possible with an ideal sine wave that produces only the single fundamental 1-kHz frequency, but ideal function generators do not exist. Stop the simulation and change the waveform generator so that it outputs a triangle wave. Leave the frequency at 1 kHz and start the simulation. You should get a THD of ~12.05 percent. A high value for THD is expected because a triangle wave contains multiple harmonics of the fundamental frequency.

What happens if a THD measurement is taken on a 2-kHz sine wave but the instrument is set to measure a fundamental frequency of 1 kHz? Change the waveform generator back to a sinusoid but with a frequency of 2 kHz. Start the simulation and obtain a THD measurement. The instrument display will show **–E–**, which indicates a measurement error.

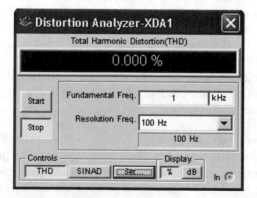

FIGURE T11-3 The display control panel for the Multisim distortion

The following Electronics Workbench™ exercises provide additional opportunities to explore the use of dB and distortion measurements to help you become more familiar with a distortion analyzer.

ELECTRONICS WORKBENCH™ EXERCISES

1. Open the file **T11-4** in your EWB CD. This circuit contains a 600-Ω audio source, a T-type attenuator, and a 600-Ω load. Measure the dB level at the output and the input and determine the amount of attenuation being provided by the attenuator.

2. Open the file **T11-5** in your EWB CD. Measure the THD introduced by the simple transmission line.

3. Open the file **T11-6** in your EWB CD. Measure the THD introduced by the sampling process. The simulation will have to run 100 ms of simulation time for the software to calculate all harmonic contributions. (6.33%).

12

TROUBLESHOOTING WITH ELECTRONICS WORKBENCH™ MULTISIM—NETWORK ANALYZER

The Smith chart was introduced in Chapter 12 of the text. In this exercise, this important impedance-calculating tool is reintroduced using Electronics Workbench™ Multisim. Multisim provides a network analyzer instrument that contains the Smith chart analysis in addition to many other useful analytical tools. A network analyzer is used to measure the parameters commonly used to characterize circuits or elements that operate at high frequencies. This exercise focuses on the Smith chart and the Z-parameter calculations. Z-parameters are the impedance values of a network expressed using its real and imaginary components. Refer to Sec. 12-8 of the text for additional Smith chart examples and a more detailed examination of their function.

Begin the exercise by opening **Fig T12-1** in your Electronics Workbench™ Multisim CD. This circuit, shown in Figure T12-1, contains a 50-Ω resistor connected to port 1 (P1) of the network analyzer, and port 2 (P2) is terminated with a 50-Ω resistor. The first circuit being examined by the network analyzer is a simple resistive cir-

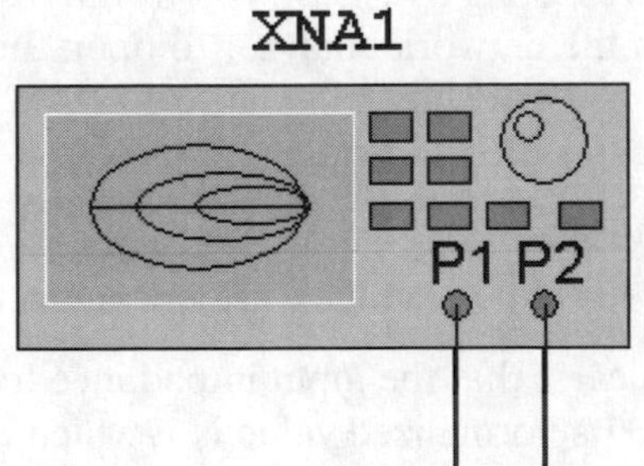

FIGURE 12-35 An example of using the Multisim Network Analyzer to analyze a 50-Ω resistor.

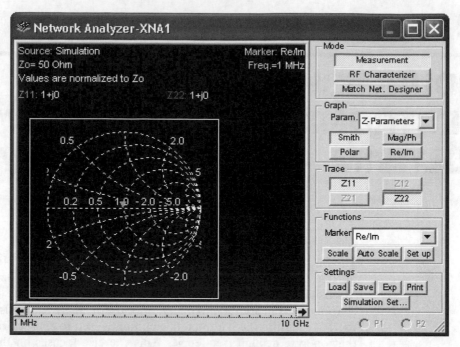

FIGURE T12-2 The Smith chart for the test of the 50-Ω resistor.

cuit. This example provides a good starting point for understanding the setup for the network analyzer and how to read the simulation results. The first circuit being tested by the network analyzer is shown in Figure T12-1.

Start the simulation. The impedance calculations performed by the network analyzer are very quick and the start-simulation button resets quickly. Before you look at the test results, predict what you will see. Based on the information you learned in Sec. 12-8 and the fact that you are testing a resistor, you would expect to see a purely resistive result. Double-click on the network analyzer to open the instrument. You should see a Smith chart similar to the one shown in Figure T12-2.

The Smith chart indicates the following:

$$Z_o = 50 \ \Omega$$
$$Z_{11} = 1 + j0 \qquad \text{Values are normalized to } Z_o$$

The value $Z_{11} = 1 + j0$ indicates that the input impedance for the network being analyzed is purely resistive and its normalized value is 1, which translates to 50 Ω. Recall that the values on a Smith chart are divided by the normalized resistance. Notice the red marker on the Smith chart located at 1.0 on the real axis. The 1.0 translates to 50 Ω, and this value is obtained by multiplying the Smith chart measured resistance of 1 Ω by the characteristic impedance of 50 Ω to obtain the actual resistance measured. In this case, the computed resistance is 50 Ω.

The frequency at which this calculation was made is shown in the upper-right corner of the Smith chart screen. In this case, a frequency of 1.0 MHz was used. Immediately to the right of the frequency is a slider that can be used to select the frequency being used to determine the impedance. Move the slider from one end to the other to see how the impedance values change through the frequency range. The frequency range is set by clicking on the **Set-up** button next to the Measurement mode at the bottom right of the network analyzer screen. Double-click on the **Set-up** button to check the settings. You will notice the following:

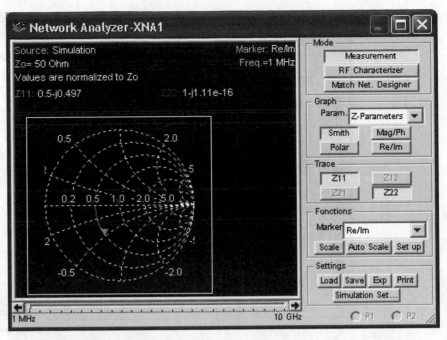

FIGURE T12-4 The Smith chart result for the simple *RC* network.

Start frequency	1 MHz
Stop frequency	10 GHz
Sweep type	Decade
Number of points per decade	25
Characteristic impedance Z_o	50 Ω

The start and stop frequencies provide control of the frequency range when testing a network. The sweep type can be either decade or linear, but decade is used most of the time. The number of points per decade enables the user to control the resolution of the plotted trace displayed, and the characteristic impedance Z_o provides for user control of the normalizing impedance.

The next two Multisim exercises provide examples of using the Multisim network analyzer to compute the impedances of simple *RC* and *RL* networks. These exercises will help you better understand the Smith chart results when analyzing complex impedances. Open the file **T12-3** in your EWB CD. This example contains a simple *RC* network of $R = 25$ Ω and $C = 6.4$ nF. The network analyzer is set to analyze the frequencies from 1 MHz to 100 MHz. The results of the simulation are shown in Figure T12-4. At 1 MHz, the normalized input impedance to the *RC* network shows that $Z_{11} = 0.5 - j0.497$. Multiplying these values by the normalized impedance of 50 Ω yields a *Z* of approximately $25 - j25$, which is the expected value for this *RC* network at 1 MHz.

Next, open the file **T12-5** in your EWB CD. This example contains a simple *RL* network of $R = 25$ Ω and $L = 4$ μH. The network analyzer is set to analyze the frequencies from 1 MHz to 10 GHz. The results of the simulation are shown in Figure T12-6. At 1 MHz, the normalized input impedance to the *RL* network shows that $Z_{11} = 0.5 + j0.5$. Multiplying these values by the normalized impedance of 50 Ω yields $Z = 25 + j25$, which is the expected value for this *RL* network at 1 MHz.

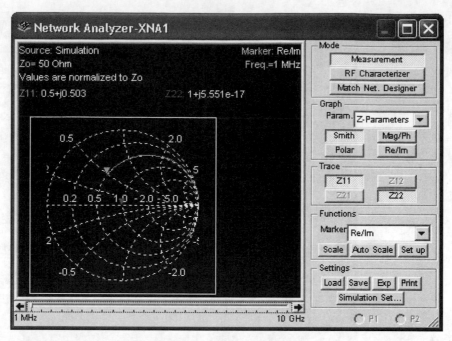

FIGURE T12-6 The Smith chart result for the simple *RL* network.

The following Electronics Workbench™ Multisim exercises provide additional experience with using the Multisim network analyzer and analyzing the results displayed on the Smith chart.

ELECTRONICS WORKBENCHTM EXERCISES

1. Open the file **T12-7** on your EWB CD. Determine the impedance of this *RC* network at 10 MHz. ($Z = 25 - j1.59$)

2. Open the file **T12-8** on your EWB CD. Determine the impedance of this *RL* network at 1 GHz and 10 GHz. *Note:* Don't forget to multiply the impedance displayed on the network analyzer by the characteristic impedance.

3. Open the file **T12-9** on your EWB CD. Use the Smith chart to determine the resonant frequency of the network. *Hint:* At resonance, a series *RLC* circuit will be resistive only. You must open the setup on the network analyzer to change the start frequency and improve the resolution of the plotted values by changing the number of points per decade to 50 so you can see at what frequency the impedance curve passes through the real axis. ($f = 50.322$ kHz)

13

TROUBLESHOOTING WITH ELECTRONICS WORKBENCH™ MULTISIM—CRYSTALS AND CRYSTAL OSCILLATORS

In this exercise, we investigate the simulation of crystals and crystal oscillators using Electronics Workbench™ Multisim. Crystals are used when greater frequency stability is required than that provided by LC oscillators. Chapter 13, of the text, focused primarily on the concepts of radio-wave propagation and the effects propagation has on the different frequencies. This is a good opportunity to explore the components used to generate these different frequencies.

The first exercise investigates the property of a crystal. Crystals and crystal oscillators were first introduced in Chapter 1 of the text, where it was mentioned that a crystal can be modeled as a series *RLC* resonant circuit with a very high Q. Refer to Fig. 1-26 in the text for a drawing of the electrical equivalent circuit of a crystal. Open the file **Fig T13-1** on your EWB Multisim CD. This circuit contains a crystal connected to the Bode plotter, a signal source, and 1-k Ω termination. The circuit is shown in Figure T13-1.

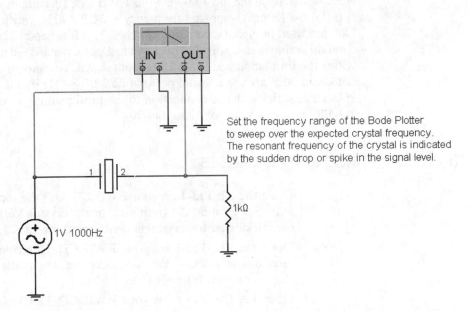

Set the frequency range of the Bode Plotter to sweep over the expected crystal frequency. The resonant frequency of the crystal is indicated by the sudden drop or spike in the signal level.

FIGURE T13-1   The test circuit for the crystal oscillator using EWB Multisim.

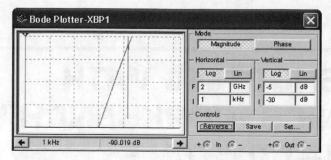

FIGURE T13-2   The frequency sweep of a crystal under test.

Recall from Chapter 1 that at the series resonant point, the crystal should have a very low resistance, whereas at other frequencies, the crystal impedance should be quite high. Based on this information, the Bode plotter provided by Multisim can be used to provide a frequency sweep of the crystal using the test circuit provided. At resonance, we should see a change or disturbance in the output response. The frequency of the crystal is not listed on the circuit, so make sure the range for the Bode plotter has been set to sweep a wide frequency range. For this example, the initial (*I*) frequency is 1 kHz and the final (*F*) frequency is 2 GHz.

Start the simulation and view the frequency-sweep results by double-clicking on the Bode plotter instrument. You should see an image similar to that shown in Figure T13-2. Move the cursor so that you can measure the frequency of the disturbance in the frequency sweep. You will find that the disturbance in the frequency sweep is at about 15 MHz. Double-click on the crystal. You should see that the crystal's frequency value is 15 MHz. Click on **Edit Model** to view how the crystal is being modeled by Multisim. The crystal is modeled by a series *LCR* circuit that is defined by the circuit nodes and the component values consisting of LS 0.005, CS 2.2e-014, and RS 210, and a parallel capacitance CO 5e-012. You can use these values to verify that the resonant frequency of the model is 15 MHz.

Next, open the file **T13-3** in your EWB CD. This circuit is an example of a Pierce crystal oscillator. The crystal frequency is 32.768 kHz, which is a common clock frequency used in digital clocks and watches. This frequency, 32.768 kHz, is equal to 2^{15}, and this value is easily divided by down to 1 pulse per second using digital logic circuits. Start the simulation and check the output signal. You should see a wave with a period of about 30.5 μS, which is the period of a 32.768-kHz signal. The RFC (RF choke) is placed in series with the connection to the power supply to minimize the coupling of oscillator noise to the power supply.

ELECTRONICS WORKBENCH™ EXERCISES

1. Open the file **T13-4** on your EWB CD. Use the technique described in the text to determine the frequency of the crystal. Verify your answer by double-clicking on the crystal and viewing the values.

2. Open the file **T13-5** on your EWB CD. Determine if the Pierce crystal oscillator is working properly. Correct any faults and retest the circuit. Report on your findings.

3. Open the file **T13-6** on your EWB CD. Determine if the Pierce crystal oscillator is working properly. Correct any faults and retest the circuit. Report on your findings.

14

TROUBLESHOOTING WITH ELECTRONICS WORKBENCH™ MULTISIM—DIPOLE ANTENNA SIMULATION AND MEASUREMENTS

The basic concepts of antennas were introduced in this chapter. A fundamental antenna that you should understand is the dipole. This exercise further investigates the half-wave dipole using the Multisim tools by incorporating the use of the network analyzer. Begin the exercise by opening **Fig T14-1** on your EWB Multisim CD. This circuit is shown in Figure T14-1.

This circuit contains a model of a 100-MHz half-wave dipole. This 100-MHz frequency is in the middle of the FM radio band. The operational characteristics of a half-wave dipole were discussed in Sec. 14-2. The 73-Ω resistor is used to model the radiation resistance of the dipole, whereas the 1-mH inductor and 2.5-pF capacitor were selected so that the resonant frequency of the antenna model is approximately 100 MHz. A network analyzer is connected to the model of the dipole for analyzing the antenna's characteristics.

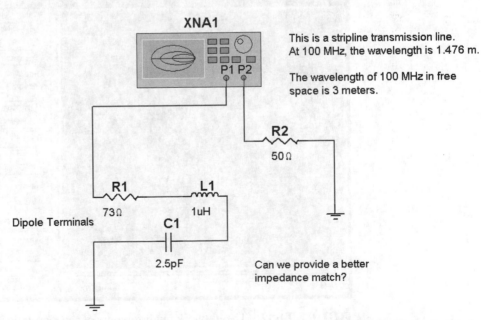

FIGURE T14-1   The Multisim circuit for modeling a 100-MHz half-wave dipole.

Before you start the simulation, double-click on the network analyzer and click on the **Setup** button next to **Measurement.** You need to set the start and stop frequencies to 90 MHz and 110 MHz, respectively. You also need to change the number of points per decade to 500. Set the characteristic impedance of the network analyzer to 50 Ω. Click **OK** to close the **Measurement setup** window. What do you expect to see on the Smith chart when the simulation is performed? At the resonant frequency of 100 MHz, you should expect the plot of the antenna on the chart to show a real or resistive component of 73 Ω, whereas frequencies above and below 100 MHz will show that the dipole is reactive. Start the simulation and view the results. You should see a display similar to that shown in Figure T14-2. Use the slider to adjust the frequency to 100 MHz. In the example shown, the normalized input impedance is $Z_{11} = 1.46 \times j$ 0.0354 at 100.5177 MHz. Multiplying gives $1.46 \times 50 = 73$ Ω, which is the characteristic impedance of the half-wave dipole. The reactive term $j0.0354$ is nearly zero, as expected.

What would need to be done if a better impedance match were needed? The next example demonstrates how a single stub tuner can be used to provide a better impedance match to an antenna. Open the file **Fig T14-3** on your EWB CD. The dipole circuit previously analyzed has been modified to include a single stub tuner. The model of the transmission line is provided by the Multisim stripline transmission line element. The dielectric constant of the stripline is $\epsilon_r = 4.13$, which results in a wavelength of 1.476 meters at 100 MHz. The wavelength of 100 MHz in free space is 3 meters. The circuit is shown in Figure T14-3. You need to double-click on the network analyzer, change the frequency range to (90 to 110) MHz, and change the number of points per decade to 500 points to get a smooth plot.

In real applications, adjusting the stub tuner is a mechanical adjustment; however, in this exercise the adjustment is provided through varying the model characteristics of the transmission line. Double-click on the ground leg of the stub tuner. You should see a menu for the **strip_line.** Click on the **Value** tab and then click on **Edit**

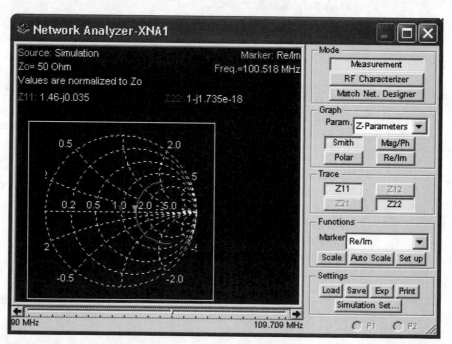

FIGURE T14-2   The network analyzer view of the simulation of a 100-MHz half-wave dipole.

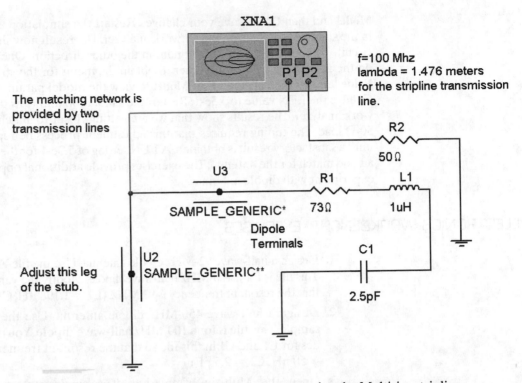

FIGURE T14-3 The model of a single stub tuner using the Multisim stripline transmission-line elements.

Model. You will see a screen image like the one in Fig. T14-4. These are the model parameters for the stripline.

To begin the tuning, make a small change to the LEN value in the model. This change effectively changes the length of the stub tuner. Remember, the wavelength of 100 MHz in the stripline is 1.476 meters. Change the value to 4.0e-1; click on **Change Part**

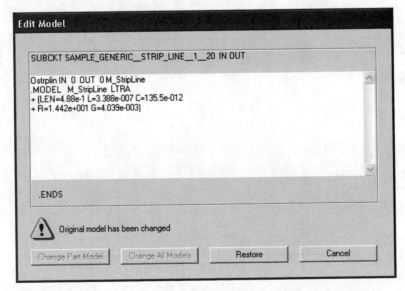

FIGURE T14-4 The model screen for the stripline element.

Model and then **OK** to save your changes. Restart the simulation and view the changes in the simulation results on the network analyzer. The result now shows a very inductive circuit. You need to try the adjustment in the other direction. Once again, double-click on the ground leg of the stub tuner to obtain the menu for the **strip_line.** Click on the **Value** tab and then click on **Edit Model** to view the model parameters for the stripline. Change the LEN value to 5.5e-1. Restart the simulation and view the results on the network analyzer. The results show that we are getting closer to matching the antenna to a 50-Ω load. The tuning requires that this adjustment process be repeated several times until a satisfactory result is obtained. A LEN setting of 5.3e-1 for the ground leg provides a good match for the antenna. The exercises provide additional opportunities for you to experiment with dipole antennas.

ELECTRONICS WORKBENCH™ EXERCISES

1. Design a half-wave 92-MHz dipole antenna. Use the file **Fig T14-1** as a sample. This file is for a 100-MHz half-wave dipole. Modify the values for L1 and C1 so that the resonant frequency is 92 MHz. (L1 = 1.198 μH, C1 = 2.5 pF)

2. Design a half-wave 450-MHz dipole antenna. Use the file **Fig T14-1** as a sample. This file is for a 100-MHz half-wave dipole. You must modify the values for L1 and C1 in this file so that the resonant frequency is 450 MHz. (L1 = 50 nH, C1 = 2.5 pF)

3. Open the Multisim simulation of a single stub tuner found in the **T14-5** file found in your EWB CD. Use the technique presented in the text to provide a match for this 100-MHz dipole antenna.

15

TROUBLESHOOTING WITH ELECTRONICS WORKBENCH™ MULTISIM—LOSSY TRANSMISSION LINES AND LOW-LOSS WAVEGUIDE

This Multisim exercise explores the properties of a lossy transmission line and a low-loss waveguide. Begin the exercise by opening **Fig T15-1** in your EWB Multisim CD. This circuit contains a sample waveguide attached to the network analyzer. The circuit is shown in Figure T15-1. Both ends of the waveguide are connected to the ports of the network analyzer. What results do you expect to see from the network analyzer?

Before starting the simulation, click on the network analyzer and change the number of points per decade to 200, the start frequency to 1 GHz, and the stop frequency to 10 GHz. This change provides a smoother plot of the simulation results and a realistic frequency range. Start the simulation and view the results on the network analyzer. You should see a result similar to the one shown in Figure T15-2.

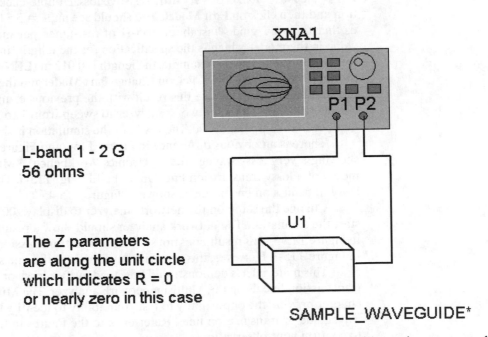

XNA1

L-band 1 - 2 G
56 ohms

The Z parameters
are along the unit circle
which indicates R = 0
or nearly zero in this case

U1

SAMPLE_WAVEGUIDE*

FIGURE T15-1   The circuit example of a low-loss waveguide section connected to a network analyzer.

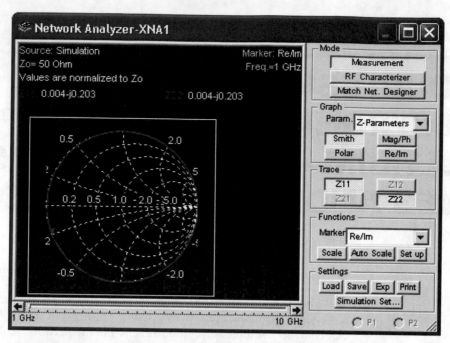

FIGURE T15-2 The simulation of a low-loss waveguide as viewed with the network analyzer.

The plot of the data is along the outside perimeter of the Smith chart, as it is in Figure T15-2. This indicates that the line is low-loss. Move the frequency marker on the network analyzer to 1 GHz. The input impedance of the waveguide at 1 GHz is $Z_{11} = 0.0040 - j0.203$ or very little resistive loss. Double-click on the waveguide section and then click on **Edit Model.** You should see an R = 5.543e-001, which is telling us that this waveguide has about 0.55-Ω of resistance per meter. Look at the **LEN** value in the model, which is the specification for the length (in meters) of the section we are analyzing. For this example, the length is 0.012 m (**LEN = 1.200e-002**). Change the value of LEN to 1.200. Click on **Change Part Model** and then click on **OK.** Restart the simulation and compare this result with the previous example. You may need to change the setup on the network analyzer to sweep from 1 to 2 GHz and change the number of data points to 800. The result of the simulation is shown in Figure T15-3.

There is an obvious difference in Figure T15-2and Figure T15-3. Figure T15-3 is showing a very lossy waveguide. Electronics Workbench™ Multisim also provides a model of a lossy transmission line. Open the file **Fig. T15-4.** The new circuit with the lossy transmission line model is shown in Figure T15-4.

Change the setup on the network analyzer to display 200 points per decade and start the simulation. The network analyzer should show a result similar to that shown in Figure T15-5. This result does not show as lossy a transmission line as the one shown in Figure T15-3. However, this result is not as good as the one shown in Figure T15-2.

This material has demonstrated how to identify a lossy or low-loss waveguide or transmission line using the Multisim network analyzer. The Multisim exercises in this chapter provide the opportunity to test your ability to identify these characteristics in waveguide or transmission lines. Refer back to the figures in this example as needed to confirm your observations.

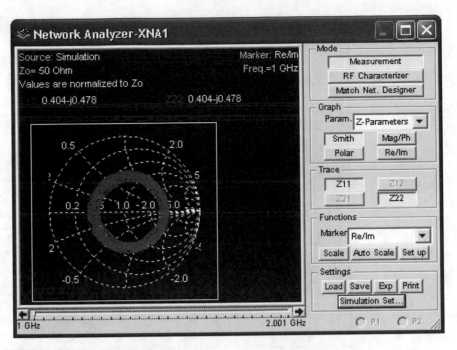

FIGURE T15-3 The simulation of a very lossy waveguide.

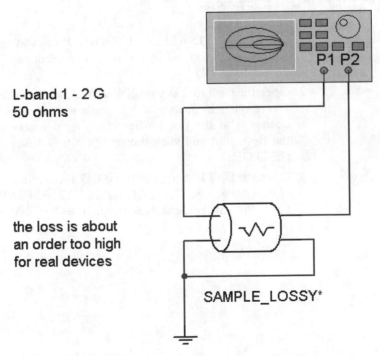

L-band 1 - 2 G
50 ohms

the loss is about
an order too high
for real devices

SAMPLE_LOSSY*

FIGURE T15-4 An example of a test on the Multisim sample lossy transmission line.

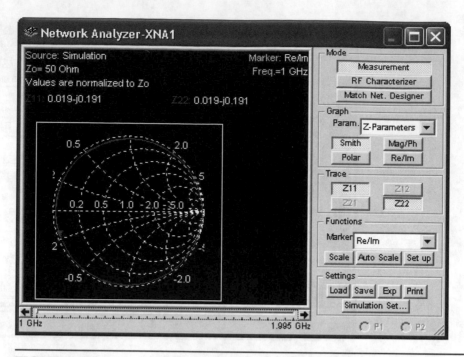

FIGURE T15-5 The simulation results of the lossy transmission line provided by EWB Multisim.

ELECTRONICS WORKBENCH™ EXERCISES

1. Open the file **T15-6** in your EWB CD. Three waveguides are shown. Use the techniques described in the text to determine which waveguide has the greatest loss. (B)

2. Open the file **T15-7** in your EWB CD. Use the Bode plotter to determine the first resonant frequency of the sample waveguide. *Hint:* The first resonant frequency is at the point where the signal reaches a maximum level. Run the Bode plot and view the results. You will see the first maximum point. (1.123 GHz)

3. Open the file **T15-8** in your EWB CD. Determine the normalized impedance of the waveguide at 1.122 GHz and at 225.16 MHz. What would you conclude about the waveguide at these frequencies? ($0.0100 - j0.0081, 0.074 - j3.487$)

16

TROUBLESHOOTING WITH ELECTRONICS WORKBENCH™ MULTISIM—CHARACTERISTICS OF HIGH-FREQUENCY DEVICES

The concept of microwave devices has been introduced in this chapter. This exercise is used to explore the characteristics of microwave devices, including the RF capacitor, the RF inductor, and the RF transistor. To begin the exercise, open the file **Fig T16-1** in your EWB Multisim CD. This file contains three circuits. Circuit A contains an ideal capacitor with a value of 0.3223 pF, whereas circuit B contains an RF capacitor of the same value. The circuit is shown in Figure T16-1. The last circuit is a component view of the model of an RF capacitor.

A Bode plotter instrument has been connected to each RC circuit and each is terminated with a 1-kΩ resistor. Start the simulation and compare the results of the two Bode plots. The Bode plots are shown in Figure T16-2. The top plot is for the ideal capacitor, whereas the bottom plot is for the RF capacitor.

The Bode plot for the ideal capacitor (circuit A) shows that it passes all frequencies above 500 MHz. This is ideal but not realistic. The RF model (circuit B) shows that at very low frequencies, the signal is attenuated by the capacitor, as ex-

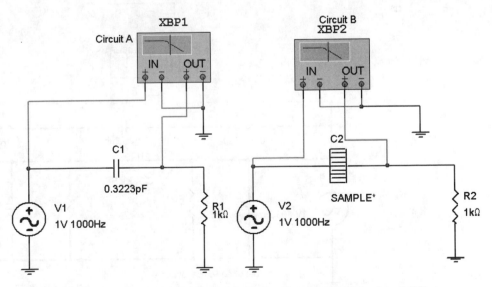

FIGURE T16-1 The simulation circuit for comparing the ideal and RF capacitors.

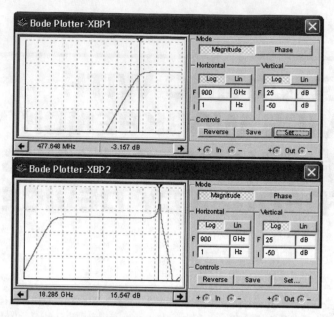

FIGURE T16-2   The Bode plots for the ideal and RF capacitors.

pected. At high frequencies, the signal has a flat response until about 11 GHz, which is the resonant frequency of the capacitor. To have a resonant frequency implies that the capacitor has an inductance. In fact, all components have resistance, capacitance, and inductance, but most of these characteristics are not significant unless you are operating the circuit at high frequencies. The component view of the RF model for a capacitor is provided in **Fig T16-1.** The circuit is also provided in Figure T16-3.

The RF capacitor is quite complex at high frequencies, as can be seen by the model. The model shows that the RF capacitor is resistive and inductive, in addition to being capacitive. This is an important concept to remember, especially when you are

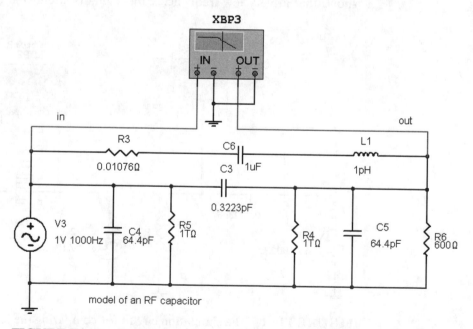

FIGURE T16-3   The component view of the model for an RF capacitor.

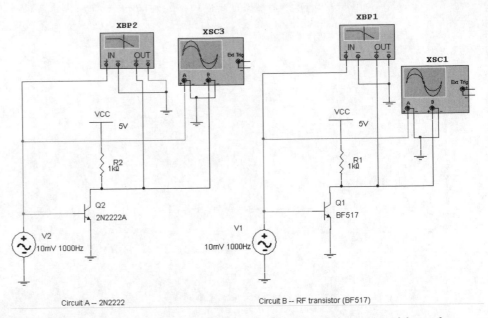

FIGURE T16-4 The example amplifier circuits that incorporate either a low-frequency or a high-frequency RF transistor.

working with high-frequency circuits. Even a simple test lead can alter the tuning of a high-frequency circuit.

The next exercise examines the characteristics of an RF amplifier. Open **Fig T16-4** in your EWB CD. This circuit contains two simple BJT common emitter amplifiers. A 2N2222 BJT transistor is used in circuit A; a BF517 RF transistor is used in circuit B. The circuit is shown in Figure T16-4. Start the simulation and verify that each amplifier is working. Use the oscilloscope to verify proper operation. You should observe gain and you should see a 180° phase inversion of the signal from input to output.

Next, generate Bode plots for each circuit. You will see that the circuit containing the 2N2222 transistor (circuit A) has a 3-dB upper cutoff frequency of about 35.5 MHz, whereas circuit B, which is using the BF517 RF transistor, has a 3-dB upper cutoff frequency of about 240 MHz. This demonstrates the vast improvement in the frequency response of an amplifier with the use of an RF circuit.

The following exercises provide you with an opportunity to explore the characteristics of an RF inductor and troubleshoot an RF amplifier.

ELECTRONICS WORKBENCH™ EXERCISES

1. Open the file **T16-5** in your EWB CD. This circuit provides a comparison of an ideal and an RF inductor. Determine the upper 3-dB cutoff frequencies for the inductors. (160 kHz, approx. 1.5 GHz)

2. Open the file **T16-6** in your EWB CD. Determine the resonant frequency of this dipole antenna. ($f = 1.071$ GHz).

3. Open the file **T16-7** in your EWB CD. Determine if the RF amplifier is working properly. If it isn't, locate and correct the fault and retry the simulation. Report on your findings.

17

TROUBLESHOOTING WITH ELECTRONICS WORKBENCH™ MULTISIM—THE NTSC TELEVISION SPECTRA

This Electronics Workbench™ Multisim exercise provides an opportunity to use a spectrum analyzer to view the UHF television spectrum. Begin the exercise by opening **Fig T17-1** on your EWB Multisim CD. The circuit is shown in Figure T17-1.

This circuit is used to demonstrate the frequency spectra for an NTSC television signal. The NTSC frequency spectra includes a visual carrier and an aural carrier. Double-click on the AM and FM sources to view the settings. The amplitude modulated visual carrier frequency has been set to 519.25 MHz. The aural carrier is a frequency-modulated signal, and the carrier frequency is 523.75 MHz. These are the visual and

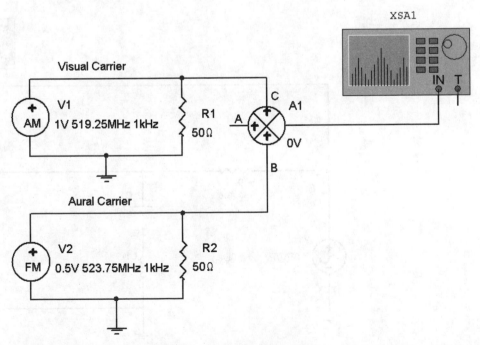

FIGURE T17-1 The Electronics Workbench™ Multisim circuit used to simulate the frequency spectra for a UHF television signal.

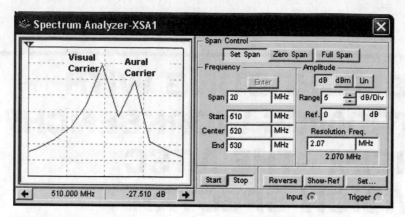

FIGURE T17-2 The Electronics Workbench™ simulation of the frequency spectra for a channel 22 television signal.

aural carriers for channel 22 in the UHF television spectrum. The two carriers are connected by a summing amplifier. The combined signal, as viewed by the spectrum analyzer, is shown in Figure T17-2. The visual carrier is shown on the left, and the aural carrier is shown on the right. Use the cursor to verify the center frequency for each carrier.

Next, open the **Fig T17-3** circuit on your EWB CD. This is called a bandstop, or wavetrap, and it is commonly used to attenuate a narrow band of frequencies. This is an example of a series resonant circuit similar to the example shown in Fig. 17-13(a). The EWB Multisim circuit is shown in Figure T17-3.

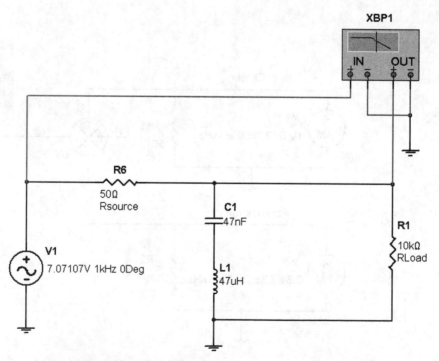

FIGURE T17-3 The Electronics Workbench™ Multisim circuit of a high-Q bandstop circuit, or wavetrap.

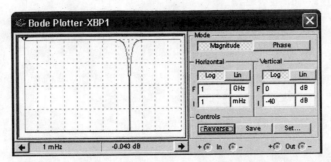

FIGURE T17-4 The Bode plotter output for the wavetrap filter.

Start the simulation and observe the output from the Bode plotter. This circuit provides more than 60 dB of attenuation at 107 kHz. Use the cursor to verify this measurement. You can also use the cursor to obtain the 3-dB corner frequencies, which are 53.7 kHz and 218.7 kHz. The output of the Bode plotter is shown in Figure T17-4.

How would the degradation of one of the filter components affect the frequency response? Open the file **T17-5** on your EWB CD. Start the simulation and observe the output of the Bode plotter. Is this circuit functioning properly? If not, troubleshoot the circuit to determine the problem. You will find that L_1 is defective. Can you explain why the Bode plot looks like it does? If the inductor, L_1, is leaky or partially shorted, then at high frequencies the inductor appears as a short or a low impedance instead of being reactive. Remember, for a properly functioning inductor, the inductive reactance increases ($X_L = 2\pi f L$) as the frequency increases. This explains why the output is severely attenuated at high frequencies.

ELECTRONICS WORKBENCH™ EXERCISES

1. Open the file **T17-6** in your EWB CD. Determine the center frequencies for the visual and aural carriers. Verify your results with the spectrum analyzer. What frequency band and television channel is this? (67.25 MHz, 71.75 MHz, VHF, channel 4)

2. Open the file **T17-7** in your EWB CD. Determine if the filter circuit is working properly. If the circuit is not working, troubleshoot it and correct the problem.

3. Open the file **T17-8** in your EWB CD. Determine if the filter circuit is working properly. If the circuit is not working, troubleshoot it and correct the problem. Explain why this type of failure might have caused the problem.

18

TROUBLESHOOTING WITH ELECTRONICS WORKBENCH™ MULTISIM—LIGHT BUDGET SIMULATION

The concept of preparing a system design for a fiber installation was presented in this chapter. This section presents a simulation exercise of a system design. Open the file **Fig T18-1** on your EWB Multisim CD. This exercise provides you with the opportunity to study a fiber-optic system design in more depth. The circuit for the light-budget simulation is shown in Figure T18-1.

Electronics Workbench™ Multisim does not contain simulation models or instruments for lightwave communications, but with a little creativity, a system design for a fiber installation can be modeled. This example is patterned after Fig. 18-23. The function generator models the output of a fiber-optic transmitter. The generator is outputting a square wave to model the pulsing of light. The settings for the function generator for three possible operating levels have been provided.

1. The maximum received signal level (RSL): −27 dBm
2. The designed operating level: −31.6 dBm
3. The minimum received signal level (RSL) for a BER of 10^{-9}: −40 dBm

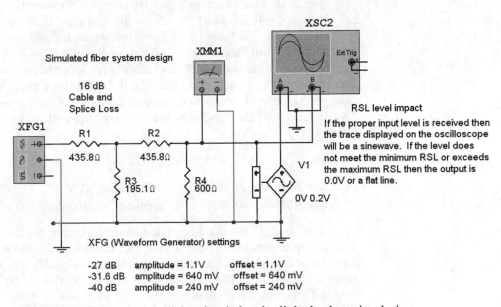

FIGURE T18-1 The Multisim circuit for the light-budget simulation.

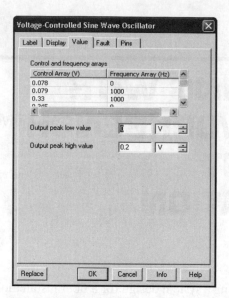

FIGURE T18-2 The settings for the voltage-controlled sine-wave generator that is being used to model an optical receiver with a minimum and maximum RSL.

A 16-dB T-type attenuator has been provided to simulate the fiber cable and splice loss. The system is terminated with a 600-Ω resistor for consistency with the analog model, but this resistor does not exist in a real optical system. A voltage-controlled sine-wave oscillator has been provided to simulate the optical receiver. The settings for the voltage-controlled sine-wave oscillator are shown in Figure T18-2. Double-click on the voltage-controlled sine-wave oscillator to view or change the settings. These settings for the voltage-controlled sine-wave oscillator provide for a sine-wave output as long as the received signal level is within the −40-dB to −27-dB operating range. If the input level falls outside this range, then the oscillator outputs a flat line.

Verify that the function generator is set for an amplitude of 640 mV and an off-set voltage of 640 mV. Start the simulation and view the level on the multimeter and the traces on the oscilloscope. The multimeter should show a −31.6-dB level, and the oscilloscope should show a pulse signal on channel B, which is the input to the volt-age-controlled sine-wave oscillator. Channel A is connected to the output of the volt-age-controlled sine-wave oscillator, and it should show a sine wave. Change the function generator levels to the maximum and minimum receive signal levels (RSLs) of − 27 dBm and −40 dBm and view the output of the voltage-controlled sine-wave oscillator.

Settings

maximum RSL = −27 dBm	amplitude = 1.1 V mV	offset = 1.1 V mV
minimum RSL = −40 dBm	amplitude = 240 mV	offset = 1.1 V

You should see a flat line on the channel A trace for both cases, which indicates that the input signal level does not meet specifications. This example demonstrates that if the input level does not meet the required input signal level specification (RSL), then some information will be lost due to an increase in the bit error rate (BER). The following Electronics Workbench™ Multisim exercises provide you with additional op-portunity to troubleshoot the fiber system model when the signal is lost. An optical time domain reflectometer (OTDR) is not available with the Multisim tools, but you can use the multimeter and the oscilloscope to measure signal levels throughout the system and verify the system for proper operation.

ELECTRONICS WORKBENCH™ EXERCISES

1. Open the file **T18-3** in your EWB CD. This is a model of the fiber system design. Determine if the system is functioning properly. If the system is not working properly, determine the cause of the fault and fix it. Rerun the simulation to verify the system is functioning properly.

2. Open the file **T18-4** in your EWB CD. This is a model of the fiber system design. Determine if the system is functioning properly. If the system is not working properly, determine the cause of the fault and fix it. Rerun the simulation to verify the system is functioning properly.

3. Open the file **T18-5** in your EWB CD. This is a model of the fiber system design. Determine if the system is functioning properly. If the system is not working properly, determine if the problem is a fault or if the problem is a system setup error. Report on your findings and return the setup levels back to proper operating points. Rerun the simulation to verify the system is functioning properly.

APPENDIX: MANUFACTURER DATA SHEETS

IRON POWDER TOROIDAL CORES

Iron Powder toroidal cores are available in numerous sizes ranging from .05 inches to more than 5 inches in outer diameter. There are two basic material groups : The Carbonyl Irons and the Hydrogen Reduced Irons.

The CARBONYL IRONS are especially noted for their stability over a wide range of temperatures and flux levels. Their permeability range is from less than 3 mu to 35 mu and can offer excellent 'Q' factors for the 50 KHz to 200 MHz frequency range. They are ideally suited for a variety of RF circuit applications where good stability and high 'Q' are essential.

The HYDROGEN REDUCED IRONS have permeabilities ranging from 35 mu to 90 mu. Somewhat lower 'Q' values can be expected from this group of cores and they are mainly used for EMI filters and low frequency chokes. In recent years they have been very much in demand for use in both input and output filters for switched-mode power supplies.

Toroidal cores, in general, are the most efficient of any core configuration. They are highly self-shielding since most of the lines of flux are contained within the toroidal form. The flux lines are essentially uniform over the entire magnetic path length and consequently stray magnetic fields will have very little effect on a toroidal inductor. It is seldom necessary to shield or isolate a toroidal inductor to prevent feedback or cross-talk. Toroidal inductors simply do not like to talk to each other.

The A_L values of Iron Powder toroidal cores will be found on the next few pages. Use these A_L values and the formula below to calculate the required number of turns for a given inductance value. The wire chart should then be consulted to determine if the required number of turns will fit on to the chosen core size.

Turns Formula

$$\text{Turns} = 100 \sqrt{\frac{\text{desired L (uh)}}{A_L \text{ (uh}/100\,t)}}$$

Key to part number

$$\underset{\text{toroid}}{T} - \underset{\text{outer-diameter}}{50} - \underset{\text{material}}{6}$$

Substantial quantities of most catalog items are maintained in stock for immediate delivery.

IRON POWDER TOROIDAL CORES
For Resonant Circuits

MATERIAL 2   Perm. 10   Freq. Range 1 - 30 MHz   Color code - Red

Core number \/	O.D. (inches)	I.D. (inches)	Hgt. (inches)	I_e (cm)	A_e (cm)^2	V_e (cm)^3	A_L Value uh/100 turns
T-12-2	.125	.062	.050	0.74	.010	.007	20
T-16-2	.160	.078	.060	0.95	.016	.015	22
T-20-2	.200	.088	.070	1.15	.025	.029	27
T-25-2	.255	.120	.096	1.50	.042	.063	34
T-30-2	.307	.151	.128	1.83	.065	.119	43
T-37-2	.375	.205	.128	2.32	.070	.162	40
T-44-2	.440	.229	.159	2.67	.107	.286	52
T-50-2	.500	.303	.190	3.03	.121	.367	49
T-68-2	.690	.370	.190	4.24	.196	.831	57
T-80-2	.795	.495	.250	5.15	.242	1.246	55
T-94-2	.942	.560	.312	6.00	.385	2.310	84
T-106-2	1.060	.570	.437	6.50	.690	4.485	135
T-130-2	1.300	.780	.437	8.29	.730	6.052	110
T-157-2	1.570	.950	.570	10.05	1.140	11.457	140
T-184-2	1.840	.950	.710	11.12	2.040	22.685	240
T-200-2	2.000	1.250	.550	12.97	1.330	17.250	120
T-200A-2	2.000	1.250	1.000	12.97	2.240	29.050	218
T-225 -2	2.250	1.405	.550	14.56	1.508	21.956	120
T-225A-2	2.250	1.485	1.000	14.56	2.730	39.749	215
T-300 -2	3.058	1.925	.500	19.83	1.810	35.892	800
T-300A-2	3.048	1.925	1.000	19.83	3.580	70.991	228
T-400 -2	4.000	2.250	.650	24.93	3.660	91.244	180
T-400A-2	4.000	2.250	1.300	24.93	7.432	185.280	360
T-520 -2	5.200	3.080	.800	33.16	5.460	181.000	207

MATERIAL 3   Perm 35   Freq. Range .05 -.5 MHz   Color code - Gray

Core number \/	O.D. (inches)	I.D. (inches)	Hgt. (inches)	I_e (cm)	A_e (cm)^2	V_e (cm)^3	A_L Value uh/100 turns
T-12-3	.125	.062	.050	0.74	.010	.007	60
T-16-3	.160	.078	.060	0.95	.016	.015	61
T-20-3	.200	.088	.070	1.15	.025	.029	90
T-25-3	.255	.120	.096	1.50	.042	.063	100
T-30-3	.307	.151	.128	1.83	.065	.119	140
T-37-3	.375	.205	.128	2.32	.070	.162	120
T-44-3	.440	.229	.159	2.67	.107	.286	180
T-50-3	.500	.303	.190	3.03	.121	.367	175
T-68-3	.690	.370	.190	4.24	.196	.831	195
T-80-3	.795	.495	.250	5.15	.242	1.246	180
T-94-3	.942	.560	.312	6.00	.385	2.310	248
T-106-3	1.060	.570	.437	6.50	.690	4.485	450
T-130-3	1.300	.780	.437	8.29	.730	6.052	350
T-157-3	1.570	.950	.570	10.05	1.140	11.457	420
T-184-3	1.840	.950	.710	11.12	2.040	22.685	720
T-200-3	2.000	1.250	.550	12.97	1.330	17.250	425
T-200A-3	2.000	1.250	1.000	12.97	2.240	29.050	460
T-225 -3	2.250	1.405	.550	14.56	1.508	21.956	425

AMIDON Associates   ·   12033 OTSEGO STREET   ·   NORTH HOLLYWOOD, CALIF. 91607

INTRODUCTION
TO CERAMIC FILTERS

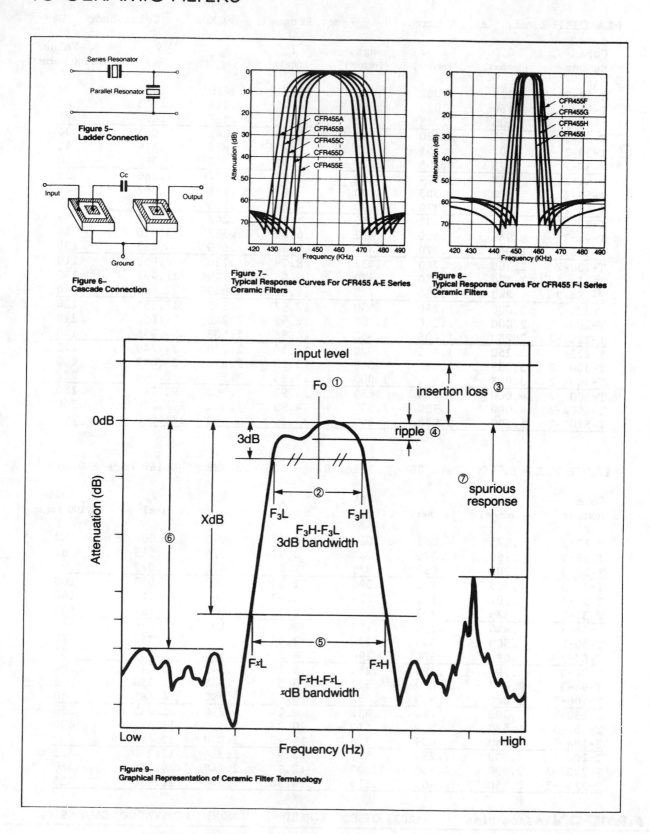

Figure 5–
Ladder Connection

Figure 6–
Cascade Connection

Figure 7–
Typical Response Curves For CFR455 A-E Series
Ceramic Filters

Figure 8–
Typical Response Curves For CFR455 F-I Series
Ceramic Filters

Figure 9–
Graphical Representation of Ceramic Filter Terminology

INTRODUCTION
TO CERAMIC FILTERS

CERAMIC FILTER TERMINOLOGY

Although the previous section has presented a concise discussion of piezoelectric theory as applied to ceramic filter technology, it is necessary that the respective terminology used in conjunction with ceramic filters be discussed before any further examination of ceramic filter technology is made.

Using Figure 9 as a typical model of a response curve for a ceramic filter, it can be seen that there are a number of relevant factors to be considered in specifying ceramic filters. These include: center frequency, pass-band-

width, insertion loss, ripple, attenuation bandwidth, stopband attenuation, spurious response and selectivity. Although not all of these factors will apply to each filter design, these are the key specifications to consider with most filters. From the symbol key shown in Table 1 below, a thorough understanding of this basic terminology should be possible.

IMPEDANCE MATCHING

As it is imperative to properly match the impedances whenever any circuit is connected to another circuit, any component to another component, or any circuit to another component, it is

also important that this be taken into account in using ceramic filters. Without proper impedance matching, the operational characteristics of the ceramic filters cannot be met.

Figure 12 illustrates a typical example of this requirement.

This example shows the changes produced in the frequency characteristics of the SFZ455A ceramic filter when the resistance values are altered. For instance, if the input/output impedances R_1 and R_2 are connected to lower values than those specified, the insertion loss increases, the center frequency shifts toward the low side and the ripple increases.

TABLE 1 - CERAMIC FILTER TERMINOLOGY CHART

Numbers In Fig. 9	Terminology	Symbol	Unit	Explanation of Term
1	Center Frequency	f_o	Hz	The frequency in the center of the pass-bandwidth. However, the center frequency for some products is expressed as the point where the loss is at its lowest point.
2	Pass-bandwidth (3dB bandwidth)	(3dB) B.W.	Hz	Signifies a difference between the two frequencies where the attenuation becomes 3dB from the level of the minimum loss point.
3	Insertion Loss	I.L.	dB	Expressed as the input/output ratio at the point of minimum loss. (The insertion loss for some products is expressed as the input/output ratio at the center frequency.) Insertion loss = 20 LOG (V_2/V_1) in dB.
4	Ripple	—	dB	If there are peaks and valleys in the pass-bandwidth, the ripple expresses the difference between the maximum peak and the minimum valley.
5	Attenuation Bandwidth (dB Bandwidth)	(20dB) B.W.	Hz	The bandwidth at a specified level of attenuation. Attenuation may be expressed as the ratio of the input signal strength to the output signal strength in decibels.
6	Stopband Attenuation	—	dB	The level of signal strength at a specified frequency outside of the passband.
7	Spurious Response	SR	dB	The difference in decibels between the insertion loss and the spurious signal in the stopband.
	Input/Output Impedance	—	Ohm	Internal impedance value of the input and output of the ceramic filter.
	Selectivity	—	dB	The ability of a filter to pass signals of one frequency and reject all others. A highly selective filter has an abrupt transition between a passband region and the stopband region. This is expressed as the shape factor—the attenuation bandwidth divided by the pass-bandwidth. The filter becomes more selective as the resultant value approaches one.

APPENDIX: MANUFACTURER DATA SHEETS   279

On the other hand, if R_1 and R_2 are connected to higher values other than those specified, the insertion loss will increase, the center frequency will shift toward the high side and the ripple will increase.

DEALING WITH SPURIOUS RESPONSE

Frequently in using 455 KHz filters, spurious will cause problems due to the fact that the resonance occurs under an alien vibrating mode or overtone deviating from the basic vibration characteristics. Among available solutions for dealing with spurious response are:

1. The use of a supplementary IFT together with the ceramic filter for suppression of the spurious.
2. The arrangement of two or more ceramic filters in parallel for the mutual cancellation of spurious.
3. The addition of a low-pass or high-pass LC filter for suppression of spurious.

Perhaps the most commonly used method of dealing with spurious is the use of a supplementary IFT in conjunction with the ceramic filter. The before and after effects of the use of an IFT are shown in Figures 10 and 11. In Figure 10, only a single SFZ455A ceramic filter is employed and spurious is a significant problem. With the addition of an IFT, the spurious problem is reduced as is shown in Figure 11.

Although spurious is a significant problem to contend with when using 455KHz ceramic filters, it is not a problem in 4.5MHz and 10.7MHz ceramic filters, as their vibration modes are significantly different.

CONSIDERATIONS FOR GAIN DISTRIBUTION

Since the impedance of both the input and output values of the ceramic filters are symmetric and small, it is necessary that the overall gain distribution within the circuit itself be taken into consideration. For instance, in the discussion concerning proper impedance matching, it was illustrated that a certain DC loss occurs if the recommended resistance values are not used. This can cause an overall reduction in the gain which could present a problem if no allowances have been made for the corresponding loss. To compensate for this problem, it is recommended that the following be done:

1. The amplifier stage should be designed to compensate for this loss.
2. The ceramic filter should be used in combination with the IFT for minimizing both matching and DC losses. The IFT should be used strictly as a matching transformer and the ceramic filter only for selectivity.

As the use of IC's has become more prevalent with ceramic filters, these considerations have been taken into account. It should be noted that few of the problems discussed above have been realized when more than three (3) IF stages have been employed.

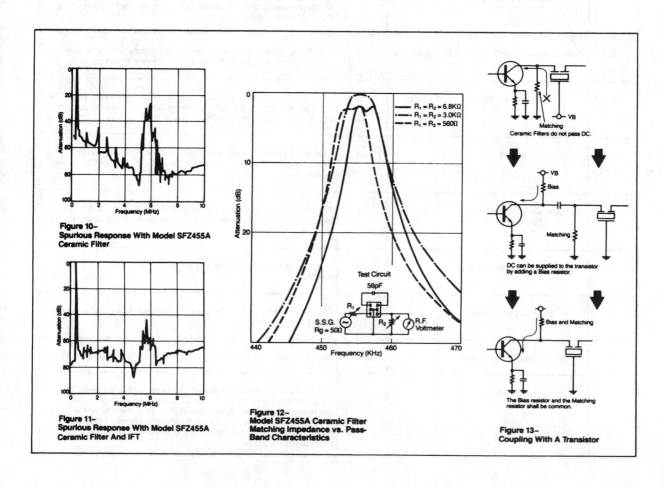

Figure 10–
Spurious Response With Model SFZ455A Ceramic Filter

Figure 11–
Spurious Response With Model SFZ455A Ceramic Filter And IFT

Figure 12–
Model SFZ455A Ceramic Filter Matching Impedance vs. Pass-Band Characteristics

Figure 13–
Coupling With A Transistor

CERAMIC FILTERS DO NOT PASS DC

It is important to note in designing circuits that ceramic filters are incapable of passing DC. As is illustrated in Figure 13, in a typical circuit where a transistor is used, a bias circuit will be required to drive the transistor. Since the ceramic filter requires matching resistance to operate properly, the matching resistor shown in the diagram can play a dual role as both a matching and bias resistor.

If the bias circuit is used, it is important that the parallel circuit of both the bias resistance and the transistor's internal resistance be taken into consideration in meeting the resistance values. This is necessary since the internal resistance of the transistor is changed by the bias resistance. However, when an IC is used, there is no need for an additional bias circuit since the IC has a bias circuit within itself.

Here it is recommended that an IFT be used for impedance matching with the ceramic filter when coupling with a mixer stage, as shown in Figure 14.

COUPLING CAPACITANCE

The SFZ455A is composed of two filter elements which must be connected by a coupling capacitor. Moreover, the frequency characteristic changes according to the coupling capacitance (Cc). As shown in Figure 15, the larger the coupling capacitance (Cc) becomes, the wider the bandwidth and more the ripple increases. Conversely, the smaller the coupling capacitance becomes, the narrower the bandwidth becomes and the more the insertion loss increases. Therefore, the specified value of the coupling capacitance in the catalog is desired in determining the specified passband characteristics.

GROUP DELAY TIME CHARACTERISTICS

Perhaps one of the most important characteristics of a transmitting element is to transmit a signal with the lowest possible distortion level. This distortion occurs when the phase shift of a signal which passes through a certain transmitting path is non-linear with respect to the frequency. For convenience, the group delay time (GDT) characteristic is used for the purpose of expressing non-linearity.

It is important to note the relationship between the amplitude and the GDT characteristics when using group delay time terminology. This relationship differs depending upon the filter characteristics. For example, in the Butterworth type, which has a relatively flat top, the passband is flat while the GDT characteristic is extremely curved, as shown in Figure 16. On the other hand, a Gaussian type, is curved in the passband, while the GDT characteristic is flat. With the flat GDT characteristics, the Gaussian type has excellent distortion characteristics.

Since the amplitude characteristics for the Butterworth type is flat in the passband the bandwidth does not change even at a low input level. With the amplitude characteristic for the Gaussian type being curved in the passband, the bandwidth becomes narrow at a low input level and the sensitivity is poor. Therefore, it should be noted that the Gaussian type has a desirable distortion factor while the Butterworth type has the desirable sensitivity.

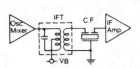

Figure 14–
Coupling From Mixer Stage

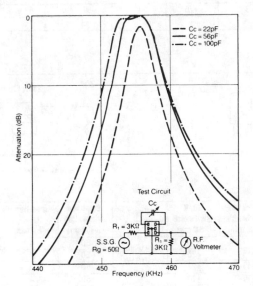

Figure 15–
Model SFZ455A Ceramic Filter
Coupling Capacitance vs. Passband
Characteristics

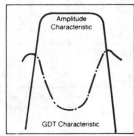

(A) Butterworth Characteristic

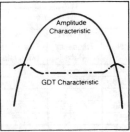

(B) Gaussian Characteristic

Figure 16–
Relationship Between Amplitude
And GDT Characteristics

muRata ERiE

455KHz

FEATURES
- High selectivity
- High ultimate attenuation
- A wide variety of pass-bandwidths
- Small size
- No peaking

CFM455

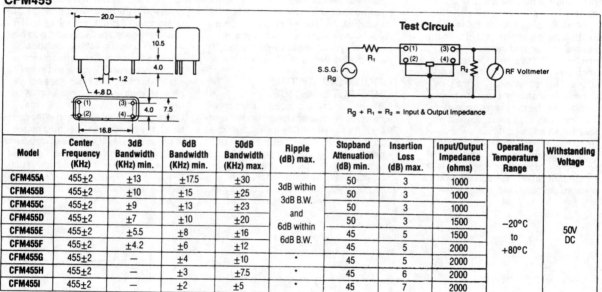

Model	Center Frequency (KHz)	3dB Bandwidth (KHz) min.	6dB Bandwidth (KHz) min.	50dB Bandwidth (KHz) max.	Ripple (dB) max.	Stopband Attenuation (dB) min.	Insertion Loss (dB) max.	Input/Output Impedance (ohms)	Operating Temperature Range	Withstanding Voltage
CFM455A	455±2	±13	±17.5	±30	3dB within 3dB B.W. and 6dB within 6dB B.W.	50	3	1000	−20°C to +80°C	50V DC
CFM455B	455±2	±10	±15	±25		50	3	1000		
CFM455C	455±2	±9	±13	±23		50	3	1000		
CFM455D	455±2	±7	±10	±20		50	3	1500		
CFM455E	455±2	±5.5	±8	±16		45	5	1500		
CFM455F	455±2	±4.2	±6	±12		45	5	2000		
CFM455G	455±2	—	±4	±10	*	45	5	2000		
CFM455H	455±2	—	±3	±7.5	*	45	6	2000		
CFM455I	455±2	—	±2	±5	*	45	7	2000		

*3dB Ripple in 6dB B.W.

CFR455

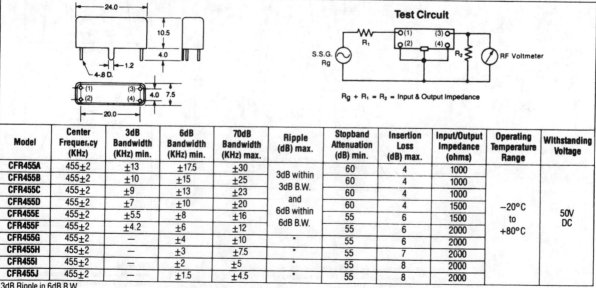

Model	Center Frequency (KHz)	3dB Bandwidth (KHz) min.	6dB Bandwidth (KHz) min.	70dB Bandwidth (KHz) max.	Ripple (dB) max.	Stopband Attenuation (dB) min.	Insertion Loss (dB) max.	Input/Output Impedance (ohms)	Operating Temperature Range	Withstanding Voltage
CFR455A	455±2	±13	±17.5	±30	3dB within 3dB B.W. and 6dB within 6dB B.W.	60	4	1000	−20°C to +80°C	50V DC
CFR455B	455±2	±10	±15	±25		60	4	1000		
CFR455C	455±2	±9	±13	±23		60	4	1000		
CFR455D	455±2	±7	±10	±20		60	4	1500		
CFR455E	455±2	±5.5	±8	±16		55	6	1500		
CFR455F	455±2	±4.2	±6	±12		55	6	2000		
CFR455G	455±2	—	±4	±10	*	55	6	2000		
CFR455H	455±2	—	±3	±7.5	*	55	7	2000		
CFR455I	455±2	—	±2	±5	*	55	8	2000		
CFR455J	455±2	—	±1.5	±4.5	*	55	8	2000		

*3dB Ripple in 6dB B.W.

National Semiconductor

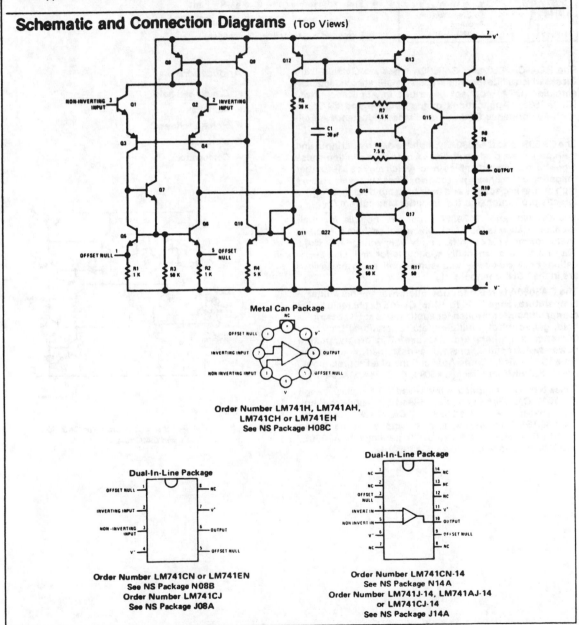

Operational Amplifiers/Buffers

LM741/LM741A/LM741C/LM741E Operational Amplifier

General Description

The LM741 series are general purpose operational amplifiers which feature improved performance over industry standards like the LM709. They are direct, plug-in replacements for the 709C, LM201, MC1439 and 748 in most applications.

The amplifiers offer many features which make their application nearly foolproof: overload pro-

tection on the input and output, no latch-up when the common mode range is exceeded, as well as freedom from oscillations.

The LM741C/LM741E are identical to the LM741/LM741A except that the LM741C/LM741E have their performance guaranteed over a 0°C to +70°C temperature range, instead of −55°C to +125°C.

Schematic and Connection Diagrams (Top Views)

Metal Can Package

Order Number LM741H, LM741AH,
LM741CH or LM741EH
See NS Package H08C

Dual-In-Line Package

Order Number LM741CN or LM741EN
See NS Package N08B
Order Number LM741CJ
See NS Package J08A

Dual-In-Line Package

Order Number LM741CN-14
See NS Package N14A
Order Number LM741J-14, LM741AJ-14
or LM741CJ-14
See NS Package J14A

Operational Transconductance Amplifiers (OTA's)

Gatable-Gain Blocks

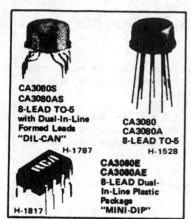

CA3080S
CA3080AS
8-LEAD TO-5
with Dual-In-Line
Formed Leads
"DIL-CAN"
H-1787

CA3080
CA3080A
8-LEAD TO-5
H-1528

CA3080E
CA3080AE
8-LEAD Dual-
In-Line Plastic
Package
"MINI-DIP"
H-1817

Features:

- Slew rate (unity gain, compensated): 50 V/μs
- Adjustable power consumption: 10μW to 30 mW
- Flexible supply voltage range: ± 2 V to ± 15 V
- Fully adjustable gain: 0 to $g_m R_L$ limit
- Tight g_m spread: CA3080 (2:1), CA3080A (1.6:1)
- Extended g_m linearity: 3 decades

The RCA-CA3080 and CA3080A types are Gatable-Gain Blocks which utilize the unique operational-transconductance-amplifier (OTA) concept described in Application Note ICAN-6668, "Applications of the CA3080 and CA3080A High-Performance Operational Transconductance Amplifiers".

The CA3080 and CA3080A types have differential input and a single-ended, push-pull, class A output. In addition, these types have an amplifier bias input which may be used either for gating or for linear gain control. These types also have a high output impedance and their transconductance (g_m) is directly proportional to the amplifier bias current (I_{ABC}).

The CA3080 and CA3080A types are notable for their excellent slew rate (50 V/μs), which makes them especially useful for multiplex and fast unity-gain voltage followers. These types are especially applicable for multiplex applications because power is consumed only when the devices are in the "ON" channel state.

The CA3080A is rated for operation over the full military-temperature range (−55 to +125°C) and its characteristics are specifically controlled for applications such as sample-hold, gain-control, multiplex, etc. Operational transconductance amplifiers are also useful in programmable power-switch applications, e.g., as described in Application Note ICAN-6048, "Some Applications of a Programmable Power Switch/Amplifier" (CA3094, CA3094A, CA3094B).

These types are supplied in the 8-lead TO-5-style package (CA3080, CA3080A), and in the 8-lead TO-5-style package with dual-in-line formed leads ("DIL-CAN", CA3080S, CA3080AS). The CA3080 is also supplied in the 8-lead dual-in-line plastic ("MINI-DIP") package (CA3080E, CA3080AE), and in chip form (CA3080H).

Applications:

- **Sample and hold**
- **Multiplex**
- **Voltage follower**
- **Multiplier**
- **Comparator**

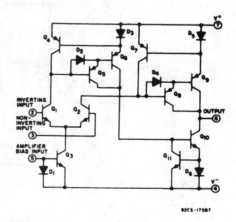

92CS-17587

Fig. 1 — Schematic diagram for CA3080 and CA3080A.

Linear Integrated Circuits
CA3080, CA3080A Types

MAXIMUM RATINGS, *Absolute-Maximum Values:*

DC SUPPLY VOLTAGE (Between V$^+$ and V$^-$ terminals)	36 V
DIFFERENTIAL INPUT VOLTAGE	±5 V
DC INPUT VOLTAGE	V$^+$ to V$^-$
INPUT SIGNAL CURRENT	1 mA
AMPLIFIER BIAS CURRENT.	2 mA
OUTPUT SHORT-CIRCUIT DURATION*	Indefinite
DEVICE DISSIPATION	125 mW

TEMPERATURE RANGE:
Operating
  CA3080, CA3080E, CA3080S . . . . 0 to + 70 °C
  CA3080A, CA3080AE, CA3080AS . . . . −55 to + 125 °C
Storage . . . . −65 to + 150 °C
LEAD TEMPERATURE (During Soldering):
  At distance 1/16 ± 1/32 in. (1.59 ± 0.79 mm)
  from case for 10 s max. . . . . + 265 °C

* Short circuit may be applied to ground or to either supply.

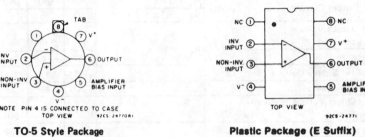

NOTE PIN 4 IS CONNECTED TO CASE
TOP VIEW   92CS 24770RI

TO-5 Style Package

TOP VIEW
92CS-24771

Plastic Package (E Suffix)

Fig.2 – Functional diagrams.

TYPICAL CHARACTERISTICS CURVES AND TEST CIRCUITS FOR THE CA3080 AND CA3080A

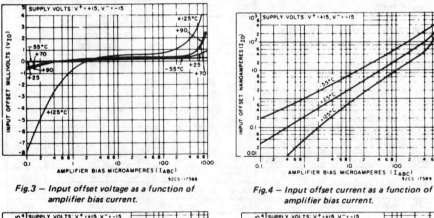

Fig.3 – Input offset voltage as a function of amplifier bias current.

Fig.4 – Input offset current as a function of amplifier bias current.

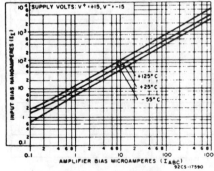

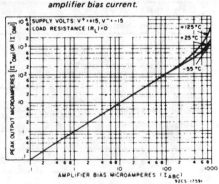

Fig.5 – Input bias current as a function of amplifier bias current.

Fig.6 – Peak output current as a function of amplifier bias current.

ELECTRICAL CHARACTERISTICS
For Equipment Design

CHARACTERISTIC		TEST CONDITIONS $V^+ = 15$ V, $V^- = -15$ V $I_{ABC} = 500$ μA $T_A = 25^{\circ}$C (unless indicated otherwise)	CA3080 CA3080E CA3080S LIMITS			UNITS
			Min.	Typ.	Max.	
Input Offset Voltage	V_{IO}		–	0.4	5	mV
		$T_A = 0$ to 70°C	–	–	6	
Input Offset Current	I_{IO}		–	0.12	0.6	μA
Input Bias Current	I_I		–	2	5	μA
		$T_A = 0$ to 70°C	–	–	7	
Forward Transconductance (large signal)	g_m		6700	9600	13000	μmho
		$T_A = 0$ to 70°C	5400	–	–	
Peak Output Current	$|I_{OM}|$	$R_L = 0$	350	500	650	μA
		$R_L = 0$, $T_A = 0$ to 70°C	300	–	–	
Peak Output Voltage:		$R_L = \infty$				V
Positive	V^+_{OM}		12	13.5	–	
Negative	V^-_{OM}		–12	–14.4	–	
Amplifier Supply Current	I_A		0.8	1	1.2	mA
Device Dissipation	P_D		24	30	36	mW
Input Offset Voltage Sensitivity:						μV/V
Positive	$\Delta V_{IO}/\Delta V^+$		–	–	150	
Negative	$\Delta V_{IO}/\Delta V^-$		–	–	150	
Common-Mode Rejection Ratio	CMRR		80	110	–	dB
Common-Mode Input-Voltage Range	V_{ICR}		12 to –12	13.6 to –14.6	–	V
Input Resistance	R_I		10	26	–	kΩ

ELECTRICAL CHARACTERISTICS
Typical Values Intended Only for Design Guidance

CA3080 CA3080E CA3080S

Input Offset Voltage	V_{IO}	$I_{ABC} = 5$ μA	0.3	mV
Input Offset Voltage Change	$|\Delta V_{IO}|$	$I_{ABC} = 500$ μA to $I_{ABC} = 5$ μA	0.2	mV
Peak Output Current	I_{OM}	$I_{ABC} = 5$ μA	5	μA
Peak Output Voltage:				V
Positive	V^+_{OM}	$I_{ABC} = 5$ μA	13.8	
Negative	V^-_{OM}		–14.5	
Magnitude of Leakage Current		$I_{ABC} = 0$, $V_{TP} = 0$	0.08	nA
		$I_{ABC} = 0$, $V_{TP} = 36$ V	0.3	
Differential Input Current		$I_{ABC} = 0$, $V_{DIFF} = 4$ V	0.008	nA
Amplifier Bias Voltage	V_{ABC}		0.71	V
Slew Rate:				V/μs
Maximum (uncompensated)	SR		75	
Unity Gain (compensated)			50	
Open-Loop Bandwidth	BW_{OL}		2	MHz
Input Capacitance	C_I	$f = 1$ MHz	3.6	pF
Output Capacitance	C_O	$f = 1$ MHz	5.6	pF
Output Resistance	R_O		15	MΩ
Input-to-Output Capacitance	C_{I-O}	$f = 1$ MHz	0.024	pF
Propagation Delay	t_{PHL}, t_{PLH}	$I_{ABC} = 500$ μA	45	ns

CA3080, CA3080A Types

ELECTRICAL CHARACTERISTICS
For Equipment Design

CHARACTERISTIC		TEST CONDITIONS V^+ = 15 V, V^- = -15 V I_{ABC} = 500 μA T_A = 25°C (unless indicated otherwise)	CA3080A CA3080AE CA3080AS LIMITS			UNITS
			Min.	Typ.	Max.	
Input Offset Voltage	V_{IO}	I_{ABC} = 5 μA	–	0.3	2	mV
			–	0.4	2	
		T_A = -55 to + 125°C	–	–	5	
Input Offset Voltage Change	$|\Delta V_{IO}|$	I_{ABC} = 500 μA to I_{ABC} = 5 μA	–	0.1	3	mV
Input Offset Current	I_{IO}		–	0.12	0.6	μA
Input Bias Current	I_I		–	2	5	μA
		T_A = -55 to + 125°C	–	–	8	
Forward Transconductance (large signal)	g_m		7700	9600	12000	μmho
		T_A = -55 to + 125°C	4000	–	–	
Peak Output Current	$|I_{OM}|$	I_{ABC} = 5 μA, R_L = 0	3	5	7	μA
		R_L = 0	350	500	650	
		R_L = 0, T_A = -55 to +125°C	300	–	–	
Peak Output Voltage: Positive	V^+_{OM}	I_{ABC} = 5 μA R_L = ∞	12	13.8	–	V
Negative	V^-_{OM}		-12	-14.5	–	
Positive	V^+_{OM}	R_L = ∞	12	13.5	–	
Negative	V^-_{OM}		-12	-14.4	–	
Amplifier Supply Current	I_A		0.8	1	1.2	mA
Device Dissipation	P_D		24	30	36	mW
Input Offset Voltage Sensitivity: Positive	$\Delta V_{IO}/\Delta V^+$		–	–	150	μV/V
Negative	$\Delta V_{IO}/\Delta V^-$		–	–	150	
Magnitude of Leakage Current		I_{ABC} = 0, V_{TP} = 0	–	0.08	5	nA
		I_{ABC} = 0, V_{TP} = 36 V	–	0.3	5	
Differential Input Current		I_{ABC} = 0, V_{DIFF} = 4 V	–	0.008	5	nA
Common-Mode Rejection Ratio	CMRR		80	110	--	dB
Common-Mode Input-Voltage Range	V_{ICR}		12 to -12	13.6 to -14.6	–	V
Input Resistance	R_I		10	26	–	kΩ

ELECTRICAL CHARACTERISTICS
Typical Values Intended Only for Design Guidance

			CA3080A CA3080AE CA3080AS	
Amplifier Bias Voltage	V_{ABC}		0.71	V
Slew Rate: Maximum (uncompensated)	SR		75	V/μs
Unity Gain (compensated)			50	
Open-Loop Bandwidth	BW_{OL}	–	2	MHz
Input Capacitance	C_I	f = 1 MHz	3.6	pF
Output Capacitance	C_O	f = 1 MHz	5.6	pF
Output Resistance	R_O		.15	MΩ
Input-to-Output Capacitance	C_{I-O}	f = 1 MHz	0.024	pF
Input Offset Voltage Temperature Drift	$\Delta V_{IO}/\Delta T$	I_{ABC} = 100 μA, T_A = -55 to +125°C	3	μV/°C
Propagation Delay	t_{PHL}, t_{PLH}	I_{ABC}=500 μA	45	ns

3N204

SILICON DUAL INSULATED-GATE FIELD-EFFECT TRANSISTOR
N-Channel Depletion Type With Integrated
Gate-Protection Circuits
For RF Amplifier Applications up to 400 MHz

RCA-40673 is an n-channel silicon, depletion type, dual insulated-gate field-effect transistor.

Special back-to-back diodes are diffused directly into the MOS* pellet and are electrically connected between each insulated gate and the FET's source. The diodes effectively bypass any voltage transients which exceed approximately ±10 volts. This protects the gates against damage in all normal handling and usage.

A feature of the back-to-back diode configuration is that it allows the 40673 to retain the wide input signal dynamic range inherent in the MOSFET. In addition, the low junction capacitance of these diodes adds little to the total capacitance shunting the signal gate.

The excellent overall performance characteristics of the RCA-40673 make it useful for a wide variety of rf-amplifier applications at frequencies up to 400 MHz. The two serially-connected channels with independent control gates make possible a greater dynamic range and lower cross-modulation than is normally achieved using devices having only a single control element.

The two gate arrangement of the 40673 also makes possible a desirable reduction in feedback capacitance by operating in the common-source configuration and ac-grounding Gate No. 2. The reduced capacitance allows operation at maximum gain *without neutralization;* and, of special importance in rf-amplifiers, it reduces local oscillator feedthrough to the antenna.

The 40673 is hermetically sealed in the metal JEDEC TO-72 package.

*Metal-Oxide-Semiconductor.

Maximum Ratings, Absolute-Maximum Values, at $T_A = 25^oC$

DRAIN-TO-SOURCE VOLTAGE, V_{DS}	-0.2 to +20	V
GATE No.1-TO-SOURCE VOLTAGE, V_{G1S}:		
Continuous (dc)	-6 to +1	V
Peak ac	-6 to +6	V
GATE No.2-TO-SOURCE VOLTAGE, V_{G2S}:		
Continuous (dc)	-6 to 30% of V_{DS}	V
Peak ac	-6 to +6	V
DRAIN-TO-GATE VOLTAGE, V_{DG1} OR V_{DG2}	+20	V
DRAIN CURRENT, I_D	50	mA
TRANSISTOR DISSIPATION, P_T:		
At ambient {up to 25°C	330	mW
temperature {above 25°C	derate linearly at 2.2 mW/°C	
AMBIENT TEMPERATURE RANGE:		
Storage and Operating	-65 to +175	°C
LEAD TEMPERATURE (During soldering):		
At distance ≥1/32 inch from seating surface for 10 seconds max.	265	°C

APPLICATIONS

- RF amplifier, mixer, and IF amplifier in military, industrial, and consumer communications equipment
- aircraft and marine vehicular receivers
- CATV and MATV equipment
- telemetry and multiplex equipment

PERFORMANCE FEATURES

- superior cross-modulation performance and greater dynamic range than bipolar or single-gate FETs
- wide dynamic range permits large-signal handling before overload
- dual-gate permits simplified agc circuitry
- virtually no agc power required
- greatly reduces spurious responses in fm receivers
- permits use of vacuum-tube biasing techniques
- excellent thermal stability

DEVICE FEATURES

- back-to-back diodes protect each gate against handling and in-circuit transients
- low gate leakage currents —— I_{G1SS} & I_{G2SS} = 20 nA(max.) at $T_A = 25^oC$
- high forward transconductance —— g_{fs} = 12,000 μmho (typ.)
- high unneutralized RF power gain —— G_{ps} = 18 dB(typ.) at 200 MHz
- low VHF noise figure —— 3.5 dB(typ.) at 200 MHz

TERMINAL DIAGRAM

LEAD 1 - DRAIN
LEAD 2 - GATE No. 2
LEAD 3 - GATE No. 1
LEAD 4 - SOURCE, SUBSTRATE AND CASE

ELECTRICAL CHARACTERISTICS, at $T_A = 25^oC$ unless otherwise specified

CHARACTERISTICS	SYMBOLS	TEST CONDITIONS	Min.	Typ.	Max.	UNITS
Gate-No.1-to-Source Cutoff Voltage	$V_{G1S(off)}$	V_{DS} = +15V, I_D = 200μA, V_{G2S} = +4V	–	-2	-4	V
Gate-No.2-to-Source Cutoff Voltage	$V_{G2S(off)}$	V_{DS} = +15V, I_D = 200μA, V_{G1S} = 0	–	-2	-4	V
Gate-No.1-Leakage Current	I_{G1SS}	V_{G1S} = +1 or -6 V, V_{DS} = 0, V_{G2S} = 0	–	–	50	nA
Gate-No.2-Leakage Current	I_{G2SS}	V_{G2S} = ±6V, V_{DS} = 0, V_{G1S} = 0	–	–	50	nA
Zero-Bias Drain Current	I_{DSS}	V_{DS} = +15V, V_{G2S} = +4V, V_{G1S} = 0	5	15	35	mA
Forward Transconductance (Gate-No.1-to-Drain)	g_{fs}	V_{DS} = +15V, I_D = 10mA, V_{G2S} = +4V, f = 1kHz	–	12,000	–	μmho
Small-Signal, Short-Circuit Input Capacitance †	C_{iss}	V_{DS} = +15V, I_D = 10mA, V_{G2S} = +4V, f=1MHz	–	6	–	pF
Small-Signal, Short-Circuit, Reverse Transfer Capacitance (Drain-to-Gate No.1) ⋄	C_{rss}		0.005	0.02	0.03	pF
Small-Signal, Short-Circuit Output Capacitance	C_{oss}		–	2.0	–	pF
Power Gain (see Fig. 1)	G_{ps}	V_{DS} = +15V, I_D = 10mA, V_{G2S} = +4V, f = 200 MHz	14	18	–	dB
Maximum Available Power Gain	MAG		–	20	–	dB
Maximum Usable Power Gain (unneutralized)	MUG		–	20*	–	dB
Noise Figure (see Fig. 1)	NF		–	3.5	6.0	dB
Magnitude of Forward Transadmittance	$|Y_{fs}|$		–	12,000	–	μmho
Phase Angle of Forward Transadmittance	θ		–	-35	–	degrees
Input Resistance	r_{iss}		–	1.0	–	kΩ
Output Resistance	r_{oss}		–	2.8	–	kΩ
Protective Diode Knee Voltage	V_{knee}	$I_{DIODE(REVERSE)}$ = ±100μA	–	±10	–	V

*Limited only by practical design considerations.
†Capacitance between Gate No. 1 and all other terminals
⋄Three-terminal measurement with Gate No. 2 and Source returned to guard terminal.

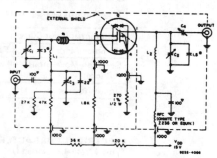

#Ferrite bead (4); Pyroferric Co. "Carbonyl J" 0.09 in. OD; 0.03 in. ID; 0.063 in. thickness.
All resistors in ohms
All capacitors in pF

Q = 40673
▼ Disc ceramic.
*Tubular ceramic.

C_1: 1.8 – 8.7 pF variable air capacitor: E.F. Johnson Type 160-104, or equivalent.
C_2: 1.5 – 5 pF variable air capacitor: E.F. Johnson Type 160-102, or equivalent.
C_3: 1 – 10 pF piston-type variable air capacitor: JFD Type VAM-010; Johanson Type 4335, or equivalent.
C_4: 0.8 – 4.5 pF piston type variable air capacitor: Erie 560-013 or equivalent.
L_1: 4 turns silver-plated 0.02-in. thick, 0.075-0.085-in. wide, copper ribbon. Internal diameter of winding = 0.25 in, winding length approx. 0.80 in.
L_2: 4½ turns silver-plated 0.02-in. thick, 0.085-0.095-in. wide, 5/16-in. ID. Coil ≈ .90 in. long.

Fig. 1. 200-MHz Power gain and noise-figure test circuit

For characteristics curves, refer to type 3N187.

288   APPENDIX

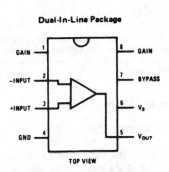

National Semiconductor

LM386 Low Voltage Audio Power Amplifier

General Description

The LM386 is a power amplifier designed for use in low voltage consumer applications. The gain is internally set to 20 to keep external part count low, but the addition of an external resistor and capacitor between pins 1 and 8 will increase the gain to any value up to 200.

The inputs are ground referenced while the output is automatically biased to one half the supply voltage. The quiescent power drain is only 24 milliwatts when operating from a 6 volt supply, making the LM386 ideal for battery operation.

Features

- Battery operation
- Minimum external parts
- Wide supply voltage range   4V−12V or 5V−18V
- Low quiescent current drain   4 mA

- Voltage gains from 20 to 200
- Ground referenced input
- Self-centering output quiescent voltage
- Low distortion
- Eight pin dual-in-line package

Applications

- AM-FM radio amplifiers
- Portable tape player amplifiers
- Intercoms
- TV sound systems
- Line drivers
- Ultrasonic drivers
- Small servo drivers
- Power converters

Equivalent Schematic and Connection Diagrams

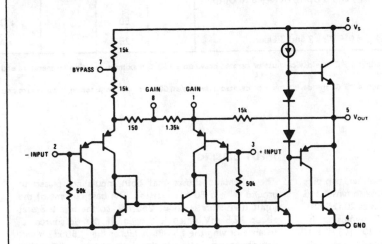

Dual-In-Line Package

TOP VIEW

**Order Number LM386N-1,
LM386N-3 or LM386N-4
See NS Package N08B**

Typical Applications

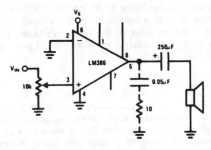

Amplifier with Gain = 20
Minimum Parts

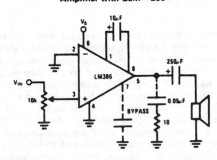

Amplifier with Gain = 200

Reprinted with permission of National Semiconductor Corp.

Absolute Maximum Ratings

Supply Voltage (LM386N)	15V	Storage Temperature	−65°C to +150°C
Supply Voltage (LM386N-4)	22V	Operating Temperature	0°C to +70°C
Package Dissipation (Note 1) (LM386N-4)	1.25W	Junction Temperature	+150°C
Package Dissipation (Note 2) (LM386)	660 mW	Lead Temperature (Soldering, 10 seconds)	+300°C
Input Voltage	±0.4V		

Electrical Characteristics $T_A = 25°C$

PARAMETER	CONDITIONS	MIN	TYP	MAX	UNITS
Operating Supply Voltage (V_S)					
LM386		4		12	V
LM386N-4		5		18	V
Quiescent Current (I_Q)	$V_S = 6V$, $V_{IN} = 0$		4	8	mA
Output Power (P_{OUT})					
LM386N-1	$V_S = 6V$, $R_L = 8\Omega$, THD = 10%	250	325		mW
LM386N-3	$V_S = 9V$, $R_L = 8\Omega$, THD = 10%	500	700		mW
LM386N-4	$V_S = 16V$, $R_L = 32\Omega$, THD = 10%	700	1000		mW
Voltage Gain (A_V)	$V_S = 6V$, f = 1 kHz		26		dB
	10μF from Pin 1 to 8		46		dB
Bandwidth (BW)	$V_S = 6V$, Pins 1 and 8 Open		300		kHz
Total Harmonic Distortion (THD)	$V_S = 6V$, $R_L = 8\Omega$, $P_{OUT} = 125$ mW f = 1 kHz, Pins 1 and 8 Open		0.2		%
Power Supply Rejection Ratio (PSRR)	$V_S = 6V$, f = 1 kHz, $C_{BYPASS} = 10\mu$F Pins 1 and 8 Open, Referred to Output		50		dB
Input Resistance (R_{IN})			50		kΩ
Input Bias Current (I_{BIAS})	$V_S = 6V$, Pins 2 and 3 Open		250		nA

Note 1: For operation in ambient temperatures above 25°C, the device must be derated based on a 150°C maximum junction temperature and a thermal resistance of 100°C/W junction to ambient.

Note 2: For operation in ambient temperatures above 25°C, the device must be derated based on a 150°C maximum junction temperature and a thermal resistance of 187°C junction to ambient.

Application Hints

GAIN CONTROL

To make the LM386 a more versatile amplifier, two pins (1 and 8) are provided for gain control. With pins 1 and 8 open the 1.35 kΩ resistor sets the gain at 20 (26 dB). If a capacitor is put from pin 1 to 8, bypassing the 1.35 kΩ resistor, the gain will go up to 200 (46 dB). If a resistor is placed in series with the capacitor, the gain can be set to any value from 20 to 200. Gain control can also be done by capacitively coupling a resistor (or FET) from pin 1 to ground.

Additional external components can be placed in parallel with the internal feedback resistors to tailor the gain and frequency response for individual applications. For example, we can compensate poor speaker bass response by frequency shaping the feedback path. This is done with a series RC from pin 1 to 5 (paralleling the internal 15kΩ resistor). For 6 dB effective bass boost: R $\cong$ 15kΩ, the lowest value for good stable operation is R = 10 kΩ if pin 8 is open. If pins 1 and 8 are bypassed then R as low as 2 kΩ can be used. This restriction is because the amplifier is only compensated for closed-loop gains greater than 9.

INPUT BIASING

The schematic shows that both inputs are biased to ground with a 50 kΩ resistor. The base current of the input transistors is about 250 nA, so the inputs are at about 12.5 mV when left open. If the dc source resistance driving the LM386 is higher than 250 kΩ it will contribute very little additional offset (about 2.5 mV at the input, 50 mV at the output). If the dc source resistance is less than 10 kΩ, then shorting the unused input to ground will keep the offset low (about 2.5 mV at the input, 50 mV at the output). For dc source resistances between these values we can eliminate excess offset by putting a resistor from the unused input to ground, equal in value to the dc source resistance. Of course all offset problems are eliminated if the input is capacitively coupled.

When using the LM386 with higher gains (bypassing the 1.35 kΩ resistor between pins 1 and 8) it is necessary to bypass the unused input, preventing degradation of gain and possible instabilities. This is done with a 0.1μF capacitor or a short to ground depending on the dc source resistance on the driven input.

Typical Performance Characteristics

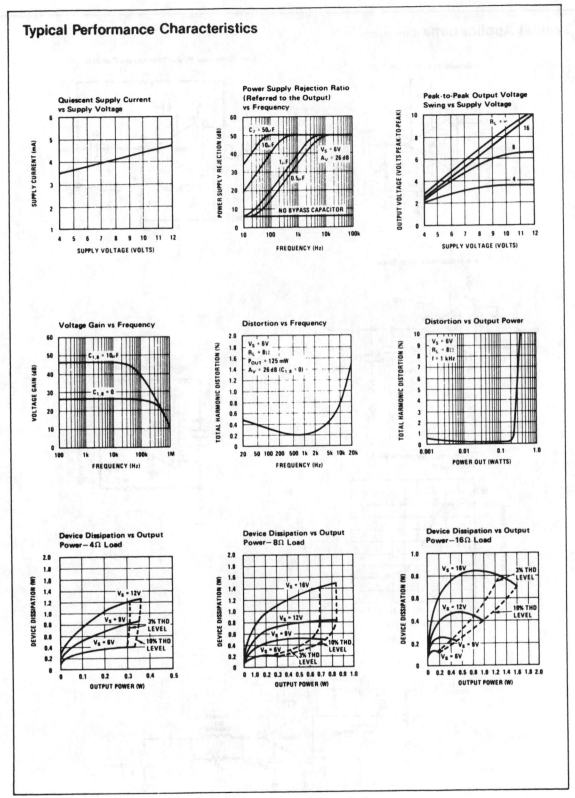

Reprinted with permission of National Semiconductor Corp.

Typical Applications (Continued)

Amplifier with Gain = 50

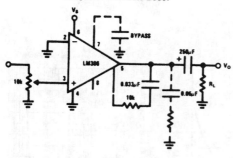

Low Distortion Power Wienbridge Oscillator

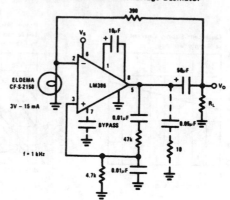

Amplifier with Bass Boost

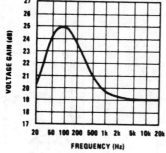

Square Wave Oscillator

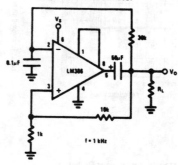

Frequency Response with Bass Boost

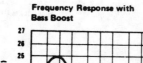

AM Radio Power Amplifier

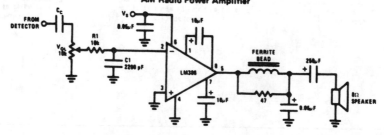

Note 1: Twist supply lead and supply ground very tightly.

Note 2: Twist speaker lead and ground very tightly.

Note 3: Ferrite bead is Ferroxcube K5-001-001/3B with 3 turns of wire.

Note 4: R1C1 band limits input signals.

Note 5: All components must be spaced very close to IC.

8-Lead TO-5-Style
"DIL-CAN" Package
H-1787

8-Lead
TO-5-Style
Package

8-Lead Dual-In-Line
Frit-Seal (Hermetic)
Package   H-1805

H-1528

DIFFERENTIAL/CASCODE AMPLIFIERS

For Communications and
Industrial Equipment at
Frequencies from DC to 120 MHz

FEATURES

- Controlled for Input Offset Voltage, Input Offset Current, and Input Bias Current (CA3028 Series only)
- Balanced Differential Amplifier Configuration with Controlled Constant-Current Source
- Single- and Dual-Ended Operation
- Operation from DC to 120 MHz
- Balanced-AGC Capability
- Wide Operating-Current Range

The CA3028A and CA3028B are differential/cascode amplifiers designed for use in communications and industrial equipment operating at frequencies from dc to 120 MHz.

The CA3028B is like the CA3028A but is capable of premium performance particularly in critical dc and differential amplifier applications requiring tight controls for input offset voltage, input offset current, and input bias current.

The CA3053 is similar to the CA3028A and CA3028B but is recommended for IF amplifier applications.

The CA3028A, CA3028B, and CA3053 are supplied in a hermetic 8-lead TO-5-style package. The "F" versions are supplied in a frit-seal TO-5 package, and the "S" versions in formed-lead (DIL-CAN) packages.

APPLICATIONS

- RF and IF Amplifiers (Differential or Cascode)
- DC, Audio, and Sense Amplifiers
- Converter in the Commercial FM Band
- Oscillator   • Mixer   • Limiter
- Companion Application Note, ICAN 5337 "Application of the RCA CA3028 Integrated Circuit Amplifier in the HF and VHF Ranges." This note covers characteristics of different operating modes, noise performance, mixer, limiter, and amplifier design considerations.

The CA3028A, CA3028B, and CA3053 are available in the packages shown below. When ordering these devices, it is important to add the appropriate suffix letter to the device.

Package 8-Lead TO-5	Suffix Letter	CA3028A	CA3028B	CA3053
TO-5	T	√	√	√
With Dual-In-Line Formed Leads (DIL-CAN)	S	√	√	√
Frit-Seal Ceramic	F	√	√	√
Beam-Lead	L	√		
Chip	H	√		

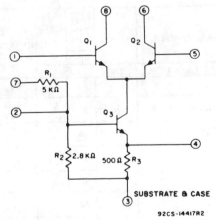

92CS-14417R2

Fig.1 - Schematic diagram for CA3028A, CA3028B and CA3053.

CA3028A, CA3028B, CA3053 Types

ABSOLUTE MAXIMUM RATINGS AT T_A = 25°C

DISSIPATION:

At T_A up to 55°C
(CA3028AF, CA3028BF,
CA3053F) . . . . 750 mW

At T_A > 55°C
(CA3028AF, CA3028BF,
CA3053F) . . . . Derate linearly 6.67 mW/°C

At T_A up to 85°C
(CA3028A, CA3028B, CA3053) . . . . 450 mW

At T_A > 85°C
(CA3028A, CA3028B, CA3053) Derate linearly 5 mW/°C

AMBIENT-TEMPERATURE RANGE:
Operating . . . . −55°C to +125°C
Storage . . . . −65°C to +150°C

LEAD TEMPERATURE (During Soldering):
At distance 1/16 ± 1/32″ (1.59 ± 0.79 mm)
from case for 10 seconds max. . . . . +265°C

MAXIMUM VOLTAGE RATINGS at T_A = 25°C

TERM-INAL No.	1	2	3	4	5	6	7	8
1		0 to -15▲	0 to -15▲	0 to -15▲	+5 to -5	*	*	+20+ to 0
2			+5 to -11	+5 to -1	+15♦ to 0	*	+15♦ to 0	*
3 ‡				+10 to 0	+15♦ to 0	+30● to 0	+15♦ to 0	+30● to 0
4					+15♦ to 0	*	*	*
5						+20+ to 0	*	*
6							*	*
7								*
8								

This chart gives the range of voltages which can be applied to the terminals listed horizontally with respect to the terminals listed vertically. For example, the voltage range of the horizontal terminal 4 with respect to terminal 2 is 1 to +5 volts.

‡ Terminal #3 is connected to the substrate and case.

* Voltages are not normally applied between these terminals. Voltages appearing between these terminals will be safe, if the specified voltage limits between all other terminals are not exceeded.

▲ Limit is -12V for CA3053

+ Limit is +15V for CA3053

♦ Limit is +12V for CA3053

● Limit is +24V for CA3028A and +18V for CA3053

MAXIMUM CURRENT RATINGS

TERM-INAL No.	I_{IN} mA	I_{OUT} mA
1	0.6	0.1
2	4	0.1
3	0.1	23
4	20	0.1
5	0.6	0.1
6	20	0.1
7	4	0.1
8	20	0.1

ELECTRICAL CHARACTERISTICS at T_A = 25°C

CHARACTERISTIC	SYMBOL	TEST CIRCUIT Fig.	SPECIAL TEST CONDITIONS $+V_{CC}$	$-V_{EE}$	LIMITS TYPE CA3028A Min.	Typ.	Max.	LIMITS TYPE CA3028B Min.	Typ.	Max.	LIMITS TYPE CA3053 Min.	Typ.	Max.	UNITS	TYPICAL CHARACTERISTICS CURVES Fig.
STATIC CHARACTERISTICS															
Input Offset Voltage	V_{IO}	2	6V 12V	6V 12V	- -	- -	- -	- -	0.98 0.89	5 5	- -	- -	- -	mV	4
Input Offset Current	I_{IO}	3a	6V 12V	6V 12V	- -	- -	- -	- -	0.56 1.06	5 6	- -	- -	- -	μA	4
Input Bias Current	I_I	3a	6V 12V	6V 12V	- -	16.6 36	70 106	- -	16.6 36	40 80	- -	- -	- -	μA	5a
		3b	9V 12V	- -	- -	- -	- -	- -	- -	- -	- -	29 36	85 125		5b
Quiescent O, rating Current	I_6 or I_8	3a	6V 12V	6V 12V	0.8 2	1.25 3.3	2 5	1 2.5	1.25 3.3	1.5 4	- -	- -	- -	mA	6a 7
		3b	9V 12V	- -	- -	- -	- -	- -	- -	- -	1.2 2.0	2.2 3.3	3.5 5.0		6b
AGC Bias Current (Into Constant-Current Source Terminal No.7)	I_7	8a	12V 12V	V_{AGC} = +9 V_{AGC} = +12	- -	1.28 1.65	- -	- -	1.28 1.65	- -	- -	- -	- -	mA	8b
			9V 12V	-	- -	- -	- -	- -	- -	- -	- -	1.15 1.55	- -		-
Input Current (Terminal No.7)	I_7	-	6V 12V	6V 12V	0.5 1	0.85 1.65	1 2.1	0.5 1	0.85 1.65	1 2.1	- -	- -	- -	mA	
Device Dissipation	P_T	3a	6V 12V	6V 12V	24 120	36 175	54 260	24 120	36 175	42 220	- -	- -	- -	mW	9
		3b	9V 12V	-	- -	- -	- -	- -	- -	- -	50 100	80 150			-

ELECTRICAL CHARACTERISTICS at $T_A = 25°C$ (cont'd)

CHARACTERISTIC	SYMBOL	TEST CIRCUIT Fig.	SPECIAL TEST CONDITIONS		LIMITS TYPE CA3028A Min.	Typ.	Max.	LIMITS TYPE CA3028B Min.	Typ.	Max.	LIMITS TYPE CA3053 Min.	Typ.	Max.	UNITS	TYPICAL CHARACTERISTICS CURVE Fig.
DYNAMIC CHARACTERISTICS															
Power Gain	G_P	10a	f = 100 MHz	Cascode	16	20	-	16	20	-	-	-	-	dB	10b
		11a,d	V_{CC} = +9V	Diff.-Ampl.	14	17	-	14	17	-	-	-	-		11b,e
		10a	f = 10.7 MHz	Cascode	35	39	-	35	39	-	35	39	-	dB	10b ✻
		11a	V_{CC} = +9V	Diff.-Ampl.	28	32	-	28	32	-	28	32	-		11b ✻
Noise Figure	NF	10a	f = 100 MHz	Cascode	-	7.2	9	-	7.2	9	-	-	-	dB	10c
		11a,d	V_{CC} = +9V	Diff.-Ampl.	-	6.7	9	-	6.7	9	-	-	-		11c,e
Input Admittance	Y_{11}	-		Cascode				-	0.6 + j 1.6	-				mmho	12
		-		Diff.-Ampl.				-	0.5 + j 0.5	-					13
Reverse Transfer Admittance	Y_{12}	-		Cascode				-	0.0003 - j0	-				mmho	14
		-	f = 10.7 MHz	Diff.-Ampl.				-	0.01 - j0.0002	-					15
Forward Transfer Admittance	Y_{21}	-	V_{CC} = +9V	Cascode				-	99 - j18	-				mmho	16
		-		Diff.-Ampl.				-	-37 + j0.5	-					17
Output Admittance	Y_{22}			Cascode				-	0. + j0.08	-				mmho	18
				Diff.-Ampl.				-	0.04 + j0.23	-					19
Power Output (Untuned)	P_o	20a	f = 10.7 MHz	Diff.-Ampl. 50 Ω Input-Output	-	5.7	-		5.7	-	-	-	-	μW	20b
AGC Range (Max. Power Gain to Full Cutoff)	AGC	21a	V_{CC} = +9V	Diff.-Ampl.	-	62	-	-	62	-	-	-	-	dB	21b
Voltage Gain at f = 10.7 MHz	A	22a	f = 10.7 MHz V_{CC} = +0V R_L = 1 kΩ	Cascode	-	40	-	-	40	-	-	40	-	dB	22b
		22c		Diff. Ampl.	-	30	-	-	30	-	-	30	-		22d
Voltage Gain Differential at f = 1 kHz		23	V_{CC} = +6V, V_{EE} = -6V, R_L = 2 kΩ		-	-	-	35	38	42	-	-	-	dB	
			V_{CC} = +12V, V_{EE} = -12V, R_L = 1.6 kΩ		-	-	-	40	42.5	45	-	-	-		
Max. Peak-to-Peak Output Voltage at f = 1 kHz	V_o(P-P)	23	V_{CC} = +6V, V_{EE} = -6V, R_L = 2 kΩ		-	-	-	7	11.5	-	-	-	-	V_{P-P}	
			V_{CC} = +12V, V_{EE} = -12V, R_L = 1.6 kΩ		-	-	-	15	23	-	-	-	-		
Bandwidth at -3 dB point	BW	23	V_{CC} = +6V, V_{EE} = -6V, R_L = 2 kΩ		-	-	-	-	7.3	-	-	-	-	MHz	
			V_{CC} = +12V, V_{EE} = -12V, R_L = 1.6 kΩ		-	-	-	-	8	-	-	-	-		
Common-Mode Input-Voltage Range	V_{CMR}	24	V_{CC} = +6V, V_{EE} = -6V		-	-	-	-2.5	(-3.2 - 4.5)	4	-	-	-	V	
			V_{CC} = +12V, V_{EE} = -12V		-	-	-	-5	(-7 - 9)	7	-	-	-		
Common-Mode Rejection Ratio	CMR	24	V_{CC} = +6V, V_{EE} = -6V		-	-	-	60	110	-	-	-	-	dB	
			V_{CC} = +12V, V_{EE} = -12V		-	-	-	60	90	-	-	-	-		
Input Impedance at f = 1 kHz	Z_{IN}		V_{CC} = +6V, V_{EE} = -6V		-	-	-	-	5.5	-	-	-	-	kΩ	
			V_{CC} = +12V, V_{EE} = -12V		-	-	-	-	3	-	-	-	-		
Peak-to-Peak Output Current	I_{P-P}		V_{CC} = +9V	f = 10.7 MHz	2	4	7	2.5	4	6	2	4	7	mA	
			V_{CC} = +12V	e_{in} = 400 mV Diff.-Ampl.	3.5	6	10	4.5	6	8	3.5	6	10		

✻ Does not apply to CA3053

CA3028A, CA3028B, CA3053 Types

DEFINITIONS OF TERMS

AGC Bias Current

The current drawn by the device from the AGC-voltage source, at maximum AGC voltage.

AGC Range

The total change in voltage gain (from maximum gain to complete cutoff) which may be achieved by application of the specified range of dc voltage to the AGC input terminal of the device.

Common-Mode Rejection Ratio

The ratio of the full differential voltage gain to the common-mode voltage gain.

Device Dissipation

The total power drain of the device with no signal applied and no external load current.

Input Bias Current

The average value (one-half the sum) of the currents at the two input terminals when the quiescent operating voltages at the two output terminals are equal.

Input Offset Current

The difference in the currents at the two input terminals when the quiescent operating voltages at the two output terminals are equal.

Input Offset Voltage

The difference in the dc voltages which must be applied to the input terminals to obtain equal quiescent operating voltages (zero output offset voltage) at the output terminals.

Noise Figure

The ratio of the total noise power of the device and a resistive signal source to the noise power of the signal source alone, the signal source representing a generator of zero impedance in series with the source resistance.

Power Gain

The ratio of the signal power developed at the output of the device to the signal power applied to the input, expressed in dB.

Quiescent Operating Current

The average (dc) value of the current in either output terminal.

Voltage Gain

The ratio of the change in output voltage at either output terminal with respect to ground, to a change in input voltage at either input terminal with respect to ground, with the other input terminal at ac ground.

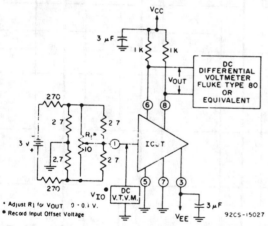

Fig.2 - Input offset voltage test circuit for CA3028B.

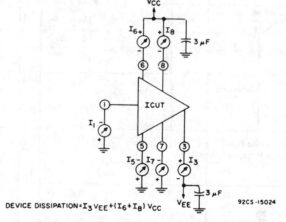

Fig.3a - Input offset current, input bias current, device dissipation, and quiescent operating current test circuit for CA3028A and CA3028B.

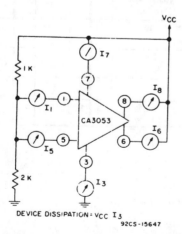

Fig.3b - Input bias current, device dissipation, and quiescent operating current test circuit for CA3053.

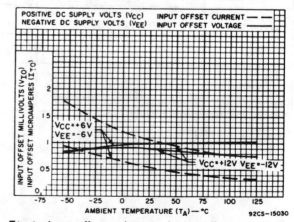

Fig.4 - Input offset voltage and input offset current for CA3028B.

ORDERING INFORMATION

Device	Temperature Range	Package
MC1496G	0°C to +70°C	Metal Can
MC1496L	0°C to +70°C	Ceramic DIP
MC1496P	0°C to +70°C	Plastic DIP
MC1596G	−55°C to +125°C	Metal Can
MC1596L	−55°C to +125°C	Ceramic DIP

MC1496
MC1596

BALANCED MODULATOR – DEMODULATOR

. . . designed for use where the output voltage is a product of an input voltage (signal) and a switching function (carrier). Typical applications include suppressed carrier and amplitude modulation, synchronous detection, FM detection, phase detection, and chopper applications. See Motorola Application Note AN-531 for additional design information.

- Excellent Carrier Suppression — 65 dB typ @ 0.5 MHz
  — 50 dB typ @ 10 MHz
- Adjustable Gain and Signal Handling
- Balanced Inputs and Outputs
- High Common Mode Rejection — 85 dB typ

BALANCED
MODULATOR – DEMODULATOR

SILICON MONOLITHIC
INTEGRATED CIRCUIT

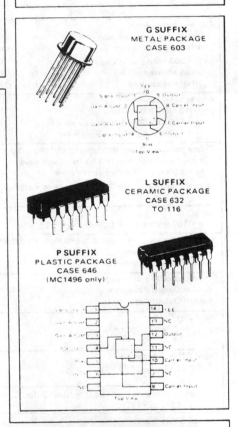

G SUFFIX
METAL PACKAGE
CASE 603

L SUFFIX
CERAMIC PACKAGE
CASE 632
TO 116

P SUFFIX
PLASTIC PACKAGE
CASE 646
(MC1496 only)

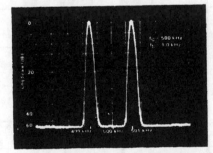

FIGURE 1
SUPPRESSED CARRIER
OUTPUT WAVEFORM

FIGURE 2
SUPPRESSED CARRIER
SPECTRUM

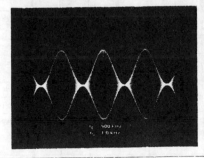

FIGURE 3 —
AMPLITUDE MODULATION
OUTPUT WAVEFORM

FIGURE 4 — AMPLITUDE MODULATION SPECTRUM

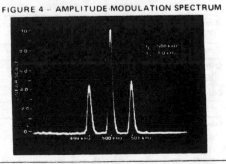

MAXIMUM RATINGS * ($T_A = +25^{\circ}C$ unless otherwise noted)

Rating	Symbol	Value	Unit
Applied Voltage $(V_6 - V_7, V_8 - V_1, V_9 - V_7, V_9 - V_8, V_7 - V_4, V_7 - V_1,$ $V_8 - V_4, V_6 - V_8, V_2 - V_5, V_3 - V_5)$	ΔV	30	Vdc
Differential Input Signal	$V_7 - V_8$ $V_4 - V_1$	$+5.0$ $\pm(5 + I_5 R_e)$	Vdc
Maximum Bias Current	I_5	10	mA

Power Dissipation (Package Limitation)
  Ceramic Dual In-Line Package
    Derate above $T_A = +25^{\circ}C$
  Metal Package
    Derate above $T_A = +25^{\circ}C$
	P_D	
		575
		3.85
		680
		4.6
			
			mW
			mW/$^{\circ}$C
			mW
			mW/$^{\circ}$C

Operating Temperature Range
  MC1496
  MC1596
	T_A	
		0 to +70
		-55 to +125
			$^{\circ}$C

Storage Temperature Range	T_{stg}	-65 to +150	$^{\circ}$C

ELECTRICAL CHARACTERISTICS * ($V_{CC} = +12$ Vdc, $V_{EE} = -8.0$ Vdc, $I_5 = 1.0$ mAdc, $R_L = 3.9$ kΩ, $R_e = 1.0$ kΩ, $T_A = +25^{\circ}C$ unless otherwise noted) (All input and output characteristics are single-ended unless otherwise noted.)

Characteristic	Fig	Note	Symbol	MC1596 Min	MC1596 Typ	MC1596 Max	MC1496 Min	MC1496 Typ	MC1496 Max	Unit
Carrier Feedthrough $V_C = 60$ mV(rms) sine wave and $\quad f_C = 1.0$ kHz offset adjusted to zero $\qquad f_C = 10$ MHz	5	1	V_{CFT}	- -	40 140	- -	- -	40 140	- -	μV(rms)
$V_C = 300$ mVp-p square wave: offset adjusted to zero $\quad f_C = 1.0$ kHz offset not adjusted $\qquad f_C = 1.0$ kHz				- -	0.04 20	0.2 100	- -	0.04 20	0.4 200	mV(rms)
Carrier Suppression $f_S = 10$ kHz, 300 mV(rms) $f_C = 500$ kHz, 60 mV(rms) sine wave $f_C = 10$ MHz, 60 mV(rms) sine wave	5	2	V_{CS}	 50 -	 65 50	 - -	 40 -	 65 50	 - -	dB k
Transadmittance Bandwidth (Magnitude) ($R_L = 50$ ohms) Carrier Input Port, $V_C = 60$ mV(rms) sine wave $f_S = 1.0$ kHz, 300 mV(rms) sine wave Signal Input Port, $V_S = 300$ mV(rms) sine wave $|V_C| = 0.5$ Vdc	8	8	BW_{3dB}	 - -	 300 80	 - -	 - -	 300 80	 - -	MHz
Signal Gain $V_S = 100$ mV(rms), $f = 1.0$ kHz, $|V_C| = 0.5$ Vdc	10	3	A_{VS}	2.5	3.5	-	2.5	3.5	-	V/V
Single-Ended Input Impedance, Signal Port, $f = 5.0$ MHz Parallel Input Resistance Parallel Input Capacitance	6	-	r_{ip} c_{ip}	- -	200 2.0	- -	- -	200 2.0	- -	kΩ pF
Single-Ended Output Impedance, $f = 10$ MHz Parallel Output Resistance Parallel Output Capacitance	6	-	r_{op} c_{op}	- -	40 5.0	- -	- -	40 5.0	- -	kΩ pF
Input Bias Current $I_{bS} = \dfrac{I_1 + I_4}{2}$; $I_{bC} = \dfrac{I_7 + I_8}{2}$	7	-	I_{bS} I_{bC}	- -	12 12	25 25	- -	12 12	30 30	μA
Input Offset Current $I_{ioS} = I_1 - I_4$; $I_{ioC} = I_7 - I_8$	7	-	$|I_{ioS}|$ $|I_{ioC}|$	- -	0.7 0.7	5.0 5.0	- -	0.7 0.7	7.0 7.0	μA
Average Temperature Coefficient of Input Offset Current ($T_A = -55^{\circ}C$ to $+125^{\circ}C$)	7	-	$|TC_{Iio}|$	-	2.0	-	-	2.0	-	nA/$^{\circ}$C
Output Offset Current ($I_6 - I_9$)	7	-	$|I_{oo}|$	-	14	50	-	14	80	μA
Average Temperature Coefficient of Output Offset Current ($T_A = -55^{\circ}C$ to $+125^{\circ}C$)	7	-	$|TC_{Ioo}|$	-	90	-	-	90	-	nA/$^{\circ}$C
Common-Mode Input Swing, Signal Port, $f_S = 1.0$ kHz	9	4	CMV	-	5.0	-	-	5.0	-	Vp-p
Common-Mode Gain, Signal Port, $f_S = 1.0$ kHz, $|V_C| = 0.5$ Vdc	9	-	ACM	-	-85	-	-	-85	-	dB
Common-Mode Quiescent Output Voltage (Pin 6 or Pin 9)	10	-	V_o	-	8.0	-	-	8.0	-	Vdc
Differential Output Voltage Swing Capability	10	-	V_{out}	-	8.0	-	-	8.0	-	Vp-p
Power Supply Current $I_6 + I_9$ I_{10}	7	6	I_{CC} I_{EE}	- -	2.0 3.0	3.0 4.0	- -	2.0 3.0	4.0 5.0	mAdc
DC Power Dissipation	7	5	P_D	-	33	-	-	33	-	mW

* Pin number references pertain to this device when packaged in a metal can. To ascertain the corresponding pin numbers for plastic or ceramic packaged devices refer to the first page of this specification sheet.

MC1496, MC1596

GENERAL OPERATING INFORMATION *

Note 1 — Carrier Feedthrough

Carrier feedthrough is defined as the output voltage at carrier frequency with only the carrier applied (signal voltage = 0).

Carrier null is achieved by balancing the currents in the differential amplifier by means of a bias trim potentiometer (R_1 of Figure 5).

Note 2 — Carrier Suppression

Carrier suppression is defined as the ratio of each sideband output to carrier output for the carrier and signal voltage levels specified.

Carrier suppression is very dependent on carrier input level, as shown in Figure 22. A low value of the carrier does not fully switch the upper switching devices, and results in lower signal gain, hence lower carrier suppression. A higher than optimum carrier level results in unnecessary device and circuit carrier feedthrough, which again degenerates the suppression figure. The MC1596 has been characterized with a 60 mV(rms) sinewave carrier input signal. This level provides optimum carrier suppression at carrier frequencies in the vicinity of 500 kHz, and is generally recommended for balanced modulator applications.

Carrier feedthrough is independent of signal level, V_S. Thus carrier suppression can be maximized by operating with large signal levels. However, a linear operating mode must be maintained in the signal-input transistor pair — or harmonics of the modulating signal will be generated and appear in the device output as spurious sidebands of the suppressed carrier. This requirement places an upper limit on input-signal amplitude (see Note 3 and Figure 20). Note also that an optimum carrier level is recommended in Figure 22 for good carrier suppression and minimum spurious sideband generation.

At higher frequencies circuit layout is very important in order to minimize carrier feedthrough. Shielding may be necessary in order to prevent capacitive coupling between the carrier input leads and the output leads.

Note 3 — Signal Gain and Maximum Input Level

Signal gain (single-ended) at low frequencies is defined as the voltage gain,

$$A_{VS} = \frac{V_o}{V_S} = \frac{R_L}{R_e + 2r_e} \text{ where } r_e = \frac{26 \text{ mV}}{I_5 \text{ (mA)}}$$

A constant dc potential is applied to the carrier input terminals to fully switch two of the upper transistors "on" and two transistors "off" (V_C = 0.5 Vdc). This in effect forms a cascode differential amplifier.

Linear operation requires that the signal input be below a critical value determined by R_E and the bias current I_5

$$V_S \leq I_5 R_E \text{ (Volts peak)}$$

Note that in the test circuit of Figure 10, V_S corresponds to a maximum value of 1 volt peak.

Note 4 — Common-Mode Swing

The common-mode swing is the voltage which may be applied to both bases of the signal differential amplifier, without saturating the current sources or without saturating the differential amplifier itself by swinging it into the upper switching devices. This swing is variable depending on the particular circuit and biasing conditions chosen (see Note 6).

Note 5 — Power Dissipation

Power dissipation, P_D, within the integrated circuit package should be calculated as the summation of the voltage-current products at each port, i.e. assuming $V_9 = V_6$, $I_5 = I_6 = I_9$ and ignoring

base current, $P_D = 2 I_5 (V_6 - V_{10}) + I_5 (V_5 - V_{10})$ where subscripts refer to pin numbers.

Note 6 — Design Equations

The following is a partial list of design equations needed to operate the circuit with other supply voltages and input conditions. See Note 3 for R_e equation.

A. Operating Current

The internal bias currents are set by the conditions at pin 5. Assume:

$$I_5 = I_6 = I_9$$

$$I_B \ll I_C \text{ for all transistors}$$

then:

$$R_5 = \frac{V^- - \phi}{I_5} - 500 \,\Omega \quad \text{where:} \quad R_5 \text{ is the resistor between pin 5 and ground}$$
$$\phi = 0.75 \text{ V at } T_A = +25^\circ C$$

The MC1596 has been characterized for the condition I_5 = 1.0 mA and is the generally recommended value.

B. Common-Mode Quiescent Output Voltage

$$V_6 = V_9 = V^+ - I_5 R_L$$

Note 7 — Biasing

The MC1596 requires three dc bias voltage levels which must be set externally. Guidelines for setting up these three levels include maintaining at least 2 volts collector-base bias on all transistors while not exceeding the voltages given in the absolute maximum rating table;

$$30 \text{ Vdc} \geq [(V_6, V_9) - (V_7, V_8)] \geq 2 \text{ Vdc}$$

$$30 \text{ Vdc} \geq [(V_7, V_8) - (V_1, V_4)] \geq 2.7 \text{ Vdc}$$

$$30 \text{ Vdc} \geq [(V_1, V_4) - (V_5)] \geq 2.7 \text{ Vdc}$$

The foregoing conditions are based on the following approximations:

$$V_6 = V_9, \quad V_7 = V_8, \quad V_1 = V_4$$

Bias currents flowing into pins 1, 4, 7, and 8 are transistor base currents and can normally be neglected if external bias dividers are designed to carry 1.0 mA or more.

Note 8 — Transadmittance Bandwidth

Carrier transadmittance bandwidth is the 3-dB bandwidth of the device forward transadmittance as defined by:

$$Y_{21C} = \frac{i_o \text{ (each sideband)}}{v_s \text{ (signal)}} \bigg|_{V_o = 0}$$

Signal transadmittance bandwidth is the 3-dB bandwidth of the device forward transadmittance as defined by:

$$Y_{21S} = \frac{i_o \text{ (signal)}}{v_s \text{ (signal)}} \bigg|_{V_C = 0.5 \text{ Vdc}, V_o = 0}$$

*Pin number references pertain to this device when packaged in a metal can. To ascertain the corresponding pin numbers for plastic or ceramic packaged devices refer to the first page of this specification sheet.

MC1496, MC1596

Note 9 — Coupling and Bypass Capacitors C_1 and C_2

Capacitors C_1 and C_2 (Figure 5) should be selected for a reactance of less than 5.0 ohms at the carrier frequency.

Note 10 — Output Signal, V_o

The output signal is taken from pins 6 and 9, either balanced or single-ended. Figure 12 shows the output levels of each of the two output sidebands resulting from variations in both the carrier and modulating signal inputs with a single-ended output connection.

Note 11 — Signal Port Stability

Under certain values of driving source impedance, oscillation may occur. In this event, an RC suppression network should be connected directly to each input using short leads. This will reduce the Q of the source-tuned circuits that cause the oscillation.

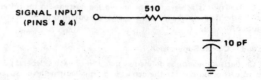

An alternate method for low-frequency applications is to insert a 1 k-ohm resistor in series with the inputs, pins 1 and 4. In this case input current drift may cause serious degradation of carrier suppression.

TEST CIRCUITS

FIGURE 5 — CARRIER REJECTION AND SUPPRESSION

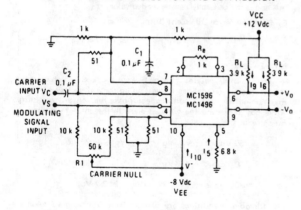

FIGURE 6 — INPUT-OUTPUT IMPEDANCE

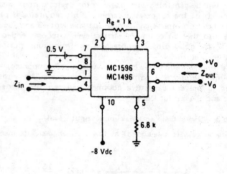

FIGURE 7 — BIAS AND OFFSET CURRENTS

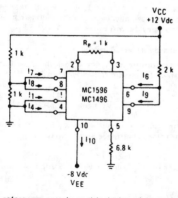

FIGURE 8 — TRANSCONDUCTANCE BANDWIDTH

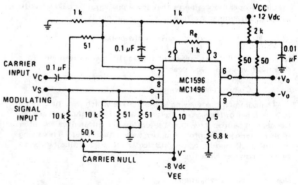

Pin number references pertain to this device when packaged in a metal can. To ascertain the corresponding pin numbers for plastic or ceramic packaged devices refer to the first page of this specification sheet.

MC1496, MC1596

TEST CIRCUITS (continued)

FIGURE 9 – COMMON-MODE GAIN

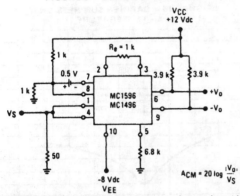

$$A_{CM} = 20 \log \frac{|V_O|}{V_S}$$

FIGURE 10 – SIGNAL GAIN AND OUTPUT SWING

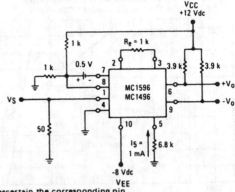

Pin number references pertain to this device when packaged in a metal can. To ascertain the corresponding pin numbers for plastic or ceramic packaged devices refer to the first page of this specification sheet.

TYPICAL CHARACTERISTICS (continued)

Typical characteristics were obtained with circuit shown in Figure 5, f_C = 500 kHz (sine wave), V_C = 60 mV(rms), f_S = 1 kHz, V_S = 300 mV(rms), T_A = +25°C unless otherwise noted.

FIGURE 11 – SIDEBAND OUTPUT versus CARRIER LEVELS

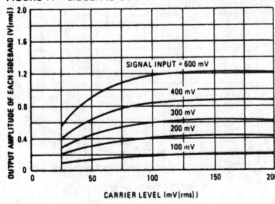

FIGURE 12 – SIGNAL-PORT PARALLEL-EQUIVALENT INPUT RESISTANCE versus FREQUENCY

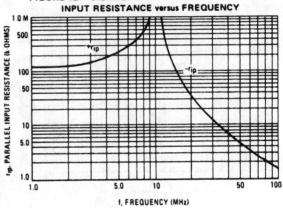

FIGURE 13 – SIGNAL-PORT PARALLEL-EQUIVALENT INPUT CAPACITANCE versus FREQUENCY

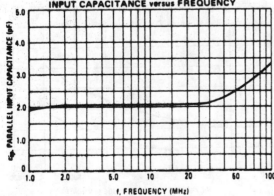

FIGURE 14 – SINGLE-ENDED OUTPUT IMPEDANCE versus FREQUENCY

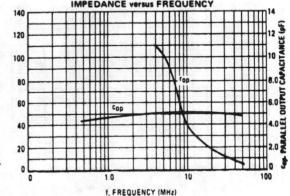

MC1496, MC1596

TYPICAL CHARACTERISTICS (continued)

Typical characteristics were obtained with circuit shown in Figure 5, f_C = 500 kHz (sine wave), V_C = 60 mV(rms), f_S = 1 kHz, V_S = 300 mV(rms), T_A = +25°C unless otherwise noted.

FIGURE 15 – SIDEBAND AND SIGNAL PORT TRANSADMITTANCES versus FREQUENCY

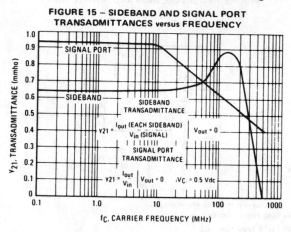

FIGURE 16 – CARRIER SUPPRESSION versus TEMPERATURE

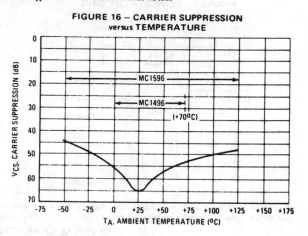

FIGURE 17 – SIGNAL-PORT FREQUENCY RESPONSE

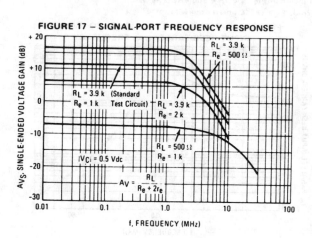

FIGURE 18 – CARRIER SUPPRESSION versus FREQUENCY

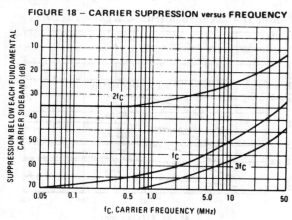

FIGURE 19 – CARRIER FEEDTHROUGH versus FREQUENCY

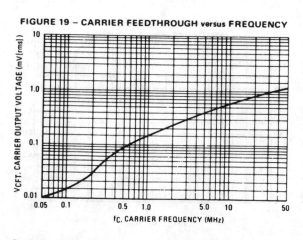

FIGURE 20 – SIDEBAND HARMONIC SUPPRESSION versus INPUT SIGNAL LEVEL

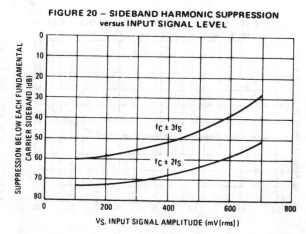

Copyright of Motorola, Inc. Used by permission.

MC1496, MC1596

TYPICAL CHARACTERISTICS (continued)

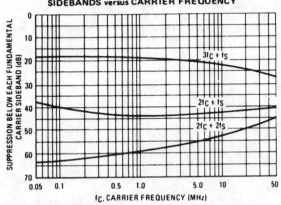

FIGURE 21 – SUPPRESSION OF CARRIER HARMONIC SIDEBANDS versus CARRIER FREQUENCY

FIGURE 22 – CARRIER SUPPRESSION versus CARRIER INPUT LEVEL

OPERATIONS INFORMATION

The MC1596/MC1496, a monolithic balanced modulator circuit, is shown in Figure 23.

This circuit consists of an upper quad differential amplifier driven by a standard differential amplifier with dual current sources. The output collectors are cross-coupled so that full-wave balanced multiplication of the two input voltages occurs. That is, the output signal is a constant times the product of the two input signals.

Mathematical analysis of linear ac signal multiplication indicates that the output spectrum will consist of only the sum and difference of the two input frequencies. Thus, the device may be used as a balanced modulator, doubly balanced mixer, product detector, frequency doubler, and other applications requiring these particular output signal characteristics.

The lower differential amplifier has its emitters connected to the package pins so that an external emitter resistance may be used. Also, external load resistors are employed at the device output.

Signal Levels

The upper quad differential amplifier may be operated either in a linear or a saturated mode. The lower differential amplifier is operated in a linear mode for most applications.

For low-level operation at both input ports, the output signal will contain sum and difference frequency components and have an amplitude which is a function of the product of the input signal amplitudes.

For high-level operation at the carrier input port and linear operation at the modulating signal port, the output signal will contain sum and difference frequency components of the modulating signal frequency and the fundamental and odd harmonics of the carrier frequency. The output amplitude will be a constant times the modulating signal amplitude. Any amplitude variations in the carrier signal will not appear in the output.

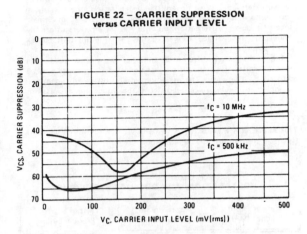

FIGURE 23 – CIRCUIT SCHEMATIC

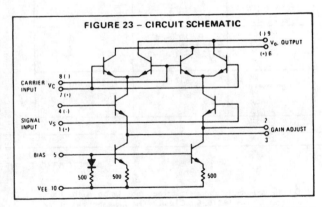

FIGURE 24 – TYPICAL MODULATOR CIRCUIT

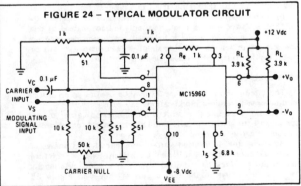

Pin number references pertain to this device when packaged in a metal can. To ascertain the corresponding pin numbers for plastic or ceramic packaged devices refer to the first page of this specification sheet.

Copyright of Motorola, Inc. Used by permission.

MC1496, MC1596

OPERATIONS INFORMATION (continued)

The linear signal handling capabilities of a differential amplifier are well defined. With no emitter degeneration, the maximum input voltage for linear operation is approximately 25 mV peak. Since the upper differential amplifier has its emitters internally connected, this voltage applies to the carrier input port for all conditions.

Since the lower differential amplifier has provisions for an external emitter resistance, its linear signal handling range may be adjusted by the user. The maximum input voltage for linear operation may be approximated from the following expression:

$$V \approx (I_5)(R_E) \text{ volts peak.}$$

This expression may be used to compute the minimum value of R_E for a given input voltage amplitude.

FIGURE 25 – TABLE 1
VOLTAGE GAIN AND OUTPUT FREQUENCIES

Carrier Input Signal (V_C)	Approximate Voltage Gain	Output Signal Frequency(s)
Low-level dc	$\dfrac{R_L V_C}{2(R_E + 2r_e)\left(\frac{KT}{q}\right)}$	f_M
High-level dc	$\dfrac{R_L}{R_E + 2r_e}$	f_M
Low-level ac	$\dfrac{R_L V_C(\text{rms})}{2\sqrt{2}\left(\frac{KT}{q}\right)(R_E + 2r_e)}$	$f_C \pm f_M$
High-level ac	$\dfrac{0.637 R_L}{R_E + 2r_e}$	$f_C \pm f_M, 3f_C \pm f_M,$ $5f_C \pm f_M, \ldots$

The gain from the modulating signal input port to the output is the MC1596/MC1496 gain parameter which is most often of interest to the designer. This gain has significance only when the lower differential amplifier is operated in a linear mode, but this includes most applications of the device.

As previously mentioned, the upper quad differential amplifier may be operated either in a linear or a saturated mode. Approximate gain expressions have been developed for the MC1596/MC1496 for a low-level modulating signal input and the following carrier input conditions:

1) Low-level dc
2) High-level dc
3) Low-level ac
4) High-level ac

These gains are summarized in Table 1, along with the frequency components contained in the output signal.

NOTES:
1. Low-level Modulating Signal, V_M, assumed in all cases. V_C is Carrier Input Voltage.
2. When the output signal contains multiple frequencies, the gain expression given is for the output amplitude of each of the two desired outputs, $f_C + f_M$ and $f_C - f_M$.
3. All gain expressions are for a single-ended output. For a differential output connection, multiply each expression by two.
4. R_L = Load resistance.
5. R_E = Emitter resistance between pins 2 and 3.
6. r_e = Transistor dynamic emitter resistance, at +25°C;

$$r_e \approx \frac{26 \text{ mV}}{I_5 \text{ (mA)}}$$

7. K = Boltzmann's Constant, T = temperature in degrees Kelvin, q = the charge on an electron.

$$\frac{KT}{q} \approx 26 \text{ mV at room temperature}$$

APPLICATIONS INFORMATION

Double sideband suppressed carrier modulation is the basic application of the MC1596/MC1496. The suggested circuit for this application is shown on the front page of this data sheet.

In some applications, it may be necessary to operate the MC1596/MC1496 with a single dc supply voltage instead of dual supplies. Figure 26 shows a balanced modulator designed for operation with a single +12 Vdc supply. Performance of this circuit is similar to that of the dual supply modulator.

AM Modulator

The circuit shown in Figure 27 may be used as an amplitude modulator with a minor modification.

All that is required to shift from suppressed carrier to AM operation is to adjust the carrier null potentiometer for the proper amount of carrier insertion in the output signal.

However, the suppressed carrier null circuitry as shown in Figure 27 does not have sufficient adjustment range. Therefore, the modulator may be modified for AM operation by changing two resistor values in the null circuit as shown in Figure 28.

Product Detector

The MC1596/MC1496 makes an excellent SSB product detector (see Figure 29).

This product detector has a sensitivity of 3.0 microvolts and a dynamic range of 90 dB when operating at an intermediate frequency of 9 MHz.

The detector is broadband for the entire high frequency range. For operation at very low intermediate frequencies down to 50 kHz the 0.1 μF capacitors on pins 7 and 8 should be increased to 1.0 μF. Also, the output filter at pin 9 can be tailored to a specific intermediate frequency and audio amplifier input impedance.

As in all applications of the MC1596/MC1496, the emitter resistance between pins 2 and 3 may be increased or decreased to adjust circuit gain, sensitivity, and dynamic range.

This circuit may also be used as an AM detector by introducing carrier signal at the carrier input and an AM signal at the SSB input.

The carrier signal may be derived from the intermediate frequency signal or generated locally. The carrier signal may be introduced with or without modulation, provided its level is sufficiently high to saturate the upper quad differential amplifier. If the carrier signal is modulated, a 300 mV(rms) input level is recommended.

Copyright of Motorola, Inc. Used by permission.

MC1496, MC1596

APPLICATIONS INFORMATION (continued)

Doubly Balanced Mixer

The MC1596/MC1496 may be used as a doubly balanced mixer with either broadband or tuned narrow band input and output networks.

The local oscillator signal is introduced at the carrier input port with a recommended amplitude of 100 mV(rms).

Figure 30 shows a mixer with a broadband input and a tuned output.

Frequency Doubler

The MC1596/MC1496 will operate as a frequency doubler by introducing the same frequency at both input ports.

Figures 31 and 32 show a broadband frequency doubler and a tuned output very high frequency (VHF) doubler, respectively.

Phase Detection and FM Detection

The MC1596/MC1496 will function as a phase detector. High-level input signals are introduced at both inputs. When both inputs are at the same frequency the MC1596/MC1496 will deliver an output which is a function of the phase difference between the two input signals.

An FM detector may be constructed by using the phase detector principle. A tuned circuit is added at one of the inputs to cause the two input signals to vary in phase as a function of frequency. The MC1596/MC1496 will then provide an output which is a function of the input signal frequency.

Pin number references pertain to this device when packaged in a metal can. To ascertain the corresponding pin numbers for plastic or ceramic packaged devices refer to the first page of this specification sheet.

TYPICAL APPLICATIONS

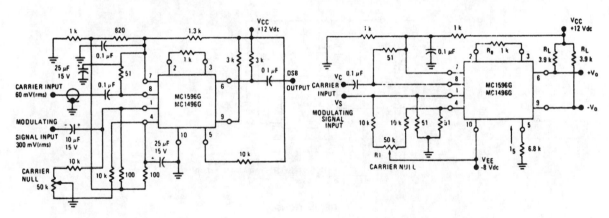

FIGURE 26 – BALANCED MODULATOR
(+12 Vdc SINGLE SUPPLY)

FIGURE 27 – BALANCED MODULATOR-DEMODULATOR

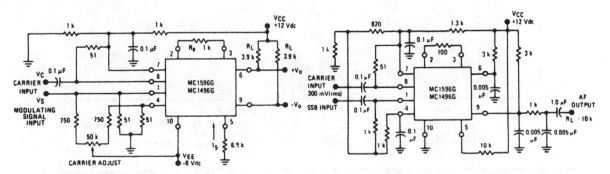

FIGURE 28 – AM MODULATOR CIRCUIT

FIGURE 29 – PRODUCT DETECTOR
(+12 Vdc SINGLE SUPPLY)

TYPICAL APPLICATIONS (continued)

FIGURE 30 – DOUBLY BALANCED MIXER (BROADBAND INPUTS, 9.0 MHz TUNED OUTPUT)

FIGURE 31 – LOW-FREQUENCY DOUBLER

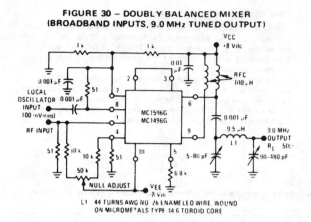

L1 44 TURNS AWG NO. 26 ENAMELED WIRE WOUND
ON MICROMETALS TYPE 44 6 TOROID CORE

FIGURE 32 – 150 to 300 MHz DOUBLER

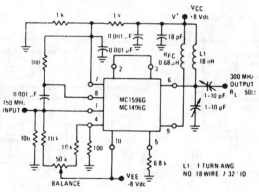

L1 1 TURN AWG
NO. 18 WIRE / 32" I.D.

DEFINITIONS

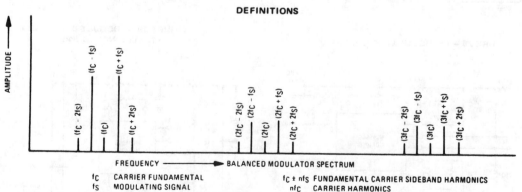

FREQUENCY ——————➤ BALANCED MODULATOR SPECTRUM

f_C	CARRIER FUNDAMENTAL	
f_S	MODULATING SIGNAL	
$f_C \pm f_S$	FUNDAMENTAL CARRIER SIDEBANDS	

$f_C \pm nf_S$	FUNDAMENTAL CARRIER SIDEBAND HARMONICS	
nf_C	CARRIER HARMONICS	
$nf_C \pm nf_S$	CARRIER HARMONIC SIDEBANDS	

Pin number references pertain to this device when packaged in a metal can. To ascertain the corresponding pin numbers for plastic or ceramic packaged devices refer to the first page of this specification sheet.

National Semiconductor

Industrial/Automotive/Functional Blocks/ Telecommunications

LM565/LM565C phase locked loop

general description

The LM565 and LM565C are general purpose phase locked loops containing a stable, highly linear voltage controlled oscillator for low distortion FM demodulation, and a double balanced phase detector with good carrier suppression. The VCO frequency is set with an external resistor and capacitor, and a tuning range of 10:1 can be obtained with the same capacitor. The characteristics of the closed loop system—bandwidth, response speed, capture and pull in range—may be adjusted over a wide range with an external resistor and capacitor. The loop may be broken between the VCO and the phase detector for insertion of a digital frequency divider to obtain frequency multiplication.

The LM565H is specified for operation over the –55°C to +125°C military temperature range. The LM565CH and LM565CN are specified for operation over the 0°C to +70°C temperature range.

features

- 200 ppm/°C frequency stability of the VCO

- Power supply range of ±5 to ±12 volts with 100 ppm/% typical
- 0.2% linearity of demodulated output
- Linear triangle wave with in phase zero crossings available
- TTL and DTL compatible phase detector input and square wave output
- Adjustable hold in range from ±1% to > ±60%.

applications

- Data and tape synchronization
- Modems
- FSK demodulation
- FM demodulation
- Frequency synthesizer
- Tone decoding
- Frequency multiplication and division
- SCA demodulators
- Telemetry receivers
- Signal regeneration
- Coherent demodulators.

schematic and connection diagrams

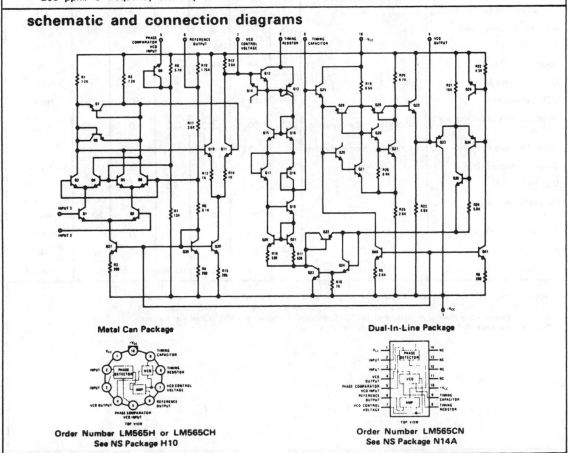

Metal Can Package

Order Number LM565H or LM565CH
See NS Package H10

Dual-In-Line Package

Order Number LM565CN
See NS Package N14A

absolute maximum ratings

Supply Voltage	±12V
Power Dissipation (Note 1)	300 mW
Differential Input Voltage	±1V
Operating Temperature Range LM565H	−55°C to +125°C
LM565CH, LM565CN	0°C to 70°C
Storage Temperature Range	−65°C to +150°C
Lead Temperature (Soldering, 10 sec)	300°C

electrical characteristics (AC Test Circuit, $T_A = 25°C$, $V_C = ±6V$)

PARAMETER	CONDITIONS	LM565			LM565C			UNITS
		MIN	TYP	MAX	MIN	TYP	MAX	
Power Supply Current			8.0	12.5		8.0	12.5	mA
Input Impedance (Pins 2, 3)	−4V < V_2, V_3 < 0V	7	10			5		kΩ
VCO Maximum Operating Frequency	C_o = 2.7 pF	300	500		250	500		kHz
Operating Frequency Temperature Coefficient			−100	300		−200	500	ppm/°C
Frequency Drift with Supply Voltage			0.01	0.1		0.05	0.2	%/V
Triangle Wave Output Voltage		2	2.4	3	2	2.4	3	V_{p-p}
Triangle Wave Output Linearity			0.2	0.75		0.5	1	%
Square Wave Output Level		4.7	5.4		4.7	5.4		V_{p-p}
Output Impedance (Pin 4)			5			5		kΩ
Square Wave Duty Cycle		45	50	55	40	50	60	%
Square Wave Rise Time			20	100		20		ns
Square Wave Fall Time			50	200		50		ns
Output Current Sink (Pin 4)		0.6	1		0.6	1		mA
VCO Sensitivity	f_o = 10 kHz	6400	6600	6800	6000	6600	7200	Hz/V
Demodulated Output Voltage (Pin 7)	±10% Frequency Deviation	250	300	350	200	300	400	mV_{pp}
Total Harmonic Distortion	±10% Frequency Deviation		0.2	0.75		0.2	1.5	%
Output Impedance (Pin 7)			3.5			3.5		kΩ
DC Level (Pin 7)		4.25	4.5	4.75	4.0	4.5	5.0	V
Output Offset Voltage $|V_7 - V_6|$			30	100		50	200	mV
Temperature Drift of $|V_7 - V_6|$			500			500		µV/°C
AM Rejection		30	40			40		dB
Phase Detector Sensitivity K_D		0.6	.68	0.9	0.55	.68	0.95	V/radian

Note 1: The maximum junction temperature of the LM565 is 150°C, while that of the LM565C and LM565CN is 100°C. For operation at elevated temperatures, devices in the TO-5 package must be derated based on a thermal resistance of 150°C/W junction to ambient or 45°C/W junction to case. Thermal resistance of the dual-in-line package is 100°C/W.

Reprinted with permission of National Semiconductor Corp.

typical performance characteristics

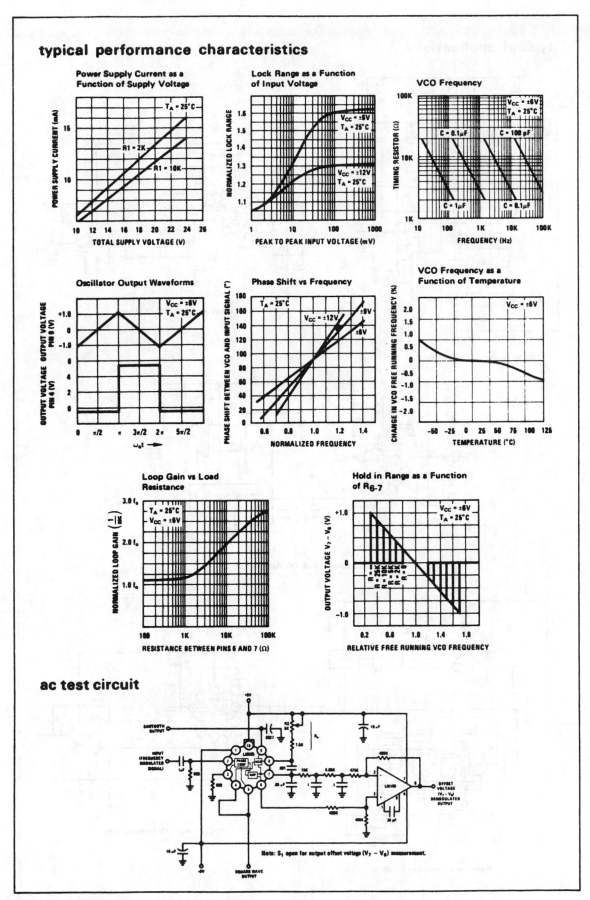

Reprinted with permission of National Semiconductor Corp.

typical applications

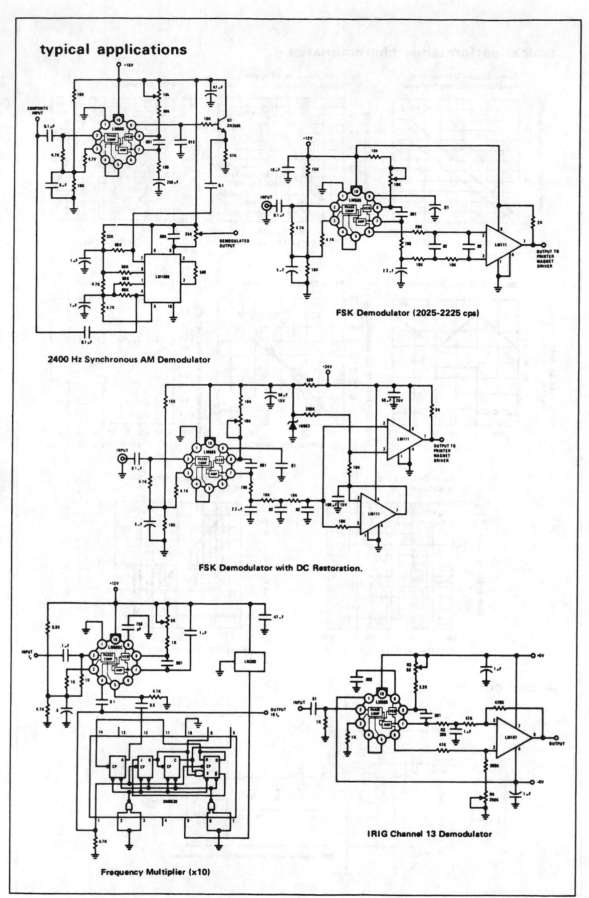

2400 Hz Synchronous AM Demodulator

FSK Demodulator (2025-2225 cps)

FSK Demodulator with DC Restoration.

Frequency Multiplier (x10)

IRIG Channel 13 Demodulator

Reprinted with permission of National Semiconductor Corp.

applications information

In designing with phase locked loops such as the LM565, the important parameters of interest are:

FREE RUNNING FREQUENCY

$$f_o \cong \frac{1}{3.7\,R_0C_0}$$

LOOP GAIN: relates the amount of phase change between the input signal and the VCO signal for a shift In input signal frequency (assuming the loop remains in lock). In servo theory, this is called the "velocity error coefficient".

$$\text{Loop gain} = K_oK_D \left(\frac{1}{\text{sec}}\right)$$

$$K_o = \text{oscillator sensitivity} \left(\frac{\text{radians/sec}}{\text{volt}}\right)$$

$$K_D = \text{phase detector sensitivity} \left(\frac{\text{volts}}{\text{radian}}\right)$$

The loop gain of the LM565 is dependent on supply voltage, and may be found from:

$$K_oK_D = \frac{33.6\,f_o}{V_c}$$

f_o = VCO frequency in Hz

V_c = total supply voltage to circuit.

Loop gain may be reduced by connecting a resistor between pins 6 and 7; this reduces the load impedance on the output amplifier and hence the loop gain.

HOLD IN RANGE: the range of frequencies that the loop will remain in lock after initially being locked.

$$f_H = \pm\,\frac{8\,f_o}{V_c}$$

f_o = free running frequency of VCO

V_c = total supply voltage to the circuit.

THE LOOP FILTER

In almost all applications, it will be desirable to filter the signal at the output of the phase detector (pin 7) this filter may take one of two forms:

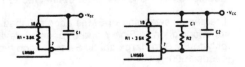

Simple Lag Filter   **Lag-Lead Filter**

A simple lag filter may be used for wide closed loop bandwidth applications such as modulation following where the frequency deviation of the carrier is fairly high (greater than 10%), or where wideband modulating signals must be followed.

The natural bandwidth of the closed loop response may be found from:

$$f_n = \frac{1}{2\pi}\sqrt{\frac{K_oK_D}{R_1C_1}}$$

Associated with this is a damping factor:

$$\delta = \frac{1}{2}\sqrt{\frac{1}{R_1C_1K_oK_D}}$$

For narrow band applications where a narrow noise bandwidth is desired, such as applications involving tracking a slowly varying carrier, a lead lag filter should be used. In general, if $1/R_1C_1 < K_oK_d$, the damping factor for the loop becomes quite small resulting in large overshoot and possible instability in the transient response of the loop. In this case, the natural frequency of the loop may be found from

$$f_n = \frac{1}{2\pi}\sqrt{\frac{K_oK_D}{\tau_1 + \tau_2}}$$

$$\tau_1 + \tau_2 = (R_1 + R_2)\,C_1$$

R_2 is selected to produce a desired damping factor δ, usually between 0.5 and 1.0. The damping factor is found from the approximation:

$$\delta \simeq \pi\,\tau_2 f_n$$

These two equations are plotted for convenience.

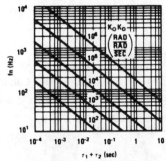

Filter Time Constant vs Natural Frequency

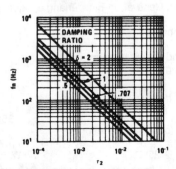

Damping Time Constant vs Natural Frequency

Capacitor C_2 should be much smaller than C_1 since its function is to provide filtering of carrier. In general $C_2 \leq 0.1\,C_1$.

Reprinted with permission of National Semiconductor Corp.

 **EXAR**

XR-8038

Precision Waveform Generator

GENERAL DESCRIPTION

The XR-8038 is a precision waveform generator IC capable of producing sine, square, triangular, sawtooth and pulse waveforms with a minimum number of external components and adjustments. Its operating frequency can be selected over nine decades of frequency, from 0.001 Hz to 1 MHz by the choice of external R-C components. The frequency of oscillation is highly stable over a wide range of temperature and supply voltage changes. The frequency control, sweep and modulation can be accomplished with an external control voltage, without affecting the quality of the output waveforms. Each of the three basic waveforms, i.e., sinewave, triangle and square wave outputs are available simultaneously, from independent output terminals.

The XR-8038 monolithic waveform generator uses advanced processing technology and Schottky-barrier diodes to enhance its frequency performance. It can be readily interfaced with a monolithic phase-detector circuit, such as the XR-2208, to form stable phase-locked loop circuits.

FEATURES

Direct Replacement for Intersil 8038
Low Frequency Drift—50 ppm/°C Max.
Simultaneous Sine, Triangle and Square-Wave Outputs
Low Distortion—THD ≃ 1%
High FM and Triangle Linearity
Wide Frequency Range—0.001 Hz to 1 MHz
Variable Duty-Cycle—2% to 98%

APPLICATIONS

Precision Waveform Generation Sine, Triangle, Square, Pulse
Sweep and FM Generation
Tone Generation
Instrumentation and Test Equipment Design
Precision PLL Design

ABSOLUTE MAXIMUM RATINGS

Power Supply	36V
Power Dissipation (package limitation)	
Ceramic package	750 mW
Derate above +25°C	6.0 mW/°C
Plastic package	625 mW
Derate above +25°C	5 mW/°C
Storage Temperature Range	−65°C to +150°C

FUNCTIONAL BLOCK DIAGRAM

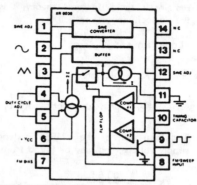

ORDERING INFORMATION

Part Number	Package	Operating Temperature
XR-8038M	Ceramic	−55°C to +125°C
XR-8038N	Ceramic	0°C to +70°C
XR-8038P	Plastic	0°C to +70°C
XR-8038CN	Ceramic	0°C to +70°C
XR-8038CP	Plastic	0°C to +70°C

SYSTEM DESCRIPTION

The XR-8038 precision waveform generator produces highly stable and sweepable square, triangle and sine waves across nine frequency decades. The device time base employs resistors and a capacitor for frequency and duty cycle determination. The generator contains dual comparators, a flip-flop driving a switch, current sources, a buffer amplifier and a sine wave converter. Three identical frequency waveforms are simultaneously available. Supply voltage can range from 10V to 30V, or ±5V with dual supplies.

Unadjusted sine wave distortion is typically less than 0.7%, with Pin 1 open and 8 kΩ from Pin 12 to Pin 11 ($-V_{EE}$ or ground). Sine wave distortion may be improved by including two 100 kΩ potentiometers between V_{CC} and V_{EE} (or ground), with one wiper connected to Pin 1 and the other connected to Pin 12.

Frequency sweeping or FM is accomplished by applying modulation to Pins 7 and 8 for small deviations, or only to Pin 8 for large shifts. Sweep range typically exceeds 1000:1.

The square wave output is an open collector transistor; output amplitude swing closely approaches the supply voltage. Triangle output amplitude is typically 1/3 of the supply, and sine wave output reaches 0.22 V_S.

XR-8038

ELECTRICAL CHARACTERISTICS

Test Conditions: $V_S = \pm 5V$ to $\pm 15V$, $T_A = 25°C$, $R_L = 1\ M\Omega$, $R_A = R_B = 10\ k\Omega$, $C_1 = 3300\ pF$, S_1 closed, unless otherwise specified. See Test Circuit of Figure 1.

PARAMETERS	XR-8038M/XR-8038			XR-8038C			UNITS	CONDITIONS
	MIN	TYP	MAX	MIN	TYP	MAX		
GENERAL CHARACTERISTICS								
Supply Voltage, V_S								
Single Supply	10		30	10		30	V	
Dual Supplies	±5		±15	±5		±15	V	
Supply Current		12	15		12	20	mA	$V_S = \pm 10V$. See Note 1.
FREQUENCY CHARACTERISTICS (Measured at Pin 9)								
Range of Adjustment								
Max. Operating Frequency		1			1		MHz	$R_A = R_B = 500\Omega$, $C_1 = 0$, $R_L = 15\ k\Omega$
Lowest Practical Frequency		0.001			0.001		Hz	$R_A = R_B = 1\ M\Omega$, $C_1 = 500\ \mu F$
Max. FM Sweep Frequency		100			100		kHz	
FM Sweep Range		1000:1			1000:1			S_1 Open. See Notes 2 and 3.
FM Linearity		0.1			0.2		%	S_1 Open. See Note 3.
Range of Timing Resistors	0.5		1000	0.5		1000	$k\Omega$	Values of R_A and R_B
Temperature Stability								
XR-8038M		20	50	—	—	—	ppm/°C	
XR-8038		50	100	—	—	—	ppm/°C	
XR-8038C	—	—	—		50		ppm/°C	
Power Supply Stability		0.05			0.05		%/V	See Note 4.
OUTPUT CHARACTERISTICS								
Square-Wave								Measured at Pin 9.
Amplitude	0.9	0.98		0.9	0.98		x V_S	$R_L = 100\ k\Omega$
Saturation Voltage		0.2	0.4		0.2	0.5	V	$I_{sink} = 2\ mA$
Rise Time		100			100		nsec	$R_L = 4.7\ k\Omega$
Fall Time		40			40		nsec	$R_L = 4.7\ k\Omega$
Duty Cycle Adj.	2		98	2		98	%	
Triangle/Sawtooth/Ramp								Measured at Pin 3.
Amplitude	0.3	0.33		0.3	0.33		x V_S	$R_L = 100\ k\Omega$
Linearity		0.05			0.1		%	
Output Impedance		200			200		Ω	$I_{out} = 5\ mA$
Sine-Wave Amplitude	0.2	0.22		0.2	0.22		x V_S	$R_L = 100\ k\Omega$
Distortion								
Unadjusted		0.7	1.5		0.8	3	%	$R_L = 1\ M\Omega$. See Note 5.
Adjusted		0.5			0.5		%	$R_L = 1\ M\Omega$

Note 1: Currents through R_A ad R_B not included.
Note 2: $V_S = 20V$, f = 10 kHz, $R_A = R_B = 10k\Omega$.
Note 3: Apply sweep voltage at Pin 8.
    $(2/3\ V_S + 2V) \leq V_{sweep} \leq V_S$
Note 4: $10V \leq V_S \leq 30V$ or $\pm 5V \leq V_S \leq \pm 15V$.
Note 5: 81 $k\Omega$ resistor connected between Pins 11 and 12.

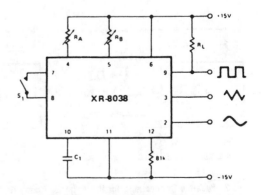

Figure 1. Generalized Test Circuit

XR-8038

CHARACTERISTIC CURVES

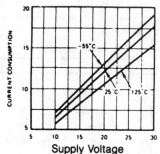

Supply Voltage
Power Dissipation vs. Supply Voltage

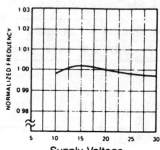

Supply Voltage
Frequency Drift vs. Power Supply

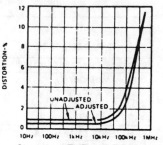

Sinewave THD vs. Frequency

WAVEFORM ADJUSTMENT

The *symmetry* of all waveforms can be adjusted with the external timing resistors. Two possible ways to accomplish this are shown in Figure 2. Best results are obtained by keeping the timing resistors R_A and R_B separate (a). R_A controls the rising portion of the triangle and sine-wave and the "Low" state of the square wave.

The magnitude of the triangle waveform is set at 1/3 V_{CC}; therefore, the duration of the rising portion of the triangle is:

$$t_1 = \frac{C \times V}{I} = \frac{C \times 1/3 \times V_{CC} \times R_A}{1/5 \times V_{CC}} = \frac{5}{3} R_A \times C$$

The duration of the falling portion of the triangle and the sinewave, and the "High" state of the square-wave is:

$$t_2 = \frac{C \times V}{I} = \frac{C \times 1/3\, V_{CC}}{\dfrac{2}{5} \times \dfrac{V_{CC}}{R_B} - \dfrac{1}{5} \times \dfrac{V_{CC}}{R_A}} = \frac{5}{3} \times \frac{R_A R_B C}{2R_A - R_B}$$

Thus a 50% duty cycle is achieved when $R_A = R_B$.

If the duty-cycle is to be varied over a small range about 50% only, the connection shown in Figure 2b is slightly more convenient. If no adjustment of the duty cycle is desired, terminals 4 and 5 can be shorted together, as shown in Figure 2c. This connection, however, carries an inherently larger variation of the duty-cycle.

With two separate timing resistors, the *frequency* is given by

$$f = \frac{1}{t_1 + t_2} = \frac{1}{\dfrac{5}{3} R_A C \left(1 + \dfrac{R_B}{2R_A - R_B}\right)}$$

or, if $R_A = R_B = R$

$$f = 0.3/RC \text{ (for Figure 2a)}$$

If a single timing resistor is used (Figures 2b and c), the frequency is

$$f = 0.15/RC$$

The frequency of oscillation is independent of supply voltage, even though none of the voltages are regulated inside the integrated circuit. This is due to the fact that both currents *and* thresholds are direct, linear function of the supply voltage and thus their effects cancel.

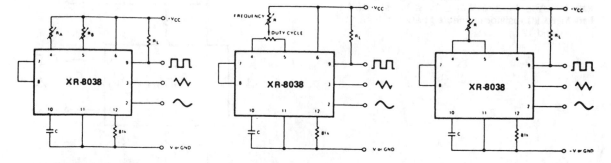

Figure 2. Possible Connections for the External Timing Resistors.

XR-8038

DISTORTION ADJUSTMENT

To minimize *sine-wave* distortion the 81 kΩ resistor between pins 11 and 12 is best made a variable one. With this arrangement distortion of less than 1% is achievable. To reduce this even further, two potentiometers can be connected as shown in Figure 3. This configuration allows a reduction of sine-wave distortion close to 0.5%

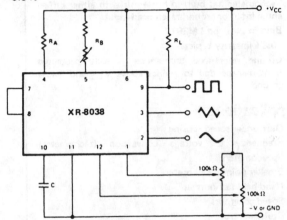

Figure 3. Connection to Achieve Minimum Sine-Wave Distortion.

SELECTING TIMING COMPONENTS

For any given output frequency, there is a wide range of RC combinations that will work. However certain constraints are placed upon the magnitude of the charging current for optimum performance. At the low end, currents of less than 0.1 μA are undesirable because circuit leakages will contribute significant errors at high temperatures. At higher currents (1 > 5 mA), transistor betas and saturation voltages will contribute increasingly larger errors. Optimum performance will be obtained for charging currents of 1 μ to 1 mA. If pins 7 and 8 are shorted together the magnitude of the charging current due to R_A can be calculated from:

$$1 = \frac{R_1 \times V_{CC}}{(R_1 + R_2)} \times \frac{1}{R_A} = \frac{V_{CC}}{5R_A}$$

A similar calculation holds for R_B.

SINGLE-SUPPLY AND SPLIT-SUPPLY OPERATION

The waveform generator can be operated either from a single power-supply (10 to 30 Volts) or a dual power-supply (±5 to ±15 Volts). With a single power-supply the average levels of the triangle and sine-wave are at exactly one-half of the supply voltage, while the square-wave alternates between +V_{CC} and ground. A split power supply has the advantage that all waveforms move symmetrically about ground.

The square-wave output is not committed. A load resistor can be connected to a different power-supply, as long as the applied voltage remains within the breakdown capability of the waveform generator (30V). In this way, the square-wave output will be TTL compatible (load resistor connected to +5 Volts) while the waveform generator itself is powered from a higher supply voltage.

FREQUENCY MODULATION AND SWEEP

The frequency of the waveform generator is a direct function of the DC voltage at terminal 8 (measured from +V_{CC}). By altering this voltage, frequency modulation is performed.

For small deviations (e.g., ±10%) the modulating signal can be applied directly to pin 8 by merely providing ac coupling with a capacitor, as shown in Figure 4a. An external resistor between pins 7 and 8 is not necessary, but it can be used to increase input impedance. Without it (i.e. terminals 7 and 8 connected together), the input impedance is 8kΩ); with it, this impedance increases to (R + 8kΩ).

For larger FM deviations or for frequency sweeping, the modulating signal is applied between the positive supply voltage and pin 8 (Figure 4b). In this way the entire bias for the current sources is created by the modulating signal and a very large (e.g., 1000:1) sweep range is obtained (f = 0 at V_{sweep} = 0). Care must be taken, however, to regulate the supply voltage; in this configuration the charge current is no longer a function of the supply voltage (yet the trigger thresholds still are) and thus the frequency becomes dependent on the supply voltage. The potential on Pin 8 may be swept from V_{CC} to 2/3 V_{CC} + 2V.

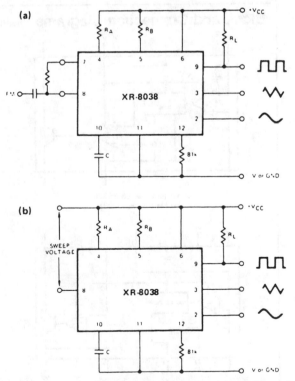

Figure 4. Connections for Frequency Modulation (a) and Sweep (b).

National Semiconductor

LM2907, LM2917 Frequency to Voltage Converter

General Description

The LM2907, LM2917 series are monolithic frequency to voltage converters with a high gain op amp/comparator designed to operate a relay, lamp, or other load when the input frequency reaches or exceeds a selected rate. The tachometer uses a charge pump technique and offers frequency doubling for low ripple, full input protection in two versions (LM2907-8, LM2917-8) and its output swings to ground for a zero frequency input.

Advantages

- Output swings to ground for zero frequency input
- Easy to use; $V_{OUT} = f_{IN} \times V_{CC} \times R1 \times C1$
- Only one RC network provides frequency doubling
- Zener regulator on chip allows accurate and stable frequency to voltage or current conversion. (LM2917)

Features

- Ground referenced tachometer input interfaces directly with variable reluctance magnetic pickups
- Op amp/comparator has floating transistor output
- 50 mA sink or source to operate relays, solenoids, meters, or LEDs

- Frequency doubling for low ripple
- Tachometer has built-in hysteresis with either differential input or ground referenced input
- Built-in zener on LM2917
- ±0.3% linearity typical
- Ground referenced tachometer is fully protected from damage due to swings above V_{CC} and below ground

Applications

- Over/under speed sensing
- Frequency to voltage conversion (tachometer)
- Speedometers
- Breaker point dwell meters
- Hand-held tachometer
- Speed governors
- Cruise control
- Automotive door lock control
- Clutch control
- Horn control
- Touch or sound switches

Block and Connection Diagrams Dual-In-Line Packages, Top Views

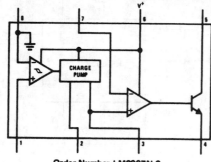

Order Number LM2907N-8
See NS Package N08B

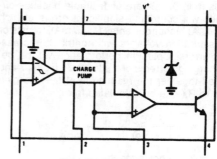

Order Number LM2917N-8
See NS Package N08B

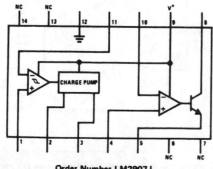

Order Number LM2907J
See NS Package J14A
Order Number LM2907N
See NS Package N14A

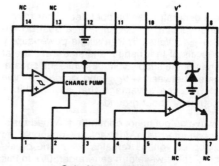

Order Number LM2917J
See NS Package J14A
Order Number LM2917N
See NS Package N14A

Reprinted with permission of National Semiconductor Corp.

LM311

National Semiconductor

Voltage Comparators

LM311 Voltage Comparator

General Description

The LM311 is a voltage comparator that has input currents more than a hundred times lower than devices like the LM306 or LM710C. It is also designed to operate over a wider range of supply voltages: from standard ±15V op amp supplies down to the single 5V supply used for IC logic. Its output is compatible with RTL, DTL and TTL as well as MOS circuits. Further, it can drive lamps or relays, switching voltages up to 40V at currents as high as 50 mA.

Features

- Operates from single 5V supply
- Maximum input current: 250 nA
- Maximum offset current: 50 nA

- Differential input voltage range: ±30V
- Power consumption: 135 mW at ±15V

Both the input and the output of the LM311 can be isolated from system ground, and the output can drive loads referred to ground, the positive supply or the negative supply. Offset balancing and strobe capability are provided and outputs can be wire OR'ed. Although slower than the LM306 and LM710C (200 ns response time vs 40 ns) the device is also much less prone to spurious oscillations. The LM311 has the same pin configuration as the LM306 and LM710C. See the "application hints" of the LM311 for application help.

Auxiliary Circuits **

**Note: Pin connections shown on schematic diagram and typical applications are for TO-5 package.

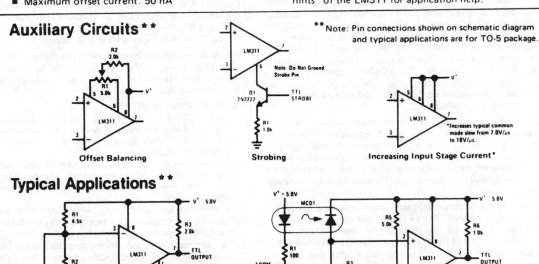

Offset Balancing

Strobing

Increasing Input Stage Current*

Typical Applications **

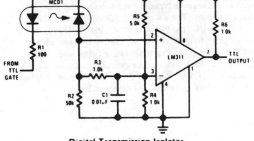

Detector for Magnetic Transducer

Digital Transmission Isolator

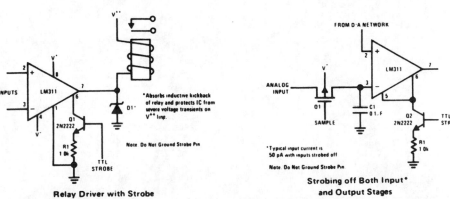

Relay Driver with Strobe

Strobing off Both Input*
and Output Stages

Reprinted with permission of National Semiconductor Corp.   5-48

APPENDIX: MANUFACTURER DATA SHEETS   317

FEATURES

Complete 8-Bit Signal Conditioning A/D Converter
  Including Instrumentation Amp and Reference
Microprocessor Bus Interface
10µs Conversion Speed
Flexible Input Stage: Instrumentation Amp Front End
  Provides Differential Inputs and High Common-Mode
  Rejection
No User Trims Required
No Missing Codes Over Temperature
Single +5V Supply Operation
Convenient Input Ranges
20-Pin DIP or Surface-Mount Package
Low Cost Monolithic Construction
MIL-STD-883B Compliant Versions Available

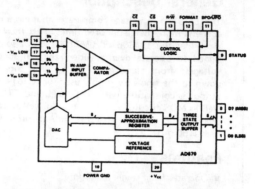

GENERAL DESCRIPTION

The AD670 is a complete 8-bit signal conditioning analog-to-digital
converter. It consists of an instrumentation amplifier front
end along with a DAC, comparator, successive approximation
register (SAR), precision voltage reference, and a three-state output
buffer on a single monolithic chip. No external components or
user trims are required to interface, with full accuracy, an analog
system to an 8-bit data bus. The AD670 will operate on the
+5V system supply. The input stage provides differential inputs
with excellent common-mode rejection and allows direct interface
to a variety of transducers.

The device is configured with input scaling resistors to permit
two input ranges: 0 to 255mV (1mV/LSB) and 0 to 2.55V
(10mV/LSB). The AD670 can be configured for both unipolar
and bipolar inputs over these ranges. The differential inputs and
common-mode rejection of this front end are useful in applications
such as conversion of transducer signals superimposed on common-
mode voltages.

The AD670 incorporates advanced circuit design and proven
processing technology. The successive approximation function is
implemented with I^2L (integrated injection logic). Thin-film
SiCr resistors provide the stability required to prevent missing
codes over the entire operating temperature range while laser
wafer trimming of the resistor ladder permits calibration of the
device to within ±1LSB. Thus, no user trims for gain or offset
are required. Conversion time of the device is 10µs.

The AD670 is available in four package types and five grades.
The J and K grades are specified over 0 to +70°C and come in
20-pin plastic DIP packages or 20-terminal PLCC packages.
The A and B grades (−40°C to +85°C) and the S grade (−55°C
to +125°C) come in 20-pin ceramic DIP packages.

The S grade is also available with optional processing to MIL-STD-
883 in 20-pin ceramic DIP or 20-terminal LCC packages. The
Analog Devices Military Products Databook should be consulted
for detailed specifications.

PRODUCT HIGHLIGHTS

1. The AD670 is a complete 8-bit A/D including three-state
   outputs and microprocessor control for direct connection to
   8-bit data buses. No external components are required to
   perform a conversion.
2. The flexible input stage features a differential instrumentation
   amp input with excellent common-mode rejection. This
   allows direct interface to a variety of transducers without
   preamplification.
3. No user trims are required for 8-bit accurate performance.
4. Operation from a single +5V supply allows the AD670 to
   run off of the microprocessor's supply.
5. Four convenient input ranges (two unipolar and two bipolar)
   are available through internal scaling resistors: 0 to 255mV
   (1mV/LSB) and 0 to 2.55V (10mV/LSB).
6. Software control of the output mode is provided. The user
   can easily select unipolar or bipolar inputs and binary or 2's
   complement output codes.

AD670

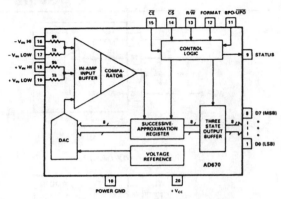

Figure 1. AD670 Block Diagram and Terminal Configuration
(All Packages)

ORDERING GUIDE

Model[1]	Temperature Range	Relative Accuracy @ +25°C	Gain Accuracy @ +25°C	Package Option[2]
AD670JN	0 to +70°C	± 1/2LSB	± 1.5LSB	Plastic DIP (N-20)
AD670JP	0 to +70°C	± 1/2LSB	± 1.5LSB	PLCC (P-20A)
AD670KN	0 to +70°C	± 1/4LSB	± 0.75LSB	Plastic DIP (N-20)
AD670KP	0 to +70°C	± 1/4LSB	± 0.75LSB	PLCC (P-20A)
AD670AD	-40°C to +85°C	± 1/2LSB	± 1.5LSB	Ceramic DIP (D-20)
AD670BD	-40°C to +85°C	± 1/4LSB	± 0.75LSB	Ceramic DIP (D-20)
AD670SD	-55°C to +125°C	± 1/2LSB	± 1.5LSB	Ceramic DIP (D-20)

NOTES
[1]For details on grade and package offerings screened in accordance with MIL-STD-883, refer to the Analog Devices Military Products Databook.
[2]D = Ceramic DIP; N = Plastic DIP; P = Plastic Leaded Chip Carrier. For outline information see Package Information section.

CIRCUIT OPERATION/FUNCTIONAL DESCRIPTION

The AD670 is a functionally complete 8-bit signal conditioning A/D converter with microprocessor compatibility. The input section uses an instrumentation amplifier to accomplish the voltage to current conversion. This front end provides a high impedance, low bias current differential amplifier. The common-mode range allows the user to directly interface the device to a variety of transducers.

The A/D conversions are controlled by R/$\overline{W}$, $\overline{CS}$, and $\overline{CE}$. The R/$\overline{W}$ line directs the converter to read or start a conversion. A minimum write/start pulse of 300ns is required on either $\overline{CE}$ or $\overline{CS}$. The STATUS line goes high, indicating that a conversion is in process. The conversion thus begun, the internal 8-bit DAC is sequenced from MSB to LSB using a novel successive approximation technique. In conventional designs, the DAC is stepped through the bits by a clock. This can be thought of as a static design since the speed at which the DAC is sequenced is determined solely by the clock. No clock is used in the AD670. Instead, a "dynamic SAR" is created consisting of a string of inverters with taps along the delay line. Sections of the delay line between taps act as one shots. The pulses are used to set and reset the DAC's bits and strobe the comparator. When strobed, the comparator then determines whether the addition of each successively weighted bit current causes the DAC current

sum to be greater or less than the input current. If the sum is less, the bit is turned off. After all bits are tested, the SAR holds an 8-bit code representing the input signal to within 1/2LSB accuracy. Ease of implementation and reduced dependence on process related variables make this an attractive approach to a successive approximation design.

The SAR provides an end-of-conversion signal to the control logic which then brings the STATUS line low. Data outputs remain in a high impedance state until R/$\overline{W}$ is brought high with $\overline{CE}$ and $\overline{CS}$ low and allows the converter to be read. Bringing $\overline{CE}$ or $\overline{CS}$ high during the valid data period ends the read cycle. The output buffers cannot be enabled during a conversion. Any convert start commands will be ignored until the conversion cycle is completed; once a conversion cycle has been started it cannot be stopped or restarted.

The AD670 provides the user with a great deal of flexibility by offering two input spans and formats and a choice of output codes. Input format and input range can each be selected. The BPO/$\overline{UPO}$ pin controls a switch which injects a bipolar offset current of a value equal to the MSB less 1/2LSB into the summing node of the comparator to offset the DAC output. Two precision 10 to 1 attenuators are included on board to provide input range selection of 0 to 2.55V or 0 to 255mV. Additional ranges of

−1.28 to 1.27V and −128 to 127mV are possible if the BPO/$\overline{UPO}$ switch is high when the conversion is started. Finally, output coding can be chosen using the FORMAT pin when the conversion is started. In the bipolar mode and with a logic 1 on FORMAT, the output is in two's complement; with a logic 0, the output is offset binary.

CONNECTING THE AD670
The AD670 has been designed for ease of use. All active components required to perform a complete A/D conversion are on board and are connected internally. In addition, all calibration trims are performed at the factory, assuring specified accuracy without user trims. There are, however, a number of options and connections that should be considered to obtain maximum flexibility from the part.

INPUT CONNECTIONS
Standard connections are shown in the figures that follow. An input range of 0 to 2.55V may be configured as shown in Figure 2a. This will provide a one LSB change for each 10mV of input change. The input range of 0 to 255mV is configured as shown in Figure 2b. In this case, each LSB represents 1mV of input change. When unipolar input signals are used, Pin 11, BPO/$\overline{UPO}$, should be grounded. Pin 11 selects the input format for either unipolar or bipolar signals. Figures 3a and 3b show the input connections for bipolar signals. Pin 11 should be tied to +V_{CC} for bipolar inputs.

Although the instrumentation amplifier has a differential input, there must be a return path to ground for the bias currents. If it is not provided, these currents will charge stray capacitances and cause internal circuit nodes to drift uncontrollably causing the digital output to change. Such a return path is provided in Figures 2a and 3a (larger input ranges) since the 1k resistor leg

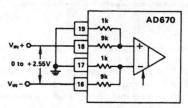

2a. 0 to 2.55V (10mV/LSB)

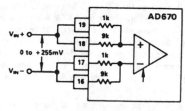

2b. 0 to 255mV (1mV/LSB)

NOTE: PIN 11, BPO/$\overline{UPO}$ SHOULD BE LOW WHEN CONVERSION IS STARTED.

Figure 2. Unipolar Input Connections

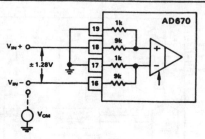

3a. ±1.28V Range

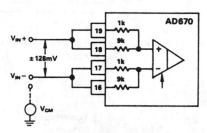

3b. ±128mV Range

NOTE: PIN 11, BPO/$\overline{UPO}$ SHOULD BE HIGH WHEN CONVERSION IS STARTED.

Figure 3. Bipolar Input Connections

is tied to ground. This is not the case for Figures 2b and 3b (the lower input ranges). When connecting the AD670 inputs to floating sources, such as transformers and ac-coupled sources, there must still be a dc path from each input to common. This can be accomplished by connecting a 10kΩ resistor from each input to ground.

Bipolar Operation
Through special design of the instrumentation amplifier, the AD670 accommodates input signal excursions below ground, even though it operates from a single 5V supply. To the user, this means that true bipolar input signals can be used without the need for any additional external components. Bipolar signals can be applied differentially across both inputs, or one of the inputs can be grounded and a bipolar signal applied to the other.

Common-Mode Performance
The AD670 is designed to reject dc and ac common-mode voltages. In some applications it is useful to apply a differential input signal V_{IN} in the presence of a dc common-mode voltage V_{CM}. The user must observe the absolute input signal limits listed in the specifications, which represent the maximum voltage V_{IN} + V_{CM} that can be applied to either input without affecting proper operation. Exceeding these limits (within the range of absolute maximum ratings), however, will not cause permanent damage.

The excellent common-mode rejection of the AD670 is due to the instrumentation amplifier front end, which maintains the differential signal until it reaches the output of the comparator. In contrast to a standard operational amplifier, the instrumentation amplifier front end provides significantly improved CMRR over a wide frequency range (Figure 4a).

**ANALOG
DEVICES**

DACPORT Low Cost, Complete µP-Compatible 8-Bit DAC

AD557

FEATURES
Complete 8-Bit DAC
Voltage Output – 0 to 2.56V
Internal Precision Band-Gap Reference
Single-Supply Operation: +5V (±10%)
Full Microprocessor Interface
Fast: 1µs Voltage Settling to ±1/2LSB
Low Power: 75mW
No User Trims Required
Guaranteed Monotonic Over Temperature
All Errors Specified T_{min} to T_{max}
Small 16-Pin DIP or 20-Pin PLCC Package
Low Cost

FUNCTIONAL BLOCK DIAGRAM

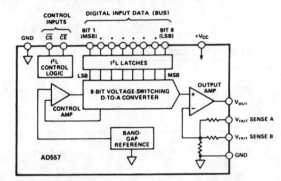

PRODUCT DESCRIPTION
The AD557 DACPORT™ is a complete voltage-output 8-bit digital-to-analog converter, including output amplifier, full microprocessor interface and precision voltage reference on a single monolithic chip. No external components or trims are required to interface, with full accuracy, an 8-bit data bus to an analog system.

The low cost and versatility of the AD557 DACPORT are the result of continued development in monolithic bipolar technologies.

The complete microprocessor interface and control logic is implemented with integrated injection logic (I^2L), an extremely dense and low-power logic structure that is process-compatible with linear bipolar fabrication. The internal precision voltage reference is the patented low-voltage band-gap circuit which permits full-accuracy performance on a single +5V power supply. Thin-film silicon-chromium resistors provide the stability required for guaranteed monotonic operation over the entire operating temperature range, while laser-wafer trimming of these thin-film resistors permits absolute calibration at the factory to within ±2.5LSB; thus, no user-trims for gain or offset are required. A new circuit design provides voltage settling to ±1/2LSB for a full-scale step in 800ns.

The AD557 is available in two package configurations. The AD557JN is packaged in a 16-pin plastic, 0.3"-wide DIP. For surface mount applications, the AD557JP is packaged in a 20-pin JEDEC standard PLCC. Both versions are specified over the operating temperature range of 0 to +70°C.

PRODUCT HIGHLIGHTS
1. The 8-bit I^2L input register and fully microprocessor-compatible control logic allow the AD557 to be directly connected to 8- or 16-bit data buses and operated with standard control signals. The latch may be disabled for direct DAC interfacing.

2. The laser-trimmed on-chip SiCr thin-film resistors are calibrated for absolute accuracy and linearity at the factory. Therefore, no user trims are necessary for full rated accuracy over the operating temperature range.

3. The inclusion of a precision low-voltage band-gap reference eliminates the need to specify and apply a separate reference source.

4. The AD557 is designed and specified to operate from a single +4.5V to +5.5V power supply.

5. Low digital input currents, 100µA max, minimize bus loading. Input thresholds are TTL/low voltage CMOS compatible.

6. The single-chip, low power I^2L design of the AD557 is inherently more reliable than hybrid multichip or conventional single-chip bipolar designs.

AD557 — SPECIFICATIONS (@ T$_A$ = +25C, V$_{CC}$ = +5V unless otherwise specified)

Model	Min	AD557J Typ	Max	Units
RESOLUTION			8	Bits
RELATIVE ACCURACY[1]				
0 to +70°C		± 1/2	1	LSB
OUTPUT				
Ranges		0 to +2.56		V
Current Source	+5			mA
Sink		Internal Passive Pull-Down to Ground[2]		
OUTPUT SETTLING TIME[3]		0.8	1.5	μs
FULL SCALE ACCURACY[4]				
@25°C		± 1.5	± 2.5	LSB
T$_{min}$ to T$_{max}$		± 2.5	± 4.0	LSB
ZERO ERROR				
@25°C			± 1	LSB
T$_{min}$ to T$_{max}$			± 3	LSB
MONOTONICITY[5]				
T$_{min}$ to T$_{max}$		Guaranteed		
DIGITAL INPUTS				
T$_{min}$ to T$_{max}$				
Input Current			± 100	μA
Data Inputs, Voltage				
Bit On – Logic "1"	2.0			V
Bit On – Logic "0"	0		0.8	V
Control Inputs, Voltage				
On – Logic "1"	2.0			V
On – Logic "0"	0		0.8	V
Input Capacitance		4		pF
TIMING[6]				
t$_W$ Strobe Pulse Width	225			ns
T$_{min}$ to T$_{max}$	300			ns
t$_{DH}$ Data Hold Time	10			ns
T$_{min}$ to T$_{max}$	10			ns
t$_{DS}$ Data Setup Time	225			ns
T$_{min}$ to T$_{max}$	300			ns
POWER SUPPLY				
Operating Voltage Range (V$_{CC}$)				
2.56 Volt Range	+4.5		+5.5	V
Current (I$_{CC}$)		15	25	mA
Rejection Ratio			0.03	%/%
POWER DISSIPATION, V$_{CC}$ = 5V		75	125	mW
OPERATING TEMPERATURE RANGE	0		+70	°C

NOTES
[1] Relative Accuracy is defined as the deviation of the code transition points from the ideal transfer point on a straight line from the offset to the full scale of the device. See "Measuring Offset Error" on AD558 data sheet.
[2] Passive pull-down resistance is 2kΩ.
[3] Settling time is specified for a positive-going full-scale step to + 1/2LSB. Negative-going steps to zero are slower, but can be improved with an external pull-down.
[4] The full-scale output voltage is 2.55V and is guaranteed with a + 5V supply.
[5] A monotonic converter has a maximum differential linearity error of ± 1LSB.
[6] See Figure 7.

Specifications shown in **boldface** are tested on all production units at final electrical test.

Specifications subject to change without notice.

PIN CONFIGURATIONS

DIP

PLCC

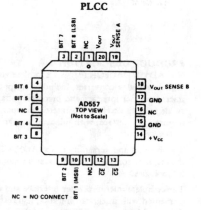

NC = NO CONNECT

ORDERING GUIDE

Model	Package Option*	Temperature
AD557JN	Plastic (N-16)	0 to +70°C
AD557JP	PLCC (P-20A)	0 to +70°C

*N = Plastic DIP; P = Plastic Leaded Chip Carrier. For outline information see Package Information section.

ABSOLUTE MAXIMUM RATINGS*

V$_{CC}$ to Ground . . . . 0V to +18V
Digital Inputs (Pins 1-10) . . . . 0 to +7.0V
V$_{OUT}$ . . . . Indefinite Short to Ground
                       Momentary Short to V$_{CC}$
Power Dissipation 450mW
Storage Temperature Range
N/P (Plastic) Packages . . . . −25°C to +100°C
Lead Temperature (soldering, 10 sec) . . . . 300°C

Thermal Resistance
Junction to Ambient/Junction to Case
N/P (Plastic) Packages . . . . 140/55°C/W

*Stresses above those listed under "Absolute Maximum Ratings" may cause permanent damage to the device. This is a stress rating only and functional operation of the device at these or any other conditions above those indicated in the operational sections of this specification is not implied. Exposure to absolute maximum rating conditions for extended periods may affect device reliability.

CIRCUIT DESCRIPTION

The AD557 consists of four major functional blocks fabricated on a single monolithic chip (see Figure 1). The main D/A converter section uses eight equally weighted laser-trimmed current sources switched into a silicon-chromium thin-film R/2R resistor ladder network to give a direct but unbuffered 0mV to 400mV output range. The transistors that form the DAC switches are PNPs; this allows direct positive-voltage logic interface and a zero-based output range.

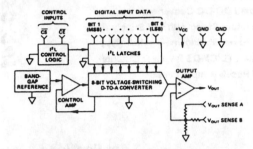

Figure 1. Functional Block Diagram

The high-speed output buffer amplifier is operated in the noninverting mode with gain determined by the user-connections at the output range select pin. The gain-setting application resistors are thin film laser trimmed to match and track the DAC resistors and to assure precise initial calibration of the output range, 0V to 2.56V. The amplifier output stage is an NPN transistor with passive pull-down for zero-based output capability with a single power supply.

The internal precision voltage reference is of the patented band-gap type. This design produces a reference voltage of 1.2V and thus, unlike 6.3V temperature-compensated zeners, may be operated from a single, low-voltage logic power supply. The microprocessor interface logic consists of an 8-bit data latch and control circuitry. Low power, small geometry and high speed are advantages of the I^2L design as applied to this section. I^2L is bipolar process compatible so that the performance of the analog sections need not be compromised to provide on-chip logic capabilities. The control logic allows the latches to be operated from a decoded microprocessor address and write signal. If the application does not involve a μP or data bus, wiring $\overline{CS}$ and $\overline{CE}$ to ground renders the latches "transparent" for direct DAC access.

Digital Input Code			Output Voltage
Binary	Hexadecimal	Decimal	
0000 0000	00	0	0
0000 0001	01	1	0.010V
0000 0010	02	2	0.020V
0000 1111	0F	15	0.150V
0001 0000	10	16	0.160V
0111 1111	7F	127	1.270V
1000 0000	80	128	1.280V
1100 0000	C0	192	1.920V
1111 1111	FF	255	2.55V

CONNECTING THE AD557

The AD557 has been configured for low cost and ease of application. All reference, output amplifier and logic connections are made internally. In addition, all calibration trims are performed at the factory assuring specified accuracy without user trims. The only connection decision to be made by the user is whether the output range desired is unipolar or bipolar. Clean circuit board layout is facilitated by isolating all digital bit inputs on one side of the package; analog outputs are on the opposite side.

UNIPOLAR 0 TO +2.56V OUTPUT RANGE

Figure 2 shows the configuration for the 0 to +2.56V full-scale output range. Because of its precise factory calibration, the AD557 is intended to be operated without user trims for gain and offset; therefore, no provisions have been made for such user trims. If a small increase in scale is required, however, it may be accomplished by slightly altering the effective gain of the output buffer. A resistor in series with V_{OUT} SENSE will increase the output range. Note that decreasing the scale by putting a resistor in series with GND will not work properly due to the code-dependent currents in GND. Adjusting offset by injecting dc at GND is not recommended for the same reason.

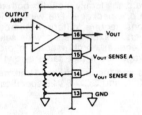

Figure 2. 0 to 2.56V Output Range

BIPOLAR −1.28V TO +1.28V OUTPUT RANGE

The AD557 was designed for operation from a single power supply and is thus capable of providing only a unipolar 0 to +2.56V output range. If a negative supply is available, bipolar output ranges may be achieved by suitable output offsetting and scaling. Figure 3 shows how a ±1.28V output range may be achieved when a −5V power supply is available. The offset is provided by the AD589 precision 1.2V reference which will operate from a +5V supply. The AD711 output amplifier can provide the necessary ±1.28V output swing from ±5V supplies. Coding is complementary offset binary.

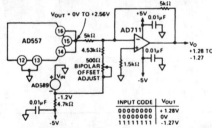

Figure 3. Bipolar Operation of AD557 from ±5V Supplies

+5V Powered
RS-232 Drivers/Receivers

General Description

Maxim's family of line drivers/receivers are intended for all RS-232 and V.28/V.24 communications interfaces, and in particular, for those applications where ±12V is not available. The MAX230, MAX236, MAX240 and MAX241 are particularly useful in battery powered systems since their low power shutdown mode reduces power dissipation to less than 5μW. The MAX233 and MAX235 use no external components and are recommended for applications where printed circuit board space is critical.

All members of the family except the MAX231 and MAX239 need only a single +5V supply for operation. The RS-232 drivers/receivers have on-board charge pump voltage converters which convert the +5V input power to the ±10V needed to generate the RS-232 output levels. The MAX231 and MAX239, designed to operate from +5V and +12V, contain a +12V to -12V charge pump voltage converter.

Since nearly all RS-232 applications need both line drivers and receivers, the family includes both receivers and drivers in one package. The wide variety of RS-232 applications require differing numbers of drivers and receivers. Maxim offers a wide selection of RS-232 driver/receiver combinations in order to minimize the package count (see table below).

Both the receivers and the line drivers (transmitters) meet all EIA RS-232C and CCITT V.28 specifications.

Features

♦ Operates from Single 5V Power Supply (+5V and +12V — MAX231 and MAX239)
♦ Meets All RS-232C and V.28 Specifications
♦ Multiple Drivers and Receivers
♦ Onboard DC-DC Converters
♦ ±9V Output Swing with +5V Supply
♦ Low Power Shutdown — <1μA (typ)
♦ 3-State TTL/CMOS Receiver Outputs
♦ ±30V Receiver Input Levels

Applications

Computers
Peripherals
Modems
Printers
Instruments

2

Selection Table

Part Number	Power Supply Voltage	No. of RS-232 Drivers	No. of RS-232 Receivers	External Components	Low Power Shutdown /TTL 3-State	No. of Pins
MAX230	+5V	5	0	4 capacitors	Yes/No	20
MAX231	+5V and +7.5V to 13.2V	2	2	2 capacitors	No/No	14
MAX232	+5V	2	2	4 capacitors	No/No	16
MAX233	+5V	2	2	None	No/No	20
MAX234	+5V	4	0	4 capacitors	No/No	16
MAX235	+5V	5	5	None	Yes/Yes	24
MAX236	+5V	4	3	4 capacitors	Yes/Yes	24
MAX237	+5V	5	3	4 capacitors	No/No	24
MAX238	+5V	4	4	4 capacitors	No/No	24
MAX239	+5V and +7.5V to 13.2V	3	5	2 capacitors	No/Yes	24
MAX240	+5V	5	5	4 capacitors	Yes/Yes	44 (Flatpak)
MAX241	+5V	4	5	4 capacitors	Yes/Yes	28 (Small Outline)

* Patent Pending

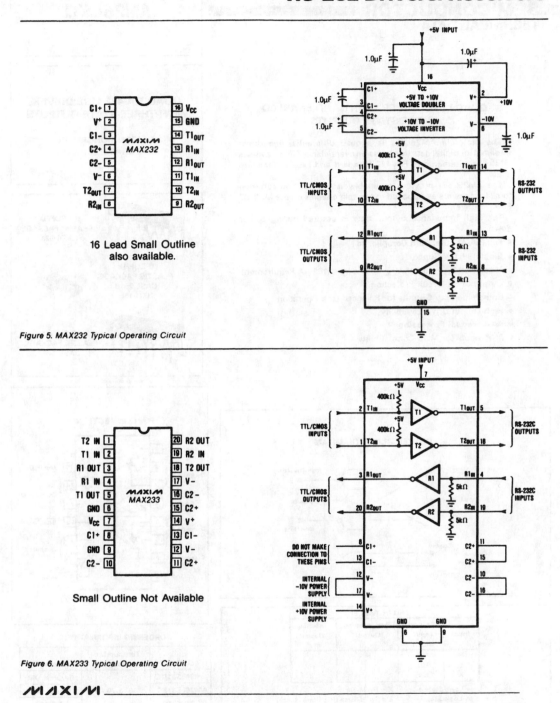

Figure 5. MAX232 Typical Operating Circuit

16 Lead Small Outline also available.

Small Outline Not Available

Figure 6. MAX233 Typical Operating Circuit

MAXIM

AM26LS31

QUAD LINE DRIVER WITH NAND ENABLED THREE-STATE OUTPUTS

The Motorola AM26LS31 is a quad differential line driver intended for digital data transmission over balanced lines. It meets all the requirements of EIA-422 Standard and Federal Standard 1020.

The AM26LS31 provides an enable/disable function common to all four drivers as opposed to the split enables on the MC3487 EIA-422 driver.

The high impedance output state is assured during power down.

- Full EIA-422 Standard Compliance
- Single +5.0 V Supply
- Meets Full V_O = 6.0 V, V_{CC} = 0 V, I_O < 100 μA Requirement
- Output Short Circuit Protection
- Complementary Outputs for Balanced Line Operation
- High Output Drive Capability
- Advanced LS Processing
- PNP Inputs for MOS Compatibility

QUAD EIA-422 LINE DRIVER WITH THREE-STATE OUTPUTS

SILICON MONOLITHIC INTEGRATED CIRCUIT

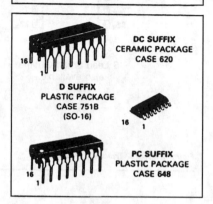

DC SUFFIX
CERAMIC PACKAGE
CASE 620

D SUFFIX
PLASTIC PACKAGE
CASE 751B
(SO-16)

PC SUFFIX
PLASTIC PACKAGE
CASE 648

DRIVER BLOCK DIAGRAM

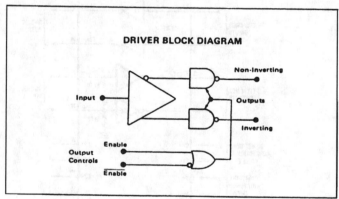

PIN CONNECTIONS

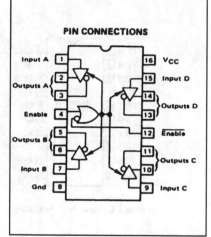

TRUTH TABLE

Input	Control Inputs (E/Ē)	Non-Inverting Output	Inverting Output
H	H/L	H	L
L	H/L	L	H
X	L/H	Z	Z

L = Low Logic State X = Irrelevant
H = High Logic State Z = Third-State (High Impedance)

ORDERING INFORMATION

Device	Temperature Range	Package
AM26LS31DC		Ceramic DIP
AM26LS31PC	0 to 70°C	Plastic DIP
MC26LS31D*		SO-16

*Note that the surface mount MC26LS31D devices use the same die as in the ceramic and plastic DIP AM26LS31DC devices, but with an MC prefix to prevent confusion with the package suffixes.

MOTOROLA LINEAR/INTERFACE ICs DEVICE DATA

MOTOROLA
■ SEMICONDUCTOR ■■■■■
TECHNICAL DATA

AM26LS32

QUAD EIA-422/423 LINE RECEIVER

Motorola's Quad EIA-422/3 Receiver features four independent receiver chains which comply with EIA Standards for the Electrical Characteristics of Balanced/Unbalanced Voltage Digital Interface Circuits. Receiver outputs are 74LS compatible, three-state structures which are forced to a high impedance state when Pin 4 is a Logic "0" and Pin 12 is a Logic "1." A PNP device buffers each output control pin to assure minimum loading for either Logic "1" or Logic "0" inputs. In addition, each receiver chain has internal hysteresis circuitry to improve noise margin and discourage output instability for slowly changing input waveforms. A summary of AM26LS32 features include:

* Four Independent Receiver Chains

* Three-State Outputs

* High Impedance Output Control Inputs (PIA Compatible)

* Internal Hysteresis — 30 mV (Typ) @ Zero Volts Common Mode

* Fast Propagation Times — 25 ns (Typ)

* TTL Compatible

* Single 5 V Supply Voltage

* Fail-Safe Input-Output Relationship. Output Always High When Inputs Are Open, Terminated or Shorted

* 6 k Minimum Input Impedance

QUAD EIA-422/3 LINE RECEIVER WITH THREE-STATE OUTPUTS

SILICON MONOLITHIC INTEGRATED CIRCUIT

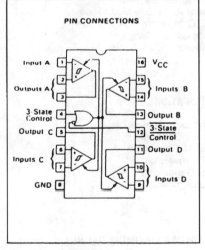

DC SUFFIX
CERAMIC PACKAGE
CASE 620

D SUFFIX
PLASTIC PACKAGE
CASE 751B
(SO-16)

PC SUFFIX
PLASTIC PACKAGE
CASE 648

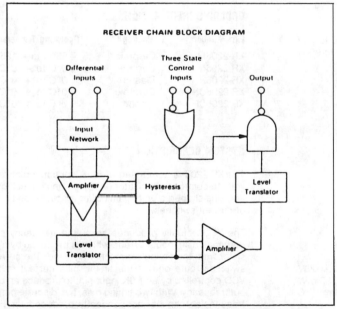

RECEIVER CHAIN BLOCK DIAGRAM

PIN CONNECTIONS

ORDERING INFORMATION

Device	Temperature	Package
AM26LS32DC		Ceramic DIP
AM26LS32PC	0 to 70°C	Plastic DIP
MC26LS32D*		SO-16

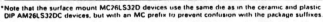

*Note that the surface mount MC26LS32D devices use the same die as in the ceramic and plastic DIP AM26LS32DC devices, but with an MC prefix to prevent confusion with the package suffixes.

MOTOROLA LINEAR/INTERFACE ICs DEVICE DATA

EXAR

XR-2206

Monolithic Function Generator

GENERAL DESCRIPTION

The XR-2206 is a monolithic function generator integrated circuit capable of producing high quality sine, square, triangle, ramp, and pulse waveforms of high-stability and accuracy. The output waveforms can be both amplitude and frequency modulated by an external voltage. Frequency of operation can be selected externally over a range of 0.01 Hz to more than 1 MHz.

The circuit is ideally suited for communications, instrumentation, and function generator applications requiring sinusoidal tone, AM, FM, or FSK generation. It has a typical drift specification of 20 ppm/°C. The oscillator frequency can be linearly swept over a 2000:1 frequency range, with an external control voltage, having a very small affect on distortion.

FEATURES

Low-Sine Wave Distortion	0.5%, Typical
Excellent Temperature Stability	20 ppm/°C, Typical
Wide Sweep Range	2000:1, Typical
Low-Supply Sensitivity	0.01%V, Typical
Linear Amplitude Modulation	
TTL Compatible FSK Controls	
Wide Supply Range	10V to 26V
Adjustable Duty Cycle	1% to 99%

APPLICATIONS

Waveform Generation
Sweep Generation
AM/FM Generation
V/F Conversion
FSK Generation
Phase-Locked Loops (VCO)

ABSOLUTE MAXIMUM RATINGS

Power Supply	26V
Power Dissipation	750 mW
Derate Above 25°C	5 mW/°C
Total Timing Current	6 mA
Storage Temperature	−65°C to +150°C

FUNCTIONAL BLOCK DIAGRAM

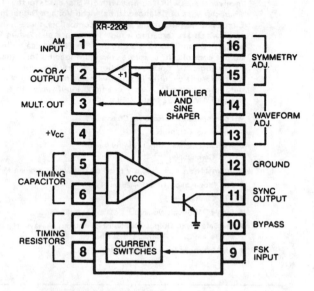

ORDERING INFORMATION

Part Number	Package	Operating Temperature
XR-2206M	Ceramic	−55°C to +125°C
XR-2206N	Ceramic	0°C to +70°C
XR-2206P	Plastic	0°C to +70°C
XR-2206CN	Ceramic	0°C to +70°C
XR-2206CP	Plastic	0°C to +70°C

SYSTEM DESCRIPTION

The XR-2206 is comprised of four functional blocks; a voltage-controlled oscillator (VCO), an analog multiplier and sine-shaper; a unity gain buffer amplifier; and a set of current switches.

The VCO actually produces an output frequency proportional to an input current, which is produced by a resistor from the timing terminals to ground. The current switches route one of the timing pins current to the VCO controlled by an FSK input pin, to produce an output frequency. With two timing pins, two discrete output frequencies can be independently produced for FSK Generation Applications.

XR-2206

ELECTRICAL CHARACTERISTICS

Test Conditions: Test Circuit of Figure 1, V^+ = 12V, T_A = 25°, C = 0.01 μF, R_1 = 100 kΩ, R_2 = 10 kΩ, R_3 = 25 kΩ unless otherwise specified. S_1 open for triangle, closed for sine wave.

PARAMETERS	XR-2206M			XR-2206C			UNITS	CONDITIONS
	MIN	TYP	MAX	MIN	TYP	MAX		
GENERAL CHARACTERISTICS								
Single Supply Voltage	10		26	10		26	V	
Split-Supply Voltage	±5		±13	±5		±13	V	
Supply Current		12	17		14	20	mA	$R_1 \geq$ 10 k Ω
OSCILLATOR SECTION								
Max. Operating Frequency	0.5	1		0.5	1		MHz	C = 1000 pF, R_1 = 1 k Ω
Lowest Practical Frequency		0.01			0.01		Hz	C = 50 μF, R_1 = 2 M Ω
Frequency Accuracy		±1	±4		±2		% of f_0	f_0 = 1/R_1C
Temperature Stability		±10	±50		±20		ppm/°C	0°C $\leq T_A \leq$ 70°C, R_1 = R_2 = 20 k Ω
Supply Sensitivity		0.01	0.1		0.01		%/V	V_{LOW} = 10V, V_{HIGH} = 20V, R_1 = R_2 = 20 k Ω
Sweep Range	1000:1	2000:1			2000:1		f_H=f_L	f_H @ R_1 = 1 k Ω f_L @ R_1 = 2 M Ω
Sweep Linearity								
10:1 Sweep		2			2		%	f_L = 1 kHz, f_H = 10 kHz
1000:1 Sweep		8			8		%	f_L = 100 kHz, f_H = 100 kHz
FM Distortion		0.1			0.1		%	±10% Deviation
Recommended Timing Components								
Timing Capacitor: C	0.001		100	0.001		100	μF	See Figure 4.
Timing Resistors: R_1 & R_2	1		2000	1		2000	k Ω	
Triangle Sine Wave Output								See Note 1, Figure 2.
Triangle Amplitude		160			160		mV/k Ω	Figure 1, S_1 Open
Sine Wave Amplitude	40	60	80		60		mV/k Ω	Figure 1, S_1 Closed
Max. Output Swing		6			6		V p-p	
Output Impedance		600			600		Ω	
Triangle Linearity		1			1		%	
Amplitude Stability		0.5			0.5		dB	For 1000:1 Sweep
Sine Wave Amplitude Stability		4800			4800		ppm/°C	See Note 2.
Sine Wave Distortion								
Without Adjustment		2.5			2.5		%	R_1 = 30 k Ω
With Adjustment		0.4	1.0		0.5	1.5	%	See Figures 6 and 7
Amplitude Modulation								
Input Impedance	50	100		50	100		k Ω	
Modulation Range		100			100		%	
Carrier Suppression		55			55		dB	
Linearity		2			2		%	For 95% modulation
Square-Wave Output								
Amplitude		12			12		V p-p	Measured at Pin 11.
Rise Time		250			250		nsec	C_L = 10 pF
Fall Time		50			50		nsec	C_L = 10 pF
Saturation Voltage		0.2	0.4		0.2	0.6	V	I_L = 2 mA
Leakage Current		0.1	20		0.1	100	μA	V_{11} = 26V
FSK Keying Level (Pin 9)	0.8	1.4	2.4	0.8	1.4	2.4	V	See section on circuit controls
Reference Bypass Voltage	2.9	3.1	3.3	2.5	3	3.5	V	Measured at Pin 10.

Note 1: Output amplitude is directly proportional to the resistance, R_3, on Pin 3. See Figure 2.
Note 2: For maximum amplitude stability, R_3 should be a positive temperature coefficient resistor.

XR-2206

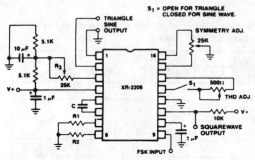

Figure 1. Basic Test Circuit.

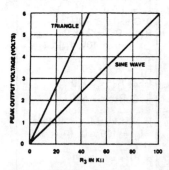

Figure 2. Output Amplitude as a Function of the Resistor, R₃, at Pin 3.

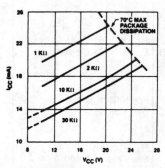

Figure 3. Supply Current versus Supply Voltage, Timing, R.

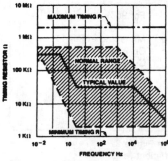

Figure 4. R versus Oscillation Frequency.

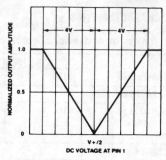

Figure 5. Normalized Output Amplitude versus DC Bias at AM Input (Pin 1).

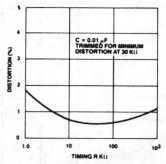

Figure 6. Trimmed Distortion versus Timing Resistor.

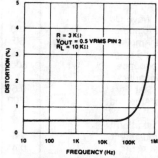

Figure 7. Sine Wave Distortion versus Operating Frequency with Timing Capacitors Varied.

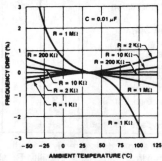

Figure 8. Frequency Drift versus Temperature.

XR-2206

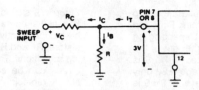

Figure 9. Circuit Connection for Frequency Sweep.

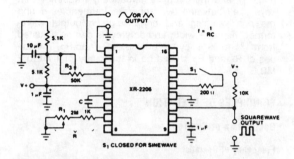

Figure 10. Circuit for Sine Wave Generation without External
Adjustment. (See Figure 2 for Choice of R₃).

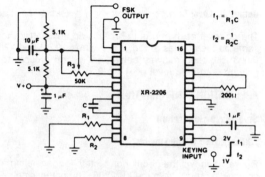

Figure 12. Sinusoidal FSK Generator.

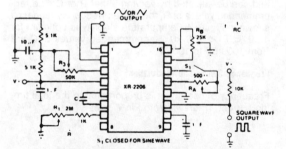

Figure 11. Circuit for Sine Wave Generation with Minimum
Harmonic Distortion. (R₃ Determines Output
Swing—See Figure 2.)

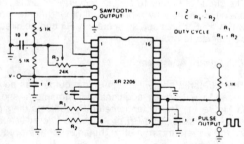

Figure 13. Circuit for Pulse and Ramp Generation.

Frequency-Shift Keying:

The XR-2206 can be operated with two separate timing resistors, R_1 and R_2, connected to the timing Pin 7 and 8, respectively, as shown in Figure 12. Depending on the polarity of the logic signal at Pin 9, either one or the other of these timing resistors is activated. If Pin 9 is open-circuited or connected to a bias voltage $\geq 2V$, only R_1 is activated. Similarly, if the voltage level at Pin 9 is $\leq 1V$, only R_2 is activated. Thus, the output frequency can be keyed between two levels, f_1 and f_2, as:

$$f_1 = 1/R_1C \text{ and } f_2 = 1/R_2C$$

For split-supply operation, the keying voltage at Pin 9 is referenced to V^-.

Output DC Level Control:

The dc level at the output (Pin 2) is approximately the same as the dc bias at Pin 3. In Figures 10, 11 and 12, Pin 3 is biased midway between V^+ and ground, to give an output dc level of $\approx V^+/2$.

APPLICATIONS INFORMATION

Sine Wave Generation

Without External Adjustment:

Figure 10 shows the circuit connection for generating a sinusoidal output from the XR-2206. The potentiometer, R_1 at Pin 7, provides the desired frequency tuning. The maximum output swing is greater than $V^+/2$, and the typical distortion (THD) is $<2.5\%$. If lower sine wave distortion is desired, additional adjustments can be provided as described in the following section.

The circuit of Figure 10 can be converted to split-supply operation, simply by replacing all ground connections with V^-. For split-supply operation, R_3 can be directly connected to ground.

With External Adjustment:

The harmonic content of sinusoidal output can be reduced to $\approx 0.5\%$ by additional adjustments as shown in Figure 11. The potentiometer, R_A, adjusts the sine-shaping resistor, and R_B provides the fine adjustment for the waveform symmetry. The adjustment procedure is as follows:

1. Set R_B at midpoint, and adjust R_A for minimum distortion.

2. With R_A set as above, adjust R_B to further reduce distortion.

Triangle Wave Generation

The circuits of Figures 10 and 11 can be converted to triangle wave generation, by simply open-circuiting Pin 13 and 14 (i.e., S_1 open). Amplitude of the triangle is approximately twice the sine wave output.

FSK Generation

Figure 12 shows the circuit connection for sinusoidal FSK signal operation. Mark and space frequencies can be independently adjusted, by the choice of timing resistors, R_1 and R_2; the output is phase-continuous during transitions. The keying signal is applied to Pin 9. The circuit can be converted to split-supply operation by simply replacing ground with V^-.

Pulse and Ramp Generation

Figure 13 shows the circuit for pulse and ramp waveform generation. In this mode of operation, the FSK keying terminal (Pin 9) is shorted to the square-wave output (Pin 11), and the circuit automatically frequency-shift keys itself between two separate frequencies during the positive-going and negative-going output waveforms. The pulse width and duty cycle can be adjusted from 1% to 99%, by the choice of R_1 and R_2. The values of R_1 and R_2 should be in the range of 1 kΩ to 2 MΩ.

PRINCIPLES OF OPERATION

Description of Controls

Frequency of Operation:

The frequency of oscillation, f_0, is determined by the external timing capacitor, C, across Pin 5 and 6, and by the timing resistor, R, connected to either Pin 7 or 8. The frequency is given as:

$$f_0 = \frac{1}{RC} \text{ Hz}$$

and can be adjusted by varying either R or C. The recommended values of R, for a given frequency range, as shown in Figure 4. Temperature stability is optimum for 4 kΩ < R < 200 kΩ. Recommended values of C are from 1000 pF to 100 μF.

Frequency Sweep and Modulation:

Frequency of oscillation is proportional to the total timing current, I_T, drawn from Pin 7 or 8:

$$f = \frac{320 \ I_T \text{ (mA)}}{C \ (\mu F)} \text{ Hz}$$

Timing terminals (Pin 7 or 8) are low-impedance points, and are internally biased at +3V, with respect to Pin 12. Frequency varies linearly with I_T, over a wide range of current values, from 1 μA to 3 mA. The frequency can be controlled by applying a control voltage, V_C, to the activated timing pin as shown in Figure 9. The frequency of oscillation is related to V_C as:

$$f = \frac{1}{RC} 1 + \frac{R}{R_C}(1 - \frac{V_C}{3}) \text{ Hz}$$

XR-2206

where V_C is in volts. The voltage-to-frequency conversion gain, K, is given as:

$$K = \partial f / \partial V_C = -\frac{0.32}{R_C C} \text{ Hz/V}$$

CAUTION: For safety operation of the circuit, I_T should be limited to ≤ 3 mA.

Output Amplitude:

Maximum output amplitude is inversely proportional to the external resistor, R_3, connected to Pin 3 (see Figure 2). For sine wave output, amplitude is approximately 60 mV peak per kΩ of R_3; for triangle, the peak amplitude is approximately 160 mV peak per kΩ of R_3. Thus, for example, $R_3 = 50$ kΩ would produce approximately ± 3V sinusoidal output amplitude.

Amplitude Modulation:

Output amplitude can be modulated by applying a dc bias and a modulating signal to Pin 1. The internal impedance at Pin 1 is approximately 100 kΩ. Output amplitude varies linearly with the applied voltage at Pin 1, for values of dc bias at this pin, within ± 4 volts of V^+/2 as shown in Figure 5. As this bias level approaches V^+/2, the phase of the output signal is reversed, and the amplitude goes through zero. This property is suitable for phase-shift keying and suppressed-carrier AM generation. Total dynamic range of amplitude modulation is approximately 55 dB.

CAUTION: AM control must be used in conjunction with a well-regulated supply, since the output amplitude now becomes a function of V^+.

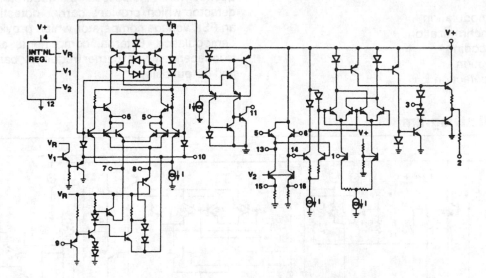

EQUIVALENT SCHEMATIC DIAGRAM

Raytheon

FSK Demodulator/
Tone Decoder

XR-2211

Features

- Wide frequency range — 0.01Hz to 300kHz
- Wide supply voltage range — 4.5V to 20V
- DTL/TTL/ECL logic compatibility
- FSK demodulation with carrier-detector
- Wide dynamic range — 2mV to $3V_{RMS}$
- Adjustable tracking range — ±1% to ±80%
- Excellent temperature stability — 20ppm/°C typical

Applications

- FSK demodulation
- Data synchronization
- Tone decoding
- FM detection
- Carrier detection

Description

The XR-2211 is a monolithic phase-locked loop (PLL) system especially designed for data communications. It is particularly well suited for FSK modem applications, and operates over a wide frequency range of 0.01Hz to 300kHz. It can accommodate analog signals between 2mV and 3V, and can interface with conventional DTL, TTL and ECL logic families. The circuit consists of a basic PLL for tracking an input signal frequency within the passband, a quadrature phase detector which provides carrier detection, and an FSK voltage comparator which provides FSK demodulation. External components are used to independently set carrier frequency, bandwidth, and output delay.

Schematic Diagram

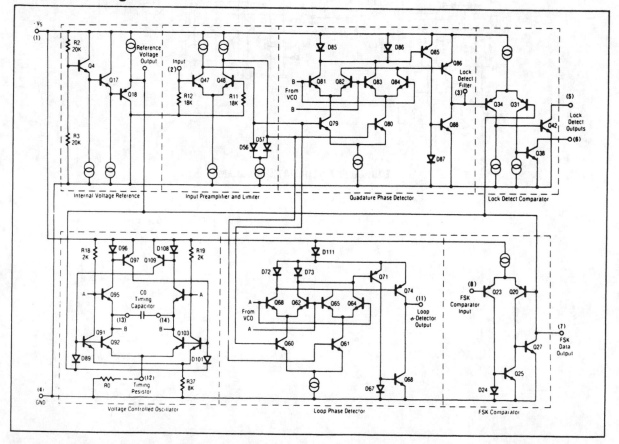

Courtesy of Ratheon Company.

XR-2211

FSK Demodulator/Tone Decoder

Mask Pattern

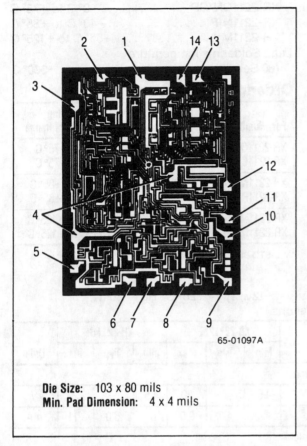

65-01097A

Die Size: 103 x 80 mils
Min. Pad Dimension: 4 x 4 mils

Connection Information

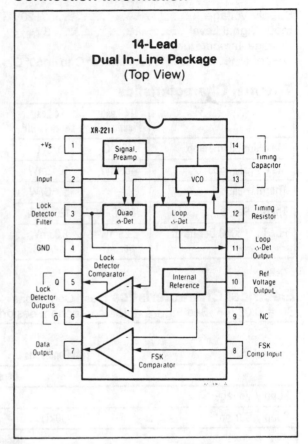

**14-Lead
Dual In-Line Package**
(Top View)

XR-2211

Pin	Label		Pin	Label
1	+Vs		14	Timing Capacitor
2	Input		13	Timing Capacitor
3	Lock Detector Filter		12	Timing Resistor
4	GND		11	Loop Φ-Det Output
5	Q Lock Detector Outputs		10	Ref Voltage Output
6	Q̄ Lock Detector Outputs		9	NC
7	Data Output		8	FSK Comp Input

Signal Preamp · VCO · Quad Φ-Det · Loop Φ-Det · Lock Detector Comparator · Internal Reference · FSK Comparator

Functional Block Diagram

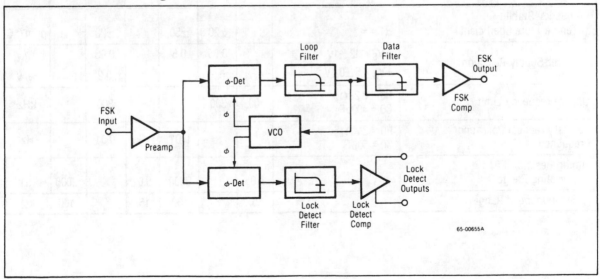

65-00655A

FSK Input — Preamp — Φ-Det — Loop Filter — Data Filter — FSK Output / FSK Comp

VCO — Φ-Det — Lock Detect Filter — Lock Detect Comp — Lock Detect Outputs

Courtesy of Ratheon Company.

Absolute Maximum Ratings

Supply Voltage .... +20V
Input Signal Level .... $3V_{RMS}$
Storage Temperature
   Range .... −65°C to +150°C

Operating Temperature Range
   XR-2211CN/CP .... 0°C to +75°C
   XR-2211N/P .... −40°C to +85°C
   XR-2211M .... −55°C to +125°C
Lead Soldering Temperature
   (60 Sec) .... +300°C

Thermal Characteristics

	14-Lead Plastic DIP	14-Lead Ceramic DIP
Max. Junction Temp.	125°C	175°C
Max. P_D T_A < 50°C	468mW	1042mW
Therm. Res. θ_{JC}	—	50°C/W
Therm. Res. θ_{JA}	160°C/W	120°C/W
For T_A > 50°C Derate at	6.25mW per °C	8.33mW per °C

Ordering Information

Part Number	Package	Operating Temperature Range
XR-2211CN	Ceramic	0°C to +75°C
XR-2211CP	Plastic	0°C to +75°C
XR-2211N	Ceramic	−40°C to +85°C
XR-2211P	Plastic	−40°C to +85°C
XR-2211M	Ceramic	−55°C to +125°C
XR-2211M/883B*	Ceramic	−55°C to +125°C

*MIL-STD-883, Level B Processing

Electrical Characteristics (Test Conditions +V_S = +12V, T_A = +25°C, R0 = 30kΩ, C0 = 0.033μF. See Figure 1 for component designations.)

Parameters	Test Conditions	XR-2211/M Min	XR-2211/M Typ	XR-2211/M Max	XR-2211C Min	XR-2211C Typ	XR-2211C Max	Units
General								
Supply Voltage		4.5		20	4.5		20	V
Supply Current	R0 ≥ 10kΩ		4.0	9.0		5.0	11	mA
Oscillator								
Frequency Accuracy	Deviation from f_0 = 1/R0C0		±1.0	±3.0		±1.0		%
Frequency Stability Temperature Coefficient	R1 = ∞		±20	±50		±20		ppm/°C
Power Supply Rejection	+V_S = 12 ±1V		0.05	0.5		0.05		%/V
	+V_S = 5 ±0.5V		0.2			0.2		%/V
Upper Frequency Limit	R0 = 8.2kΩ, C0 = 400pF	100	300			300		kHz
Lowest Practical Operating Frequency	R0 = 2MΩ C0 = 50μF			0.01		0.01		Hz
Timing Resistor, R0 Operating Range		5.0		2000	5.0		2000	kΩ
Recommended Range		15		100	15		100	kΩ

Courtesy of Raytheon Company.

Electrical Characteristics (Continued)

(V_S = +12V, T_A = +25° C, R0 = 30kΩ, C0 = 0.033μF. See Figure 1 for component designations.)

Parameters	Test Conditions	XR-2211/M			XR-2211C			Units
		Min	Typ	Max	Min	Typ	Max	
Loop Phase Detector								
Peak Output Current	Meas. at Pin 11	±150	±200	±300	±100	±200	±300	μA
Output Offset Current			±1.0			±2.0		μA
Output Impedance			1.0			1.0		MΩ
Maximum Swing	Ref. to Pin 10	±4.0	±5.0		±4.0	±5.0		V
Quadrature Phase Detector								
Peak Output Current	Meas. at Pin 3	100	150			150		μA
Output Impedance			1.0			1.0		MΩ
Maximum Swing			11			11		V_{p-p}
Input Preamp								
Input Impedance	Meas. at Pin 2		20			20		kΩ
Input Signal Voltage Required to Cause Limiting			2.0	10		2.0		mV_{RMS}
Voltage Comparator								
Input Impedance	Meas. at Pins 3 & 8		2.0			2.0		MΩ
Input Bias Current			100			100		nA
Voltage Gain	R_L = 5.1kΩ	55	70		55	70		dB
Output Voltage Low	I_C = 3mA		300			300		mV
Output Leakage Current	V_O = 12V		0.01			0.01		μA
Internal Reference								
Voltage Level	Meas. at Pin 10	4.9	5.3	5.7	4.75	5.3	5.85	V
Output Impedance			100			100		Ω

Courtesy of Raytheon Company.

Description of Circuit Controls

Signal Input (Pin 2)
The input signal is AC coupled to this terminal. The internal impedance at pin 2 is 20kΩ. Recommended input signal level is in the range of 10mV_{RMS} to 3V_{RMS}.

Quadrature Phase Detector Output (Pin 3)
This is the high-impedance output of the quadrature phase detector, and is internally connected to the input of lock-detect voltage comparator. In tone detection applications, pin 3 is connected to ground through a parallel combination of R_D and C_D (see Figure 1) to eliminate chatter at the lock-detect outputs. If this tone-detect section is not used, pin 3 can be left open circuited.

Lock-Detect Output, Q (Pin 5)
The output at pin 5 is at a "high" state when the PLL is out of lock and goes to a "low" or conducting state when the PLL is locked. It is an open collector type output and requires a pull-up resistor, R_L, to $+V_S$ for proper operation. In the "low" state it can sink up to 5mA of load current.

Lock-Detect Complement, Q̄ (Pin 6)
The output at pin 6 is the logic complement of the lock-detect output at pin 5. This output is also an open collector type stage which can sink 5mA of load current in the low or "on" state.

FSK Data Output (Pin 7)
This output is an open collector logic stage which requires a pull-up resistor, R_L, to $+V_S$ for proper operation. It can sink 5mA of load current. When decoding FSK signals the FSK data output will switch to a "high" or off state for low input frequency, and will switch to a "low" or on state for high input frequency. If no input signal is present, the logic state at pin 7 is indeterminate.

FSK Comparator Input (Pin 8)
This is the high-impedance input to the FSK voltage comparator. Normally, an FSK post-detection or data filter is connected between this terminal and the PLL phase-detector output (pin 11). This data filter is formed by R_F and C_F of Figure 1. The threshold voltage of the comparator is set by the internal reference voltage, V_R, available at pin 10.

Reference Voltage, V_R (Pin 10)
This pin is internally biased at the reference voltage level, V_R; $V_R = V+/2 - 650\text{mV}$. The DC voltage level at this pin forms an internal reference

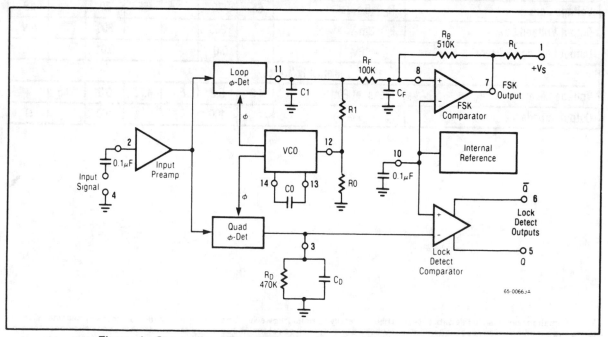

Figure 1. Generalized Circuit Connection for FSK and Tone Detection

for the voltage levels at pin 3, 8, 11, and 12. Pin 10 must be bypassed to ground with a 0.1μF capacitor.

Loop Phase Detector Output (Pin 11)
This terminal provides a high impedance output for the loop phase-detector. The PLL loop filter is formed by R1 and C1 connected to pin 11 (see Figure 1). With no input signal, or with no phase error within the PLL, the DC level at pin 11 is very nearly equal to V_R. The peak voltage swing available at the phase detector output is equal to $\pm V_R$.

VCO Control Input (Pin 12)
VCO free-running frequency is determined by external timing resistor, R0, connected from this terminal to ground. The VCO free-running frequency, f_0, is given by:

$$f_0(Hz) = \frac{1}{R0C0}$$

where C0 is the timing capacitor across pins 13 and 14. For optimum temperature stability R0 must be in the range of 10kΩ to 100kΩ (see Typical Electrical Characteristics).

This terminal is a low impedance point, and is internally biased at a DC level equal to V_R. The maximum timing current drawn from pin 12 must be limited to $\leq$3mA for proper operation of the circuit.

VCO Timing Capacitor (Pins 13 and 14)
VCO frequency is inversely proportional to the external timing capacitor, C0, connected across these terminals. C0 must be non-polarized, and in the range of 200pF to 10μF.

VCO Frequency Adjustment
VCO can be fine tuned by connecting a potentiometer, R_X, in series with R0 at pin 12 (see Figure 2).

VCO Free-Running Frequency, f_0
The XR-2211 does not have a separate VCO output terminal. Instead, the VCO outputs are internally connected to the phase-detector sections of the circuit. However, for setup or adjustment purposes, the VCO free-running frequency can be measured at pin 3 (with C_D disconnected) with no input and with pin 2 shorted to pin 10.

Design Equations
See Figure 1 for Definitions of Components.

1. VCO Center Frequency, f_0:

$$f_0(Hz) = \frac{1}{R0C0}$$

2. Internal Reference Voltage, V_R (measured at pin 10):

$$V_R = \left(\frac{+V_S}{2}\right) - 650mV$$

3. Loop Lowpass Filter Time Constant, τ:

$$\tau = R1C1$$

4. Loop Damping, ζ:

$$\zeta = \left(\sqrt{\frac{C0}{C1}}\right)\left(\frac{1}{4}\right)$$

5. Loop Tracking Bandwidth, $\pm\Delta f/f_0$:

$$\Delta f/f_0 = R0/R1$$

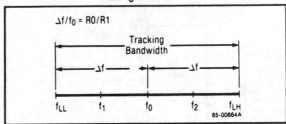

6. FSK Data Filter Time Constant, τ_F:

$$\tau_F = R_F C_F$$

7. Loop Phase Detector Conversion Gain, K_ϕ: (K_ϕ is the differential DC voltage across pins 10 and 11, per unit of phase error at phase-detector input):

$$K\phi \text{ (in volts per radian)} = \frac{(-2)(V_R)}{\pi}$$

8. VCO Conversion Gain, K0, is the amount of change in VCO frequency per unit of DC voltage change at pin 11:

$$K0 \text{ (in Hertz per volt)} = \frac{-1}{C0R1V_R}$$

9. Total Loop Gain, K_T:

$$K_T \text{ (in radians per second per volt)} = 2\pi K\phi K0$$
$$= 4/C0R1$$

10. Peak Phase-Detector Current, I_A:

$$I_A \text{ (mA)} = \frac{V_R}{25}$$

FSK Demodulator/Tone Decoder

XR-2211

Applications

FSK Decoding

Figure 2 shows the basic circuit connection for FSK decoding. With reference to Figures 1 and 2, the functions of external components are defined as follows: R0 and C0 set the PLL center frequency, R1 sets the system bandwidth, and C1 sets the loop filter time constant and the loop damping factor. C_F and R_F form a one pole post-detection filter for the FSK data output. The resistor R_B (= 510kΩ) from pin 7 to pin 8 introduces positive feedback across FSK comparator to facilitate rapid transition between output logic states.

Recommended component values for some of the most commonly used FSK bauds are given in Table 1.

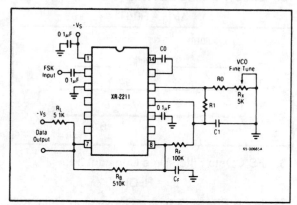

Figure 2. Circuit Connection for FSK Decoding

**Table 1. Recommended Component Values
for Commonly Used FSK Bands**
(See Circuit of Figure 2)

FSK Band	Component Values
300 Baud	C0 = 0.039μF C_F = 0.005μF
f_1 = 1070Hz	C1 = 0.01μF R0 = 18kΩ
f_2 = 1270Hz	R1 = 100kΩ
300 Baud	C0 = 0.022μF C_F = 0.005μF
f_1 = 2025Hz	C1 = 0.0047μF R1 = 18kΩ
f_2 = 2225Hz	R1 = 200kΩ
1200 Baud	C0 = 0.027μF C_F = 0.0022μF
f_1 = 1200Hz	C1 = 0.01μF R0 = 18kΩ
f_2 = 2200Hz	R1 = 30kΩ

Courtesy of Ratheon Company.

Design Instructions

The circuit of Figure 2 can be tailored for any FSK decoding application by the choice of five key circuit components; R0, R1, C0, C1 and C_F. For a given set of FSK mark and space frequencies, f_1 and f_2, these parameters can be calculated as follows:

1. Calculate PLL center frequency, f_0

$$f_0 = \frac{f_1 + f_2}{2}$$

2. Choose a value of timing resistor R0 to be in the range of 10kΩ to 100kΩ. This choice is arbitrary. The recommended value is R0 $\cong$ 20kΩ. The final value of R0 is normally fine-tuned with the series potentiometer, R_X.

3. Calculate value of C0 from Design Equation No. 1 or from Typical Performance Characteristics:

$$C0 = 1/R0f_0$$

4. Calculate R1 to give a Δf equal to the mark-space deviation:
$$R1 = R0 \, [f_0/(f_1 - f_2)]$$

5. Calculate C1 to set loop damping. (See Design Equation No. 4.)
Normally, $\zeta \approx 1/2$ is recommended
Then: C1 = C0/4 for $\zeta = 1/2$

6. Calculate Data Filter Capacitance, C_F:
For R_F = 100kΩ, R_B = 510kΩ, the recommended value of C_F is:

$$C_F \text{ (in } \mu F) = \frac{3}{\text{Baud Rate}}$$

Note: All calculated component values except R0 can be rounded off to the nearest standard value, and R0 can be varied to fine-tune center frequency through a series potentiometer, R_X (see Figure 2).

Design Example

75 Baud FSK demodulator with mark/space frequencies of 1110/1170Hz:

Step 1: Calculate f_0:
f_0 = (1110 + 1170) (1/2) = 1140Hz

Step 2: Choose R0 = 20kΩ (18kΩ fixed resistor in series with 5kΩ potentiometer)

Step 3: Calculate C0 from V_{CO} Frequency vs. Timing Capacitor: C0 = 0.044μF

Step 4: Calculate R1: R1 = R0 (2240/60) = 380kΩ

Step 5: Calculate C1: C1 = C0/4 = 0.011μF

Note: All values except R0 can be rounded off to nearest standard value.

FSK Decoding With Carrier Detect

The lock-detect section of the XR-2211 can be used as a carrier detect option for FSK decoding. The recommended circuit connection for this application is shown in Figure 3. The open-collector lock-detect output, pin 6, is shorted to the data output (pin 7). Thus, the data output will be disabled at "low" state, until there is a carrier within the detection band of the PLL, and the pin 6 output goes "high" to enable the data output.

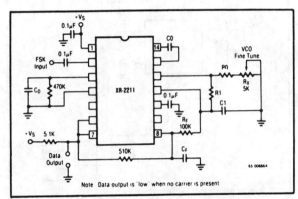

Figure 3. External Connectors for FSK Demodulation With Carrier Detect Capability

The minimum value of the lock-detect filter capacitance C_D is inversely proportional to the capture range, $\pm\Delta f_c$. This is the range of incoming frequencies over which the loop can acquire lock and is always less than the tracking range. It is further limited by C1. For most applications, $\Delta f_c < \Delta f/2$. For $R_D = 470k\Omega$, the approximate minimum value of C_D can be determined by:

$$C_D(\mu F) \geq 16/\text{capture range in Hz}$$

With values of C_D that are too small, chatter can be observed on the lock-detect output as an incoming signal frequency approaches the capture bandwidth. Excessively large values of C_D will slow the response time of the lock-detect output.

Tone Detection

Figure 4 shows the generalized circuit connection for tone detection. The logic outputs, Q and $\overline{Q}$ at pins 5 and 6 are normally at "high" and "low" logic states, respectively. When a tone is

present within the detection band of the PLL, the logic state at these outputs becomes reversed for the duration of the input tone. Each logic output can sink 5mA of load current.

Both logic outputs at pins 5 and 6 are open-collector type stages, and require external pull-up resistors R_{L1} and R_{L2} as shown in Figure 4.

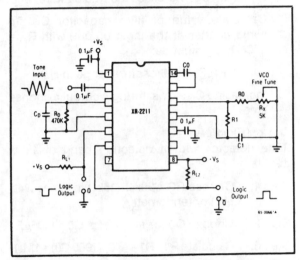

Figure 4. Circuit Connection for Tone Detection

With reference to Figures 1 and 4, the function of the external circuit components can be explained as follows: R0 and C0 set VCO center frequency, R1 sets the detection bandwidth, C1 sets the lowpass-loop filter time constant and the loop damping factor, and R_{L1} and R_{L2} are the respective pull-up resistors for the Q and $\overline{Q}$ logic outputs.

Design Instructions

The circuit of Figure 4 can be optimized for any tone-detection application by the choice of five key circuit components: R0, R1, C0, C1, and C_D. For a given input tone frequency, f_S, these parameters are calculated as follows:

1. Choose R0 to be in the range of 15kΩ to 100kΩ. This choice is arbitrary.

2. Calculate C0 to set center frequency, f_0 equal to f_S: C0 = 1/R0f_S.

3. Calculate R1 to set bandwidth $\pm\Delta f$ (see Design Equation No. 5): R1 = R0($f_0/\Delta f$)

Note: The total detection bandwidth covers the frequency range of $f_0 \pm \Delta f$.

Courtesy of Ratheon Company.

4. Calculate value of C1 for a given loop damping factor:

$$C1 = C0/16\zeta^2$$

Normally $\zeta \approx 1/2$ is optimum for most tone-detector applications, giving C1 = 0.25 C0.

Increasing C1 improves the out-of-band signal rejection, but increases the PLL capture time.

5. Calculate value of filter capacitor C_D. To avoid chatter at the logic output, with R_D = 470kΩ, C_D must be:

$$C_D(\mu F) \geq (16/\text{capture range in Hz})$$

Increasing C_D slows the logic output response time.

Design Examples
Tone detector with a detection band of 1kHz ±20Hz:

Step 1: Choose R0 = 20kΩ (18kΩ in series with 5kΩ potentiometer).

Step 2: Choose C0 for f_0 = 1kHz: C0 = 0.05μF.

Step 3: Calculate R1: R1 = (R0) (1000/20) = 1MΩ.

Step 4: Calculate C1: for ζ = 1/2, C1 = 0.25μF, C0 = 0.013μF.

Step 5: Calculate C_D: C_D = 16/38 = 0.42μF.

Step 6: Fine tune the center frequency with the 5kΩ potentiometer, R_X.

Linear FM Detection

The XR-2211 can be used as a linear FM detector for a wide range of analog communications and telemetry applications. The recommended circuit connection for the application is shown

in Figure 5. The demodulated output is taken from the loop phase detector output (pin 11), through a post detection filter made up of R_F and C_F, and an external buffer amplifier. This buffer amplifier is necessary because of the high impedance output at pin 11. Normally, a non-inverting unity gain op amp can be used as a buffer amplifier, as shown in Figure 5.

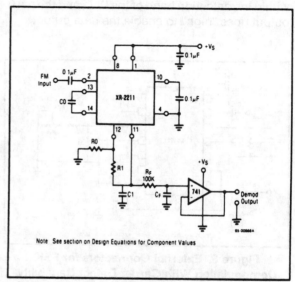

Figure 5. Linear FM Detector Using XR-2211 and an External Op Amp

The FM detector gain, i.e., the output voltage change per unit of FM deviation, can be given as:

$$V_{OUT} = R1 \ V_R/100 \ R0 \ \text{Volts/\% deviation}$$

where V_R is the internal reference voltage. For the choice of external components R1, R0, C_D, C1 and C_F, see the section on Design Equations.

Typical Performance Characteristics

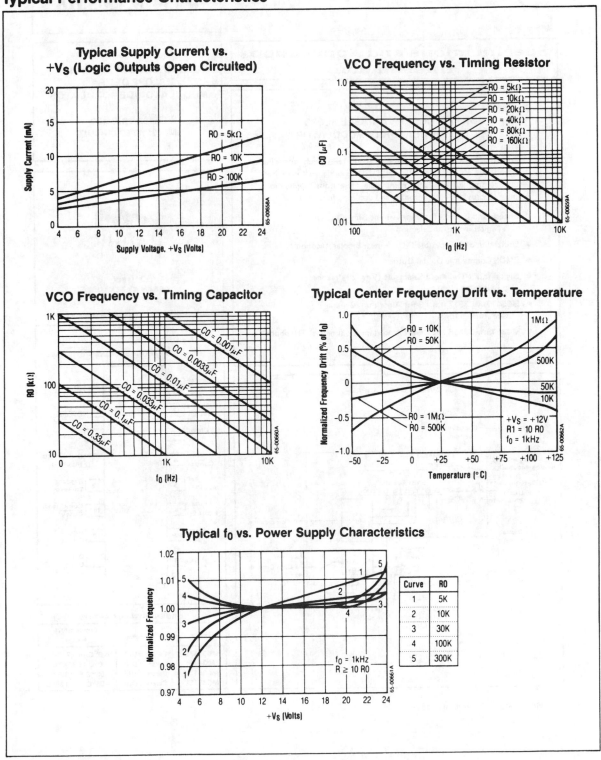

Courtesy of Ratheon Company.

 **MOTOROLA**

Specifications and Applications Information

CONTINUOUSLY VARIABLE SLOPE MODULATOR/DEMODULATOR

LASER-TRIMMED INTEGRATED CIRCUIT

CONTINUOUSLY VARIABLE SLOPE DELTA MODULATOR/DEMODULATOR

Providing a simplified approach to digital speech encoding/ decoding, the MC3517/18 series of CVSDs is designed for military secure communication and commercial telephone applications. A single IC provides both encoding and decoding functions.

- Encode and Decode Functions on the Same Chip with a Digital Input for Selection
- Utilization of Compatible I^2L — Linear Bipolar Technology
- CMOS Compatible Digital Output
- Digital Input Threshold Selectable ($V_{CC}/2$ reference provided on chip)
- MC3417/MC3517 has a 3-Bit Algorithm (General Communications)
- MC3418/MC3518 has a 4-Bit Algorithm (Commercial Telephone)

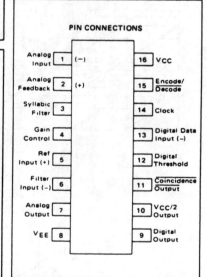

L SUFFIX
CERAMIC PACKAGE
CASE 620

PIN CONNECTIONS

Analog Input	1	(−)	16	VCC
Analog Feedback	2	(+)	15	Encode/Decode
Syllabic Filter	3		14	Clock
Gain Control	4		13	Digital Data Input (−)
Ref Input (+)	5		12	Digital Threshold
Filter Input (−)	6		11	Coincidence Output
Analog Output	7		10	VCC/2 Output
VEE	8		9	Digital Output

CVSD BLOCK DIAGRAM

ORDERING INFORMATION

Device	Package	Temperature Range
MC3417L	Ceramic DIP	0°C to +70°C
MC3418L	Ceramic DIP	0°C to +70°C
MC3517L	Ceramic DIP	−55°C to +125°C
MC3518L	Ceramic DIP	−55°C to +125°C

MC3417, MC3517, MC3418, MC3518

DEFINITIONS AND FUNCTION OF PINS

Pin 1 — Analog Input

This is the analog comparator inverting input where the voice signal is applied. It may be ac or dc coupled depending on the application. If the voice signal is to be level shifted to the internal reference voltage, then a bias resistor between pins 1 and 10 is used. The resistor is used to establish the reference as the new dc average of the ac coupled signal. The analog comparator was designed for low hysteresis (typically less than 0.1 mV) and high gain (typically 70 dB).

Pin 2 — Analog Feedback

This is the non-inverting input to the analog signal comparator within the IC. In an encoder application it should be connected to the analog output of the encoder circuit. This may be pin 7 or a low pass filter output connected to pin 7. In a decode circuit pin 2 is not used and may be tied to $V_{CC}/2$ on pin 10, ground or left open.

The analog input comparator has bias currents of 1.5 μA max, thus the driving impedances of pins 1 and 2 should be equal to avoid disturbing the idle channel characteristics of the encoder.

Pin 3 — Syllabic Filter

This is the point at which the syllabic filter voltage is returned to the IC in order to control the integrator step size. It is an NPN input to an op amp. The syllabic filter consists of an RC network between pins 11 and 3. Typical time constant values of 6 ms to 50 ms are used in voice codecs.

Pin 4 — Gain Control Input

The syllabic filter voltage appears across C_S of the syllabic filter and is the voltage between V_{CC} and pin 3. The active voltage to current (V–I) converter drives pin 4 to the same voltage at a slew rate of typically 0.5 V/μs. Thus the current injected into pin 4 (I_{GC}) is the syllabic filter voltage divided by the R_x resistance. Figure 6 shows the relationship between I_{GC} (x-axis) and the integrating current, I_{Int} (y-axis). The discrepancy, which is most significant at very low currents, is due to circuitry within the slope polarity switch which enables trimming to a low total loop offset. The R_x resistor is then varied to adjust the loop gain of the codec, but should be no larger than 5.0 kΩ to maintain stability.

Pin 5 — Reference Input

This pin is the non-inverting input of the integrator amplifier. It is used to reference the dc level of the output signal. In an encoder circuit it must reference the same voltage as pin 1 and is tied to pin 10.

Pin 6 — Filter Input

This inverting op amp input is used to connect the integrator external components. The integrating current (I_{Int}) flows into pin 6 when the analog input (pin 1) is high with respect to the analog feedback (pin 2) in the encode mode or when the digital data input (pin 13) is high in the decode mode. For the opposite states, I_{Int} flows out of Pin 6. Single integration systems require a capacitor and resistor between pins 6 and 7. Multipole configurations will have different circuitry. The resistance between pins 6 and 7 should always be between 8 kΩ and 13 kΩ to maintain good idle channel characteristics.

Pin 7 — Analog Output

This is the integrator op amp output. It is capable of driving a 600-ohm load referenced to $V_{CC}/2$ to +6 dBm and can otherwise be treated as an op amp output. Pins 5, 6, and 7 provide full access to the integrator op amp for designing integration filter networks. The slew rate of the internally compensated integrator op amp is typically 0.5 V/μs. Pin 7 output is current limited for both polarities of current flow at typically 30 mA.

Pin 8 — V_{EE}

The circuit is designed to work in either single or dual power supply applications. Pin 8 is always connected to the most negative supply.

Pin 9 — Digital Output

The digital output provides the results of the delta modulator's conversion. It swings between V_{CC} and V_{EE} and is CMOS or TTL compatible. Pin 9 is inverting with respect to pin 1 and non-inverting with respect to pin 2. It is clocked on the falling edge of pin 14. The typical 10% to 90% rise and fall times are 250 ns and 50 ns respectively for V_{CC} = 12 V and C_L = 25 pF to ground.

Pin 10 — $V_{CC}/2$ Output

An internal low impedance mid-supply reference is provided for use of the MC3417/18 in single supply applications. The internal regulator is a current source and must be loaded with a resistor to insure its sinking capability. If a +6 dBmo signal is expected across a 600 ohm input bias resistor, then pin 10 must sink 2.2 V/600 Ω = 3.66 mA. This is only possible if pin 10 sources 3.66 mA into a resistor normally and will source only the difference under peak load. The reference load resistor is chosen accordingly. A 0.1 μF bypass capacitor from pin 10 to V_{EE} is also recommended. The $V_{CC}/2$ reference is capable of sourcing 10 mA and can be used as a reference elsewhere in the system circuitry.

Pin 11 — Coincidence Output

The duty cycle of this pin is proportional to the voltage across C_S. The coincidence output will be low whenever the content of the internal shift register is all 1s or all 0s. In the MC3417 the register is 3 bits long

MC3417, MC3517, MC3418, MC3518

DEFINITIONS AND FUNCTIONS OF PINS (continued)

while the MC3418 contains a 4 bit register. Pin 11 is an open collector of an NPN device and requires a pull-up resistor. If the syllabic filter is to have equal charge and discharge time constants, the value of R_P should be much less than R_S. In systems requiring different charge and discharge constants, the charging constant is $R_S C_S$ while the decaying constant is $(R_S + R_P)C_S$. Thus longer decays are easily achievable. The NPN device should not be required to sink more than 3 mA in any configuration. The typical 10% to 90% rise and fall times are 200 ns and 100 ns respectively for $R_L = 4$ kΩ to +12 V and $C_L = 25$ pF to ground.

Pin 12 — Digital Threshold

This input sets the switching threshold for pins 13, 14, and 15. It is intended to aid in interfacing different logic families without external parts. Often it is connected to the $V_{CC}/2$ reference for CMOS interface or can be biased two diode drops above V_{EE} for TTL interface.

Pin 13 — Digital Data Input

In a decode application, the digital data stream is applied to pin 13. In an encoder it may be unused or may be used to transmit signaling message under the control of pin 15. It is an inverting input with respect to pin 9. When pins 9 and 13 are connected, a toggle flip-flop is formed and a forced idle channel pattern

can be transmitted. The digital data input level should be maintained for 0.5 μs before and after the clock trigger for proper clocking.

Pin 14 — Clock Input

The clock input determines the data rate of the codec circuit. A 32K bit rate requires a 32 kHz clock. The switching threshold of the clock input is set by pin 12. The shift register circuit toggles on the falling edge of the clock input. The minimum width for a positive-going pulse on the clock input is 300 ns, whereas for a negative-going pulse, it is 900 ns.

Pin 15 — Encode/$\overline{\text{Decode}}$

This pin controls the connection of the analog input comparator and the digital input comparator to the internal shift register. If high, the result of the analog comparison will be clocked into the register on the falling edge at pin 14. If low, the digital input state will be entered. This allows use of the IC as an encoder/decoder or simplex codec without external parts. Furthermore, it allows non-voice patterns to be forced onto the transmission line through pin 13 in an encoder.

Pin 16 — V_{CC}

The power supply range is from 4.75 to 16.5 volts between pin V_{CC} and V_{EE}.

FIGURE 1 — POWER SUPPLY CURRENT

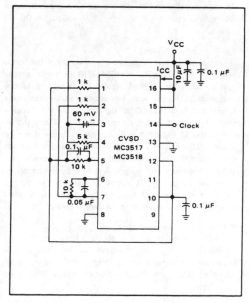

FIGURE 2 — I_{GCR}, GAIN CONTROL RANGE and I_{Int} — INTEGRATING CURRENT

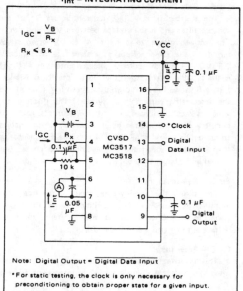

Note: Digital Output = $\overline{\text{Digital Data Input}}$

*For static testing, the clock is only necessary for preconditioning to obtain proper state for a given input.

National Semiconductor

January 1990

TP5089 DTMF (TOUCH-TONE) Generator

General Description

The TP5089 is a low threshold voltage, field-implanted, metal gate CMOS integrated circuit. It interfaces directly to a standard telephone keypad and generates all dual tone multi-frequency pairs required in tone-dialing systems. The tone synthesizers are locked to an on-chip reference oscillator using an inexpensive 3.579545 MHz crystal for high tone accuracy. The crystal and an output load resistor are the only external components required for tone generation. A MUTE OUT logic signal, which changes state when any key is depressed, is also provided.

Features

- 3.5V–10V operation when generating tones
- 2V operation of keyscan and MUTE logic
- Static sensing of key closures or logic inputs
- On-chip 3.579545 MHz crystal-controlled oscillator
- Output amplitudes proportional to supply voltage
- High group pre-emphasis
- Low harmonic distortion
- Open emitter-follower low-impedance output
- SINGLE TONE INHIBIT pin

Block Diagram

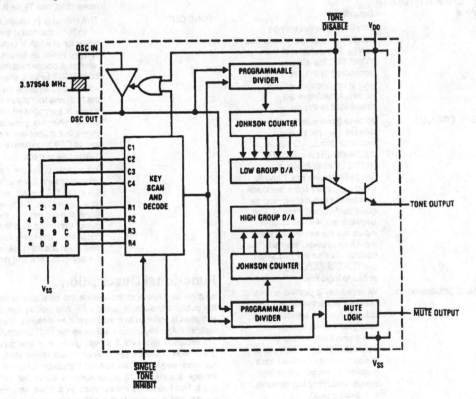

FIGURE 1

Connection Diagram

Dual-In-Line Package

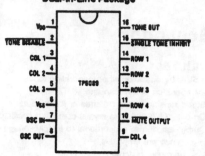

TL/H/5057–2

Top View

Order Number TP5089N
See NS Package N16A

Pin Descriptions

Symbol	Description
V_{DD}	This is the positive voltage supply to the device, referenced to V_{SS}. The collector of the TONE OUT transistor is connected to this pin.
V_{SS}	This is the negative voltage supply. All voltages are referenced to this pin.
OSC IN, OSC OUT	All tone generation timing is derived from the on-chip oscillator circuit. A low cost 3.579545 MHz A-cut crystal (NTSC TV color-burst) is needed between pins 7 and 8. Load capacitors and a feedback resistor are included on-chip for good start-up and stability. The oscillator stops when column inputs are sensed with no valid input having been detected. The oscillator is also stopped when the TONE DISABLE input is pulled to logic low.
Row and Column Inputs	When no key is pushed, pull-up resistors are active on row and column inputs. A key closure is recognized when a single row and a single column are connected to V_{SS}, which starts the oscillator and initiates tone generation. Negative-true logic signals simulating key closures can also be used.
TONE DISABLE Input	The TONE DISABLE input has an internal pull-up resistor. When this input is open or at logic high, the normal tone output mode will occur. When TONE DISABLE input is at logic low, the device will be in the inactive mode, TONE OUT will be at an open circuit state.

Symbol	Description
MUTE Output	The MUTE output is an open-drain N-channel device that sinks current to V_{SS} with any key input and is open when no key input is sensed. The MUTE output will switch regardless of the state of the SINGLE TONE INHIBIT input.
SINGLE TONE INHIBIT Input	The SINGLE TONE INHIBIT input is used to inhibit the generation of other than valid tone pairs due to multiple row-column closures. It has a pull-down resistor to V_{SS}, and when left open or tied to V_{SS} any input condition that would normally result in a single tone will now result in no tone, with all other functions operating normally. When tied to V_{DD}, single or dual tones may be generated, see Table II.
TONE OUT	This output is the open emitter of an NPN transistor, the collector of which is connected to V_{DD}. When an external load resistor is connected from TONE OUT to V_{SS}, the output voltage on this pin is the sum of the high and low group sine-waves superimposed on a DC offset. When not generating tones, this output transistor is turned OFF to minimize the device idle current.

Adjustment of the emitter load resistor results in variation of the mean DC current during tone generation, the sinewave signal current through the output transistor, and the output distortion. Increasing values of load resistance decrease both the signal current and distortion. |

Functional Description

With no key inputs to the device the oscillator is inhibited, the output transistor is pulled OFF and device current consumption is reduced to a minimum. Key closures are sensed statically. Any key closure activates the MUTE output, starts the oscillator and sets the high group and low group programmable counters to the appropriate divide ratio. These counters sequence two ratioed-capacitor D/A converters through a series of 28 equal duration steps per sine-wave cycle. The two tones are summed by a mixer amplifier, with pre-emphasis applied to the high group tone. The output is an NPN emitter-follower requiring the addition of an external load resistor to V_{SS}. This resistor facilitates adjustment of the signal current flowing from V_{DD} through the output transistor.

The amplitude of the output tones is directly proportional to the device supply voltage.

Reprinted with permission of National Semiconductor Corporation.

TABLE I. Output Frequency Accuracy

Tone Group	Valid Input	Standard DTMF (Hz)	Tone Output Frequency	% Deviation from Standard
Low Group f_L	R1	697	694.8	−0.32
	R2	770	770.1	+0.02
	R3	852	852.4	+0.03
	R4	941	940.0	−0.11
High Group f_H	C1	1209	1206.0	−0.24
	C2	1336	1331.7	−0.32
	C3	1477	1486.5	+0.64
	C4	1633	1639.0	+0.37

TABLE II. Functional Truth Table

SINGLE TONE INHIBIT	TONE DISABLE	ROW	COLUMN	TONE OUT Low	TONE OUT High	MUTE
X	O	O/C	O/C	0V	0V	O/C
X	X	O/C	O/C	0V	0V	O/C
X	0	One	One	V_{OS}	V_{OS}	O
X	1	One	One	f_L	f_H	O
1	1	2 or More	One	—	f_H	O
1	1	One	2 or More	f_L	—	O
1	1	2 or More	2 or More	V_{OS}	V_{OS}	O
0	1	2 or More	One	V_{OS}	V_{OS}	O
0	1	One	2 or More	V_{OS}	V_{OS}	O
0	1	2 or More	2 or More	V_{OS}	V_{OS}	O

Note 1: X is don't care state.

Note 2: V_{OS} is the output offset voltage.

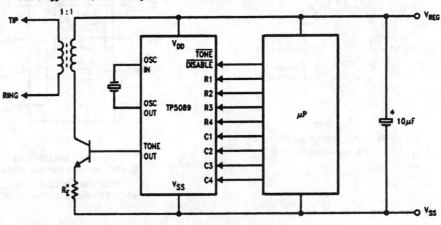

*Adjust R_E for desired tone amplitude.

FIGURE 2. Typical Application

LIFE SUPPORT POLICY.

NATIONAL'S PRODUCTS ARE NOT AUTHORIZED FOR USE AS CRITICAL COMPONENTS IN LIFE SUPPORT DEVICES OR SYSTEMS WITHOUT THE EXPRESS WRITTEN APPROVAL OF THE PRESIDENT OF NATIONAL SEMICONDUCTOR CORPORATION. As used herein:

1. Life support devices or systems are devices or systems which, (a) are intended for surgical implant into the body, or (b) support or sustain life, and whose failure to perform, when properly used in accordance with instructions for use provided in the labeling, can be reasonably expected to result in a significant injury to the user.

2. A critical component is any component of a life support device or system whose failure to perform can be reasonably expected to cause the failure of the life support device or system, or to affect its safety or effectiveness.

Reprinted with permission of National Semiconductor Corporation.

National
Semiconductor
Corporation

LM567/LM567C Tone Decoder

General Description

The LM567 and LM567C are general purpose tone decoders designed to provide a saturated transistor switch to ground when an input signal is present within the passband. The circuit consists of an I and Q detector driven by a voltage controlled oscillator which determines the center frequency of the decoder. External components are used to independently set center frequency, bandwidth and output delay.

Features

■ 20 to 1 frequency range with an external resistor
■ Logic compatible output with 100 mA current sinking capability

■ Bandwidth adjustable from 0 to 14%
■ High rejection of out of band signals and noise
■ Immunity to false signals
■ Highly stable center frequency
■ Center frequency adjustable from 0.01 Hz to 500 kHz

Applications

■ Touch tone decoding
■ Precision oscillator
■ Frequency monitoring and control
■ Wide band FSK demodulation
■ Ultrasonic controls
■ Carrier current remote controls
■ Communications paging decoders

Connection Diagrams

Metal Can Package

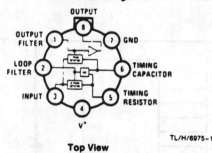

Top View

TL/H/6975–1

Order Number LM567H or LM567CH
See NS Package Number H08C

Dual-In-Line and Small Outline Packages

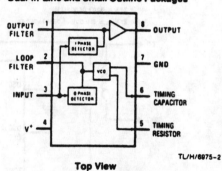

TL/H/6975–2

Top View

Order Number LM567CM
See NS Package Number M08A
Order Number LM567CN
See NS Package Number N08E

LM567

LM567/LM567C

Absolute Maximum Ratings

If Military/Aerospace specified devices are required, contact the National Semiconductor Sales Office/Distributors for availability and specifications.

Supply Voltage Pin	9V
Power Dissipation (Note 1)	1100 mW
V_8	15V
V_3	−10V
V_3	$V_4 + 0.5V$
Storage Temperature Range	−65°C to +150°C
Operating Temperature Range	
LM567H	−55°C to +125°C
LM567CH, LM567CM, LM567CN	0°C to +70°C

Soldering Information
Dual-In-Line Package
  Soldering (10 sec.)   260°C
Small Outline Package
  Vapor Phase (60 sec.)   215°C
  Infrared (15 sec.)   220°C
See AN-450 "Surface Mounting Methods and Their Effect on Product Reliability" for other methods of soldering surface mount devices.

Electrical Characteristics AC Test Circuit, $T_A = 25$°C, $V^+ = 5V$

Parameters	Conditions	LM567 Min	LM567 Typ	LM567 Max	LM567C/LM567CM Min	LM567C/LM567CM Typ	LM567C/LM567CM Max	Units
Power Supply Voltage Range		4.75	5.0	9.0	4.75	5.0	9.0	V
Power Supply Current Quiescent	$R_L = 20k$		6	8		7	10	mA
Power Supply Current Activated	$R_L = 20k$		11	13		12	15	mA
Input Resistance		18	20		15	20		kΩ
Smallest Detectable Input Voltage	$I_L = 100$ mA, $f_i = f_o$		20	25		20	25	mVrms
Largest No Output Input Voltage	$I_C = 100$ mA, $f_i = f_o$	10	15		10	15		mVrms
Largest Simultaneous Outband Signal to Inband Signal Ratio			6			6		dB
Minimum Input Signal to Wideband Noise Ratio	$B_n = 140$ kHz		−6			−6		dB
Largest Detection Bandwidth		12	14	16	10	14	18	% of f_o
Largest Detection Bandwidth Skew			1	2		2	3	% of f_o
Largest Detection Bandwidth Variation with Temperature			±0.1			±0.1		%/°C
Largest Detection Bandwidth Variation with Supply Voltage	4.75 − 6.75V		±1	±2		±1	±5	%V
Highest Center Frequency		100	500		100	500		kHz
Center Frequency Stability (4.75−5.75V)	$0 < T_A < 70$ $−55 < T_A < +125$		35 ± 60 35 ± 140			35 ±60 35 ± 140		ppm/°C ppm/°C
Center Frequency Shift with Supply Voltage	4.75V − 6.75V 4.75V − 9V		0.5	1.0 2.0		0.4	2.0 2.0	%/V %/V
Fastest ON-OFF Cycling Rate			$f_o/20$			$f_o/20$		
Output Leakage Current	$V_8 = 15V$		0.01	25		0.01	25	µA
Output Saturation Voltage	$e_i = 25$ mV, $I_8 = 30$ mA $e_i = 25$ mV, $I_8 = 100$ mA		0.2 0.6	0.4 1.0		0.2 0.6	0.4 1.0	V
Output Fall Time			30			30		ns
Output Rise Time			150			150		ns

Note 1: The maximum junction temperature of the LM567 and LM567C is 150°C. For operating at elevated temperatures, devices in the TO-5 package must be derated based on a thermal resistance of 150°C/W, junction to ambient or 45°C/W, junction to case. For the DIP the device must be derated based on a thermal resistance of 110°C/W, junction to ambient. For the Small Outline package, the device must be derated based on a thermal resistance of 160°C/W, junction to ambient.

Note 2: Refer to RETS567X drawing for specifications of military LM567H version.

LM567

Typical Applications

Touch-Tone Decoder

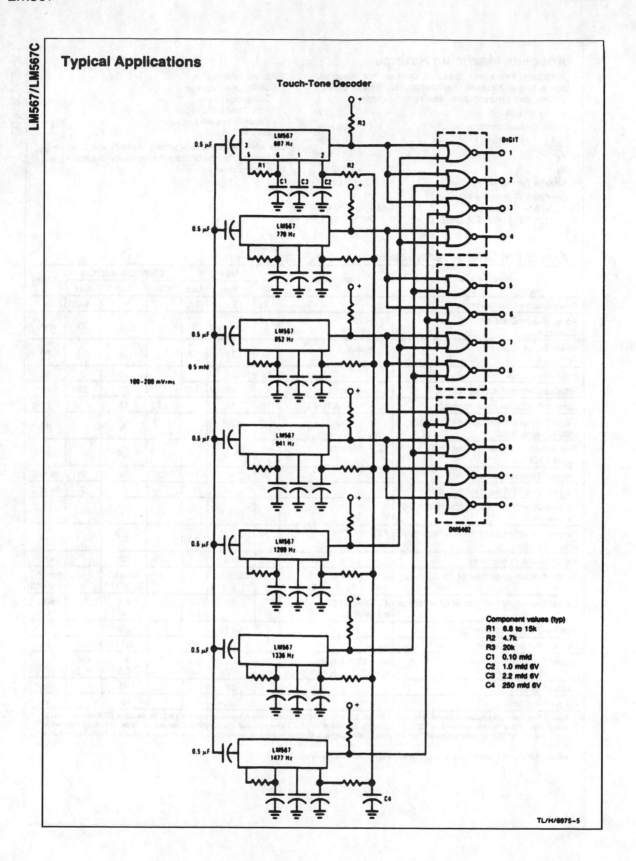

Component values (typ)
R1 6.8 to 15k
R2 4.7k
R3 20k
C1 0.10 mfd
C2 1.0 mfd 6V
C3 2.2 mfd 6V
C4 250 mfd 6V

TL/H/6975–5

LM567

Typical Applications (Continued)

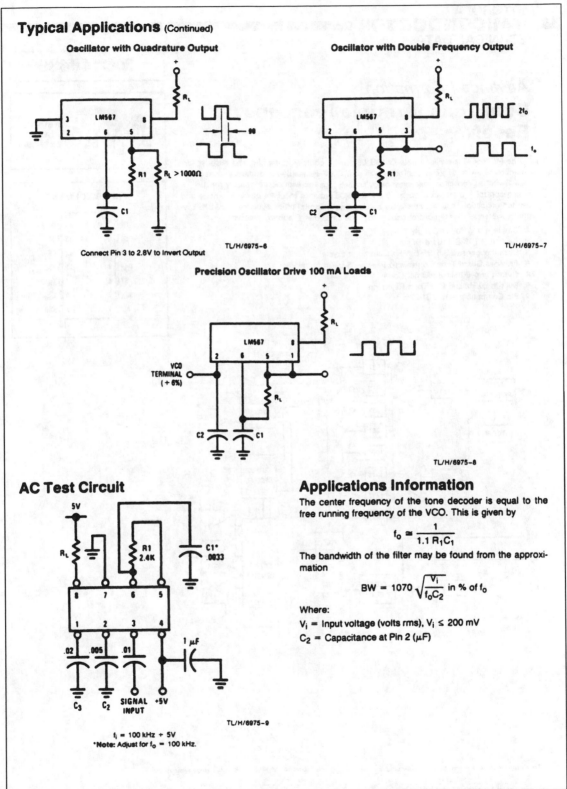

Oscillator with Quadrature Output

TL/H/6975-6

Connect Pin 3 to 2.8V to Invert Output

Oscillator with Double Frequency Output

TL/H/6975-7

Precision Oscillator Drive 100 mA Loads

TL/H/6975-8

AC Test Circuit

$f_i = 100$ kHz $\div$ 5V
*Note: Adjust for $f_0 = 100$ kHz.

TL/H/6975-9

Applications Information

The center frequency of the tone decoder is equal to the free running frequency of the VCO. This is given by

$$f_0 \simeq \frac{1}{1.1\,R_1 C_1}$$

The bandwidth of the filter may be found from the approximation

$$BW = 1070 \sqrt{\frac{V_i}{f_0 C_2}} \text{ in } \% \text{ of } f_0$$

Where:

V_i = Input voltage (volts rms), $V_i \leq 200$ mV

C_2 = Capacitance at Pin 2 (μF)

MOTOROLA
■ SEMICONDUCTOR ■■■■■■
TECHNICAL DATA

Advance Information
Dual Tone Multiple Frequency Receiver

The MC145436 is a silicon-gate CMOS LSI device containing the filter and decoder for detection of a pair of tones conforming to the DTMF standard with outputs in hexadecimal. Switched capacitor filter technology is used together with digital circuitry for the timing control and output circuits. The MC145436 provides excellent power-line noise and dial tone rejection, and is suitable for applications in central office equipment, PABX, keyphone systems, remote control equipment, and consumer telephony products.

- Single +5 V Power Supply
- Detects All 16 Standard Digits
- Uses Inexpensive 3.579545 MHz Colorburst Crystal
- Provides Guard Time Controls to Improve Speech Immunity
- Output in 4-Bit Hexadecimal Code
- Built-In 60 Hz and Dial Tone Rejection
- Pin Compatible with SSI-204

MC145436

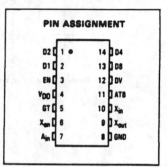

P SUFFIX
PLASTIC
CASE 646

PIN ASSIGNMENT

D2	1 ●	14	D4
D1	2	13	D8
EN	3	12	DV
V_{DD}	4	11	ATB
GT	5	10	X_{in}
X_{en}	6	9	X_{out}
A_{in}	7	8	GND

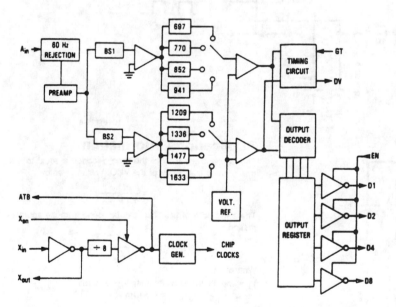

MC145436

ABSOLUTE MAXIMUM RATINGS
(Voltages Referenced to GND Unless Otherwise Noted)

Rating	Symbol	Value	Unit
DC Supply Voltage	V_{DD}	-0.5 to $+6.0$	V
Input Voltage, Any Pin Except A_{in}	V_{in}	-0.5 to $V_{DD} + 0.5$	V
Input Voltage, A_{in}	V_{in}	$V_{DD} - 10$ to $V_{DD} + 0.5$	V
DC Current Drain per Pin	I	± 10	mA
Operating Temperature Range	T_A	-40 to $+85$	°C
Storage Temperature Range	T_{stg}	-65 to $+150$	°C

This device contains circuitry to protect the inputs against damage due to high static voltages or electric fields; however, it is advised that normal precautions be taken to avoid applications of any voltage higher than the maximum rated voltages to this high impedance circuit.

For proper operation it is recommended that V_{in} and V_{out} be constrained to the range $V_{SS} \leq (V_{in}$ or $V_{out}) \leq V_{DD}$. Reliability of operation is enhanced if unused inputs are tied to an appropriate logic voltage level (e.g., either V_{SS} or V_{DD}).

ELECTRICAL CHARACTERISTICS
(All Polarities Referenced to $V_{DD} = 5.0$ V $\pm 10\%$, $T_A = -40$ to $+85°C$ Unless Otherwise Noted)

Parameter		Symbol	Min	Typ	Max	Unit
DC Supply Voltage		V_{DD}	4.5	5	5.5	V
Supply Current ($f_{CLK} = 3.58$ MHz)		I_{DD}	–	7	15	mA
Input Current	GT	I_{in}	–	–	200	μA
	EN, X_{in}, X_{en}		–	–	± 1	
Input Voltage Low	EN, GT, X_{en}	V_{IL}	–	–	1.5	V
Input Voltage High	EN, GT, X_{en}	V_{IH}	3.5	–	–	V
High Level Output Current ($V_{OH} = V_{DD} - 0.5$ V; Source)	Data, DV	I_{OH}	800	–	–	μA
Low Level Output Current ($V_{OL} = 0.4$ V; Sink)	Data, DV	I_{OL}	1.0	–	–	mA
Input Impedance	A_{in}	R_{in}	90	100	–	kΩ
Fanout	ATB	FO	–	–	10	
Input Capacitance	X_{en}, EN	C_{in}	–	6	–	pF

ANALOG CHARACTERISTICS ($V_{DD} = 5.0$ V $\pm 10\%$, $T_A = -40$ to $+85°C$)

Parameter	Min	Typ	Max	Unit
Signal Level for Detection (A_{in})	-32	–	-2	dBm
Twist = High Tone/Low Tone	-10	–	10	dB
Frequency Detect Bandwidth (Notes 1 and 2)	$\pm (1.5 + 2$ Hz)	± 2.5	± 3.5	% f_C
60 Hz Tolerance	–	–	0.8	Vrms
Dial Tone Tolerance (Note 3) (Dial Tone 330 + 440)	–	–	0	dB
Noise Tolerance (Notes 3 and 4)	–	–	-12	dB
Power Supply Noise (Wide Band)	–	–	10	mV p-p
Talk Off (Mitel Tape #CM7290)	–	2	–	Hits

NOTES:
1. f_C is center frequency of bandpass filters.
2. Maximum frequency detect bandwidth of the 1477 Hz filter is $+3.5\%$ to -4%.
3. Referenced to lower amplitude tone.
4. Bandwidth limited (0 to 3.4 kHz) Gaussian noise.

MOTOROLA TELECOMMUNICATIONS DEVICE DATA

MC145436

AC CHARACTERISTICS (V_{DD} = 5.0 V ± 10%, T_A = −40 to +85°C)

Characteristic		Symbol	Min	Typ	Max	Unit
Tone On Time	For Detection	$Tone_{on}$	40	–	–	ms
	For Rejection		–	–	20	
Pause Time	For Detection	$Tone_{off}$	40	–	–	ms
	For Rejection		–	–	20	
Detect Time	GT = 0	t_{det}	22	–	40	ms
	GT = 1		32	–	50	
Release Time	GT = 0	t_{rel}	28	–	40	ms
	GT = 1		18	–	30	
Data Setup Time		t_{su}	7	–	–	μs
Data Hold Time		t_h	4.2	4.6	5	ms
Pulse Width	GT	$t_{w(GT)}$	18	–	–	μs
DV Reset Lag Time		$t_{lag(DV)}$	–	–	5	ms
Enable High to Output Data Valid		t_{EHDV}	–	200	–	ns
Enable Low to Output High-Z		t_{ELDZ}	–	150	–	ns

TIMING

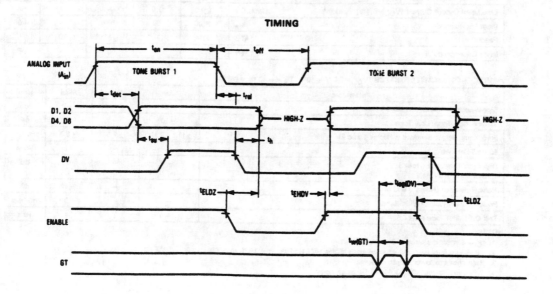

MOTOROLA TELECOMMUNICATIONS DEVICE DATA

MC145436

MC145436

PIN DESCRIPTION

D1, D2, D4, D8—DATA OUTPUT

These digital outputs provide the hexadecimal codes corresponding to the detected digit (see Table 1). The digital outputs become valid after a tone pair has been detected, and are cleared when a valid pause is timed. These output pins are high impedance when Enable is at a logic 0.

EN—ENABLE

Outputs D1, D2, D4, D8 are enabled when EN is at a logic 1, and high impedance (disabled) when EN is at a logic 0.

GT—GUARD TIME

The Guard Time control input provides two sets of detected time and release time, both within the allowed ranges of tone on and tone off. A longer tone detect time rejects signals too short to be considered valid. With GT = 1, talk off performance is improved, since it reduces the probability that tones simulated by speech will maintain signal conditions long enough to be accepted. In addition, a shorter release time reduces the probability that a pause simulated by an interruption in speech will be detected as a valid pause. On the other hand, a shorter tone detect time with a long release time would be appropriate for an extremely noisy environment where fast acquisition time and immunity to drop-outs would be required. In general, the tone signal time generated by a telephone is 100 ms, nominal, followed by a pause of about 100 ms. A high-to-low, or low-to-high transition on the GT pin resets the internal logic, and the MC145436 is immediately ready to accept a new tone input.

X$_{en}$—OSCILLATOR ENABLE

A logic 1 on X$_{en}$ enables the on-chip crystal oscillator. When using alternate time base from the ATB pin, X$_{en}$ should be tied to GND.

A$_{in}$—ANALOG INPUT

This pin accepts the analog input, and is internally biased so that the input signal may be ac coupled. The input may be dc coupled so long as it does not exceed the positive supply. (See Figure 1.)

X$_{in}$/X$_{out}$—OSCILLATOR IN AND OSCILLATOR OUT

These pins connect to an internal crystal oscillator. In operation, a parallel resonant crystal is connected from X$_{in}$ to X$_{out}$, as well as a 1 MΩ resistor in parallel with the crystal. When using the alternate clock source from ATB, X$_{in}$ should be tied to V$_{DD}$.

ATB—ALTERNATE TIME BASE

This pin serves as a frequency reference when more than one MC145436 is used, so that only one crystal is required for multiple MC145436s. In this case, all ATB pins should be tied together as shown in Figure 2. When only one MC145436 is used, this pin should be left unconnected. The output frequency of ATB is 447.4 kHz.

DV—DATA VALID

DV signals a detection by going high after a valid tone pair is sensed and decoded at output pins D1, D2, D4, D8. DV remains high until a loss of the current DTMF signal occurs, or until a transition in GT occurs.

V$_{DD}$—POSITIVE POWER SUPPLY

The digital supply pin, which is connected to the positive side of the power supply.

GND—GROUND

Ground return pin is typically connected to the system ground.

Table 1. Hexadecimal Codes

Digit	Output Code			
	D8	D4	D2	D1
1	0	0	0	1
2	0	0	1	0
3	0	0	1	1
4	0	1	0	0
5	0	1	0	1
6	0	1	1	0
7	0	1	1	1
8	1	0	0	0
9	1	0	0	1
0	1	0	1	0
*	1	0	1	1
#	1	1	0	0
A	1	1	0	1
B	1	1	1	0
C	1	1	1	1
D	0	0	0	0

OPERATIONAL INFORMATION

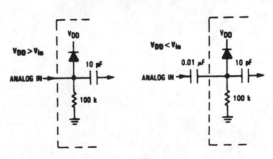

Figure 1. Analog Input

MC145436

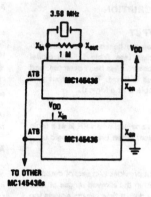

3.58 MHz

Figure 2. Multiple MC145436s

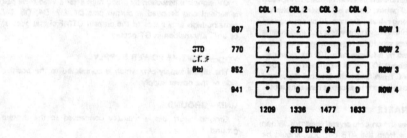

	COL 1	COL 2	COL 3	COL 4	
697	1	2	3	A	ROW 1
770	4	5	6	B	ROW 2
852	7	8	9	C	ROW 3
941	*	0	#	D	ROW 4
	1209	1336	1477	1633	

STD DTMF (Hz)

Figure 3. 4 x 4 Keyboard Matrix

Signetics

Linear Products

NE5533/5533A
NE/SA/SE5534/5534A
Dual and Single Low Noise Op Amp

Product Specification

DESCRIPTION

The 5533/5534 are dual and single high-performance low noise operational amplifiers. Compared to other operational amplifiers, such as TL083, they show better noise performance, improved output drive capability and considerably higher small-signal and power bandwidths.

This makes the devices especially suitable for application in high quality and professional audio equipment, in instrumentation and control circuits and telephone channel amplifiers. The op amps are internally compensated for gain equal to, or higher than, three. The frequency response can be optimized with an external compensation capacitor for various applications (unity gain amplifier, capacitive load, slew rate, low overshoot, etc.) If very low noise is of prime importance, it is recommended that the 5533A/5534A version be used which has guaranteed noise specifications.

FEATURES

- Small-signal bandwidth: 10MHz
- Output drive capability: 600Ω, 10V$_{RMS}$ at V$_S$ = ± 18V
- Input noise voltage: 4nV/$\sqrt{Hz}$
- DC voltage gain: 100000
- AC voltage gain: 6000 at 10kHz
- Power bandwidth: 200kHz
- Slew rate: 13V/μs
- Large supply voltage range: ± 3 to ± 20V

PIN CONFIGURATIONS

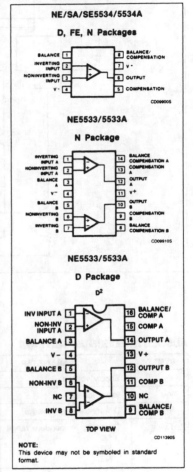

NE/SA/SE5534/5534A
D, FE, N Packages

NE5533/5533A
N Package

NE5533/5533A
D Package

TOP VIEW

NOTE:
This device may not be symboled in standard format.

ORDERING INFORMATION

DESCRIPTION	TEMPERATURE RANGE	ORDER CODE
14-Pin Plastic DIP	0 to +70°C	NE5533N
16-Pin Plastic SO package	0 to +70°C	NE5533AD
14-Pin Plastic DIP	0 to +70°C	NE5533AN
16-Pin Plastic SO package	0 to +70°C	NE5533D
8-Pin Plastic SO package	0 to +70°C	NE5534D
8-Pin Hermetic Cerdip	0 to +70°C	NE5534FE
8-Pin Plastic DIP	0 to +70°C	NE5534N
8-Pin Plastic SO package	0 to +70°C	NE5534AD
8-Pin Hermetic Cerdip	0 to +70°C	NE5534AFE
8-Pin Plastic DIP	0 to +70°C	NE5534AN
8-Pin Plastic DIP	−40°C to +85°C	SA5534N
8-Pin Plastic DIP	−40°C to +85°C	SA5534AN
8-Pin Hermetic Cerdip	−55°C to +125°C	SE5534AFE
8-Pin Plastic DIP	−55°C to +125°C	SE5534N
8-Pin Hermetic Cerdip	−55°C to +125°C	SE5534AFE
8-Pin Plastic DIP	−55°C to +125°C	SE5534AN

Dual and Single Low Noise Op Amp

NE5533/5533A
NE/SA/SE5534/5534A

EQUIVALENT SCHEMATIC

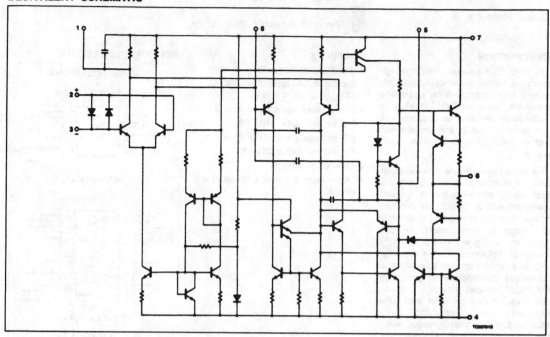

ABSOLUTE MAXIMUM RATINGS

SYMBOL	PARAMETER	RATING	UNIT
V_S	Supply voltage	± 22	V
V_{IN}	Input voltage	± V supply	V
V_{DIFF}	Differential input voltage[1]	± 0.5	V
T_A	Operating temperature range SE SA NE	−55 to +125 −40 to +85 0 to +70	°C °C °C
T_{STG}	Storage temperature range	−65 to +150	°C
T_J	Junction temperature	150	°C
P_D	Power dissipation at 25°C[2] 5533N, 5534N, 5534FE	800	mW
	Output short-circuit duration[3]	Indefinite	
T_{SOLD}	Lead soldering temperature (10sec max)	300	°C

NOTES:
1. Diodes protect the inputs against over voltage. Therefore, unless current-limiting resistors are used, large currents will flow if the differential input voltage exceeds 0.6V. Maximum current should be limited to ±10mA.
2. For operation at elevated temperature, derate packages based on the following junction-to-ambient thermal resistance:
   8-pin ceramic DIP 150°C/W
   8-pin plastic DIP 105°C/W
   8-pin plastic SO 160°C/W
   14-pin ceramic DIP 100°C/W
   14-pin plastic DIP 80°C/W
   16-pin plastic SO 90°C/W
3. Output may be shorted to ground at $V_S = ±15V$, $T_A = 25°C$. Temperature and/or supply voltages must be limited to ensure dissipation rating is not exceeded.

Dual and Single Low Noise Op Amp

NE5533/5533A
NE/SA/SE5534/5534A

DC ELECTRICAL CHARACTERISTICS $T_A = 25°C$, $V_S = \pm 15V$, unless otherwise specified. [1, 2]

SYMBOL	PARAMETER	TEST CONDITIONS	SE5534/5534A Min	Typ	Max	NE5533/5533A/ 5534/5534A Min	Typ	Max	UNIT
V_{OS}	Offset voltage	Over temperature		0.5	2 3		0.5	4 5	mV mV
$\Delta V_{OS}/\Delta T$				5			5		$\mu V/°C$
I_{OS}	Offset current	Over temperature		10	200 500		20	300 400	nA nA
$\Delta I_{OS}/\Delta T$				200			200		pA/°C
I_B	Input current	Over temperature		400	800 1500		500	1500 2000	nA nA
$\Delta I_B/\Delta T$				5			5		nA/°C
I_{CC}	Supply current per op amp	Over temperature		4	6.5 9		4	8 10	mA mA
V_{CM}	Common mode input range		± 12	± 13		± 12	± 13		V
CMRR	Common mode rejection ratio		80	100		70	100		dB
PSRR	Power supply rejection ratio			10	50		10	100	$\mu V/V$
A_{VOL}	Large-signal voltage gain	$R_L \geq 600\Omega$, $V_O = \pm 10V$ Over temperature	50 25	100		25 15	100		V/mV V/mV
V_{OUT}	Output swing 5534 only	$R_L \geq 600\Omega$ Over temperature $R_L \geq 600\Omega$, $V_S = \pm 18V$ $R_L \geq 2k\Omega$ Over temperature	± 12 ± 10 ± 15 ± 13 ± 12	± 13 ± 12 ± 16 ± 13.5 ± 12.5		± 12 ± 10 ± 15 ± 13 ± 12	± 13 ± 12 ± 16 ± 13.5 ± 12.5		V V V V V
R_{IN}	Input resistance		50	100		30	100		$k\Omega$
I_{SC}	Output short circuit current			38			38		mA

NOTES:
1. For NE5533/5533A/5534/5534A, $T_{MIN} = 0°C$, $T_{MAX} = 70°C$.
2. For SE5534/5534A, $T_{MIN} = -55°C$, $T_{MAX} = +125°C$.

AC ELECTRICAL CHARACTERISTICS $T_A = 25°C$, $V_S = 15V$, unless otherwise specified.

SYMBOL	PARAMETER	TEST CONDITIONS	SE5534/5534A Min	Typ	Max	NE5533/5533A/ 5534/5534A Min	Typ	Max	UNIT
R_{OUT}	Output resistance	$A_V = 30dB$ closed-loop $f = 10kHz$, $R_L = 600\Omega$, $C_C = 22pF$		0.3			0.3		Ω
	Transient response	Voltage-follower, $V_{IN} = 50mV$ $R_L = 600\Omega$, $C_C = 22pF$, $C_L = 100pF$							
t_R	Rise time			20			20		ns
	Overshoot			20			20		%
	Transient response	$V_{IN} = 50mV$, $R_L = 600\Omega$ $C_C = 47pF$, $C_L = 500pF$							
t_R	Rise time			50			50		ns
	Overshoot			35			35		%
A_V	Gain	$f = 10kHz$, $C_C = 0$ $f = 10kHz$, $C_C = 22pF$		6 2.2			6 2.2		V/mV V/mV
BW	Gain bandwidth product	$C_C = 22pF$, $C_L = 100pF$		10			10		mHz
SR	Slew rate	$C_C = 0$ $C_C = 22pF$		13 6			13 6		V/μs V/μs
	Power bandwidth	$V_{OUT} = \pm 10V$, $C_C = 0$ $V_{OUT} = \pm 10V$, $C_C = 22pF$ $V_{OUT} = \pm 14V$, $R_L = 600\Omega$ $C_C = 22pF$, $V_{CC} = \pm 18V$		200 95 70			200 95 70		kHz kHz kHz

ELECTRICAL CHARACTERISTICS $T_A = 25°C$, $V_S = 15V$, unless otherwise specified.

SYMBOL	PARAMETER	TEST CONDITIONS	5533/5534 Min	Typ	Max	5533A/5534A Min	Typ	Max	UNIT
V_{NOISE}	Input noise voltage	$f_O = 30Hz$ $f_O = 1kHz$		7 4			5.5 3.5	7 4.5	nV/$\sqrt{Hz}$ nV/$\sqrt{Hz}$
I_{NOISE}	Input noise current	$f_O = 30Hz$ $f_O = 1kHz$		2.5 0.6			1.5 0.4		pA/$\sqrt{Hz}$ pA/$\sqrt{Hz}$
	Broadband noise figure	$f = 10Hz - 20kHz$, $R_S = 5k\Omega$					0.9		dB
	Channel separation	$f = 1kHz$, $R_S = 5k\Omega$		110			110		dB

Dual and Single Low Noise Op Amp

NE5533/5533A
NE/SA/SE5534/5534A

TYPICAL PERFORMANCE CHARACTERISTICS

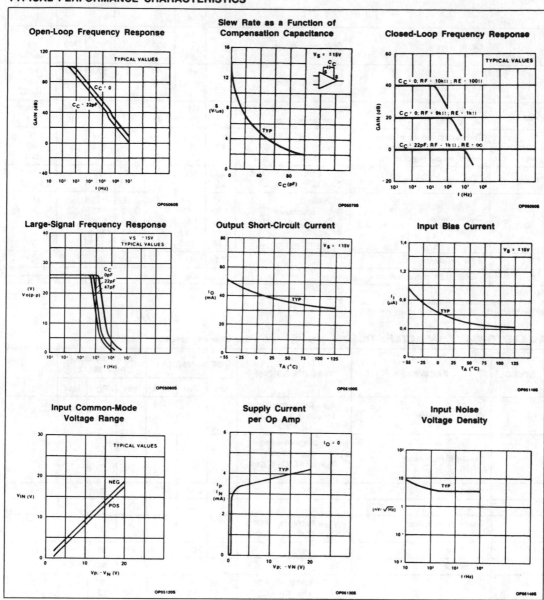

Dual and Single Low
Noise Op Amp

TYPICAL PERFORMANCE CHARACTERISTICS (Continued)

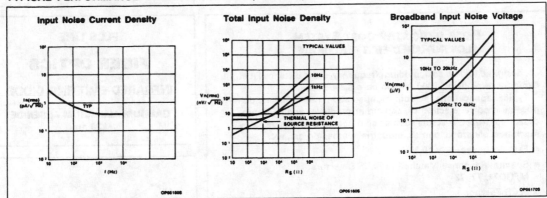

TEST LOAD CIRCUITS

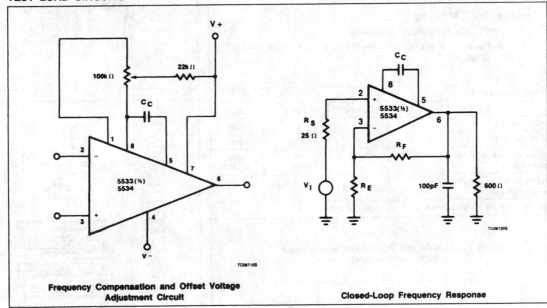

Frequency Compensation and Offset Voltage
Adjustment Circuit

Closed-Loop Frequency Response

MOTOROLA

FIBER OPTIC LOW COST SYSTEM
FLCS INFRARED-EMITTING DIODE

. . . designed for low cost, medium frequency, short distance Fiber Optic Systems using 1000 micron core plastic fiber.

Typical applications include: high isolation interconnects, disposable medical electronics, consumer products, and microprocessor controlled systems such as coin operated machines, copy machines, electronic games, industrial clothes dryers, etc.

- Fast Response — > 10 MHz
- Spectral Response Matched to FLCS Detectors: MFOD71, 72, 73
- FLCS Package
  - Low Cost
  - Includes Connector
  - Simple Fiber Termination and Connection
  - Easy Board Mounting
  - Molded Lens for Efficient Coupling
  - Mates with 1000 Micron Core Plastic Fiber (DuPont OE1040, Eska SH4001)

FLCS LINE
FIBER OPTICS
INFRARED-EMITTING DIODE
GALLIUM ALUMINUM ARSENIDE
820 nm

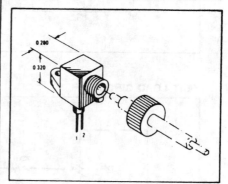

MAXIMUM RATINGS

Rating	Symbol	Value	Unit
Reverse Voltage	V_R	6.0	Volts
Forward Current	I_F	150	mA
Total Power Dissipation @ T_A = 25°C Derate above 25°C	$P_D(1)$	150 2.5	mW mW/°C
Operating and Storage Junction Temperature Range	T_J, T_{stg}	−40 to +85	°C

(1) Measured with the device soldered into a typical printed circuit board.

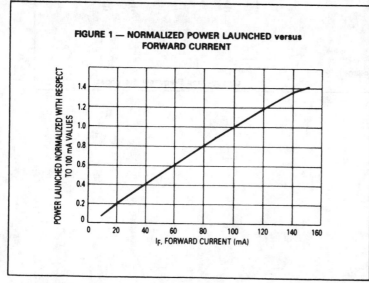

FIGURE 1 — NORMALIZED POWER LAUNCHED versus FORWARD CURRENT

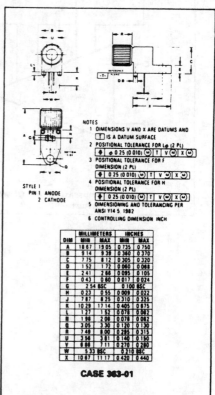

NOTES
1. DIMENSIONS V AND X ARE DATUMS AND ⊡ IS A DATUM SURFACE
2. POSITIONAL TOLERANCE FOR Lφ (2 PL)
3. POSITIONAL TOLERANCE FOR F DIMENSION (2 PL)
4. POSITIONAL TOLERANCE FOR H DIMENSION (2 PL)
5. DIMENSIONING AND TOLERANCING PER ANSI Y14.5, 1982
6. CONTROLLING DIMENSION: INCH

STYLE 1
PIN 1 ANODE
     2 CATHODE

DIM	MILLIMETERS MIN	MILLIMETERS MAX	INCHES MIN	INCHES MAX
A	18.67	19.05	0.735	0.750
B	9.14	9.39	0.360	0.370
C	7.75	8.12	0.305	0.320
D	1.52	1.72	0.060	0.068
E	2.41	2.66	0.095	0.105
F	0.43	0.60	0.017	0.024
G	2.54 BSC		0.100 BSC	
H	0.23	0.55	0.009	0.022
J	7.87	8.25	0.310	0.325
K	10.29	17.14	0.405	0.675
L	1.27	1.52	0.078	0.082
M	1.98	2.08	0.078	0.082
Q	3.05	3.30	0.120	0.130
R	7.49	8.00	0.295	0.315
U	3.56	3.81	0.140	0.150
V	6.86	7.11	0.270	0.280
W	5.33 BSC		0.210 BSC	
X	10.67	11.17	0.420	0.440

CASE 363-01

MFOE71

ELECTRICAL CHARACTERISTICS (T_A = 25°C unless otherwise noted)

Characteristic	Fig. No.	Symbol	Min	Typ	Max	Unit
Reverse Breakdown Voltage (I_R = 100 μA)	—	$V_{(BR)R}$	2.0	4.0	—	Volts
Forward Voltage (I_F = 100 mA)	—	V_F	—	1.5	2.0	Volts

OPTICAL CHARACTERISTICS (T_A = 25°C unless otherwise noted)

Characteristic	Fig. No.	Symbol	Min	Typ	Max	Unit
Power Launched	2, 4	P_L	110	165	—	μW
Optical Rise and Fall Time	3	t_r, t_f	—	25	35	ns
Peak Wavelength (I_F = 100 mA)	1	λ_P	—	820	—	nm

For simple fiber termination instructions, see the MFOD71, 72 and 73 data sheet.

FIGURE 2 — POWER LAUNCHED TEST SET

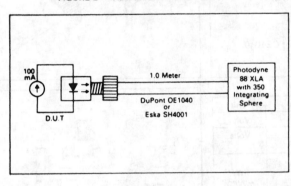

FIGURE 3 — POWER LAUNCHED (P_L) versus FIBER LENGTH

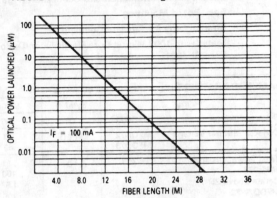

FIGURE 4 — OPTICAL RISE AND FALL TIME TEST SET (10%–90%)

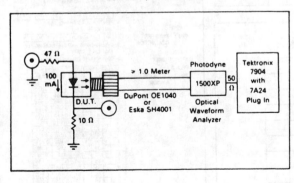

FIGURE 5 — TYPICAL SPECTRAL OUTPUT versus WAVELENGTH

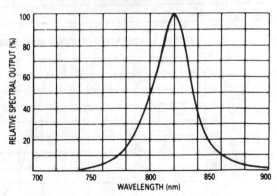

 **MOTOROLA**

MFOD71
MFOD72
MFOD73

FIBER OPTIC LOW COST SYSTEM
FLCS DETECTORS

... designed for low cost, short distance Fiber Optic Systems using 1000 micron core plastic fiber.

Typical applications include: high isolation interconnects, disposable medical electronics, consumer products, and microprocessor controlled systems such as coin operated machines, copy machines, electronic games, industrial clothes dryers, etc.

- Fast PIN Photodiode: Response Time <5.0 ns
- Standard Phototransistor
- High Sensitivity Photodarlington
- Spectral Response Matched to MFOE71 LED
- Annular Passivated Structure for Stability and Reliability
- FLCS Package
  - Includes Connector
  - Simple Fiber Termination and Connection (Figure 4)
  - Easy Board Mounting
  - Molded Lens for Efficient Coupling
  - Mates with 1000 Micron Core Plastic Fiber (DuPont OE1040, Eska SH4001)

FLCS LINE

FIBER OPTICS

DETECTORS

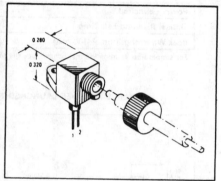

MAXIMUM RATINGS (T_A = 25°C unless otherwise noted)

Rating		Symbol	Value	Unit
Reverse Voltage	MFOD71	V_R	100	Volts
Collector-Emitter Voltage	MFOD72	V_{CEO}	30	Volts
	MFOD73		60	
Total Power Dissipation @ T_A = 25°C		P_D		
MFOD71			100	mW
Derate above 25°C			1.67	mW/°C
MFOD72/73			150	mW
Derate above 25°C			2.5	mW/°C
Operating and Storage Junction Temperature Range		T_J, T_{stg}	−40 to +85	°C

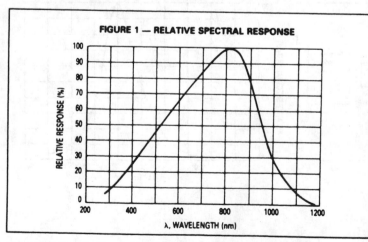

FIGURE 1 — RELATIVE SPECTRAL RESPONSE

(Graph: RELATIVE RESPONSE (%) vs λ, WAVELENGTH (nm), ranging 200 to 1200 nm)

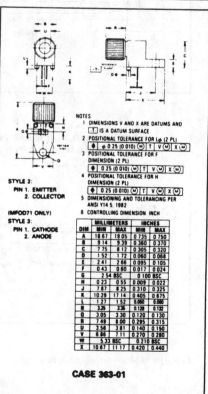

NOTES
1. DIMENSIONS V AND X ARE DATUMS AND [T] IS A DATUM SURFACE
2. POSITIONAL TOLERANCE FOR Lφ (2 PL) [φ|0 25 (0 010)(M)|T|V(M)|X(M)]
3. POSITIONAL TOLERANCE FOR F DIMENSION (2 PL) [φ|0 25 (0 010)(M)|T|V(M)|X(M)]
4. POSITIONAL TOLERANCE FOR H DIMENSION (2 PL) [φ|0 25 (0 010)(M)|T|V(M)|X(M)]
5. DIMENSIONING AND TOLERANCING PER ANSI Y14 5, 1982
6. CONTROLLING DIMENSION INCH

STYLE 2:
PIN 1. EMITTER
2. COLLECTOR

(MFOD71 ONLY)
STYLE 3:
PIN 1. CATHODE
2. ANODE

DIM	MILLIMETERS		INCHES	
	MIN	MAX	MIN	MAX
A	18 67	19 05	0 735	0 750
B	9 14	9 39	0 360	0 370
C	7 75	8 12	0 305	0 320
D	1 52	1 72	0 060	0 068
E	2 41	2 66	0 095	0 105
F	0 43	0 60	0 017	0 024
G	2 54 BSC		0 100 BSC	
H	0 23	0 55	0 009	0 022
J	7 87	8 25	0 310	0 325
K	10 29	17 14	0 405	0 675
L	1 27	1 52	0 050	0 080
N	3 25	3 36	0 128	0 132
Q	3 05	3 30	0 120	0 130
R	7 49	8 00	0 295	0 315
U	3 56	3 81	0 140	0 150
V	6 86	7 11	0 270	0 280
W	5 33 BSC		0 210 BSC	
X	10 67	11 17	0 420	0 440

CASE 363-01

MFOD71, MFOD72, MFOD73

STATIC ELECTRICAL CHARACTERISTICS (T_A = 25°C unless otherwise noted)

Characteristic	Symbol	Min	Typ	Max	Unit
Dark Current (V_R = 20 V, R_L = 1.0 MΩ) T_A = 25°C T_A = 85°C	I_D	— —	0.06 10	10 —	nA
Reverse Breakdown Voltage (I_R = 10 μA)	$V_{(BR)R}$	50	100	—	Volts
Forward Voltage (I_F = 50 mA)	V_F	—	—	1.1	Volts
Series Resistance (I_F = 50 mA)	R_s	—	8.0	—	ohms
Total Capacitance (V_R = 20 V; f = 1.0 MHz)	C_T	—	3.0	—	pF

OPTICAL CHARACTERISTICS (T_A = 25°C)

	Symbol	Min	Typ	Max	Unit
Responsivity (V_R = 5.0 V, Figure 2)	R	0.15	0.2	—	μA/μW
Response Time (V_R = 5.0 V, R_L = 50 Ω)	$t_{(resp)}$	—	5.0	—	ns

MFOD72/MFOD73

STATIC ELECTRICAL CHARACTERISTICS

		Symbol	Min	Typ	Max	Unit
Collector Dark Current (V_{CE} = 10 V)		I_D	—	—	100	nA
Collector-Emitter Breakdown Voltage (I_C = 10 mA)	MFOD72 MFOD73	$V_{(BR)CEO}$	30 60	— —	— —	Volts

OPTICAL CHARACTERISTICS (T_A = 25°C unless otherwise noted)

			Symbol	Min	Typ	Max	Unit
Responsivity (V_{CC} = 5.0 V, Figure 2)		MFOD72 MFOD73	R	80 1,000	125 1,500	— —	μA/μW
Saturation Voltage (λ = 820 nm, V_{CC} = 5.0 V) (P_{in} = 10 μW, I_C = 1.0 mA) (P_{in} = 1.0 μW, I_C = 2.0 mA)		MFOD72 MFOD73	$V_{CE(sat)}$	— —	0.25 0.75	0.4 1.0	Volts
Turn-On Time	R_L = 2.4 kΩ, P_{in} = 10 μW, λ = 820 nm, V_{CC} = 5.0 V	MFOD72	t_{on}	—	10	—	μs
Turn-Off Time			t_{off}	—	60	—	μs
Turn-On Time	R_L = 100 Ω, P_{in} = 1.0 μW, λ = 820 nm, V_{CC} = 5.0 V	MFOD73	t_{on}	—	125	—	μs
Turn-Off Time			t_{off}	—	150	—	μs

TYPICAL COUPLED CHARACTERISTICS

FIGURE 2 — RESPONSIVITY TEST CONFIGURATION

FIGURE 3 — DETECTOR CURRENT versus FIBER LENGTH

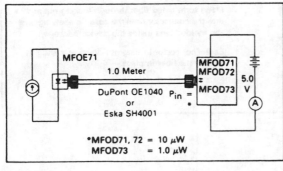

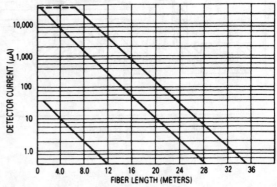

MFOD71, MFOD72, MFOD73

FLCS WORKING DISTANCES

The system length achieved with a FLCS emitter and detector using the 1000 micron core fiber optic cable depends upon the forward current through the LED and the Responsivity of the detector chosen. Each emitter/detector combination will work at any cable length up to the maximum length shown.

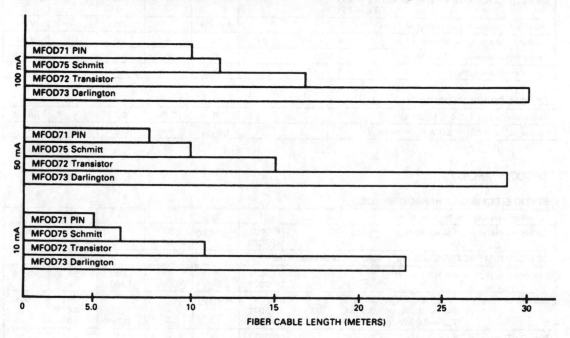

FIBER CABLE LENGTH (METERS)

FIGURE 4 — FO CABLE TERMINATION AND ASSEMBLY

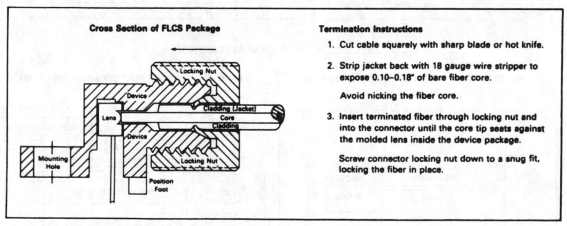

Cross Section of FLCS Package

Termination Instructions

1. Cut cable squarely with sharp blade or hot knife.

2. Strip jacket back with 18 gauge wire stripper to expose 0.10–0.18″ of bare fiber core.

   Avoid nicking the fiber core.

3. Insert terminated fiber through locking nut and into the connector until the core tip seats against the molded lens inside the device package.

   Screw connector locking nut down to a snug fit, locking the fiber in place.

MFOD71, MFOD72, MFOD73

Input Signal Conditioning
The following circuits are suggested to provide the desired forward current through the emitter.

TTL TRANSMITTERS

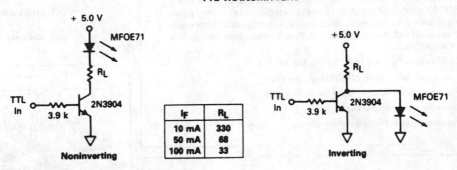

I$_F$	R$_L$
10 mA	330
50 mA	68
100 mA	33

Noninverting

Inverting

Output Signal Conditioning
The following circuits are suggested to take the FLCS detector output and condition it to drive TTL with an acceptable bit error rate.

TTL RECEIVERS

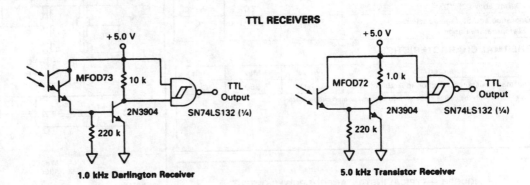

1.0 kHz Darlington Receiver

5.0 kHz Transistor Receiver

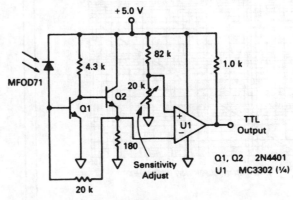

1.0 MHz PIN Receiver

 **MOTOROLA**

INFRARED-EMITTING DIODE

. . . designed for infrared remote control applications for use with the MRD701 phototransistor in optical slotted coupler/interrupter module applications, and for industrial processing and control applications such as light modulators, shaft or position encoders, end of tape detectors.

● Continuous P_O = 2.5 mW (Typ) @ I_F = 50 mA
● Low Cost, Miniature, Clear Plastic Package
● Package Designed for Accurate Positioning
● Lens Molded into Package
● Narrow Spatial Radiation Pattern

INFRARED-EMITTING DIODE

PN GALLIUM ARSENIDE

940 nm

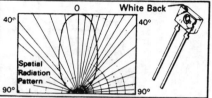

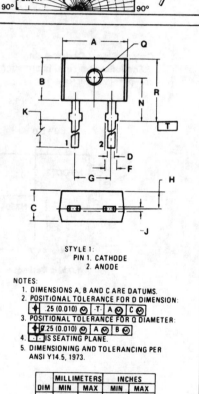

MAXIMUM RATINGS

Rating	Symbol	Value	Unit
Reverse Voltage	V_R	6.0	Volts
Forward Current — Continuous	I_F	50	mA
Total Power Dissipation @ T_A = 25°C Derate above 25°C	P_D(1)	150 2.0	mW mW/°C
Operating and Storage Junction Temperature Range	T_J, T_{stg}	–40 to +100	°C

THERMAL CHARACTERISTICS

Characteristic	Symbol	Max	Unit
Thermal Resistance Junction to Ambient	$R_{\theta JA}$(1)	350	°C/W

(1)Measured with the device soldered into a typical printed circuit board.

STYLE 1:
PIN 1. CATHODE
2. ANODE

NOTES:
1. DIMENSIONS A, B AND C ARE DATUMS.
2. POSITIONAL TOLERANCE FOR D DIMENSION:
   .25 (0.010) ⓜ ·T· A ⓜ C ⓜ
3. POSITIONAL TOLERANCE FOR Q DIAMETER:
   ⌀.25 (0.010) ⓜ A ⓜ B ⓜ
4. ⌷ IS SEATING PLANE.
5. DIMENSIONING AND TOLERANCING PER ANSI Y14.5, 1973.

DIM	MILLIMETERS		INCHES	
	MIN	MAX	MIN	MAX
A	3.43	4.60	0.135	0.185
B	2.79	3.30	0.110	0.130
C	2.03	3.18	0.080	0.125
D	0.43	0.60	0.017	0.024
F	1.14	1.40	0.045	0.055
G	2.54 BSC		0.100 BSC	
H	1.52 BSC		0.060 BSC	
J	0.23	0.56	0.009	0.022
K	12.83	19.05	0.505	0.750
N	3.05	3.30	0.120	0.130
Q	0.76	1.52	0.030	0.060
R	3.81	4.60	0.150	0.185

CASE 349-01

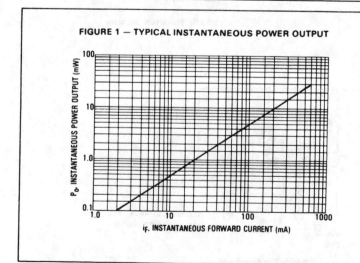

FIGURE 1 — TYPICAL INSTANTANEOUS POWER OUTPUT

MLED71

ELECTRICAL CHARACTERISTICS ($T_A = 25°C$ unless otherwise noted)

Characteristic	Fig. No.	Symbol	Min	Typ	Max	Unit
Reverse Leakage Current ($V_R = 6.0$ V, $R_L = 1.0$ Megohm)	—	I_R	—	50	—	nA
Reverse Breakdown Voltage ($I_R = 100$ μA)	—	$V_{(BR)R}$	6.0	—	—	Volts
Instantaneous Forward Voltage ($I_F = 50$ mA)	2	v_F	—	1.3	1.8	Volts
Total Capacitance ($V_R = 0$ V, f = 1.0 MHz)	—	C_T	—	25	—	pF

OPTICAL CHARACTERISTICS ($T_A = 25°C$ unless otherwise noted)

Characteristic	Fig. No.	Symbol	Min	Typ	Max	Unit
Continuous Power Out, Note 1 ($I_F = 50$ mA)	—	P_O	2.0	2.5	—	mW
Instantaneous Power Out, Note 1 ($I_F = 100$ mA, 100 pps –100 μs pw)	1	P_O	—	5.0	—	mW
Radiant Intensity ($I_F = 100$ mA)		I_o	—	3.5	—	mW/st
Optical Turn-On Turn-Off Time	—	t_{on}, t_{off}	—	1.0	—	μs

Note 1. Power out measurements were made using a SPECTRA-1000 photometer with an integrated sphere.

TYPICAL ELECTRICAL CHARACTERISTICS

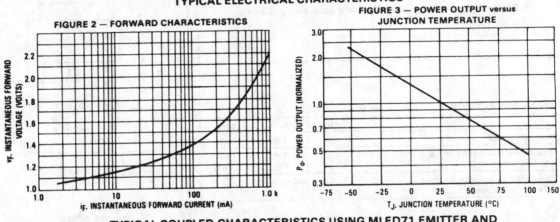

FIGURE 2 — FORWARD CHARACTERISTICS

FIGURE 3 — POWER OUTPUT versus JUNCTION TEMPERATURE

TYPICAL COUPLED CHARACTERISTICS USING MLED71 EMITTER AND MRD701 PHOTOTRANSISTOR DETECTOR

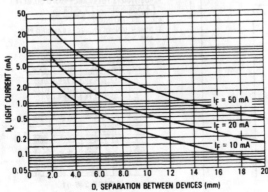

FIGURE 4 — CONTINUOUS MRD701 COLLECTOR LIGHT CURRENT versus DISTANCE FROM MLED71

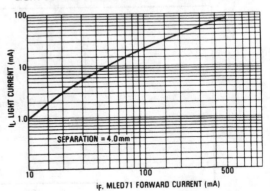

FIGURE 5 — INSTANTANEOUS MRD701 COLLECTOR LIGHT CURRENT versus MLED71 FORWARD CURRENT

 **MOTOROLA**

PIN SILICON PHOTO DIODE

PIN PHOTO DIODE

100 VOLT

... designed for application in laser detection, light demodulation, detection of visible and near infrared light-emitting diodes, shaft or position encoders, switching and logic circuits, or any design requiring radiation sensitivity, ultra high-speed, and stable characteristics.

- Ultra Fast Response — (<1.0 ns Typ)
- Sensitive Throughout Visible and Near Infrared Spectral Range for Wide Application
- Annular Passivated Structure for Stability and Reliability
- Economical, Low Profile, Miniature Plastic Package
- Lense Molded Into Package
- Designed for Automatic Handling and Accurate Positioning

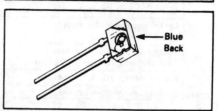
Blue Back

MAXIMUM RATINGS (T_A = 25°C unless otherwise noted)

Rating	Symbol	Value	Unit
Reverse Voltage	V_R	100	Volts
Total Power Dissipation @ T_A = 25°C Derate above 25°C	P_D	100 1.33	mW mW/°C
Operating and Storage Junction Temperature Range	T_J, T_{stg}	–40 to +100	°C

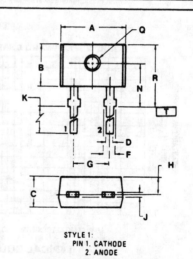

STYLE 1:
PIN 1. CATHODE
2. ANODE

NOTES:
1. DIMENSIONS A, B AND C ARE DATUMS.
2. POSITIONAL TOLERANCE FOR D DIMENSION:
   ⊕ .25 (0.010) Ⓜ ·T· Ⓐ Ⓜ C Ⓜ
3. POSITIONAL TOLERANCE FOR Q DIAMETER:
   ⊕ ⌀.25 (0.010) Ⓜ Ⓐ Ⓜ B Ⓜ
4. ⊤ IS SEATING PLANE.
5. DIMENSIONING AND TOLERANCING PER ANSI Y14.5, 1973.

DIM	MILLIMETERS		INCHES	
	MIN	MAX	MIN	MAX
A	3.43	4.60	0.135	0.185
B	2.79	3.30	0.110	0.130
C	2.03	3.18	0.080	0.125
D	0.43	0.60	0.017	0.024
F	1.14	1.40	0.045	0.055
G	2.54 BSC		0.100 BSC	
H	1.52 BSC		0.060 BSC	
J	0.23	0.56	0.009	0.022
K	12.83	19.05	0.505	0.750
N	3.05	3.30	0.120	0.130
Q	0.76	1.52	0.030	0.060
R	3.81	4.60	0.150	0.185

CASE 349-01

FIGURE 1 — TYPICAL OPERATING CIRCUIT

+V

H

V_{signal}

50 Ω

MRD721

STATIC ELECTRICAL CHARACTERISTICS ($T_A = 25°C$ unless otherwise noted)

Characteristic	Fig. No.	Symbol	Min	Typ	Max	Unit
Dark Current ($V_R = 20$ V, $R_L = 1.0$ MΩ; Note 2) $\quad T_A = 25°C$ $\quad T_A = 100°C$	3 and 4	I_D	— —	0.06 14	10 —	nA
Reverse Breakdown Voltage ($I_R = 10$ μA)	—	$V_{(BR)R}$	100	200	—	Volts
Forward Voltage ($I_F = 50$ mA)	—	V_F	—	—	1.1	Volts
Series Resistance ($I_F = 50$ mA)	—	R_S	—	8.0	—	ohms
Total Capacitance ($V_R = 20$ V; f = 1.0 MHz)	5	C_T	—	3.0	—	pF

OPTICAL CHARACTERISTICS ($T_A = 25°C$)

Characteristic	Fig. No.	Symbol	Min	Typ	Max	Unit
Light Current ($V_R = 20$ V, Note 1)	2	I_L	1.5	4.0	—	μA
Sensitivity ($V_R = 20$ V, Note 3)	— —	$S(\lambda = 0.8\ \mu m)$ $S(\lambda = 0.94\ \mu m)$	— —	5.0 1.2	— —	μA/mW/cm^2
Response Time ($V_R = 20$ V, $R_L = 50$ Ω)	—	$t_{(resp)}$	—	1.0	—	ns
Wavelength of Peak Spectral Response	6	λ_S	—	0.8	—	μm

NOTES: 1. Radiation Flux Density (H) equal to 5.0 mW/cm^2 emitted from a tungsten source at a color temperature of 2870 K.
     2. Measured under dark conditions. (H $\approx$ 0)
     3. Radiation Flux Density (H) equal to 0.5 mW/cm^2

MRD721

FIGURE 2 — IRRADIATED VOLTAGE — CURRENT CHARACTERISTIC

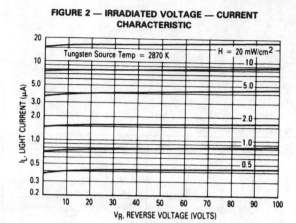

FIGURE 3 — DARK CURRENT versus TEMPERATURE

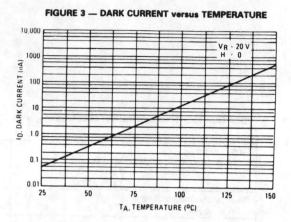

FIGURE 4 — DARK CURRENT versus REVERSE VOLTAGE

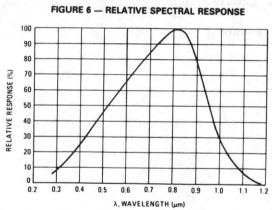

FIGURE 5 — CAPACITANCE versus VOLTAGE

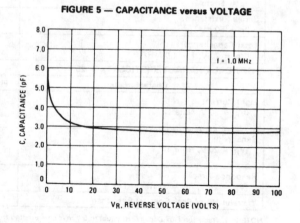

FIGURE 6 — RELATIVE SPECTRAL RESPONSE

Copyright of Motorola, Inc. Used by permission.

T-1 3/4 (5mm) LOW PROFILE SOLID STATE LAMPS

RED ●	HLMP-3200 SERIES
HIGH EFFICIENCY RED ●	HLMP-3350 SERIES
YELLOW ●	HLMP-3450 SERIES
HIGH PERFORMANCE GREEN ●	HLMP-3550 SERIES

TECHNICAL DATA   JANUARY 1984

Features

- **HIGH INTENSITY**
- **LOW PROFILE: 5.8mm (0.23 in) NOMINAL**
- **T-1¾ DIAMETER PACKAGE**
- **LIGHT OUTPUT CATEGORIES**
- **DIFFUSED AND NON-DIFFUSED TYPES**
- **GENERAL PURPOSE LEADS**
- **IC COMPATIBLE/LOW CURRENT REQUIREMENTS**
- **RELIABLE AND RUGGED**

Description

The HLMP-3200 Series are Gallium Arsenide Phosphide Red Light Emitting Diodes with a red diffused lens.

The HLMP-3350 Series are Gallium Arsenide Phosphide on Gallium Phosphide High Efficiency Red Light Emitting Diodes.

The HLMP-3450 Series are Gallium Arsenide Phosphide on Gallium Phosphide Yellow Light Emitting Diodes.

The HLMP-3550 Series are Gallium Phosphide Green Light Emitting Diodes.

The Low Profile T-1¾ package provides space savings and is excellent for backlighting applications.

Package Dimensions

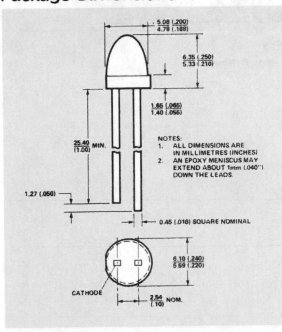

Part Number HLMP-	Application	Lens	Color
3200	Indicator — General Purpose	Tinted Diffused Wide Angle	Red
3201	Indicator — High Brightness		
3350	Indicator — General Purpose	Tinted Diffused Wide Angle	High Efficiency Red
3351	Indicator — High Brightness		
3365	General Purpose Point Source	Tinted Non-diffused Narrow Angle	
3366	High Brightness Annunciator		
3450	Indicator — General Purpose	Tinted Diffused Wide Angle	Yellow
3451	Indicator — High Brightness		
3465	General Purpose Point Source	Tinted Non-diffused Narrow Angle	
3466	High Brightness Annunciator		
3553	Indicator — General Purpose	Tinted Diffused Wide Angle	Green
3554	Indicator — High Brightness		
3567	General Purpose Point Source	Tinted Non-diffused Narrow Angle	
3568	High Brightness Annunciator		

Absolute Maximum Ratings at $T_A = 25°C$

Parameter	3200 Series	3350 Series	3450 Series	3550 Series	Units
Peak Forward Current	1000	90	60	90	mA
Average Forward Current[1]	50	25	20	25	mA
DC Current[2]	50	30	20	30	mA
Power Dissipation[3]	100	135	85	135	mW
Operating Temperature Range	−55 to +100	−55 to +100	−55 to +100	−40 to +100	C°
Storage Temperature Range				−55 to +100	
Lead Soldering Temperature (1.6 mm (0.063 in.) from body)	260°C for 5 seconds				

NOTES:
1. See Figure 5 (Red), 10 (High Efficiency Red), 15 (Yellow) or 20 (Green) to establish pulsed operating conditions.
2. For High Efficiency Red and Green Series derate linearly from 50°C at 0.5 mA/°C. For Red and Yellow Series derate linearly from 50°C at 0.2 mA/°C.
3. For High Efficiency Red and Green Series derate power linearly from 25°C at 1.8 mW/°C. For Red and Yellow Series derate power linearly from 50°C at 1.6 mW/°C.

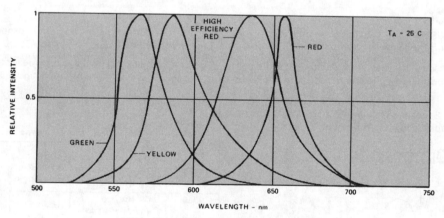

Figure 1. Relative Intensity versus Wavelength.

RED HLMP-3200 SERIES
Electrical Specifications at T_A=25°C

Symbol	Description	Device HLMP-	Min.	Typ.	Max.	Units	Test Conditions
I_v	Axial Luminous Intensity	3200	1.0	2.0		mcd	I_F = 20mA (Fig. 3)
		3201	2.0	4.0			
$2\theta_{\frac{1}{2}}$	Included Angle Between Half Luminous Intensity Points			60		deg.	Note 1 (Fig. 6)
λ_{PEAK}	Peak Wavelength			655		nm	Measurement @ Peak (Fig. 1)
λ_d	Dominant Wavelength			648		nm	Note 2
τ_S	Speed of Response			15		ns	
C	Capacitance			100		pF	V_F = 0; f = 1 MHz
θ_{JC}	Thermal Resistance			125		°C/W	Junction to Cathode Lead 1.6 mm (0.063 in.) from Body
V_F	Forward Voltage		1.4	1.6	2.0	V	I_F = 20mA (Fig. 2)
V_{BR}	Reverse Breakdown Voltage		3	10		V	I_R = 100µA
η_v	Luminous Efficacy			55		lm/W	Note 3

Notes: 1. $\theta_{\frac{1}{2}}$ is the off-axis angle at which the luminous intensity is half the axial luminous intensity. 2. Dominant wavelength, λ_d, is derived from the CIE chromaticity diagram and represents the single wavelength which defines the color of the device. 3. Radiant Intensity I_e, in watts/steradian may be found from the equation $I_e = I_v/\eta_v$, where I_v is the luminous intensity in candelas and η_v is the luminous efficacy in lumens/watt.

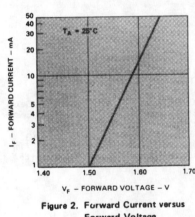

Figure 2. Forward Current versus Forward Voltage.

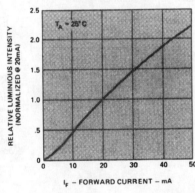

Figure 3. Relative Luminous Intensity versus Forward Current.

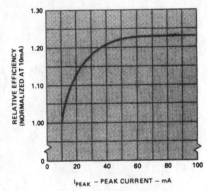

Figure 4. Relative Efficiency (Luminous Intensity per Unit Current) versus Peak Current.

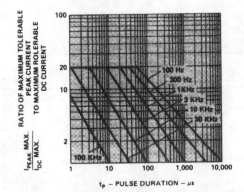

Figure 5. Maximum Tolerable Peak Current versus Pulse Duration. (I_{DC} MAX as per MAX Ratings)

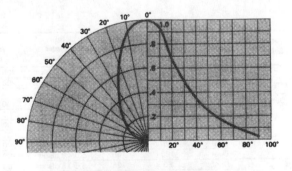

Figure 6. Relative Luminous Intensity versus Angular Displacement.

AMP

OPTIMATE
Fiber Optic Cables
(Continued)

Dimensioning:
Unless otherwise specified, dimensions are in millimeters and inches.

Values in brackets are equivalent U.S. customary units.

Plenum Grade—Dual Channel

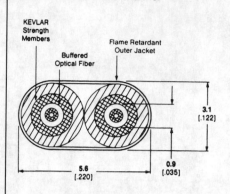

KEVLAR Strength Members

Buffered Optical Fiber

Flame Retardant Outer Jacket

3.1 [.122]

5.6 [.220]

0.9 [.035]

Specifications

No. of Fibers	2
Fiber Type	Glass Multimode
Core Diameter	See Chart, Below
Cladding Diameter	See Chart, Below
Cable Weight	34 kg/km
Max. Installation Load	1000 N [224.8 lb]
Max. Operational Load	200 N [45.0 lb]
Min. Bend Radius (Unloaded)	10.0 cm [3.94 in]
Operating Temperature Range	0°C to +50°C

Plastic Grade—Single Channel

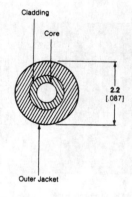

Cladding

Core

2.2 [.087]

Outer Jacket

Specifications

No. of Fibers	1
Fiber Type	Plastic Multimode
Core Diameter	See Chart, Below
Cladding Diameter	See Chart, Below
Cable Weight	4 kg/km
Tensile Strength—Break	10 to 12 kg
Min. Bend Radius (Unloaded)	2.0 cm [.787 in]
Operating Temperature Range	−40°C to +85°C

Note: See page 49 for undercarpet fiber optic cables

Cable Grade	Channels	Core Dia. μm	Cladding Dia. μm	Max Attenuation 850/1300 nm	Min Bandwidth 850 nm	Part Numbers Length - m[ft]			
						25 [82.03]	50 [164.05]	100 [328.1]	1000 [3281.0]
Light Duty	Single	50	125	4.0/2.5 dB/km	400 MHz-km	501110-1	501110-2	501110-3	501110-4
	Single	85	125	5.0/3.5 dB/km	200 MHz-km	501111-1	501111-2	501111-3	501111-4
	Single	100	140	5.0/4.0 dB/km	100 MHz-km	501112-1	501112-2	501112-3	501112-4
	Dual	50	125	4.0/2.5 dB/km	400 MHz-km	501113-1	501113-2	501113-3	501113-4
	Dual	85	125	5.0/3.5 dB/km	200 MHz-km	501114-1	501114-2	501114-3	501114-4
	Dual	100	140	5.0/4.0 dB/km	100 MHz-km	501115-1	501115-2	501115-3	501115-4
Heavy Duty	Dual	50	125	4.0/2.5 dB/km	400 MHz-km	501116-1	501116-2	501116-3	501116-4
	Dual	85	125	5.0/3.5 dB/km	200 MHz-km	501117-1	501117-2	501117-3	501117-4
	Dual	100	140	5.0/4.0 dB/km	100 MHz-km	501118-1	501118-2	501118-3	501118-4
Plenum Duty	Dual	50	125	5.0/3.5 dB/km	400 MHz-km	501119-1	501119-2	501119-3	501119-4
	Dual	85	125	5.0/3.5 dB/km	200 MHz-km	501120-1	501120-2	501120-3	501120-4
	Dual	100	140	7.0/5.5 dB/km	100 MHz-km	501121-1	501121-2	501121-3	501121-4
Plastic	Single	980	1000	—	—	501232-1	501232-2	501232-3	501232-4

AMP

OPTIMATE DNP (Dry Non-Polish) Connectors

Dimensioning:
Values in brackets are equivalent U.S. customary units.

Features

- Performance and reliability at low cost
- No adhesive
- No polishing
- Simple field assembly
- Designed for low cost plastic fibers
- Quick connect/ disconnect with audible snap action
- Repeatable coupling efficiency
- Dual position polarized
- Designer Kit available

Technical Documents

AMP Instruction Sheet:
IS 2974—Dry Non-Polish Connectors

AMP Product Specification:
108-45000

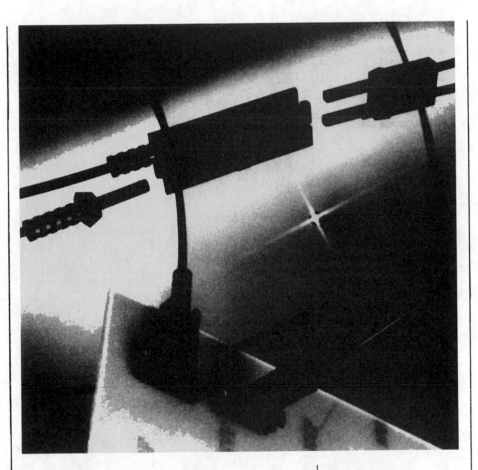

The AMP OPTIMATE DNP Fiber Optic Connectors provide for the assembly of both dual and single channel cables as well as the interface to emitters and detectors. The product family includes the following:

- Splice
- Single Position Plug
- Single Position Device Mount (Honeywell Low-Cost Plastic Sweetspot™)
- Single Position Device Mount (TO-92)
- Single Position Bulkhead Receptacle
- Dual Position Bulkhead Receptacle
- Dual Position Plug

When used in conjunction with low cost plastic fiber of 1000 microns in diameter and low cost active devices, the AMP family of OPTIMATE DNP

Connectors can provide a reliable and cost effective electro-optics system.

Optical Characteristics

Insertion Loss:
2 dB, Ref: FOTP 34 Method C

Environmental Characteristics

Temperature Range:
−40°C to +60°C

Mechanical Characteristics

Insertion Force:
13.34 N [3 lb] (plug to receptacle)

Cable Retention in Plug:
8.89N [12 lb]

Materials

Retention Clip:
Copper Alloy, plated

Splice:
Copper Alloy, plated

Connectors:
Thermoplastic

APPENDIX: MANUFACTURER DATA SHEETS   379

OPTIMATE DNP
(Dry Non-Polish)
Connectors
(Continued)

Dimensioning:
Dimensions are in millimetres and inches.
Values in brackets are equivalent U.S.
customary units.

Features

- Performance and reliability at low cost
- No adhesive
- No polishing
- Simple field assembly
- Designed for low cost plastic fibers
- Quick connect/ disconnect with audible snap action
- Low loss—less than 2 dB
- Repeatable coupling efficiency
- Semiautomatic application

Technical Documents

IS 2974—Dry Non-Polish Connectors

AMP Product Specification: 108-45000

Use With:

Single Position Device Mounts, pp. 28 & 29

Single Position Bulkhead Receptacle, p. 30

Dual Position Bulkhead Receptacle, p. 31

AMP Plastic Fiber Optic Cable, p. 37

Splice and Retention Clip
Splice—Part No. 228051-1
Retention Clip—Part No. 228046-1

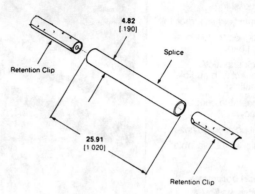

Single Position
Plug Assembly
Part No. 228087-1[1]

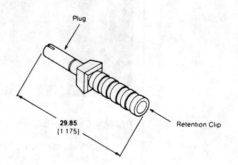

Dual Position
Plug Assembly
Part No. 228088-1[2]

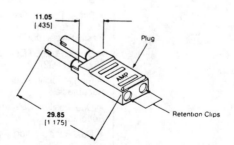

[1]Cutting Tool Fixture Part No. 228837-1 required for proper termination

[2]Cutting Tool Fixture Part No. 228836-1 required for proper termination

AMP

OPTIMATE DNP
(Dry Non-Polish)
Connectors
(Continued)

Dimensioning:
Dimensions are in millimetres and inches.
Values in brackets are equivalent U.S. customary units.

Single Position Device Mounts

For TO-92 Device—
Part No. 228040-1

For .085 x .180 Device—
Part No. 228709-1

Features

■ Performance and reliability at low cost

■ No adhesive

■ No polishing

■ Simple field assembly

■ Designed for low cost plastic fibers

■ Quick connect/disconnect with audible snap action

■ Low loss—less than 2 dB

■ Repeatable coupling efficiency

■ Semiautomatic application

Technical Documents

IS 2974—Dry Non-Polish Connectors

AMP Product Specification: 108-45000

Use With:

Single Position Plug Assembly p. 27

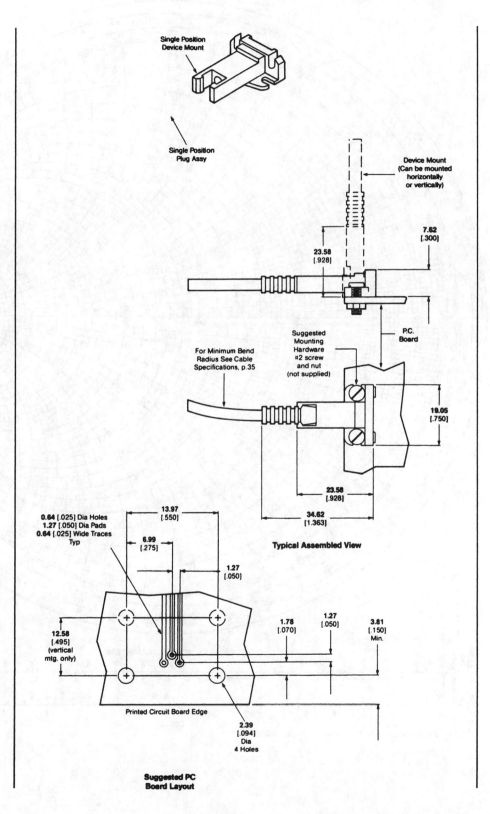

Single Position Device Mount

Single Position Plug Assy

Device Mount
(Can be mounted horizontally or vertically)

7.62 [.300]

23.58 [.928]

P.C. Board

Suggested Mounting Hardware #2 screw and nut (not supplied)

For Minimum Bend Radius See Cable Specifications, p.35

19.05 [.750]

23.58 [.928]

34.62 [1.363]

Typical Assembled View

0.64 [.025] Dia Holes
1.27 [.050] Dia Pads
0.64 [.025] Wide Traces Typ

13.97 [.550]

6.99 [.275]

1.27 [.050]

12.58 [.495] (vertical mtg. only)

1.78 [.070]

1.27 [.050]

3.81 [.150] Min.

Printed Circuit Board Edge

2.39 [.094] Dia 4 Holes

Suggested PC Board Layout

NAME

TITLE

DWG. NO.

DATE

SMITH CHART FORM 82BSPR (2-49)   KAY ELECTRIC COMPANY, PINE BROOK, N.J. ©1949   PRINTED IN U.S.A.

Supersedes G.R. Form 5301-7560 N

IMPEDANCE OR ADMITTANCE COORDINATES

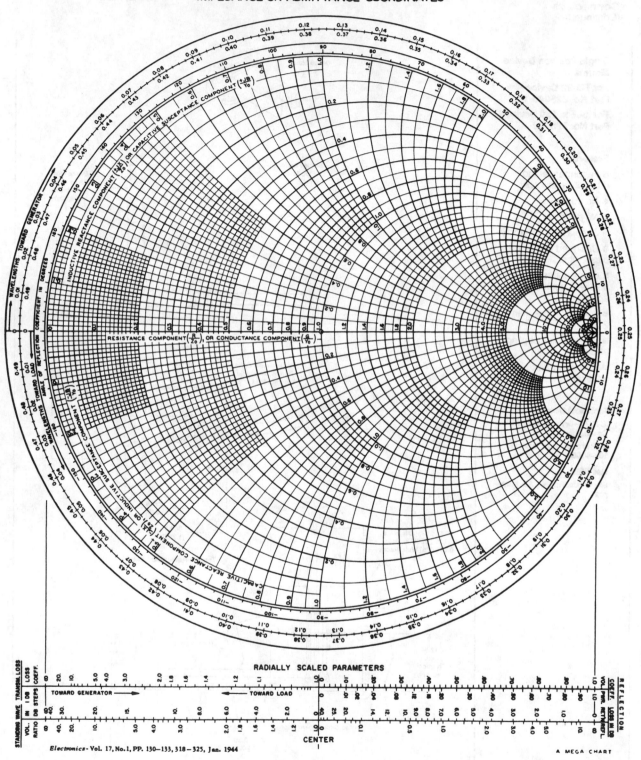

RADIALLY SCALED PARAMETERS

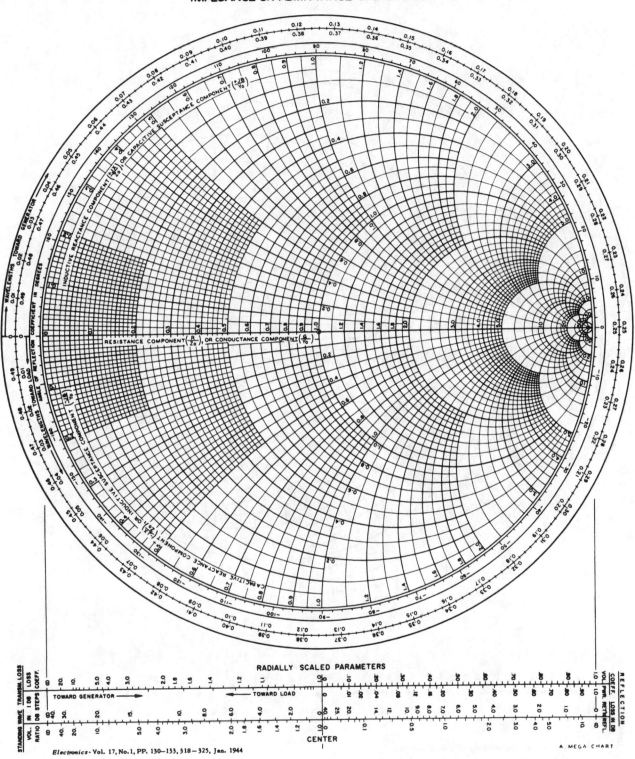

IMPEDANCE OR ADMITTANCE COORDINATES

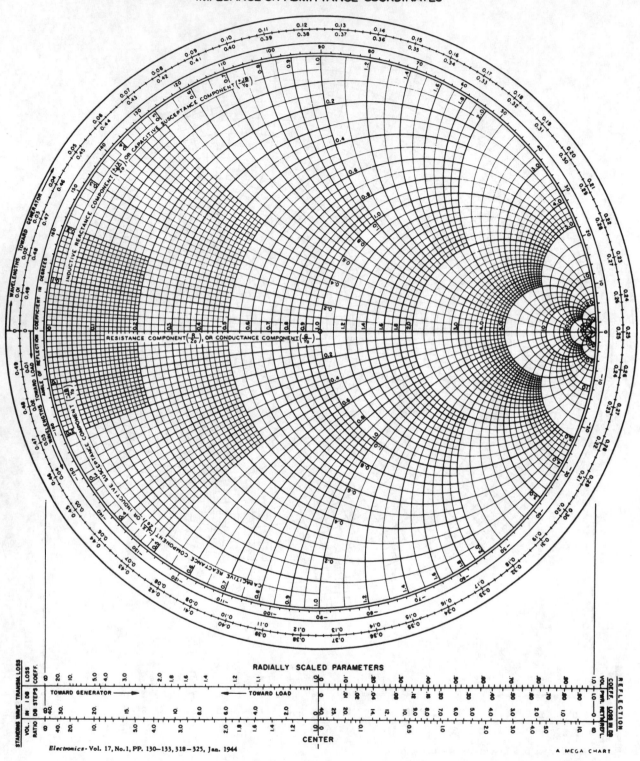

RADIALLY SCALED PARAMETERS

Electronics - Vol. 17, No. 1, PP. 130—133, 318—325, Jan. 1944

A MEGA CHART

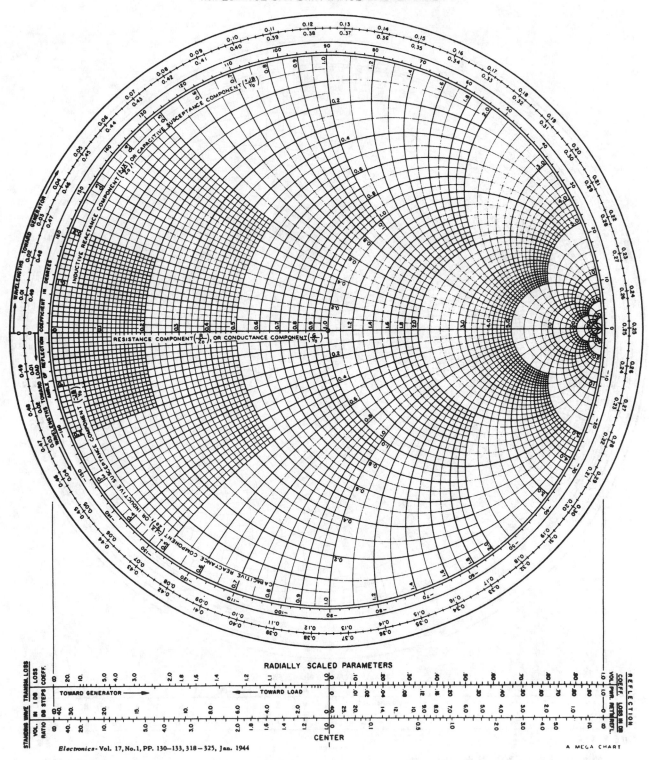

IMPEDANCE OR ADMITTANCE COORDINATES

RADIALLY SCALED PARAMETERS

IMPEDANCE OR ADMITTANCE COORDINATES

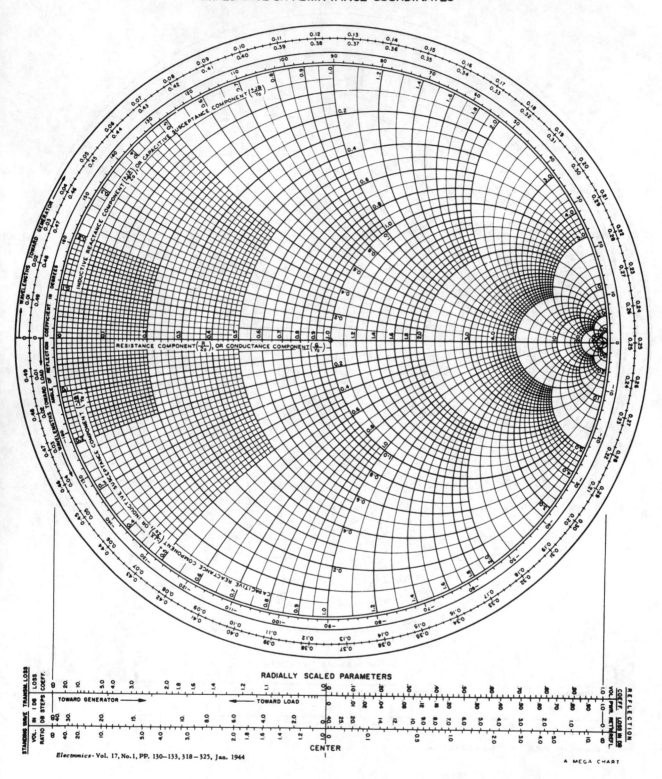

RADIALLY SCALED PARAMETERS

Electronics · Vol. 17, No. 1, PP. 130—133, 318—325, Jan. 1944

A MEGA CHART